Comic Transactions

Comic Transactions

Literature, Humor, and the Politics of Community in Twentieth-Century Britain

JAMES F. ENGLISH

Cornell University Press

Ithaca and London

First published 1994 by Cornell University Press.

Library of Congress Cataloging-in-Publication Data

English, James F., 1958–
    Comic transactions : literature, humor, and the politics of
community in 20th-century Britain / by James F. English.
        p.   cm.
    Includes bibliographical references and index.
    ISBN 0-8014-2953-6 (alk. paper)
        1. English wit and humor—20th century—History and criticism.
    2. Community life—Political aspects—Great Britain—History—20th
century. 3. Politics and literature—Great Britain—History—20th
century. 4. English literature—20th century—History and
criticism. 5. Humerous stories, English—History and criticism.
    6. Comic, The, in literature. I. Title.
    PR937.E54 1994
    827.009—dc20   93-42073

Printed in the United States of America

Excerpts from *Between the Acts* by Virginia Woolf, copyright 1941 by Harcourt Brace & Company and renewed 1969 by Leonard Woolf, reprinted by permission of the publisher. Published in the U.K. by the Hogarth Press.

Excerpts from *Lucky Jim* by Kingsley Amis copyright © 1954 by Kingsley Amis, used by permission of Doubleday, a division of Bantam Doubleday Dell Publishing Group, Inc., and Victor Gollancz.

Excerpts from *The Golden Notebook* by Doris Lessing copyright © 1962 by Doris Lessing, copyright renewed © 1990 by Doris Lessing, reprinted by permission of Simon and Schuster, Inc. Published 1962 by Michael Joseph, London, and reproduced by permission of Michael Joseph Ltd.

∞The paper in this book meets the minimum requirements of the American National Standard for Information Sciences— Permanence of Paper for Printed Library Materials, ANSI Z39.48-1984.

For ARTURO

♠ ♥ ♦ ♣

The increasing seriousness
of things, then—that's
the great opportunity
of jokes.

—HENRY JAMES, *Portrait of a Lady*

Contents

Five

Six

Preface

While this book is hardly unique in approaching questions about literature and culture by means of an inquiry into the comic, it does not conceive of that project in the usual ways. As a consequence, readers may at first find the unfolding of the book somewhat obscure. The Introduction begins with a tendentious survey of humor studies and some notes toward a theory of "comic transaction," then turns to consider, on no less summary and abstract a level, the paradoxes of "community" and the role of communitarian logics in securing the stability and intelligibility of the social field in modern times. From this point on, the book consists largely of historical and literary-critical analysis, working chronologically through six relatively well known but not necessarily "comic" twentieth-century British novels and the varying cultural contexts of their production. I am hopeful that the linkages between and among the different parts and chapters will become clear enough to any careful reader of the entire book from beginning to end. But in anticipation of readers who skip from this preface to a later moment in the discussion I will briefly sketch here what I am trying to accomplish.

To begin with, despite my initial emphases on humor studies and on the theory of community, my primary objective is not to make contributions in these areas but to contribute something to our understanding of the politics of literature in twentieth-century Britain. In pursuing this objective, however, I have found it necessary to formulate an approach to literary politics which brings both humor and community into play. It is an approach in terms of *work* done on a *field*, where the work invariably takes a *witty* form—is, in fact, coextensive with what Freud called "joke-work"—and the field is that of a social imaginary organized according to the logic of "community," which is to say, a field on which all social and political thought must be cast in the terms of communitarian discourse. The starting point for my readings in the modern British novel, in other words, is the recognition that a literary text is a political event inasmuch as its underlying function is to engage with the problematic of community—and hence the very logic of the modern social imaginary—in a series of witty operations. Or, to put this more provocatively, the reason literature is important, socially and politically, is because it is always making jokes. And one way or another, what its jokes are "about" is community.

Like humor and laughter, "community" is approached here in a spirit of analysis and critique, not of celebration. Those who would wish to see community once again waved as properly and uniquely the banner of an emergent left opposition, or who imagine that the political catastrophes of this century can be accounted for by a *lack* of powerful communitarian ideas and initiatives, will be disappointed. But so, too, will those who might hope to see community disposed of, supplanted by some new logic, some new politics that would lift us beyond the communitarian horizon. Community is a paradox whose logic informs, in both enabling and disabling ways, every system of political thought, every movement or bloc, every significant intervention that has occurred on the social field in modern memory. And part of the paradox is its continuing exigency in the face of manifest failure, the fact that our most radical and utopian hopes cannot be separated from the very structures of thought and feeling which have repeatedly unraveled and defeated them. My objective in this book is not directly to advance the ongoing theoretical discussion of this problematic, but to present a few microhistories of cultural struggle in twentieth-century Britain which might gain us some useful, some *strategic* knowledge about the functions and effects of communitarian thinking. Only with a better, more concrete understanding of the kinds of work, or joke-work, which have been done in and through the concept of community can we hope to clarify the problems we face in attempting to rethink it.

The six novels I focus on are not more thoroughly, or more profoundly, or even more amusingly bound up with the politics of community than are others I might have selected. But they do offer good opportunities for the exploration of the communitarian field on which literature, politics, and humor converge in twentieth-century Britain. Each novel addresses itself more or less explicitly to important strains of British communitarianism, to major communitarian strategies that have been called upon to manage difference and construct lines of identity and unity across the British social imaginary: liberal nationalism, radical anarchism, British fascism, social feminism, Leavisism, New Left culturism, postwar feminism, Powell/Thatcherite cultural racism, black British community activism, and others. Each novel, moreover, can be usefully articulated with the century's major literary moments or categories—modernism, postmodernism, and postcolonialism—an articulation that makes it possible to rethink these in terms of the fundamental struggle over who or what constitutes the "community."

And each novel demonstrates how thoroughly the literary text's engagement with this struggle, and hence how thoroughly the whole political dimension of literary practice, depends on ostensibly nonserious forms of symbolic exchange.

Although my discussion of these novels is less a series of close readings or new interpretations than an extended meditation on literary and cultural politics, I have tried to take into account and to contribute something to the debates that have shaped existing critical literature on the individual novels and their authors. I hope that participants in those debates will find my individual chapters useful. Nevertheless, *Comic Transactions* is a book, not a series of articles. It unfolds its main arguments across seven chapters, and performs detailed analysis of individual texts only as a way of assisting a broader and more polemical engagement with literary history and cultural politics in twentieth-century Britain. It is on this level that the book's real merits, and of course its equally real limitations, will make themselves evident.

I am indebted to many individuals and groups for their assistance. The Research Institute of the University of Pennsylvania provided a generous summer research grant in 1989. The University of Pennsylvania also supported me financially during a leave of absence in 1991–92. My research that year was greatly facilitated by a postdoctoral fellowship arranged by Richard Brodhead of the English Department of Yale University and by an electronic link to the Internet arranged by Gregg TeHennepe of Connecticut College. The library staffs at Stanford University, University of California at Berkeley, University of Pennsylvania, Yale University, and Connecticut College have all contributed extensive and invaluable guidance. Bernhard Kendler and Kay Scheuer of Cornell University Press have been wonderfully helpful and efficient editors.

Among the friends and colleagues who helped to bring *Comic Transactions* through its several manuscript phases, I owe a special debt to the late Arturo Islas, whose early encouragement, unflagging attentiveness, and honest criticism not only contributed much to this book but have served for me as a model of pedagogical excellence and a continuing inspiration. The contributions of Albert Guerard, Robert Polhemus, William Todd, and Ian Watt were instrumental in preparing the initial version of the book; the rethinking and rewriting I have done over the last several years have been greatly enhanced by my contact and collaboration with graduate students and colleagues at the University of Pennsylvania—who I hope will forgive me for not listing them all here. Rex Bossert, Heesok Chang, and John Unsworth have for many years helped to shape my general thinking about literary and cultural politics; without their friendships this would have been a very different book. My parents, Isabelle and Jim, have provided unwavering support; most recently, they housed me and kept me company in Connecticut while I did final work on the manuscript. Finally, I am grateful to Sue Zemka and Basie "Mister Base Man" Zemka for paying me so many visits despite their shared aversion to air travel.

Grateful acknowledgment is made to the following for permission to reprint previously published material.

Black Sparrow Press. Material from: *Apes of God* Copyright © 1981; *The Art of Being Ruled* Copyright © 1989; *Blast* 1 Copyright © 1981; *Men Without Art* Copyright © 1987; *Complete Wild Body* Copyright © 1982; *Rude Assignment* Copyright © 1984, all by the estate of Mrs. G. A. Wyndham Lewis. Reprinted by permission of Black Sparrow Press.

Conradiana. Material from "Scientist, Moralist, Humorist: A Bergsonian Reading of *The Secret Agent,*" by James F. English. *Conradiana* 19 (Summer 1987).

Genre. Material from "The Laughing Reader: A New Direction for Studies of the Comic," by James F. English. *Genre* 19 (Summer 1986).

Purdue Research Foundation. Material from "Conrad's 'Counterrevolutionary' Modernism and the *Witz* of the Political Unconscious," by James F. English. *Modern Fiction Studies* 38 (Fall 1992), Copyright © 1993, Purdue Research Foundation, West Lafayette, Indiana 47907. All rights reserved.

Philadelphia   JAMES F. ENGLISH

Comic Transactions

Introduction: Humor, Politics, Community

> To understand laughter, we must put it back into its natural
> environment, which is society, and above all must we deter-
> mine the utility of its function, which is a social one.
>
> —Henri Bergson, *Laughter*

My starting point is the observation that humor is a social practice, an activity by means of which work is performed within and upon a concrete and historically specific social situation. This is a banal enough observation, scarcely novel even in 1900, when Henri Bergson published *Le Rire*,[1] yet it is one that has generally been denied, neglected, or systematically bracketed in the vast literature of humor studies.[2] Since the nineteenth century this literature, though diverse, has been dominated by narrow formalisms. From linguistics we have models of the "joke" as a distinct class of *énoncé*, a special arrangement of syntactic and/or semantic elements whose pragmatic dimensions (uses, effects, social functions) are regarded as strictly ancillary and nonconstitutive.[3] From literary criticism and aesthetics we have models of the "comic text" or its various subspecies (comedy, travesty, farce, burlesque, parody, caricature, grotesque, and so forth) as distinct genres, particular formal

1. Henri Bergson, *Laughter* (1900), trans. Wylie Sypher, in *Comedy*, ed. Wylie Sypher (Garden City, N.Y., 1956).

2. For the fullest English-language bibliography of humor studies through 1975, see Jeffrey H. Goldstein et al., "Humour, Laughter, and Comedy: A Bibliography of Empirical and Nonempirical Analyses in the English Language," in *It's a Funny Thing, Humour: International Conference on Humour and Laughter*, ed. Antony J. Chapman and Hugh C. Foot (Oxford, 1977). A useful summary and overview of this work can be found in Norman Holland, *Laughing: A Psychology of Humor* (Ithaca, 1982) 15–103.

3. For a recent overview of linguistic approaches to humor, see Victor Raskin, *Semantic Mechanisms of Humor* (Boston, 1985). In developing his own highly formalistic theory of "opposed scripts," Raskin acknowledges that not all the scripts involved in a joke are strictly "linguistic" in character and that what he calls "non-linguistic scripts"—i.e., codes, rules, or patterns of association which obtain on the level of pragmatics and hence cannot be extrapolated from the language system itself—must be taken into consideration (65–66, 135–37.).

arrangements of thematic, narrative, or visual elements, which bear no necessary relation either to the manifestly *trans*generic phenomenon of laughter or to the particulars of its social circulation.[4] From cognitive psychology, gestalt psychology, behavioral psychology, pop psychology, philosophy, and cybernetics we have endless variants of the "incongruity" or "incongruity-and-resolution" model of "humor appreciation," in terms of which the joke is seen mainly as a cognitive problem that an idealized human mind submits to universal problem-solving procedures.[5]

4. As early as the mid-eighteenth century, when the generic paradigm was first emerging, Samuel Johnson complained that the scholars of genre had severed the connection between comedy and laughter, producing elaborate but arid definitions that left out the one essential thing. See Samuel Johnson, "On the Difficulty of Defining 'Comedy'" (1751), *The Rambler*, 4 vols. (London, 1794) 3: 112–14, rpt. *The Comic in Theory and Practice*, ed. John J. Enck et al. (Englewood Cliffs, N.J., 1960) 10–11. A telling instance of this myopia is Northrop Frye's monumental study of literary genres, *The Anatomy of Criticism* (Princeton, 1957), the exhaustive index to which contains not one entry under "humor," "laughter," or "mirth." More recently, there have been attempts on the one hand to rethink the comic genres in less formalistic terms, and on the other hand to take nongeneric approaches to literary humor. An early example of the former is Philip Thomson's useful monograph *The Grotesque*, Critical Idiom Series 24 (London, 1972), which, like Tzvetan Todorov's better-known book *The Fantastic* (Ithaca, 1973), anticipates the project of the Konstanz school, and in particular of Hans Robert Jauss, to rewrite genre studies "from the receptive side." Among the studies of literary humor which shift the emphasis away from the whole question of genre and form, some particularly provocative instances are Leah S. Marcus, *The Politics of Mirth* (Chicago, 1986), Jerry Aline Flieger, *The Purloined Punch Line: Freud's Comic Theory and the Postmodern Text* (Baltimore, 1991), and Daniel Cottom, *Text and Culture: The Politics of Interpretation* (Minneapolis, 1989), especially chapter 1, "What Is a Joke?" Also of interest is Richard Keller Simon, *The Labyrinth of the Comic: Theory and Practice from Fielding to Freud* (Tallahassee, Fla., 1985), which contests the generic distinction between comic literature and theory of the comic.

5. Immanuel Kant is usually credited with the first statement of the incongruity and resolution theory for his unelaborated remark in the *Critique of Judgment* (trans. J. H. Bernard [New York, 1951]) that "laughter *is an affection arising from sudden transformation of a strained expectation into nothing*" (177). Arthur Schopenhauer gives this view of the comic its first systematic elaboration in *The World as Will and Idea*, trans. R. B. Haldane and John Kemp (London, 1957). Schopenhauer initially sketches his "theory of the ludicrous" in vol. 1, book 1, sec. 13; he then adds an important Supplement to Book I in vol. 2, chap. 8. Some typical examples of contemporary tinkerings with the incongruity-and-resolution theory can be found in *The Psychology of Humor*, ed. Jeffrey H. Goldstein and Paul E. McGhee (New York, 1972); see in particular Jerry Suls, "A Two-Stage Model for the Appreciation of Jokes and Cartoons: An Information-Processing Analysis" 80–92. Suls states the theory this way: "In the first stage the perceiver finds his expectations about the text disconfirmed by the ending of the joke. . . . In other words, the recipient encounters an incongruity—the punch line. In the second stage, the perceiver engages in a form of

More varied and valuable studies have come from anthropology, sociology, and psychoanalysis. But even in these disciplines scholars have been drawn into quasi-formalist frameworks that obscure the radically social character of their object. Anthropologists have tended to accentuate the transhistorical, transcultural features of such comic phenomena as the trickster figure and the joking relationship;[6] sociologists have developed group-interaction models of comic exchange which attempt to map the concrete dynamics of identification and group formation onto a simple grid of static and discrete membership positions;[7] psychoanalytic critics have tended to focus so exclusively on the interplay between an *énoncé* and its (more or less idealized) individual recipient that the complex social process Freud termed "joke-work" becomes a mere translation of the joke-text's internal structure or "technique" onto an affective register.[8]

---

problem solving to find a cognitive rule which makes the punch line follow the main part of the joke and reconciles the incongruous parts" (81).

6. For a useful, though necessarily superficial, overview of the anthropological literature, see Mahadev L. Apte, *Humor and Laughter: An Anthropological Approach* (Ithaca, 1985).

7. A summary and bibliography of various sociological approaches to humor is Gary Allen Fine, "Sociological Approaches to the Study of Humor," in *Handbook of Humor Research*, 2 vols., ed. Paul E. McGhee and Jeffrey H. Goldstein (New York, 1983) 1: 159–82. Some sociologists, following Lawrence La Fave, have used the "identification class" rather than the membership class as the basic category of comic analysis. This practice is only a very modest improvement since it still idealizes the individual recipient and reduces the complex process of identification to a "positive" or "negative" subjective orientation that has already been settled before the joke takes place and to which the joke-work can contribute nothing.

8. To a certain extent, Freud's *Jokes and Their Relation to the Unconscious* (1905) seems to invite this reductiveness. For several chapters the book follows standard humor-theory practice, tracing the abstract technique of the joke across the mental topography of an idealized receiving psyche (an incongruity is encountered; a resolution is supplied from the reservoir of the unconscious, etc.), and effectively limiting analysis of the joke to a kind of close reading transposed into the language of affect and reception. In chapter 3 ("The Purposes of Jokes"), however, and especially in chapter 5 ("The Motives of Jokes—Jokes as Social Process"), the text begins to backtrack and reconsider in the characteristic Freudian manner, dismantling and reformulating much of the rather synthetic discussion with which it began. The notion that the "essential character of the joke" is to be found in its technique is discarded, and the figure of the individual respondent, mechanically processing the joke-text, is drawn into a complex, and indeed paradoxical, social dynamic with other participants in the exchange. My citations of Sigmund Freud, with the title abbreviated *JRU* where necessary, are included parenthetically. They refer to the James Strachey translation (New York, 1960).

In his useful and highly readable book *Laughing*, the psychoanalytic literary critic Norman Holland undertakes what would appear to be a welcome departure from the

This is not to say that one learns nothing—that I have learned nothing—from humor studies. The present book is in many ways indebted to the major texts of that field, which include the contributions of Hobbes, Hegel, Schopenhauer, Spencer, Kierkegaard, Nietzsche, Bergson, Freud, Bataille, Bakhtin, Radcliffe-Brown, Bateson, Derrida, Eco, Cixous, and other writers whom it would be absurd to dismiss either individually or collectively. My point is simply that "humor studies," precisely because the term indicates such a broad and heterogeneous scholarly terrain, has been vulnerable to a certain anxiety concerning its proper object. And this anxiety has produced a widespread formalistic tendency, a misguided determination to define or construct a model of the *joke-as-such*, the text that is comic by virtue of its special combination of intrinsic properties, its determinative formal features. This tendency has been, in my view, a crippling one particularly ruinous where humor studies overlaps with linguistics and literary criticism, for here it has met with some all too congenial disciplinary predispositions, and indeed managed to sustain these where humor is concerned even as both disciplines have on the whole begun to reconfigure themselves along more sociopolitical and historicist lines.

A thorough survey and systematic critique of humor studies would over-burden this introduction and misplace the overall emphasis of the book, a book intended not as an intervention in humor theory which happens to draw examples from modern British literature, but as a contribution to literary criticism and cultural history which makes its approach to certain persistent problematics in modern British culture by way of literary humor. What I propose to do here is first to present, in rather unsystematic fashion, a series of brief "position statements" intended to suggest the basic contours of my approach to humor as a social practice. Then, in the second half of the chapter, I raise the question of "community," a question that is in some way at issue in every joke discussed in this book and that serves to anchor or

---

mechanistic, stimulus-and-response conception of joke-work. By observing and investi-gating his subjects' responses to contemporary cartoons, Holland refutes empirically the assumption that the joke-text, by virtue of its particular technique or internal design, provokes and organizes a single set of mental operations for virtually all recipients. But while Holland's approach is useful in opening the joke to the fractured, heterogeneous context(s) of its reception, it is compromised by his commitment to the profoundly non-Freudian idea of the individual "identity theme" (129). Ultimately his analysis can be as reductive as its alternative, simply reducing joke-work to the automatic reproduction of an inherent identity theme rather than to the automatic reproduction of the joke's inherent design.

organize much of what I have to say about literature, humor, and politics in twentieth-century Britain.

Humor as Social Practice: Rethinking Joke-Work

> The riot of carnival, the impudence of inversion, the cackling of iconoclasm: these for historical materialism are moments within, not alternatives to, that deeper comedy which is the joke of contradiction and its pleasurable release.
>
> —Terry Eagleton, *Walter Benjamin; or, Towards a Revolutionary Criticism*

1. *Humor is an event, not an utterance.* Humor, wit, comedy, jokes: these terms, between and among which one cannot rigorously distinguish,[9] refer to certain kinds of events or *énonciations*, to whole scenes and systems of symbolic exchange whose determining feature is simply the involvement of laughter. The words spoken, the gestures made, do not in themselves constitute a joke—or, to introduce a less misleading term, a "comic transaction."[10] The opening of a door and the announcement "Honey, I'm home," may or may

9. The most important attempt rigorously to distinguish these categories of the laughable is Freud's. In *Jokes and Their Relation*, he declares that wit, or joking, requires at least three participants (a joker, a laugher, and an object of laughter), that the comic requires at least two participants (a laugher and an object of laughter), and that humor, "the most easily satisfied among the species of the comic," requires only one participant, the subject of "humorous pleasure" (229). This system of head-counting doesn't stand up for a minute; as Freud's own analysis makes brilliantly clear, there are always more people involved in laughter than at first appears, and the roles of subject and object are themselves shared out or divided among multiple participants. In any case, few scholars have adopted Freud's definitions, and most today would accept "humor" and "comic" as virtually synonymous umbrella terms covering the whole range of laughable phenomena. Wherever mirth arises we are in the domain of the comic, or of humor. In showing a certain preference for "humor" as the root term of the domain, I follow the example of recent scholarship as well as the standard usage in America (according to an ethnosemantic study discussed in Apte, *Humor and Laughter* 206–10).

10. I have taken this term from Holland, *Laughing*. But it should be clear that our uses of the term are quite different. For Holland, comic transactions are receptive events whereby "we recreate our identities by means of a stimulus" (170). His analysis of humor consists in providing a "holistic explanation" of a particular individual's laughter in terms of that individual's personal "identity theme" (129), a further application of the model of reading he developed in *5 Readers Reading* (New Haven, 1975). This is something of a departure from the practice of other reader-response critics of the 1970s, whose analysis of reading-events was little more than a way to dress up the formalist platitudes of a

not be part of a comic transaction; if these actions are implicated in some-body's mirth (amusement, laughter—here again no rigorous distinctions are possible) then we must say that a joke is taking place. But we can scrutinize the opening of the door and the utterance "Honey, I'm home" as thoroughly as we like and never come any closer to an understanding of the humor. For the comic transaction, the humor-event, might in this case include an exten-sive and somewhat imperiled system of social norms regarding gender roles, familial organization, and the sexual distribution of labor. It might include a set of popular cultural texts with which the utterance "Honey, I'm home," or near variants of this utterance, would be closely associated. It might include a prior recognition, on the part of the participants, of shared, or partly shared, attitudes toward this system of social norms and this set of popular texts, and perhaps even recognition that the shared, or partly shared, attitude toward the one (bitter, oppositional) is not fully reconcilable with the shared, or partly shared, attitude towards the other (indulgent, nostalgic). These norms and texts and attitudes are not "background," they are not "context"; they are part of what constitutes the comic transaction as a comic transaction. Leave out these kinds of sociohistorical, cultural, and interpersonal consid-erations and there is simply nothing to talk about, no joke to examine. And given that this is the case, one obviously never completes the examination, never exhausts the scene of the joke. The analysis can go on forever because, to adapt the well-worn but not always well-understood phrase, there is no "outside" the joke.

Thus when we focus the inquiry into humor on particular utterances or *énoncés*, on "texts" in the formalist sense, we are misdirected from the very start. For there is no utterance that is always and everywhere laughable; there is no universal joke-text. And by the same token, there is no utterance that could not somewhere and sometime be produced and/or received with laughter. The formalist is obliged to introduce arbitrary limits or boundaries on the comic text (e.g., constraints of genre, such as the imperatives of the so-called comic ending) because, strictly speaking, there are no formalist grounds for excluding *any* text from the category of the comic.[11]

---

waning New Criticism in the novel terminology of aesthetic reception. But Holland's invocation of the "identity theme" which ostensibly secures the "wholeness of one chang-ing and unchanging individual" (*Laughing* 129) strikes me as a kind of New Critical practice as well, with the individual subject replacing the individual text as the object whose wholeness and self-identity are affirmed through interpretation. In any case, my view of the comic transaction subordinates the individual "laughing reader" to the subjec-tive organization of all the joke's participants and to the social functions of this positioning.

11. It should, for example, be regarded as a most profound embarrassment to the

2. *Comic incongruity is social contradiction.* Virtually all humor theory is built on the premises of the so-called incongruity or incongruity-and-resolution theory: humor depends on a sudden juxtaposition or "bisociation" of incompatible rules, codes, or logics (or "associative fields," "frames of reference," "universes of discourse," "circles of ideas," "semantic scripts"),[12] the negotiation of which entails an initial bewilderment followed by rapid adjustment and recovery—a "two-stage process" that somehow (under certain conditions) triggers mirth.[13] The debate whether the bewilderment or incongruity must be brought to a satisfactory resolution to be perceived as funny, or can in itself surprise one into laughter, is actually a trivial one, because every incongruity is resolved in some sense.[14] A joke that cannot be resolved in the

---

classificatory system of Northrop Frye that comedy turns out to be formally identical with melodrama. That the greatest critic of literary genres is obliged to remark that melodrama is "comedy without humor" (*Anatomy* 167), thus tacitly acknowledging the lack of any rigorous or necessary connection between comedy as a formal category and the phenomenon of humor/laughter, seems to me to discredit the entire enterprise.

12. The term "bisociation," which comes from Arthur Koestler's chapter on humor in *The Act of Creation* (New York, 1964) 35, reflects the misleading diadic emphasis of most incongruity theories. In fact, as some of my examples below indicate, humor works with contradictions between or among at least two frames of reference. Koestler uses the terms "associative field" and "frame of reference" interchangeably; he also employs the Boolean term "universe of discourse" or "discursive universe," apparently following D. H. Monro, *Argument of Laughter* (Melbourne, 1951), though he never cites this work. "Circle of ideas," or "circle of thoughts," is the term preferred by Freud (e.g., *JRU* 151), though he, too, uses "frame of reference." "Semantic scripts" is from Raskin, *Semantic Mechanisms*; "symbolic axes" is from G. B. Milner, "Homo Ridens: Towards a Semiotic Theory of Humour and Laughter," *Semiotica* 5 (1972): 1–30.

13. Because this two-stage process as described by Suls and other proponents of the incongruity-and-resolution theory cannot be distinguished from problem solving in general, many scholars have coupled the theory to certain affective and social preconditions: the recipient must be in a playful mood, sufficiently but not overly invested in the "thought-material" of the joke; the joker must not be threatening to the recipient, and other such factors. The trouble is that these various qualifying factors ultimately build up so substantial a layer of social accretions on the cognitive model as to suggest a kind of discursive version of "stone soup" (i.e., the wanderer's miraculous stone-and-water concoction, which is "improved" to perfection as fascinated villagers each volunteer a little something from their garden or larder). For an overview of "factor-analysis" studies, see Christopher Wilson, *Jokes: Form, Content, Use and Function* (London, 1979) 78–149; the "arousal theories," which focus on the recipient's degree of psychic investment in the material, are discussed on pp. 41–59.

14. Insistence on the "two-stage" model provides the polemical basis for work such as Suls's. Gregory Bateson, and his disciple William Fry, are among those who have constructed models of humor without relying on the idea of resolution. For Bateson, laughter is a response to the essentially "paradoxical" form of humorous stimulae, which, precisely

usual way—a joke with a nonsense punch line, a shaggy-dog tale—is simply resolved on the next level, as a metajoke, a joke about jokes.[15] But even in these cases, in which the comic incongruity arises partly out of expectations concerning comic practice itself, the joke is not reducible to a mere self-contained *énoncé*. On the contrary, precisely because humor *is* a social practice, self-reflexive or metajokes involve incongruities of a profoundly social character: they work, if they do work, because they are inserted into a system of social codes governing conversational behavior and into a scene of social relations (relations of power) marked by various lines of tension and strain. Indeed, a cultural outsider has even more difficulty participating in this kind of transaction than in other forms of comic exchange. (And, as anthropologists have observed, humor poses perhaps the most substantial cultural obstacles, or barriers to entry, of any everyday discursive practice.)[16]

In general we need to recognize that the incongruity that virtually every commentator has found at the heart of the comic transaction is a particular aspect of, or moment within, some binding tension or contradiction on the level of the social. The clash between incompatible scripts or universes which a joke brings about is not the product of some abstract comic essence lying within or beneath the social situation, or of an external comic principle

---

because they cannot be entirely resolved, set up a kind of mental "oscillation" on the part of the recipient. "I am always prepared to say that an electric buzzer is laughing," remarks Bateson ("The Position of Humor in Human Communication," in *Cybernetics: Circular Causal and Feedback Mechanisms in Biological and Social Systems*, Transactions of the Ninth Conference, ed. Heinz Von Foerster [New York, 1953] 11). "Paradox," wrote Fry in *Sweet Madness: A Study of Humor* (Palo Alto, Calif., 1963), "has been demonstrated to be so involved in the architecture [of humor] as to constitute its very essence" (138).

15. In a footnote to *Jokes and Their Relation*, Freud gives a fine example of one such joke: "A man at the dinner table who was being handed fish dipped his two hands twice in the mayonnaise and then ran them through his hair. When his neighbour looked at him in astonishment, he seemed to notice his mistake and apologized: 'I'm so sorry, I thought it was spinach'" (138–39). Freud rather humorlessly denounces this production as an example of "idiocy masquerading as a joke." But reflexive humor is no more idiotic than other forms; it is simply the humor proper to social fields that have become saturated with "ordinary" jokes. The craving for novelty in humor, which Freud mentions, often produces waves or cycles of jokes whose whole enjoyment depends on their apparent deviation from the rules governing normative comic exchange.

16. Apte quotes E. T. Hall, *The Silent Language*, to the effect that outsiders do not begin to gain any mastery of humor until they have become intimately familiar with a society's other practices: "People laugh and tell jokes, and if you can learn the humor of a people and really control it, you know that you are also in control of nearly everything else" (*Humor and Laughter* 17).

or comic vision imposed on the situation. It is but one version or phase of a contradiction that is itself partly constitutive of that situation. Jokes occur because society is structured in contradiction; there are no jokes in paradise, or in the telos of the good society.

3. *Humor is never "innocent."* Bergson expressed the social character of the joke by remarking that "our laughter is always the laughter of the group" (64). Comic practice is always on some level or in some measure an assertion of group against group, an effect and an event of struggle, a form of symbolic violence. The inescapable heterogeneity of society, the ceaseless conflict of social life, the multiple and irreconcilable patterns of identification within which relationships of solidarity and hierarchy must be negotiated—these are what our laughter is "about." Hence the collapse and abandonment, in Freud's text, of the distinction between "tendentious" and "non-ten-dentious" jokes, between "aggressive" jokes that draw on intergroup hostility and "innocent" jokes whose social function is a neutral one. "Even if the thought contained in them is non-tendentious," Freud belatedly acknowl-edges, "jokes . . . are in fact never non-tendentious" (132).

That is to say, the putative innocence of certain jokes dissolves once we recognize that their social character is not to be located in the supposed content of the utterances but throughout the scene of comic transaction. Even the most trivial piece of wordplay or seemingly nonsensical comic reiteration can function as a sort of rudimentary "dividing practice" (Fou-cault), as an "understanding test" (Thompson) to distinguish an "ingroup" from an "outgroup" (Martineau) affirming some cultural or subcultural identity (avant-garde, adolescent, cosmopolitan, etc.) and asserting a certain superiority over nonlaughing others.[17] (This is what Thomas Hobbes called the "sudden glory" of the laugher).[18] The point is made concisely in Don DeLillo's novel *Mao II*: "'Measure your head before ordering.' The line says everything—all the more appropriate and all the funnier because outsiders

17. Michel Foucault's term is from "The Subject and Power," Afterword to Hubert L. Dreyfus and Paul Rabinow, *Michel Foucault: Beyond Structuralism and Hermeneutics* (Chicago, 1982): "I have studied the objectivizing of the subject in what I shall call 'dividing practices.' The subject is either divided inside himself or divided from others. This process objectivizes him" (208). On humor as an understanding test, see John B. Thompson, *Studies in the Theory of Ideology* (Berkeley, 1984) 115. On ingroup/outgroup analysis of humor, see William H. Martineau, "A Model of the Social Functions of Humor," in Goldstein and McGhee, eds., *The Psychology of Humor* 117–25.

18. Thomas Hobbes, *Leviathan* (1651), *The English Works of Thomas Hobbes*, vol. 3, ed. Sir William Molesworth (London, 1840).

did not understand and all the better finally because there was nothing to understand."[19]

4. *"We do not know what we are laughing at."* Once one recognizes that humor is a group practice by means of which hostility, aggression, violent energy are inserted into a specific (but inexhaustable) social situation, there is a temptation grossly to simplify the status of the comic object, the butt or target of the joke. The comic object, one wants to say, is a particular group or segment of society whose symbolic denigration or exclusion provokes the laughter of a group hostile to it. But as the DeLillo passage indicates, neither the target group nor the group of laughers is necessarily specified at all directly; the participating groups are embedded in the transaction in complex and often highly unstable ways. This is the case because, while humor seeks to shore up identifications and solidarities, it does so by working on those very contradictions of "society" which assure that all such identifications and solidarities will be provisional, negotiable, unsettled. If we could always pin down exactly what target group was represented by a particular figure or statement in a joke, exactly where the lines of identity and difference must be drawn, then jokes themselves would cease to exist.

A Monty Python skit dating from 1969 depicts "a new kind of crime" on English streets: gangs of elderly women attacking respectable citizens, beating young men to the ground with their purses, riding their motorbikes through yarn shops, marking their turf with spray-painted slogans such as "Make Tea Not Love."[20] The comic object here is not any one particular group. In these Hell's Grannies we perceive at least two groups incongruously conflated: elderly women, whom we are expected to recognize as the proper victims rather than as perpetrators of crime, a group incapable of any but the most benign and docile forms of social behavior (and who in this sense are mocked by their unlikely transformation); and adolescent males, whom we are expected to identify as the genuine criminal class, the authentic subjects of this new crime on the streets (and who are themselves made reassuringly laughable through comic reduction, or what Herbert Spencer called *"descending* incongruity").[21] It may even be possible that in 1969, just

19. Don DeLillo, *Mao II* (New York, 1991) 170.

20. Graham Chapman et al., "Hell's Grannies" skit, "Full Frontal Nudity" episode, *Monty Python's Flying Circus* (London, 1969).

21. Herbert Spencer, "The Physiology of Laughter" (1860), in *Essays: Scientific, Political, and Speculative*, 3 vols. (London, 1868) 1:206. Spencer's famous distinction between "descending" and "ascending" incongruity (the latter, he remarks with confidence, "fails to cause laughter") is in fact rather problematic. The Monty Python skit begins with the

prior to the mugging panic in England (the panic whose construction and manipulation by cultural authorities enabled crime to be purposively articulated with "race"),[22] the joke of the elderly white woman criminal is a way of evoking and managing the threat of the young black male criminal—the quintessential mugger—and that hostility toward blacks, despite their being nowhere mentioned or depicted in the content of the skit, is nonetheless an important part of the transaction. Finally, the Hell's Granny is readable as a caricature of the sort of object which is produced through the (then-emergent) BBC television documentary approach to social problems, with its combination of simplistic, alarmist declarations, sensational images, and reassuringly banal "expert" analyses (proffered here by Eric Idle as the soundbite sociologist). As such, the skit's target is not any particular class of criminals (or victims) but the cultural apparatus by means of which criminal classes are constructed in the first place—and, by implication, the group of people (the documentary-watching bourgeoisie) who accept these mythological constructions as reality.

But the point is that none of these potential targets of derisive laughter—elderly women, rebellious young men, black youths, media experts, credulous middlebrows—constitutes *the* object of the comic transaction. The comic object—the Hell's Granny—is what Freud calls a "nodal point," a

---

image of a leather-clad young man walking through town while the documentary voice-over warns about the "new kind of crime on the streets." Suddenly, a gang of elderly women appears and beats up the youth. Who exactly is "descending" here? And what is this a descent *from*? If the youth's sudden transformation from dangerous thug to helpless victim is a comic *descent*, then what do we say of the little old ladies' transformation from helpless victims to dangerous thugs? Do the Spencerian notions of ascent and descent refer to social status, to shifting positions on a status hierarchy? The Aristotelian pedigree of such a standpoint cannot obviate the confusion it causes in regard to such classes as "criminals" and "victims": why should a mugged youth be lower (or higher) in status than a youthful mugger? One might, rather, read Spencer's formulation as referring to some sort of affective scale, to transformations from *something* (frightening, troubling, awesome, admirable) to *nothing much*. This would establish its links not to Aristotle's but to Kant's remark, quoted earlier: "Laughter *is an affection arising from sudden transformation of a strained expectation into nothing*" (*Critique of Judgment* 177). But this does not account for the apparent countermovement within the comic, from relatively neutral representations (ordinary elderly women) to loaded ones (violent elderly women). In any case, Spencer's brief text leaves all these doubts and questions unaddressed.

22. The founding text on "race" and policing in the postwar period is the Center for Contemporary Cultural Studies' *Policing the Crisis: Mugging, the State, and Law and Order*, coauthored by Stuart Hall, Charles Critcher, Tony Jefferson, John Clarke, and Brian Roberts (London, 1978). These issues are taken up in the first part of my Chapter 6.

site of condensation and overdetermination (*JRU* 163). This overdetermination of the object is one reason why, as Freud repeatedly insists, "we do not know what we are laughing at" (102, 154). We are always laughing at something too complex, too multiple and divided, to be given a proper name.

5. *Our laughter is the laughter of others.* One should add to this remark of Freud's that we don't know who the "we" is that is laughing, either. A Powellite racist (hostile to emergent social groups that, as the Python sociologist says of the Grannies, "reject *our* values") and a black cultural materialist (hostile to the hegemonic institutions that construct convenient "new" forms of crime and classes of criminal) might both laugh at the Hell's Grannies skit, but the fact that they laugh "together," and that this laughter must involve in both cases a sense of solidarity with other laughers, should not mislead us: the group that laughs is as divided and unstable as the target of laughter.

We cannot overcome this complication by invoking the intentions of the joker; a comic transaction is not controlled by the conscious and/or unconscious purposes of its speaking subject or author. We cannot restrict our analysis to instances of "successful" comic exchange or "authorized" laughter. Harvey Sacks and his colleagues have performed a discourse analysis of a joke about oral sex, told by a twelve-year-old girl to her teenage brother. The joke involves a young bride explaining to her inquisitive mother why there was such silence behind the bedroom door on the wedding night: "But Mom, you *told* me it was impolite to talk with my mouth full." Sacks notes that the joke is specifically geared to the purposes of a twelve-year-old girl, for the punch line "effects a squelch of the mother by the daughter: it says, effectively, 'if I violated a rule, I did so by reference to some other rule which *you* told me to follow.'"[23] Commenting on Sacks's analysis, however, John B. Thompson points out that the joke might serve a very different psychic purpose for the teenage brother. Because it presents women "as objects of pleasure whose capacity to satisfy male desire is enhanced by their incapacity to distinguish between a dinner table and a bed," the joke permits the satisfaction of repressed hostility toward women.[24] In an analysis of this transaction, the point is not to decide which set of hostilities, intergenerational or misogynistic, the joke is *meant* to provoke and manage but to

23. Harvey Sacks, "Some Technical Considerations of a Dirty Joke," in *Studies in the Organization of Conversational Interaction*, ed. Jim Schenkein (New York, 1978) 249–69. My discussion is based on a summary of Sacks's argument provided by Thompson, *Studies in the Theory of Ideology* 117.

24. Thompson, *Studies in the Theory of Ideology* 117.

recognize that it makes intergenerational conflict among women available to men in veiled misogynistic form, thus effecting a specious concord across lines of sexual difference.

This example points to a more general problem concerning the identity and authority of the subject of the joke. Here, a young woman who, as the speaking subject of the joke, experiences a kind of emancipation from adult authority is also and simultaneously made a target, a (sexual) object of a recipient's laughter; the one transaction effects her empowerment as subject and her domination as object. But, as Samuel Weber has pointed out in his widely influential reading of *Jokes and Their Relation to the Unconscious*, even Freud, whose analysis of the dirty joke as a male practice leaves no room for the possibility of woman-as-subject, begins to wonder about the speaker's status within the enunciation. For the dirty joker, Freud remarks, cannot succeed, cannot effect the joke-work of indirect "seduction," without the assistance of his listener. And so "the part played by the third person, the listener," is in a sense of even "great[er] importance" than that of the speaker himself (*JRU* 99). Nor is this the case only in connection with obscene jokes. Freud generalizes the point, noting that no enunciation can be called a joke without the "completion" of a "process" which "requires the participation of someone else" in addition to the speaker and the object, a "third person" whose collaboration turns out to be decisive (179).

Weber rightly sees in this economy of required collaboration an encroachment by the third person upon the position of the first person, a (Lacanian) reversal of the assumed relation of power in symbolic exchange: "For the joke-teller, it is the *third* person who, although fundamentally 'passive,' is decisive. A joke is only jocular, *witzig*, if the listener laughs. . . . The third person, as listener, decides whether or not the joke is successful—i.e. whether it is a joke or not—and thus, whether or not the *first* person really is a first person, an ego, the author, or at least the teller of a true joke. The 'decision' of the third person, therefore . . . determines the status of the joke, and with it, that of the ego telling it.[25] This is a further reason why we cannot appeal to the joker's intentions as a way of narrowing the joke's true or proper audience, its legitimate laughers. Strictly speaking, the joke has no one author; the role of subject is shared out or contested within the transac-

25. Samuel Weber, "The Divaricator: Remarks on Freud's *Witz*," *Glyph* 1 (1977): 25–26. While, as Joseph H. Smith suggests in his brief Foreword to Weber's *Legend of Freud* (Minneapolis, 1982), Weber would probably prefer that his work on Freud be characterized as Derridean rather than Lacanian (xii), there is no question that in this instance his commentary runs parallel to Lacan's.

tion. The joking subject is itself a construction of and within a process of exchange from which it is always already too late to withdraw or set aside inconvenient third persons.

The inconvenience of third persons can take more forms than Freud's discussion suggests. Like most commentators, Freud imagines that the third person's laughter completes and closes a communicative process: once the listener laughs, the subject positions are stabilized and the nature of the joke-work performed becomes clear. The only problem is posed by non-laughers, who can never be ruled out of the transaction since, as a dividing practice and an understanding test, humor always presupposes a fractured audience. But as the Hells Grannies and wedding-night jokes illustrate, the group of laughers is itself divided in any number of ways. Laughing together is not the same as reaching agreement: a listener's laughter can be a means of contesting as well as affirming the speaker's position as subject of the transaction. Humor is not a matter of "successful" or "unsuccessful" communication, but rather a practice that disrupts and problematizes what Jacques Lacan has called the "elaborate idiocy" of the communications paradigm.[26] This is why we need to regard quite skeptically the common-sensical assumption that, as Freud puts it, "laughing at the same jokes is evidence of far-reaching psychical conformity" (*JRU* 151). Humor makes us laugh not merely with our allies but with our enemies, with those whose psychical organization—whose orientation in regard to the social imaginary, the ideological repertoire—is radically irreconcilable with our own. Indeed, a very important feature of the work performed through comic exchange is that even while the transaction intensifies certain lines of difference and antagonism it selectively obscures other such lines, effecting false consensus, overlaying a scene of necessary and ongoing conflict with the illusions of identity (community) and agreement (communication).

6. *Joke-work is the "most social" form of dream-work.* Despite this and many other limitations of Freud's *Jokes and Their Relation to the Unconscious*, I have found it to offer more promising starting points than do the other founding texts of humor studies because it presents a theory of processes and not of

26. Jacques Lacan, "Sign, Symbol, Imaginary," in *On Signs*, ed. Marshall Blonsky (Baltimore, 1985) 203. Lacan's full-scale assault on the idea of communication is "Function and Field of Speech and Language," *Ecrits*, trans. Alan Sheridan (New York, 1977) 30–113, esp. 77–107. These interventions did not kill communications studies for poststructuralism, as the work of Lacan's first translator, Anthony Wilden, attests. See for example Wilden's unwieldy but provocative *System and Structure: Essays in Communication and Exchange* (London, 1972).

contents; it recognizes that what jokes *do* (their "work") is more important than what they *say* (their "meaning"), and that what they do is to transform, manipulate, reorganize, resituate the psychosymbolic material with which they are concerned. Freud's text is also, in spite of its initially misleading emphasis on the "techniques" of jokes and the minute operations of the individual psyche, ultimately clear on the point that this joke-work is an interactive social process, governed not by the needs or intentions of any one person but by the relations among all the participants and groups in the exchange. Indeed, this interaction is what distinguishes joke-work from dream-work: despite the "very far-reaching agreement" between the two processes—both of which Freud describes in terms of condensation, displacement, secondary elaboration, and "regression"[27]—the dream may be regarded as "a completely asocial mental product" while the joke is the "most social" of such products (159, 179). Of course, as Freud later spells out in *Group Psychology and the Analysis of the Ego* (1922), all psychic activity, including the dream, is social: "In the individual's mental life someone else is invariably involved, as a model, as an object, as a helper, as an opponent."[28] But joke-work is a social process in the further sense that it is always operating on more than one person at a time, fulfilling more than one set of needs and desires; it is a "Janus-like" process of production/reception (*JRU* 155), a transaction that restructures not merely the joker's underlying "thought-material" but the distinct thought-material of the listener(s), as well as the relations of joker to listener(s) and of both to the various groups compressed in the comic object.

Joke-work is thus best understood in terms of subjective positioning and of patterns of identification. The processes it involves—the condensation of various objects of hostility or anxiety on or through a nodal point, the displacement of a particular tension or contradiction onto a less threatening field of association, the circumvention of a taboo through indirect representation, representation by nonsense, and so forth—all amount to renegotiations of the

27. That is, regression "from the region of thought-structures to that of sensory perceptions," the *unthinking* of a set of ideas (and of their problematic relations to one another) which "change[s] them back into sensory images" and thus makes them representable within the scene of the dream or the joke (*JRU* 162, 163). Freud is already expressing reservations about this terminology of earlier and later "regions," which he advises "is not to be taken anatomically" or as a literal guide to the "topography of the mental apparatus" (162).

28. Sigmund Freud, *Group Psychology and the Analysis of the Ego* (1922), trans. James Strachey (New York, 1959) 1.

(relational) positions of the subjects and objects of exchange. What the joke *does* is to intervene in a particular system of social relationships, putting into circulation a "mutilated and altered transcript" of certain of the system's elements, a "most strange revision" of the problems or contradictions that bind those elements within the system (*JRU* 160, 162). And this intervention must always entail certain shifts in subjective alignment or identification, momentary adjustments along the axes of hierarchy and solidarity. Freud tries, at least intermittently, to relegate these subjective repositionings to the status of epiphenomena. But it will be my practice throughout this book to regard them as part of the joke-work itself, as necessary and indeed fundamental moments in this "mental process," which, it is the strength of Freud's text to recognize, is also a "social process"—a process that simply cannot take place without the participation of others.

7. *Politics is a joke . . . but does the joke have a politics?* The larger argument of *Jokes and Their Relation* concerns the centrality of *Witz* to unconscious processes in general. The reason his interpretations of dreams can strike critics as overly clever and indeed "in the nature of a joke," Freud argues, is that wit is the underlying process or "method" of the unconscious itself (*JRU* 173).[29] This thesis can be combined with a more recent intervention in psychoanalysis to produce the rather disconcerting conclusion that the politics of a text is a joke. I am referring to Fredric Jameson's influential argument that "the unmasking of cultural artifacts as socially symbolic acts" requires the assertion and analysis of a "political unconscious" at work in those artifacts.[30] If we accept both this thesis and Freud's, then it must be that, read on the level of the political, that is, as a "socially symbolic act," the cultural artifact—the literary text, for example—is encountered as a series of jokes. Or, to put this differently, the politics of a text has to be understood in terms of the joke-work (the socialized dream-work) it performs or enables— the redistribution of energies and repositioning of subjects it effects through processes of "condensation, displacement, indirect representation, and so on" (*JRU* 95)—and not in terms of a stable and altogether "serious" partisanship.

29. As Weber points out in *The Legend of Freud* (84–86), this is no minor point in the unfolding of Freud's work. In making the case for the "wit of all unconscious processes" Freud was defending psychoanalysis against the sweeping charge that has always dogged it: that it supplies the very symptoms it seeks to explain, that what the analysis unfailingly "reveals" are its own assumptions and procedures—its own cleverness.

30. Fredric Jameson, *The Political Unconscious: Narrative as a Socially Symbolic Act* (Ithaca, 1981) 21.

This is not politics in the sense that most commentators intend when they discuss the politics of humor or the politics of laughter. Humor and laughter have no politics—that is to say, they have no automatic hegemonic or oppositional trajectory, no global connection with practices either of domination or of subversion. Indeed, even the local instance, the particular comic transaction, is not much illuminated by the kind of analysis which insists on reading it as a "conservative" or a "progressive" event. V. N. Volosinov's emphasis on the "social *multiaccentuality*" of discourse serves us better in approaching comic transactions than does the insufficiently tempered impulse in the work of his alter-ego, M. M. Bakhtin, to embrace laughter as the liberating practice par excellence.[31]

I do not mean to deny the seemingly unavoidable strategic imperative to undertake a calculus of effects, however rough and provisional a one. While every comic transaction performs work of a complex and multivalenced kind, none can be said to induce a perfectly self-canceling set of political effects; indeed, the illusion of comic neutrality—which bears a special connection to the practice of irony—is itself a political effect to be reckoned with. An awareness of humor's social multiaccentuality should not make us apologists for the cultural dirty work, the work of domination and exclusion, which is often the special province of comic practice. Nor should it make us simply disdainful of the various utopianisms of comedy, or of the hope that Nietzsche, among many others, has expressed that "our laughter may yet have a future."[32] But if our commitment to what Michel Foucault has called strate-

---

31. V. N. Volosinov, *Marxism and the Philosophy of Language* (1929), trans. Ladislav Matejka and I. R. Titunik (Cambridge, Mass., 1986) 23; Mikhail Bakhtin, *Rabelais and His World* (1965), trans. Hélène Iswolsky (Bloomington, Ind., 1984). Such a characterization is not altogether fair to Bakhtin, who traces laughter's changing functions over time, embraces it quite selectively, and values in particular its multiaccentuality, its "multiplicity of meaning, its complex relation to the object" (142; here quoting L. E. Pinsky). Indeed, most of the major statements linking laughter either to domination or to liberation are more nuanced than we care to admit. Bergson, for example, is widely associated with the Aristotelian view of laughter as a repressive social mechanism, a means of punishing deviance. Yet what laughter "singles out and represses," according to Bergson's paradoxical analysis (117), is the tendency toward rigidity, inflexibility, or excessively rule-bound behavior; laughter is a form of social control or constraint, but it is aimed at those whose deviance consists in a *lack* of spontaneity, spirit, and freedom of behavior. Neither Bergson's nor Bakhtin's analysis is without serious problems, but both are preferable to the one-dimensional comic utopianisms that have been proliferating in recent years.

32. Friedrich Nietzsche, *Beyond Good and Evil: Prelude to a Philosophy of the Future*, trans. Walter Kaufmann (New York, 1966) 150.

gic knowledge[33] leads us at times to weigh things up, to say that a joke's political effects are *on the whole* progressive or regressive, it should also keep us somewhat skeptical of the analytical framework within which such a calculus is carried out. For strategy can be advanced only just so far where struggle continues to be thought in binary terms, where politics is always a matter of an oppressive system or a reified power and its outside or opposite, of a utopian freedom that would be achieved through subversion of authority, transgression of the law, inversion of the established order, and so forth.

What I am suggesting is that even when we decide to decide, to sum up and situate a comic transaction on this or that side of "the struggle," we should keep one eye on those places where the joke simply fails to conform to an inside/outside, two-side topography of the social field. Instead of calling upon jokes always and simply to confirm the familiar logics of inside and outside, containment and transgression, hybridization across a border, and so on, we should allow them sometimes to suggest a stranger politics than such frameworks can accommodate. In this way we can arrive at certain provisional strategic conclusions while respecting what seems to me the most urgent theoretical task now facing radical scholarship: namely, the production of new cognitive maps, new cartographies of social space itself.[34] This is not a task which my book can hope to assist except in the most glancing and incidental ways. But it should be understood that my aim in what follows is less to raise questions for humor theory than to raise questions for cultural politics—and that these must include questions about how to map a political "event," how to determine the scale of its effects, and how to connect it to other events on other levels or registers.

The most important line of connection among the many scattered comic events or transactions I will be examining is that which can be indicated by the term "community." "All literature," Jameson remarks in *The Political*

---

33. Michel Foucault, "Powers and Strategies," written interview, trans. Colin Gordon et al., *Power/Knowledge: Selected Interviews and Other Writings*, ed. Colin Gordon (New York, 1980) 145.

34. The most strenuous and exuberant effort along these lines is that represented by Gilles Deleuze and Félix Guattari, *A Thousand Plateaus: Capitalism and Schizophrenia 2*, trans. Brian Massumi (Minneapolis, 1987). One should keep in mind, too, Deleuze's reading of Foucault as "the new cartographer" in his *Foucault* (trans. Sean Hand [Minneapolis, 1988] 23–44). This reading is a valuable corrective to the many appropriations of Foucault's texts as narratives of subversion-and-containment, i.e., as dead-end elaborations of a naive cartography.

Unconscious, "must be read as a symbolic meditation on the destiny of community" (70). If we take "symbolic" in its fullest sense here, we could add that literature must be read as a concrete intervention in the politics of community, in the struggle for and over community, in the whole array of social practices—violent, exclusionary, utopian, paradoxical—which are organized around the term, the concept, the telos of "community." And, keeping in mind what has already been said, we should add as well that the literary intervention in "community" will be a witty one: in the literary text the contradictions of community will take the form of a joke; "community" will be not simply an object of meditation but a problematic within and upon which joke-work takes place.

These are in any case the presuppositions I bring, in the chapters that follow, to certain texts of Joseph Conrad, Wyndham Lewis, Virginia Woolf, Kingsley Amis, Doris Lessing, and Salman Rushdie. Whether these texts qualify as comic novels from the standpoint of genre theory is of no particular concern to me here. The important thing is to try to say what they do, what work they perform, as social and political events. And my overarching assumptions will be, first, that some of the most important work they perform is "in the nature of a joke" and therefore needs to be addressed as comic practice and, second, that from *The Secret Agent* in 1907 to *The Satanic Verses* in 1988 the specific conditions and contradictions upon which this work is performed are without exception and at the most fundamental level interwoven with the problematic of "community."

Community: The Politics of a Paradox

> *Community* can be the warmly persuasive word to describe an existing set of relationships, or the warmly persuasive word to describe an alternative set of relationships. What is most important, perhaps, is that unlike all other terms of social organization (*state*, *nation*, *society*, etc.) it seems never to be used unfavourably, and never to be given any positive opposing or distinguishing term.
>
> —Raymond Williams, *Keywords*

> Community therefore occupies a singular place; it assumes the impossibility of its own immanence, the impossibility of a communitarian being in the form of a subject. In a certain sense community acknowledges and inscribes—this is its peculiar gesture—the impossibility of community.
>
> —Jean-Luc Nancy, *The Inoperative Community*

The very ubiquity of "community" in modern social and political thought makes it at once an obtrusive and an elusive object of inquiry. For under the least scrutiny the discourse of community begins to break apart, shattering into a thousand microdiscourses, each with its own declared aims and affiliations. Nationalism, of course, is a discourse of community;[35] but so are the internationalisms (feminist, pacifist, socialist, green) that have struggled to resist the nationalist hegemony of the modern period. Communism would appear to be the discourse of community par excellence, but when we turn to fascism we find a telos of community no less fundamental or insistent. Christianity, with its promise of an ultimate communion, and liberal humanism, with its ideology of the *com-munis* or social contract and its orientation toward an ideally rational consensus (i.e., toward the *communicative* ideal), are likewise discourses of community—ways of thinking the many as one, the members of society as the fragments of a lost or immanent unity whose recovery or realization is the highest goal of humanity and the proper end of history.[36]

And this is only to mention some of the broadest movements, the most prominent names under which communitarianism has been thought and practiced. The fact is, community does not refer to a particular political option, to a discursive umbrella under which just one set of political doctrines is gathered, but to the very horizon of sociopolitical thought in our time. But while this means that we cannot simply dispense with community (even if we wanted to), it does not mean that we, too, must engage in what Georges Van Den Abbeele calls "the all but universal use of the term as an unquestioned value."[37] The more useful contributions will come, as Abbeele remarks in his introduction to the first anthology of such efforts, from those who "seek to rethink what it is that *we* mean by community when both the New Left and the New Right claim for themselves the enthusiastic appeal the notion still garners."[38]

Among those who have undertaken this rethinking of community and of the "we" that it invokes and is invoked by, Jean-Luc Nancy occupies something like a central position, though his sinuous and demanding text must be

35. Benedict Anderson, *Imagined Communities: Reflections on the Origin and Spread of Nationalism* (London, 1983).

36. See Jean-Luc Nancy, "The Inoperative Community," trans. Peter Connor, in Nancy, *The Inoperative Community*, ed. Peter Connor (Minneapolis, 1991) 1–42. Subsequent references to this book will be included parenthetically, with the title abbreviated *IC* where necessary.

37. Georges Van Den Abbeele, "Introduction" to *Community at Loose Ends*, ed. Miami Theory Collective (Minneapolis, 1991) ix.

38. Ibid.

read as a kind of thinking *with* Georges Bataille and Maurice Blanchot. this meditation, community is no longer upheld as the proper aim of so labor, as the work in whose collective production society realizes its immanent self. The work or project of community is no longer presented as the solution to the political problem (the problem of the loss of community), but as a problem in its own right—a site of much historical error and a dangerous impasse for contemporary political thought. The yearning or trajectory of all the various discourses of *immanent* community, of community as return and as destiny, from Christianity to National Socialism, is understood by Nancy and Blanchot to be death; the whole "communal system" of thought, predicated as it is on the "nostalgia for a communal being" that can never be realized in historical time, is "at the same time the desire for a work of death"; it is the thinking of "death . . . as the work of common life" (*IC* 17). In contrast, the *life* of community (to which, it must be understood, Nancy and Blanchot are themselves profoundly committed) is to be coaxed out of the endless paradoxes of its impossibility—its "negative" or "unworking" or "unavowable" character,[39] its "infinite resistance to everything that would bring it to completion" (*IC* 81). For Nancy, community must be thought in terms of the ecstatic *unworking* of any work (discursive, technical, institutional) of community building, in terms of the very "singularity" or "passion of being" which interrupts the communitarian myth and frustrates the communitarian project (*IC* 33). And what Nancy's thinking demands of us in the way of a politics is some "way of opening community to itself, rather than to a destiny or to a future" (*IC* 80).

In a different and more relaxed idiom, the neo-Gramscian "post-Marxists" Ernesto Laclau and Chantal Mouffe have also attempted to address community as a necessary impossibility, a site of interlocking paradoxes rather than a safe haven.[40] As Mouffe points out, the communitarian aim of

39. Georges Bataille, "The College of Sociology" (1939), in *Visions of Excess: Selected Writings, 1927–1939*, ed. Allan Stoekl, trans. Allan Stoekl, Carl R. Lovitt, and Donald M. Leslie, Jr. (Minneapolis, 1985) 246–53; Bataille, *The Accursed Share*, vol. 1, trans. Robert Hurley (New York, 1988), and *The Accursed Share*, vols. 2 and 3, trans. Robert Hurley (Cambridge, 1992); Nancy, essays in *The Inoperative Community*, and "Of Being-in-Common," in *Community at Loose Ends* 1–12; Maurice Blanchot, "The Negative Community," in Blanchot, *The Unavowable Community*, trans. Pierre Joris (Barrytown, N.Y., 1983) 1–27. "Unworking" is an alternative to "inoperative" as a translation of Blanchot's term *désoeuvrement*, which becomes a key motif in Nancy's text. See translators' comments in *Unavowable Community* (xxiv–xxv) and *Inoperative Community* (154n).

40. Relevant texts include Ernesto Laclau, "Community and Its Paradoxes," and Chantal Mouffe, "Democratic Citizenship and the Political Community," in *Community at Loose Ends* (83–98 and 70–82, respectively); Laclau, "The Impossibility of Society," *Cana-*

social unity is irredeemably divisive and exclusionary: "a fully inclusive political community and a final unity can never be realized since there will permanently be a 'constitutive outside,' an exterior to the community that makes its existence possible."[41] Moreover, this necessary boundary separating an inside from an outside can be erected and maintained only by means of a certain violence. The "first paradox of a free community," writes Laclau, is that "that which constitutes its condition of impossibility (violence) constitutes at the same time its condition of possibility. . . . A totally free society and a totally determined society would be . . . exactly the same."[42]

In Laclau and Mouffe's work, as also in Nancy and Blanchot's, the communitarianism that remains blind to its own violent and totalitarian dimensions is always a kind of identity politics—that is, a politics that misconceives the question of identity, failing to incorporate either "the psychoanalytic insight that all identities are forms of identification"[43] or the lessons of deconstruction in regard to the "radically relational character of all identity" and the false self-presence of the unitary subject.[44] But while Laclau and Mouffe completely reject such a politics (and, it must be added, pursue the continuing exigency of community less deeply and vigorously than Bataille/Blanchot/ Nancy), this rejection does not constitute a simple refusal of community. On the contrary, it is by opening the question of identity to psychoanalysis and deconstruction that Laclau and Mouffe begin to "open community to itself" and hence to pose it as a question, a problem and a puzzle, rather than to deploy it as a means of anticipating the end and foreclosing the political as such.

The same can be said of those feminist and postcolonial writers who have refused the convenience (the apparent tactical efficacy) of an identity politics as well as the comfort of a communitarian telos. Feminism cannot simply invoke the communitarian ideal, writes Iris Marion Young, for it is an ideal that "participates in the metaphysics of presence" and hence absorbs any politics of gender difference into a totalitarian framework of identity: "It conceives that subjects no longer need be exterior to one another. They no

---

dian Journal of Political and Social Theory 7.12 (1983): 21–24; Laclau and Mouffe, *Hegemony and Socialist Strategy: Towards a Radical Democratic Politics*, trans. Winston Moore and Paul Cammack (London, 1985).

41. Mouffe, "Democratic Citizenship" 78.

42. Laclau, "Community and Its Paradoxes" 92.

43. Mouffe, "Democratic Citizenship" 80.

44. "The point . . . at which deconstruction becomes central for a theory of politics," writes Laclau, is that of "the radically relational character of all identity." "Community and Its Paradoxes" 94.

longer outrun one another in directions they do not mutually understand and affirm. The ideal, moreover, extends this mutuality to its conception of the good society as a telos, an end to the conflict and violence of human interaction. Community here is conceived as a totality."[45] But this emphatic rejection of the communitarian ideal does not mean that feminism, even a poststructuralist feminism, has simply done with community. On the contrary, insofar as it poses a new conception of the political agent not as a unitary subject but as a precarious and negotiable articulation of subject positions, and hence as an agent constituted in difference and antagonism, poststructuralist feminism raises the very question that communitarianisms have historically shut out: the question of a *different* community, a community in and of difference, a community, as Nancy expresses it, "formed by an articulation of 'particularities,' and not founded in any autonomous essence that would subsist by itself and that would reabsorb or assume singular beings into itself" (*IC* 75).

Recent postcolonialist interventions have gestured in the same direction. Homi Bhabha installs "cultural difference" within the problematic of identity "not merely to change the 'object' of analysis—to focus, for instance, on race rather than gender or native knowledges rather than metropolitan myths . . . [but] to transform the scenario of articulation" and the whole system of "alignment of subject and object in the culture of community."[46] A true politics of cultural *différance* such as Bhabha envisions must be, as Mouffe says, "a matter not of establishing a mere alliance between given interests but of actually modifying the very identity of these forces."[47] And Bhabha recognizes that this politics, a postcolonial politics of transformative articulations across irreducible lags and differences, would entail "rethink[ing] the question of community and communication *without* the moment of transcendence,"[48] that is, without the moment of the many-as-one, without the moment when the immanent or scattered or lost "black community" is finally (re)achieved.

It is no doubt unwise to collapse together these demanding and very different writings on the problematic of community, treating the participants in this ongoing conversation as though they themselves formed an "interpre-

45. Iris Marion Young, "The Ideal of Community and the Politics of Difference," in *Feminism/Postmodernism*, ed. Linda J. Nicholson (London, 1990) 308.

46. Homi K. Bhabha, "DissemiNation," in *Nation and Narration*, ed. Bhabha (London, 1990) 312.

47. Mouffe, "Democratic Citizenship" 80.

48. Bhabha, "DissemiNation" 304.

tive community" in the liberal sense. What is taking place in and through these writings is less a charting of common ground than a necessary struggle. But one can say, quite broadly, that what informs them all and differentiates them from more banal meditations on both the left and the right is a critical and historical awareness of the catastrophes in which "community" has been fundamentally implicated; a strategic refusal to participate in the uncritical communitarianisms of the present day; and, at the same time, an acknowledgment that the political exigency, here and now, is to open community up as a paradox and a problem, and in this way to fight for its "life," rather than to deny the horizon within which it still inscribes "us" and our aspirations.

My own study shares these several inclinations, but brings them to bear in a more piecemeal, local, and historicist manner. What I have aimed to do through my readings in the politics of literary humor is to trace out intermittently, from about 1900 to the present, some of the paths community has taken through British cultural life and, more specifically, some of the mechanisms of its construction and deployment in twentieth-century literature. I have tried, that is, to perform contextualized close readings of literary texts that, in their concern with the sociopolitical dimensions of joke-work, might serve as microhistories of community.

The chronological scope of the undertaking has, however, necessitated a certain amount of macro- or broad-brush historical argument. To begin with, I have had to indicate rather roughly the context of contemporaneous discourses and debates on community against which my readings take place; and it is obviously not possible very fully to illuminate, say, liberal nationalism, anarchism, fascism, or communism—or even more manageably local communitarianisms such as Leavisism, British social feminism, New Left Culturism, Thatcherism, or black British community activism—in so cursory a fashion. In addition, I have tried to situate both the texts themselves and these various modes of communitarian discourse in relation to the broadest movements or developments in literary culture—those which have gone by the names of literary modernism, postmodernism, and postcolonialism. In this connection my work is meant as a corrective to a certain tendency in leftist cultural criticism to employ "community" as the stick with which to beat "modernism." One should not follow Raymond Williams in critiquing the politics of modernism on the grounds of an ostensible hostility or indifference to community, a lofty contempt for the social, an aesthetic of transcendent individualism, and so forth. It is precisely modernism's agitated concern with community—with problems of inclusion and exclusion, belonging and exile, solidarity and hierarchy, social essence and social destiny—which shapes its politics. What is needed is not the rejection of modernism in favor of a bright (albeit still unrealized) postmodern "future in which community may be imagined again,"[49] but a more thorough understanding of the ways community is imagined and deployed in modernism itself: the modernist text's characteristic strategies of suturing and scapegoating, the imagined patterns of social unity it conjures forth in managing such categories of social difference as nation, region, religion, ethnicity, class, and gender. That is to say, we need to stop positing community as the missing term of value whose restoration will assure the improvement of culture, and begin to understand it as a problematic term that is always already there and in relation to which the cultural work of the text (modernist or otherwise) is already being performed.

Indeed, it will be one of the general strains of argument running through this book that *post*modernism in Britain is best understood as referring not to a literature of (feminist, postcolonial, ecopolitical, or working-class subcultural) "community" which emerges with the discrediting of modernist (and white male *faux*-postmodernist) "individualism" or "elitism," but on the contrary to a kind of self-conscious stalling within the communitarian paradigm itself, which emerges with the gradual recognition of modernism's imbrication with fascist, Christian, and nationalist-imperial ideologies. This is not to say either that a modernist text such as Lewis's *Apes of God* (1930) should be read as unproblematically supporting the project of fascist community or that a postmodern/postcolonial text such as Lessing's *Golden Notebook* (1962) should be applauded for cleansing itself of modernist taint and freeing itself of all entanglement with communitarian logics. Neither the communitarian work of modernism nor the unworking of this work in the texts of postmodernism and postcolonialism is fully achieved; we are dealing here with a compromised, incomplete, and indeed manifestly impossible project of communitarian construction and with the no less uncertain and unfinished process of its deconstruction. There is indeed an important shift or turning in British literature on the question of community; I have tried to mark the turning point with Woolf's *Between the Acts* (1941). But the paradoxical character of any political thinking that takes place within the horizon of community, the constitution of its proper subjects and objects in terms of their impossibility, may be sharply illuminated by literary events on either side of this turning.

49. Raymond Williams, *The Politics of Modernism: Against the New Conformists* (London, 1989) 35.

Obviously these kinds of sweeping statements, and indeed the sweeping terms themselves (modernism, postmodernism, postcolonialism), are of only limited—and largely polemical—value. I have tried for the most part to address more finely discriminated historical conjunctures, to situate specific works of twentieth-century British fiction at specific moments of struggle over the proper meaning and destiny of community. Such moments are not reducible to the rise or fall of particular communitarian doctrines—of British fascism or social feminism or Powellism—nor does the literary text's participation in them necessarily involve any explicit invocations of "community." The readings that follow constitute neither a history of the word "community" nor a survey of the organized political movements that have occurred within its horizon. Their engagement with the problematic of community consists rather in an attempt to clarify the emergence and abeyance of particular unifying frameworks or patterns of articulation within the British social imaginary, particular strategies for managing difference and constructing identity.

These communitarian strategies are obviously multifaceted; however one makes one's way into their analysis, one encounters substantial complexities. One might begin, for example (as I begin the next chapter), with the setting or siting of national community, the geographics of England and Englishness, the management of such categories of difference as country and city, north and south, cosmopolitan and provincial. As Martin Wiener and others have shown, since the mid-nineteenth century there have been constant attempts to install the largely urban and industrial population of England within the British social imaginary as essentially a pastoral, village community: a community whose true center or authentic home is in the country.[50] This projection of the national community onto an idealized small country village is in itself open-ended, capable of being incorporated into politically quite divergent cultural projects. Where it appears in the work of, say, E. M. Forster or D. H. Lawrence, it resonates on the one hand with neofeudalist reaction (the concerted effort, from about 1800 on, to counter the nation's potentially destabilizing self-image as the most advanced and innovative of industrial societies by inventing a counterimage of "old" England anchored to "traditional" English values), and on the other hand with the line of nostalgic, anti-industrial socialism which can be traced from Robert Owen through Robert Blatchford to postwar leftists such as Richard Hoggart and

50. Martin J. Wiener, *English Culture and the Decline of the Industrial Spirit, 1850–1980* (Cambridge, 1981); see also Raymond Williams, *The Country and the City* (London, 1973).

even Raymond Williams. Where this rustic community appears in the work of women modernists such as H. D., Dorothy Richardson, or Woolf, it on the one hand contributes to a feminist polemic against the perceived male modernist embrace of technologism and warfare, and on the other hand reproduces one of the most characteristic of male modernist topoi. For while we tend to associate high modernism with the metropolis, the ideal of the village community circulates through it in the form of what Russell Berman calls a "typically modernist antimodernism." In modernist texts, says Berman, one can observe a kind of reflexive antitechnologism which seems to "follow logically [from any] account of the English countryside" and which contains "a yearning not essentially for pastness but for a genuine community of pleasure, loyalty, and freedom, a charismatic community."[51] Again, in the postwar period, one finds women authors such as Elizabeth Bowen and Iris Murdoch, as well as social feminists and Campaign for Nuclear Disarmament (CND) activists, invoking the village-type community as an organic or "green" alternative to the techno-patriarchy of the nuclear age, even while other feminist writers (e.g., Doris Lessing) are indicating as the most glaringly patriarchal element of the mainstream left its continued attachment to a myth of the village community which invariably freezes women into the traditional, self-sacrificing role of "good mother."

The point is that we can't say anything about the geographics of community in a literary text until we consider the particular structure of articulations which this setting or siting enables. The identification of an immanent national community with the country village is strategically useful precisely because it affords all manner of displacements: almost any of the real contradictions of modern industrial existence can be projected onto, and "resolved" in, the mythological village community. By the same token, the rustic setting can be used effectively to marginalize (as un-English) or to scapegoat (as threats or impediments to community) any group associated with the city—which, in a country as urbanized as England, means virtually any segment of the population. In the literature of the past century we find the valorization of the country over the city in attacks not only on the "degenerate" poor but on the "parasitic" bankers, not only on the "lazy," unemployed Irish (or West Indians) but on the "aggressive," job-stealing Jews (or subcontinental Indians), not only on the "subversive" intellectuals or artists but on the "hegemonic" cultural elite and their pacifying art industry. In each case

51. Russell A. Berman, *Modern Culture and Critical Theory: Art, Politics and the Legacy of the Frankfurt School* (Madison, Wis., 1989) 122.

the opposition between small country village and vast metropolis plays a necessary, though never a sufficient, role in organizing a particular framework of solidarities and exclusions.

What holds for the site of an imagined community holds equally for its gender, or for its racial, religious, or class complexion: while such elements are never "innocent," neither is their political valence simply given, independently of their positive and negative articulation along other axes of difference. A literary criticism that addresses questions of cultural politics in terms of communitarian strategies must be attentive both to the complex array of identifications which gets packed into a particular idea of the good society and to the peculiar double-edgedness of this process, to the violent exclusionism on which the warm vision of community depends. Communitarian strategies have served historically not simply to represent difference as identity and to repress or selectively to transform those elements which cannot be assimilated to an ideal of social unity, but also and simultaneously to reinforce and exaggerate the lines of difference which function as the community's proper boundaries and mark off the alien spaces of its constitutive outside. Every community, which is to say every "imagined community,"[52] has its scapegoat, the figure of absolute and unassimilable difference onto which the unsurmountable impediments to communitarian aims have been projected. As Slavoj Žižek has put it, the scapegoat—historically, for Europe, the Jew—appears precisely because community is impossible; the scapegoat is the "symptom" of this impossibility.[53]

Though he does not stress the fact, Žižek (who is himself the most exuberantly comic of theoreticians) is clearly aware that the whole psychosocial process of communification and scapegoat-production could be described in terms of joke-work. The Jew of the fascist imaginary, he observes, is an overdetermined fantasy figure, a figure of "displacement . . . supported by condensation"; and through this figure the fundamental blockage or bind in communitarian ideology—its self-canceling logic, its commitment to a life-in-death, its "impossibility"—is given a kind of "positive, palpable existence," an existence *as object*, which effects an "eruption of enjoyment in the

52. The phrase comes from Anderson's fine and influential study of print culture and the rise of nationalisms, *Imagined Communities*. "In fact," writes Anderson, "all communities larger than primordial villages of face-to-face contact (and perhaps even these) are imagined. Communities are to be distinguished, not by their falsity/genuineness, but by the style in which they are imagined" (15).

53. Slavoj Žižek, *The Sublime Object of Ideology* (London, 1989) 125.

social field."[54] This is just another way of saying that the Jew is the object of fascist joke-work and, more generally, that the scapegoat is the comic object that the discourse of community, seeking with all the desperate wit of the political unconscious to manage its contradictions and those of society, cannot help but produce. And in saying this we are not trivializing (treating as a joke) the actual predicament of the actual Jew or any other victim of the scapegoating process but, on the contrary, beginning to take the full measure of the violence that can be involved in comic transactions and in the pleasures they make available.

I am aware that the intertwining of literature, humor, politics, and community in this project may be troubling to some readers. If one is prepared to regard community as the contemporary horizon of the political, the political as the unconscious work of the literary text, and wit as the form or method of all unconscious processes, then one must in effect approach every piece of text (every literary event) as in some sense a joke of or about community. A study of "humor and the politics of community" would seem thereby to forfeit any claim to specificity and merge with the study of cultural politics in general.

This is a valid, but not, it seems to me, a disabling objection. The essays that follow are indeed widely scattered engagements with cultural politics. As I said earlier, they are not intended to offer a new theory of humor, a rigorous genealogy of community, or a survey of the modern cultural and political movements in whose manifestos "community" has explicitly enjoyed a place of special privilege. They are meant, rather, to show how profoundly, and often problematically, the British novel of the past century has been bound up with certain strategic patterns of inclusion and exclusion, certain visions of the good society, certain constructions of the outside and the Other. "Community" is simply the most adequate term for naming the paradigm or horizon within which these patterns, visions, constructions have appeared; "humor" (or "joke-work") the most adequate term for naming the treacherous, seductive processes of their engagement and transformation by the literary text. Taken together, humor and community provide a new and, I believe, particularly fruitful way to assess the modern British novel as a socially symbolic event.

54. Žižek, *Sublime Object of Ideology* 125, 126.

One

Covert Operations: The Unworking of the "Working Community" in *The Secret Agent*

> Conservatism is the anarchism of the fortunate, anarchism the conservatism of the deprived.
> —Irving Howe, "Conrad: Order and Anarchy"

> The true anarchist . . . is the millionaire.
> —Joseph Conrad, letter to R. B. Cunninghame Graham

> The criminal has always been bourgeois.
> —Theodor W. Adorno and Max Horkheimer, "A Theory of Crime"

Community needs to be sited; it requires a place, a geography, a putative center and periphery. One would have thought that community would be where the people are, where the business of society is conducted. But the briefest reflection on the kinds of images which are routinely used to evoke communitarian feelings about England and Englishness—images of the depopulated pastoral countryside or village green—reminds us that "community" expresses a yearning and a dream, not a concrete reality. The relation between discourses of community and the actual geographics of social arrangement has always been a complex and indirect one in Britain, such that the population centers—and even the population itself—have served more often than not as putative obstacles to the communitarian ideal. They occupy the center of anxious attention, and as such appear to be the central problem or even the problem *at the center*, but the true center of the community's self-immanence is somehow always to be located elsewhere.

By the turn of the last century, the great heavy-industrial cities of the North could no longer serve even as the center of attention for the ongoing debates over what was wrong with the condition of England. The British economy's gradual transition to what Tom Nairn has called the "new imperialism," whereby the nation staked out a dominant position in the world's financial markets as compensation for a domestic manufacturing base severely eroded by foreign competition, had reestablished London as the place from which both the fortunes of the nation and those of Empire depended.[1] This change had been accompanied by an ideological disavowal of England's thoroughly industrial character, in the form of a collective reimagining of Englishness as essentially southern and rural (hedgerows, village greens, thatched roofs)—that is, as precisely the opposite of northern urbanindustrial, which now came to constitute the very definition of "provincial."[2] Needless to say, even the relatively light-industrial character of London was a far cry from this dominant rural ideal of authentic England. Though it effectively muted Victorian uneasiness over conditions in Manchester and the North, the myth of the "South country" simply substituted London as the new site of condensation for the social and cultural anxieties of an empire in the early stages of legitimation crisis.

Nearly every commentator of the day agreed that the most pressing problems facing English society were traceable to London. The difficulty was in sorting out causes and effects, identifying the villains and victims, and especially situating "outcast" groups in relation to intrinsic problems. Conservatives, following the tradition of Burke, Coleridge, Carlyle, and Arnold, embraced the ideal of organic community conceived in nostalgic and quasifeudalist terms. A village model of stable and orderly community was thereby opposed to the perceived squalor, sprawl, and disarray of London, with particular horror and disgust focused on the "degenerating" masses of the East End. But it was never clear whether these degenerates were themselves "the English" or rather some sort of alien virus on the social body. Confused environmental-eugenic analyses simultaneously "otherized" the poor as a genetically separate group and took them as the leading indicator of an

1. Tom Nairn, *The Break-up of Britain: Crisis and Neo-Nationalism* (London, 1977): "As the 'industrial revolution' waned from the mid-19th century onwards the more conscious and systematic exploitation of these advantages [of "developmental priority"] compensated for domestic backwardness. A 'New Imperialism' took over from the old, with the establishment of financial control of the world market as its core" (21).

2. See Wiener, *English Culture*; also Alun Howkins, "The Discovery of Rural England," in *Englishness: Politics and Culture 1880–1920*, ed. Robert Colls and Philip Dodd (London, 1986) 62–88. As these and other commentators have pointed out, a very specific image of rural England is operative here: the depopulated, postenclosure countryside of a thoroughly industrialized nation.

urban-induced decay threatening the "racial vigour" of the (ostensibly rural) English populace itself.[3] More charity-oriented Whig liberals frequently ran up against similar uncertainties. Calling upon a broader version of the organicist tradition (substituting, where convenient, Ruskin or Dickens for Carlyle, Eliot or Hardy for Arnold, and so forth), Whigs underscored the degraded environmental and moral conditions of city life and the need for social programs or even relocation to salvage and redeem the increasingly isolated London poor. But whether the objects of such charity were themselves the proper subjects of degeneration, or whether the degenerative urban environment was in fact attributable to a decadence of the London middle and upper classes, was a point of contention and confusion in Whig social commentary. Even for radical socialists, the roots of decay proved difficult to locate in social terms. Their own nostalgia for preindustrial village life readily apparent in the work of such writers as William Morris and Robert Blatchford,[4] the socialists were a good deal clearer about the fact that a rejection of industrialization and mass urbanization meant a rejection of capitalism, and they were more willing to denounce the corruption and parasitism of the London bourgeoisie. But they participated in the general symptomatology at least to the point of bracketing the issue of Empire while sharing certain suspicions and resentments toward the (mostly union-resistant) "casual poor" of London.[5]

This whole situation was exacerbated by the South African War (1899–1902), which initially swept many key liberals and some socialists into the rising tide of Late Victorian jingoism[6] and then, as the conflict wore on, led to the widespread view that even the Empire's military debacles were a consequence of hereditary urban degeneration: it was believed that because London (and the other large cities) had increasingly to supply the pool of

---

3. See Richard Solloway, "Counting the Degenerates: The Statistics of Race Deterioration in Edwardian England," *Journal of Contemporary History* 17 (January 1982): 155.

4. Robert Blatchford, whose sermon-like anti-industrial tract *Merrie England* ranks among the most influential pieces of socialist writing in British history (it sold some 750,000 copies in 1894), made no secret of the fact that, as he saw it, socialist thought in England owed much less to Marx than to the organicist strain of liberalism; the socialist movement, he said, is "largely the result of the labours of Darwin, Carlyle, Ruskin, Dickens, Thoreau, and Walt Whitman." Quoted in John Callaghan, *Socialism in England since 1884* (Oxford, 1990) 57.

5. See Gareth Stedman Jones, *Outcast London: A Study in the Relationship between Classes in Victorian Society* (Clarendon, 1971) 337–49; also Callaghan, *Socialism in Britain* 10–29.

6. See Richard N. Price, "Society, Status, and Jingoism: The Social Roots of Lower Middle Class Patriotism, 1870–1900," in *The Lower Middle Class in Britain, 1870–1914*, ed. Geoffrey Crossick (New York, 1977) 89–112.

potential recruits, Britain's army was becoming less and less fit to defend the realm from competing powers.[7] In sum, wherever they appeared on the political spectrum, and in no matter what specific articulation, anxieties about the disintegration of the community, the deterioration of the populace, and the decline of the Empire converged on the denizens of London, who served as the necessary nodal point for turn-of-the-century moral panics and political myths.

Such a situation—which not infrequently gave rise to Roman analogies on the model of Gibbon ("a great Empire, overextended, hugely wealthy, and relying increasingly on native and colonial peoples to maintain its wealth, [is] destroyed because of decay at the center")[8]—could be expected to foster the production of satire, an essentially urban literature of alarm and recrimination. And yet satire did not flourish at the turn of the century. Edwardian condition-of-England literature, in both its popular and elite forms, tended to proceed indirectly, focusing on what might be called the remote center, the rustic community of an imperiled authentic England—even when, as with Hardy or Forster (though not with Kipling), these refuges were at least partly understood to be compromised or illusory.[9] Joseph Conrad's seemingly routine decision, in 1904–5, to write a London political satire entirely devoid of pastoral idyll—*The Secret Agent*[10]—was thus something of a deviation from dominant literary practice; in a paradox that marks the new "social situation" of British literature in the twentieth century, Conrad's self-consciously marginal, outsider relation to the dominant culture enabled an unusually direct and unsettling engagement with the perceived crises of the national community.[11]

7. See Stedman Jones, *Outcast London* 78; Solloway, "Counting the Degenerates."

8. Howkins, "The Discovery of Rural England" 65.

9. See Wiener, "The 'English Way of Life'?" in Wiener, *English Culture* 41–80; Peter Brooker and Peter Widdowson, "A Literature for England," in Colls and Dodd, eds., *Englishness* 116–63, esp. 126–41; Raymond Williams, *The English Novel from Dickens to Lawrence* (London, 1971) 115–68.

10. Joseph Conrad, *The Secret Agent* (1907; Garden City, N.Y., 1954). Subsequent references to this edition will be included parenthetically, with the title abbreviated *TSA* where necessary. I should note here that the fantasy of a nonurban, preindustrial land where the Englishman authentically belongs does appear in the novel, in the Assistant Commissioner's brief nostalgic reveries of colonial life, "in a jungle many thousands of miles away from departmental desks and official inkstands" (130). As the example of Kipling's later novels makes clear, the communitarian myth of the South Country was curiously intertwined with colonial fantasies of adventure and self-reliance.

11. On the new cultural role of the social outsider, see Raymond Williams, *The Long*

I am aware that to call *The Secret Agent* a satire invites objections. It is not simply that established critical practice has situated Conrad's work in general at a fair remove from the comic, or even that *The Secret Agent* in particular has often been judged a painfully mirthless production. Every comic transaction is after all characterized by divisions among (as well as within) its participants. The pronounced split, manifest in the earliest reviews and persisting to the present day, between readers who take *The Secret Agent* to be a hugely comic "entertainment" and those who find it rather a "sombre," "bleak," or even a "repulsive" novel,[12] merely throws into especially sharp relief the contestatory and uncertain status of humor in general. The specific lines of division which have appeared in the readership of *The Secret Agent* around the question of humor—and their relation to larger instabilities in the reception of Conrad—will certainly be of interest here, but they do not in themselves constitute a special obstacle to analysis of the novel's joke-work. The weightier objections to approaching *The Secret Agent* as satire are, first, that for reasons outlined in my introductory chapter, this sort of generic category can be a dubious and misleading tool of comic study and, second, that as a typical modernist instance of sustained ironic discourse *The Secret Agent* is a text that insists on *not* being read, beyond a certain point, as satire—that is, as partisan mockery. I take both these points, and indeed am concerned neither to demonstrate the novel's conformity to some set of generic criteria nor to evade the problems posed by its notoriously thoroughgoing irony. Nevertheless, I begin with some rather narrow questions about the novel's "satiric" target(s): what group on the political field of turn-of-the-century England supplies the text's primary comic objects—the scapegoats of its communitarian logic—and what are the means of their comic objectification? But

---

Revolution (1961; Westport, Conn., 1975) 239–45. In his valuable essay "Romanticism, the Self, and the City: *The Secret Agent* in Literary History," *Boundary 2* 9 (Fall 1980): 75–89, Jonathan Arac connects both Conrad's anxious relation to the urban experience and his "off-center" relation to the dominant culture with a broadly romanticist legacy. For Arac, Conrad figures as one of the "belated Romantics who have yearned for the unified culture, the order of tradition, that Rome represents, but who must seek their goal as demonic adversaries, not suppliants" (88).

12. "Entertainment" is taken from Albert Guerard, *Conrad the Novelist* (Cambridge, Mass., 1958) 222; "sombre" from an unsigned review, *New York Times Book Review* (21 September 1907), rpt. in *The Secret Agent: A Casebook*, ed. Ian Watt, Casebook Series (London, 1973) 55; "bleak" from an unsigned review, *Putnam's Monthly*, December 1907, rpt. in Watt, ed., *Casebook* 55; and "repulsive" from an unsigned article, "On Ugliness in Fiction," *Edinburgh Review*, April 1908, excerpts rpt. in *Conrad: The Critical Heritage*, ed. Norman Sherry, Critical Heritage Series (London, 1973) 202.

this line of questioning is meant to highlight the considerable difficulties involved in specifying either the objects or the effects of the novel's satiric procedures, and ultimately to force open the category of satire rather than to secure or stabilize it. In the second part of the chapter I take up the further difficulties introduced by what Conrad called his "ironic method,"[13] a practice that has frequently been taken as constitutive of literary modernism in general. This discussion does not, however, simply confirm the impossibility of locating ideologically a practice that consists in ceaseless movement or slippage among incompatible positions. Rather, my attempt is to specify the work irony can perform on social and historical terrain, even while the ironist refuses any fixed place on that terrain. I will try to show that in *The Secret Agent* the joke-work connected with irony is in fact far more conservative, exclusionist, and narrowing of community than is the joke-work performed through transactions that approximate more readily to the model of reactionary satire. A wider implication of this argument is that the hegemonic liberal-imperial conception of the English community which sustained itself in the face of considerable anxiety, discontent, and active resistance in the late nineteenth and early- to mid-twentieth centuries may have operated most effectively not through overt vehicles of counterrevolution but through various "apolitical" discourses, of which modernist irony was a rapidly emergent instance.

Anarchy in the Flesh

> On the whole, my idea is that he was much more of an anarchist than he confessed to me or to himself.
>
> —Joseph Conrad, "An Anarchist"

Walter Benjamin once remarked of Baudelaire: "It seems of little value to give his work a position on the most advanced ramparts of the human struggle for liberation. From the beginning, it appears much more promising to follow him in his machinations where he is without doubt at home: in the enemy camp. These machinations are a blessing for the enemy only in the rarest of cases. [He] was a secret agent, an agent of the secret discontent of his class with its own rule."[14]

13. Conrad, "Author's Note" (*TSA* 12). Hereafter cited parenthetically as AN.
14. Walter Benjamin, quoted by Herbert Marcuse, *The Aesthetic Dimension* (Boston, 1977) 20.

To begin to see how this description might be usefully extended to the author of *The Secret Agent*, we need to think about the novel's comic objects *as objects*, that is, to consider the precise means of their objectification. For in his attempts to render the anarchists of Late Victorian London laughable, to make them the scapegoats of his discourse of community, Conrad indeed performs some machinations in the conservative camp which are at best a mixed blessing for the forces of reaction.

A particularly conspicuous and significant means of comic objectification in the novel is the association of anarchism with fatness. As J. Hillis Miller has remarked, it comes as "something of a shock" to realize just "how many of the characters in *The Secret Agent* are fat."[15] But because not all these characters profess to be anarchists, and not all their bodies afford the same kind of comic shock, Miller and others have tended to view the novel as presenting us in effect with a fat "world," rather than a specific logic of association through which the body of the anarchist becomes, in Bergson's terms, a comical encrustation of flesh on the vital spirit of anarchism (anarchy, if you will, *in* the flesh).[16] Such a logic becomes apparent, however, if we begin to construct a rough typology of large bodies in the text—some of these providing a more pronounced and resonant shock of comic incongruity than others.

The "vast . . . bulk and stature" of Sir Ethelred (118), the novel's "great personage" of the ruling class, for example, is not at all of a kind with the "monstrous" physique of Michaelis (96), the book's most voluble anarchist proselytizer. Modeled on Sir William Harcourt, the ambitious secretary of state whose mammoth size made him a favorite subject for late-nineteenth-century political cartoons, Conrad's "great personage" confirms first of all a normative association between big men and power. That Sir Ethelred gives the impression of actually "expanding" may be, as the narrator remarks, "unfortunate from a tailoring point of view" (118), but it is an appropriate and desirable impression for a politician to make, inasmuch as it suggests that his power, however extensive, has yet to reach its full scope. (Harcourt, incidentally, had managed to convey this impression in 1894, the year the novel is set, for there was a general expectation that he would succeed William Gladstone that year as prime minister.)[17] Sir Ethelred's "big and

---

15. J. Hillis Miller, *Poets of Reality: Six Twentieth-Century Writers* (Cambridge, Mass., 1965) 50.

16. Bergson, *Laughter* 92–93.

17. See Norman Sherry, *Conrad's Western World* (Cambridge, 1971) 294. My discussion of the political background of *The Secret Agent* owes much to the latter half of this major study.

rustic presence" is likened to that of an oak, immediately triggering the association with lineage: "indeed the unbroken record of that man's descent surpassed in the number of centuries the age of the oldest oak in the country" (119). A large body in this instance means a good blood line, which chimes exactly with the terms of the ongoing hereditary-degeneration panic. According to the logic of degeneration, large = robust = rustic, while small = sickly = urban; the frequently bogus or mishandled statistical studies of the period emphasize above all the "stunted growth" of the degenerating urban masses as against the fine statures of the country-bred folk.[18]

Conrad has as much fun with his caricature of Sir William Harcourt as did Sir John Tenniel and other Late Victorian cartoonists, but the size of the great personage is not really shocking or incongruous. Like the *DNB* entry that describes Harcourt's "robust proportions" as "eminently suited to his vigorous and aggressive temperament,"[19] *The Secret Agent* marks his enormous size as perfectly fitting his station. Nor is "fatness" really an issue here; Sir Ethelred is referred to constantly as a big man, never as a fat one. In this respect a very sharp contrast emerges between the treatment of the home secretary and that of Michaelis, the one anarchist who rivals Sir Ethelred for sheer size. As the "apostle of utopian hopes" within the London anarchist movement, Michaelis suggests Pëtr Kropotkin as a model (though his "saintly" socialism, more evangelical than philosophical, is recognizably English), but physically his resemblance is to Mikhail Bakunin, the anarchist "Apostle of Destruction."[20] Michaelis is described as utterly "monstrous," a figure of "grotesque and incurable obesity" (96), "round like a tub, with an enormous stomach and distended cheeks of a pale, semi-transparent complexion" (46). The extraordinary dimensions that enhance Sir Ethelred, offering a reassuringly "big and rustic Presence," carry negative value in the case of Michaelis, making him "quite startling" to look at, and "virtually a cripple" (99). Michaelis is big, but emphatically not of sound blood line; like all the novel's anarchists (but unlike Ethelred/Harcourt) he is childless, and his obesity is consistently associated with impotence—with the declining reproductive capacity (i.e., "racial vigour") of a sickly society—rather than with the fecundity of the material body. This, to invoke Mikhail Bakhtin, is the "new bodily

18. *23rd Annual Report of the Poor Law Board*, quoted by Stedman Jones, *Outcast London* 129.

19. Quoted in Sherry, *Conrad's Western World* 292.

20. See Sherry, *Conrad's Western World* 260–73. Bakunin (1814–76) had in fact died eighteen years before the Greenwich outrage (and thirty years before publication of *The Secret Agent*).

canon of art" with a vengeance: a "grotesque system of images" in which the "purely satirical, that is, negative" predominates, and the renewing, regenerative meanings of the "true grotesque" have been all but completely eliminated.[21]

The contrasting treatment of Sir Ethelred and Michaelis, both modeled after notoriously oversized figures on the Late Victorian political scene, suggests that the novel is concerned to establish a specific symbolic association between radicalism and fatness and that the comic shock effects felt by many readers have more to do with this association than with a general preponderance of large-bodied characters. When the delegates to the International Red Committee meet in Verloc's house in chapter three, there is scarcely a normative or "healthy" body under the roof. Verloc, the secret agent, is "very corpulent" (28), a "fat . . . animal" (30), "burly in a fat-pig style" (24). Comrade Ossipon is so extremely "robust" that the word becomes a descriptive tag; Conrad repeats it dozens of times. Even Karl Yundt, the self-declared "terrorist," a dried-up, wasted little man, is "deformed by . . . swellings" (47); in this respect he resembles several other characters who, while not actually fat, are somehow "marred by too much flesh" (103).

The novel's rather careful distribution of fatness among its large-bodied characters might seem to confirm the unity and stability of its comic object and to invite a simple translation of Conrad's obesity jokes into the language of sober reaction against the anarchist movement. But identifying the fat anarchist as the novel's primary comic object does not really settle anything, for as Freud emphasizes, we still "do not know what we are laughing at" (*JRU* 102). The fat anarchist is a *witty* construction, a complex and contradictory figure that is not reducible to the anarchist as such. And despite being unthinkable outside the processes of joke-work, this figure is not an alternative *comic* version or translation of a political thought but a particular moment within a politics that is itself, precisely, a witty negotiation of internalized but unassimilable contradictions in the social order.

The "what" we are laughing at here is neither an object of fixed identity nor a simple condensation of two incompatible objects of fixed identity. It is the kind of complex condensation that D. H. Monro, Arthur Koestler, and other humor theorists have described in terms of bisociated discursive "universes": it puts into play a whole series of related incongruities along such axes as the literary, the social, the ideological. As regards the literary dimension, for example, it is evident throughout Conrad's work that the notion of

21. Bakhtin, *Rabelais and His World* 319, 306.

fatness invokes for him a more general semantic code of inactivity, whose terms include idleness, indolence, gluttony, lethargy, immobility, inertness, complacency, domesticity, leisure—all key words of *The Secret Agent* (a novel built, in Jamesian fashion, on key words). The anarchists in the novel simply don't *do* much; they are "constitutionally averse to every superfluous exertion" (24). Their tendency toward corpulence thus constitutes a flagrant violation of the generic code of action invoked by the title and (intermittently) by the thematics of the novel. Mark Conroy is correct to say that in *The Secret Agent* "the now familiar ethos of espionage novels is [already] developed fully."[22] But it must also be said that the novel constantly transgresses the very norms it helped to make familiar, creating through the bathos of obesity a series of "descending incongruities" which disappoint generic expectations.[23] This ostensible action novel of "Diplomatic Intrigue and Anarchist Treachery" (as the American publishers had it)[24] slides continually into a

22. Mark Conroy, *Modernism and Authority: Strategies of Legitimation in Flaubert and Conrad* (Baltimore, 1985) 140.

23. One should exercise caution, however, in assuming the *unique* orientation of a comic incongruity. As I mentioned in the Introduction, Spencer's well-known rule that such incongruities "descend," bringing low the high and mighty, tends to obscure the range of hostilities and desires that joke-work is called upon to manage, as well as the multiplicity of subject positions which a joke opens to its readers or listeners. On this question of genre, for example, one could say that Conrad's "bisociation" of the code of action with the code of leisure, the spy novel with the domestic drama, brings the "high" world of global politics together with the "low" world of petit-bourgeois family life. But the novel is not on that account reducible to either a parody of espionage fiction or a satire of the Anglo-European political scene. From one vantage, *The Secret Agent* reads as parody of Victorian domestic realism and as satire of conventional Victorian familial relations, which hold the husband's role as breadwinner and the wife's as caregiver separate from and inaccessible to each other. The great secrecy required of secret agent Verloc, and the corresponding duplicity of Winnie (who married him only to gain financial security for her brother Stevie), produce a hyperbolic—and, in the climactic murder scene, wickedly funny—version of this mutual isolation and lack of communication, of the "respectable" but "undemonstrative" Victorian marriage that Conrad satirizes briefly in *Typhoon* and elsewhere. Certainly during the writing of *The Secret Agent* the emotional and financial demands of marriage and fatherhood caused Conrad far more distress than any he might have suffered in connection with the London political underground. He seems at any rate to have been peculiarly fascinated around this time by the (more or less false) idea that anarchists "preached the dissolution of all . . . domestic ties" ("The Informer" in Joseph Conrad, *A Set of Six* [1908; Garden City, N.Y., 1922] 89), an idea expressed at various moments in *The Secret Agent* by Vladimir, Ethelred, and the Assistant Commissioner.

24. In a 7 November 1906 letter to Algernon Methuen, Conrad reports this phrase from posters advertising the Amercian serialized version of the novel. *The Collected Letters of Joseph Conrad*, ed. Frederick R. Karl and Laurence Davies (Cambridge, 1988) 3: 370–71.

novel about marital relations and domestic routines, a novel in which eating and sleeping provide much of the line-by-line "action," while "the disposal of a few tables and chairs" belonging to one's mother-in-law can assume the character of a major event (133). It reaches its climax when the "domestic carving knife" (217) puts an end to the "domestic tiff" (212) between Verloc and his wife; in the end, the corpse of the "invaluable Secret Agent" (235) resembles nothing so much as "Mr. Verloc in the fulness of his domestic ease reposing on the sofa" (233).

This generic conflation of imperial and domestic themes is a "literary" joke, but, as Martin Green and Daniel Bivona have shown, such interleavings always operate as part of a larger economy of contradictions and evasions. Conrad's comic figure of "inert fanaticism, or perhaps rather . . . fanatical inertness" (24) is a way of evoking and managing certain key contradictions in the late-imperial social order, particularly those centered on the question of labor. Ian Watt has shown how crucially labor operates in Conrad's "code of solidarity"; work binds the community together, while "resentment . . . against work" is *the* major threat to social cohesion.[25] From this standpoint (which accounts for Conrad's rather surprising professions of solidarity with the emergent Labour party, the party of "British working men"),[26] not to work is to force others to do your work for you; it is to withdraw more than you invest. Hence for Conrad the indolent man is a social parasite; and just as his antagonism to the "working community" (as Raymond Williams rightly terms Conrad's ideal social unit)[27] is typically represented in Conrad's texts as foreignness or "un-Englishness" (usually of a Russian or Germanic stripe), so is his excessive concern for his own comfort typically represented by a fat body, symbolically the body of one who takes more in than he gives out.

The (Germanic) captain of the *Patna* in *Lord Jim* (1900) exemplifies this type and his function: it is not just that he is "the fattest man in the whole blessed tropical belt," resembling "a trained baby elephant walking on hind legs" but that he is "larger of girth than any living man *has a right to be*" (my emphasis).[28] The manifest excess of his consumption over his production violates the "code of solidarity" from which the very rights of social man are derived. Although there are problems with Bergson's analysis of obesity in *Le Rire* (a text contemporaneous with *The Secret Agent*), he was right to see the

25. Ian Watt, *Conrad in the Nineteenth Century* (Berkeley, 1979) 103.
26. Quoted in Avrom Fleishman, *Conrad's Politics: Community and Anarchy in the Fiction of Joseph Conrad* (Baltimore, 1967) 47.
27. Williams, *The English Novel* 141.
28. Joseph Conrad, *Lord Jim* (1900), ed. Thomas Moser (New York, 1968) 23.

comedy of bodily excess as an index of some perceived threat to the solidarity and survival of the laughing group.[29] In the recurring Conradian figure of the flabby seaman, the nonworking member of the idealized working community of the ship—a figure of which the fat anarchist is merely an urban variant—one can readily make out the "soft spot" of an imperial society increasingly anxious about its own fatal parasitism: "They loved short passages, good deck chairs, large native crews, and the distinction of being white. They shuddered at the thought of hard work . . . and in all they said—in their actions, in their looks, in their persons—could be detected the soft spot, the place of decay" (*Lord Jim* 9). In *The Secret Agent* Conrad, like so many social commentators of the day, displaces his representatives of the cultural "soft spot" or "place of decay" to the squalid neighborhoods of London, but these prevailing anxieties about imperialism remain very much a part of the landscape. In this respect the text captures a key displacement in the discourse of national/racial decline. The oft-asserted degeneration of the urban populace, though centered on casual laborers and other poor, was often linked in a scientifically empty but ideologically powerful way to a blood-thinning urban atmosphere of decadence and nonproductivity whose subject, at least implicitly, was the bourgeoisie of late-imperial capitalism. A typical liberal diagnosis of the period, J. A. Hobson's *Imperialism* (1902), depicted London as a place of "plush parasitism," where great comfort was enjoyed by precisely those who kept themselves at furthest remove from the actual sites of productive labor—the northern cities and the colonies.[30] As with Conrad, who speaks of London in his "Author's Note" to *The Secret Agent* as an "enormous," "monstrous . . . devourer" (11), the city itself seems in such analyses to have grown larger than it "has any right to be" by lounging in the good deck chairs of global, European-controlled capital. The relation between the overweight citizen and the overgrown city is in this sense homologous as well as synechdocal, and fraught with the tensions of a late-imperial bourgeoisie whose professed valorization of work and of the working community only half conceals a global mode of production in which rewards accrue to the nonlaboring few.

Also put into play by the novel's bisociation of action with inaction is a set of contradictions involving the concepts of theory and practice as these informed contemporary political thinking. The dubious distinction, so often and opportunistically employed to typologize (and to divide) the anarchist

29. Bergson, *Laughter* 93.
30. Quoted in Nairn, *Break-up of Britain* 23.

movement,[31] between the political agent who "acts" and the one who "merely" talks or writes, is a highly visible one in Conrad. The fat anarchist is, of course, a comic figure because his failure in the realm of praxis is so continually on display: his revolutionism is "purely" theoretical and therefore self-contradictory. But the terms of this joke, which oppose practice to theory in a simple high/low binarism, involve their own contradictions and failures. The joke must necessarily evoke a certain yearning for revolutionary action as such, for the "pure" practice that can move the world—in whatever direction. The denigration of anarchy *in* the flesh, of encrusted and immobilized anarchy, entails a certain positive investment in an anarchy *of* the flesh, in the idea of anarchy materially achieved. The joke of the fat anarchist thus depends on a profound ambivalence toward the existing social order, an order that the "revolutionary spirit" is resented both for threatening in theory and for failing to threaten in practice.[32]

The farcical generic slippage between espionage novel and domestic melodrama is thus also a slippage between worker and parasite, colonized and colonizer, genuine *révolté* and mere radical *philosophe*. What makes *The Secret Agent* funny, in other words, what makes it work as satire, is not its ostensibly hostile or abusive disposition toward some group that one can firmly situate in social terms, but rather its dependence on a highly overdetermined and condensed figure the very appearance of which depends on ceaseless internal play. It is not only that Conrad's fat anarchists are "a lazy lot" (54) who find revolutionary theory more congenial than revolutionary practice and who are content to reap the benefits of a European colonial order, but that they are so "thoroughly domesticated" (19), so devoted to their personal "repose . . . and security" (54), that their first response to any manifestation of revolutionary activism is to mount a defense of the status quo. Such "anarchists" as these are hard to distinguish from the law-abiding, self-interested, and complacent bourgeoises of London, who make their

31. Marie Flemming, in *The Anarchist Way to Socialism: Elisée Reclus and Nineteenth-Century European Anarchism* (London, 1979) 208–13, traces attempts to distinguish the "*practiciens*" from the "*philosophes*" of anarchism from the late 1890s into the early twentieth century, and shows why any strict distinction along these lines "is not valid" historically (23). Flemming does not mention the most strenuous attempts to legitimate this distinction "scientifically," which were made by Cesare Lombroso, the major theoretician of degeneracy, whose work is constantly invoked by Comrade Ossipon in *The Secret Agent*. See Cesare Lombroso, *Crime: Its Causes and Remedies* (Boston, 1911) 227–28.

32. Conrad, "A Familiar Preface" to *A Personal Record*, in Conrad, *"The Mirror of the Sea" and "A Personal Record,"* ed. Morton Dauwen Zabel (Garden City, N.Y., 1960) 192.

little profit off the labor of others. The "fat-pig" anarchist, as Conrad puts it, might be taken for "anything from a picture-frame maker to a locksmith; an employer of labour in a small way" (24). The whole system of images in which the anarchists are embedded can thus be smoothly transposed into a left-liberal or radical critique of the English middle class. Indeed, these are exactly the terms in which the anarchist leader Mr. X rails against the bourgeoisie in "The Informer," which Conrad composed not long before *The Secret Agent*: "the idle and selfish class . . . the well-fed bourgeoisie . . . the overfed taskmasters of the poor . . . the bourgeoisie, the smug, overfed lot . . . these gorged brutes."[33]

This condensation or overdetermination in the comic object is emphatically not reducible to a simple figure of hypocrisy. The object here is rather a figure of *ressentiment*, which Jameson has rightly called "the fundamental conceptual category" of counterrevolutionary modernist thought from Nietzsche to Wyndham Lewis and George Orwell.[34] By asserting the *ressentiment* of society's losers and have-nots, their poisonous envy and their desperate recurrence to dreams of destructive vengeance, these modernist writers have tried to account on a psychological level for phenomena of mass resistance (such as anarchism) which they cannot or will not address on a material level, that is, as effects of profound social and economic oppression. What we see in *The Secret Agent* is that the logic of *ressentiment* as an explanatory category is what in philosophy one would call a paradox, in the visual arts an optical illusion, and in literature a joke. For the object of anti-*ressentiment* discourse (the slave bent on a miserable revenge of the weak over the strong), presumed to be the subject of *ressentiment* proper, must always become identified with the *object* of *ressentiment* (the dominant class, for the slaves are resentfully perceived as the true masters of a decadent contemporary situation) and hence with the presumed subject of the anti-*ressentiment* discourse. In short, what the explanatory category explains is the explanation itself. The effect is not one of simple inversion, but of an "oscillation [which] . . . has no stable state"—Gregory Bateson's cybernetic definition of the psychic state provoked by joke-work.[35]

To reduce *The Secret Agent* to an attack on hypocrisy, then, is entirely inadequate. Nor is one justified in separating out from the logic of *ressenti-*

33. In Conrad, *A Set of Six* 78–86.

34. Fredric Jameson, *Fables of Aggression: Wyndham Lewis, the Modernist as Fascist* (Berkeley, 1979) 131. Jameson's more extended discussion of this concept, and of its importance to Conrad in particular, is found in *The Political Unconscious* 200–205, 267–71.

35. Bateson, "The Position of Humor" 11.

ment those descriptive phrases ("fat-pig," and so on) that refer to Verloc, on the grounds that *he* is not an anarchist but, on the contrary, an agent of Scotland Yard and of the tsar—a man whose "mission in life [is] the protection of the social mechanism, not its perfectionment or even its criticism" (26). Verloc is scarcely alone in his "instinct for conventional respectability" (55), his identification with those who hold power, and his desire to "protect" London's "opulence and luxury," indeed "the whole social order favorable to [the] hygienic idleness [of the wealthy]," from the encroachments of "unhygienic labour" (24). For according to the joke-logic of the novel this attachment to and identification with idleness as against labor constitute "a temperamental defect" which Verloc shares "with a large proportion of revolutionary reformers"; despite his role as police spy, he is said to be "temperamentally identical with his associates" in the anarchist underground (55).

These shady associates may be less clear about their interest in protecting "the whole social order," but they are, in practice, every bit as domesticated and bourgeois as Verloc. While Verloc is the only one who actually commits the anarchist "apostasy" of marriage (42), all of them are set up domestically in the care of women. Even the Professor, an uncompromising outsider (even in respect to the anarchist circle) and the one anarchist who is not marred by too much flesh, depends on his spinster landladies to keep the premises of his little "home industry" (241) "clean" and "respectable" (245).

Michaelis is the latest celebrity freak of London society; when not engaged in the writing of his utopian manifesto (for which a "fashionable publisher has offered him five hundred pounds") or "luxuriating in the country somewhere" (73), he is generally on display in the drawing room of his wealthy "lady patroness." Her patronage lends him respectability (to the point that the Assistant Commissioner would find it "inconvenient" to arrest him), while testifying to her own liberal views and her "lofty position" "above" mere politics (97).

Comrade Ossipon, whose patronesses ("silly girls with savings-bank books" [55]) are less wealthy but more numerous than Michaelis's, makes his own bid for respectability by falsely claiming the title of "Doctor." (In this, he follows the example of the self-titled Professor, who is likewise concerned "to raise himself in the social scale" [72].) Scarcely a foe of law and order, Ossipon draws on his knowledge of the eugenist-criminologist Lombroso to condemn "deviants" (such as Verloc's half-wit brother-in-law, Stevie), whose genetic criminality can be read on "the lobes of [their] ears" (50). When "the even tenor of his revolutionary life [is] menaced" by signs of violent revolutionary activity, Ossipon feels "something resembling virtuous indignation" (75).

Karl Yundt, who is quite literally "supported" by a woman (he is "nursed by a blear-eyed old woman" who "help[s] him out of the bus" and leads him on his daily "constitutional crawl" [55]), at least commands the rhetoric of uncompromising opposition. But he is no more committed to a revolutionary practice than are his comrades; "no man of action," this "famous terrorist had never in his life raised personally as much as his little finger against the social edifice" (51). As is the case with all the other anarchists, the excess flesh that attaches to Yundt (in the form of "gouty swellings") serves as an index of his "inactivity." He, too, is a parasite, a violator of the code of solidarity, an impediment to the "working community" and an enemy of the only social class Conrad ever openly embraced, an ostensibly class-transcendent "class of workers."[36]

With the possible exception of the Professor, none of these characters is a more genuine anarchist than the police spy Verloc. Wherever we look for "real" anarchists in the novel, we turn up plump, domesticated frauds like Verloc, who "haven't got even the physique of [their] profession," and could "never" pass as "desperate socialist[s]" or "member[s] of a starving prole-tariat" (30). This difficulty in producing a "real" anarchist is widespread in early twentieth-century texts and marks a decided shift from the texts of just a decade earlier. In the eighties and nineties, during the brief era of anarchist "propaganda by deed," the several fatal bombing attacks and assassination attempts on the Continent, as well as the Greenwich outrage and the Walsall incident in England, left little room for ambiguity in either popular or official representations of "the anarchist."

In political cartoons of this earlier period one can observe a certain dis-tinction between bomb-throwers and intellectuals, but there is no sign of the fat/bourgeois anarchist. The practical revolutionaries are rendered as sinis-ter hooded figures carrying spherical bombs (as later immortalized in the "Pip, Squeak, and Wilfred" cartoons), the radical philosophers as small-bodied men with large, bearded, foreign-looking heads (often coded "Jew-ish"). Even these alien-intellectual figures are sometimes clutching bombs, and in the few cases in which one of them is fat the body serves an identifica-tional function (usually indicating Johann Most or, even after his death in 1876, Bakunin) rather than a symbolic one. In allegorical cartoons, such as those of Sir John Tenniel (the Tory artist who, as one historian notes, "changed *Punch* from one of the ruck of comic papers to a National Institu-tion"),[37] anarchism is a snake, lizard, dragon, or, more rarely, a Fury with a

36. Conrad, quoted in Fleishman, *Conrad's Politics* 47.
37. Richard Geoffrey George Price, *A History of Punch* (London, 1957) 74. Tenniel,

snake-covered head (i.e., chaos): it is represented as a real threat to "civilization." In the one Tenniel cartoon that attempts to point up anarchist hypocrisy, the joke is not that of the radical philosopher who, like Conrad's Michaelis, "luxuriat[es] in the country someplace," but rather of the "down-with-everything" demonstrator who, set upon by a violent mob of outraged (but of course highly respectable-looking) citizens, ends up howling for law and order.[38]

The novels of these decades are similarly untroubled by any confusion between "real" anarchists and pretenders. It has often been said that James's *Princess Casimassima* (1886) and Zola's *Paris* (1896–97) ridicule anarchists in the same fashion that *The Secret Agent* does. But though both novels contain caricatures that clearly influenced Conrad's own practice, James and Zola do not have Conrad's difficulty in representing a proletarian revolutionary sincerely committed to the destruction of the existing social order. Some of their anarchists are frauds or silly pipe dreamers, but one is given grounds for distinguishing the "true" anarchists from the bourgeoisie, as one is even in *The Possessed* of Dostoevsky (1871).

It is only after the mid-nineties, when the anarchist movement entered a period of decline which was to last until the years just preceding the Great War,[39] that the representation of "real" anarchists becomes a problem. The decimation of the movement was partly a consequence of police infiltrations, international restrictions, fierce reprisals, and the new *lois scélérates* or "wicked laws" in France (which culminated in the 1894 Trial of the Thirty); but it also pointed up the catastrophic failure of "propaganda by deed," which had driven away potential supporters while supplying abundant material for the propaganda machines of reaction.

"the Pride of Mr. Punch and the delight of the British Public" was a key figure in raising the status not only of *Punch* but of political cartoons as a genre. For a contemporary account see H. H. Spielman, *History of Punch* (London, 1895) 471–75; quotation, p. 475.

38. This cartoon, from the 21 July 1894 *Punch*, probably refers to the aftermath of the Greenwich Bomb Outrage—the event on which Conrad based his story—when angry mobs attacked the funeral party of the bombing's perpetrator and sole victim, Martial Bourdin, and the police had to move in to protect Bourdin's friends and sympathizers. The funeral riot is described in John Quail, *The Slow Burning Fuse: The Lost History of the British Anarchists* (London, 1978) 165–66. Conrad's use of the Greenwich bombing in *The Secret Agent* is ably discussed by Sherry in *Conrad's Western World*.

39. The standard general introduction to the history of anarchism is still George Woodcock, *Anarchism: A History of Libertarian Movements and Ideas* (New York, 1962). The only full-length studies of the anarchist movement in England are Quail, *The Slow Burning Fuse*, and Hermia Oliver, *The International Anarchist Movement in Late Victorian London* (New York, 1983).

Indeed, it was the nearly universal abandonment of propaganda by deed (a doctrine whose defenders had in any case never been more than a faction within the movement), which contributed most to the increasing confusion about anarchists in these years. The public imagination still held the image of the nineties' *dynamitards*, but the movement now consisted of a few utopianist philosophers and a handful of followers clustered in and around London, the only remaining "open" city.[40] Whereas in the early nineties all anarchists were presumed "real," even the least violent and most respectable of them a potential bomb-thrower or assassin, by 1907 the bombers were being dismissed by the voices of official reason as mere "common criminals," unwarrantedly granted the status of anarchists by "the newspaper and the novel," while the "real" anarchists turned out not to be so real, either, since they "never do anything . . . at all except talk and write."[41]

In Isabel Meredith's *Girl among the Anarchists* (1903), the pseudonymous roman à clef by former anarchists Olive and Helen Rossetti, and in W. C. Hart's bitter memoir, *Confessions of an Anarchist* (1906), virtually identical anarchist typologies are offered which, as Norman Sherry has pointed out, seem to consist entirely of false or fraudulent types. Perhaps the "fanatics" are an exception, though their "practical work" is laughed off as "useless"; but the other main types of anarchist are said to be the "deluded fools," the "criminals," and the "police spies."[42] The joke of the "thoroughly domesticated" anarchist is given considerable play in the Rossettis' novel, as in the scene in which a "formidable preacher of dynamite and disaster" is pounced upon, denounced, and dragged away from an anarchist meeting by his domineering wife.[43] Helen Rossetti herself served as the model for Conrad's "girl anarchist" in "The Informer" (1906), another anarchist story in which one searches in vain for the genuine article. In this "ironic tale," the heroine is a well-off and beautiful young woman whose anarchism, though said to be "sincerely" professed, is also exposed as a mere series of charming "gestures" which she, in her "innocence," has taken up to enhance her feminine

40. For estimates of the size of the movement in 1890, 1894, and 1900, see Quail, *Slow Burning Fuse* 193–99.

41. From a March 1907 *TLS* review of Kropotkin's *Conquest of Bread*, quoted in Roderick Kedward, *The Anarchists: The Men Who Shocked an Era* (New York, 1971) 53. This book from the Library of the Twentieth Century series is of interest only for its illustrations.

42. See Sherry, *Conrad's Western World* 251.

43. Isabel Meredith [Isabel Rossetti and Olive Rossetti], *A Girl among the Anarchists* (London, 1903) 53.

appeal. She becomes infatuated with the "guiding spirit" of the movement, a supposed "fanatic of social revolution" named Sevrin, who turns out to be yet another reactionary spy.[44] The whole tale is recounted by another supposed anarchist leader, the extraordinarily well-bred and "fashionable" Mr. X, who, however, appears at the end to be less a revolutionary than some kind of aristocratic practical joker. G. K. Chesterton's novel *The Man Who Was Thursday* (1909) imagines the entire inner circle of the London anarchist movement as consisting of special agents for Scotland Yard who chase each other about in a great daisychain of fatuity. The anarchist leader, the enormously fat "Sunday," turns out to be the very man at Scotland Yard who assigned these agents to the case: the slippage has carried to the point where the novel's Michaelis *is* its Sir Ethelred.

This sudden and seemingly ubiquitous appearance of the fat anarchist at a time when anarchism itself had been effectively swept from the political field is typical of the overly witty (*witzelnd*) processes that are set to work in a political unconscious on the verge of desperation. (And the political unconscious is always a little desperate.) The important thing is to come to some recognition of the contradictory fears and desires that this joke-work has been called upon to "manage" (in Norman Holland's sense), and not to attempt to arrest the multiple slippages or oscillations it entails.[45] There is certainly a sense in which we can say, as Benjamin says of Baudelaire, that the Conrad of *The Secret Agent* was himself "a secret agent, an agent of the secret discontent of his class with its own rule." But Benjamin knew, too, that such an agent was far from dependable: his "home" would always be "the enemy camp," and "to give his work a place on the most advanced ramparts of the struggle for human liberation" would be an exercise "of little value." At the same time, however, one cannot accept as adequate Irving Howe's remark that "where Conrad presumes to render the London anarchists . . . he drops to a coarse-spirited burlesque." Conrad's estimate of Kropotkin, Bakunin, Elisée Reclus, and their movement may indeed, as Howe says, have been "a fabulous vulgarity." But the "malice," "vindictive[ness]," and "cruel[ty]" of which Howe complains circulate in a far more involved psychosymbolic economy, and perform far more complex ideological tasks than such a reading can recognize.[46] The view of *The Secret Agent* as

44. Conrad, *A Set of Six* 75.

45. Norman Holland, *The Dynamics of Literary Response* (New York, 1968) 289; cited by Jameson, *Political Unconscious* 267.

46. Irving Howe, *Politics and the Novel* (New York, 1957) 97.

simply, in Jameson's words, a "powerful counterrevolutionary tract"[47] sup-
presses more fully than does the novel itself a certain positive valuation of
anarchist aims and an underlying contempt for counterrevolutionary positions. We can agree that the radical displacements that constitute the text's
joke-work (anarchist-as-bourgeois being merely the prime instance of a
vastly extended system of such displacements) effectively contain this discontent, redirecting the self-critical and potentially counterhegemonic impulses of an imperial bourgeoisie uncertain of its own legitimacy, channeling
expressions of hostility onto officially sanctioned paths. But one can also see
the recklessness of a narrative strategy that depends on such comic transactions. For it is not only Conrad, but also his laughing readers, who must at
certain moments of the book occupy the position of "extreme revolutionist"
("Author's Note" 12).

This is why *The Secret Agent* should not be set apart from the modernist
project as Jameson sees it embodied in *Lord Jim*: "The modernist project
is . . . the intent . . . to 'manage' historical and social, deeply political impulses, that is to say, to defuse them, to prepare substitute gratifications for
them, and the like. But we must add that such impulses cannot be managed
until they are aroused; this is the delicate part of the modernist project."[48]
Of course modernism is not the only cultural project whose effectivity is
problematic in this way, nor is there anything new, in 1907, about a comic
practice that generates the very energies it aims to proscribe and punish. But
this is not simply an inevitable bivalence, either. Classical humor theory tells
us that the satirist's only strategic imperative is to render the specific vice in
question ultimately "harmless" (Aristotle) and the practitioners themselves
"weak and unable to retaliate" (Plato).[49] Conrad evidently succeeds here; it
is this diminishment of the putative threat posed by anarchism which enables
a release, in laughter, of the fear connected with violence, loss of personal
property, and radical change or upheaval generally. In this sense, psychoanalytic critics are correct to say that Conrad's humor functions as a sort of
"protective . . . screen" or "defense mechanism,"[50] just as Howe is right to
argue that Conrad's presentation of the anarchists "removes any reasonable

47. Jameson, *Political Unconscious* 268.
48. Ibid. 266.
49. Aristotle, *Nicomachean Ethics*, 4.8. Plato, *Philebus* 48–50. Both rpt. in *The Philosophy of Laughter and Humor*, ed. John Morreall (Albany, 1987) 12, 15.
50. See Thomas Moser, *Joseph Conrad: Achievement and Decline* (1957; Hamden,
Conn., 1966) 94; Norman Holland, "Style as Character in *The Secret Agent*," *Modern
Fiction Studies* 12 (1966): 221–31.

ground for the fear they . . . arouse in him."[51] It is the nature of joke-work to fulfill such psychic functions.

But as the novels and cartoons of the early nineties attest, there are many ways to disperse the grounds of this fear, and Howe simplifies misleadingly when he says that Conrad's strategic purpose was to portray the anarchists "as garrulous fools."[52] *The Secret Agent* could represent its anarchists as fools without calling forth the very images of radical social critique. There could be active, committed revolutionaries whose stupidity renders them both "harmless" (laughable in terms of classical theory) and "mechanical" (laughable in Bergson's terms, for "mindless action" presents the key Bergsonian opposition). Or there could be determined fanatics of revolution, rendered harmless by their lack of local, pragmatic knowledge and political savvy, and mechanically controlled, as Bergson puts it, "like puppets" by an overly abstract and inflexible *idée fixe* (*Laughter* 80). Indeed, the Professor is approached in something like this fashion.

Either of these comic strategies could do the job of counterrevolutionary cultural production more efficiently than Conrad's relentless domestication and bourgeoisification of the anarchist. But neither strategy could have established much resonance with the social imaginary of turn-of-the-century England, where anxieties about community enjoyed a complex circulation with only the most indirect linkages to the anarchist movement as such. What should be clear by now is that what the modernist novel had to "manage" or "defuse" in 1907 was not fear of a largely continental and by then largely obliterated revolutionary movement but fear of a certain "soft spot" at the heart of the Empire, a growing cavity of degeneration/deterioration/parasitism which was the projection onto the domestic landscape of an essentially global problematic (namely an emergent legitimation crisis in the colonial order). Such fear was productive of a whole range of sometimes contradictory hostilities, which an effective satire might ultimately intensify or neutralize, but had in any case to arouse. On the one hand were hostilities directed downward into the supposed abyss of resentment; rather than acknowledge the claims London's outcasts might make on the community, one could secure their exclusion by means of various dividing practices and "otherizing" discourses that marked them out as the radically *unworkable* elements in what would otherwise be a working system or systematic work of solidary and cooperative relations. On the other hand were hostilities directed across or

51. Howe, *Politics and the Novel* 97.
52. Ibid.

upward at the too-comfortable bourgeoisie, whose parasitic relation to the social body could be seen as justifying their removal by more legitimate members of this same not-yet-working "working community."

To laugh at the fat anarchist in 1907 is thus really to experience the crisis or impossibility of a discursive system—of, you could say, England's way of talking about England. It is a system that attempts to articulate and to stabilize social relations through an idea of the "working community," which is itself ultimately the most unworkable and destabilizing element. This impossibility at the heart of the liberal/nationalist idea of community—this traffic jam in the social imaginary which results from the routing of fundamentally opposed or divergent (and often extranational) social energies through the mirage of a common "center" and toward an illusory common goal or communitarian "work"—is what anarchism, at its most radical moments, had in fact recognized and taken as the starting point of a new thinking, a thinking that would be taken up between the wars by Georges Bataille and the Acéphaliste group. As we turn now to the question of Conrad's "ironic method," we can note this singular irony—that anarchism, all but swept from the field of political struggle during the first two decades of the century, should have found its secret refuge in the joke-work of counterrevolution.

Ironic Reaction

> Ironical humour . . . makes the bourgeois feel safe in Wapping.
>
> —William Empson, *Some Versions of Pastoral*

Most critics who discuss the humor of *The Secret Agent* are inclined to overlook what Howe sees as the "coarse-spirited burlesque" of the fat anarchists and concentrate on the seemingly more artful comic pleasures associated with Conrad's intended "ironic method" of composition. In his retrospective "Author's Note" Conrad averred that the rigorous application of such a method was the primary task that he, as a conscious craftsman, had set out to perform in the novel and that he had largely succeeded in achieving this "purely artistic purpose": "Even the purely artistic purpose, that of applying an ironic method to a subject of that kind, was formulated with deliberation and in the earnest belief that ironic treatment alone would enable me to say all I felt I would have to say. . . . It is one of the minor satisfactions of my writing life that having taken that resolve I did manage, it seems to me, to carry it right through to the end" (AN 12). The expression of artisanal pride here rests on a conception of irony as control which runs through much of the commentary on *The Secret Agent* and indeed on literary modernism generally. The idea is that only a quite deliberate and resolute artist can sustain an "ironic treatment" as unrelentingly as Conrad does in this novel and that his implicit command over ironic distance provides a reassuring sense of stability amid the "mass of oppressive doubts" that he himself sees as "haunt[ing]" the work (AN 12). Variations on this view of irony have led critics to speak of Conrad's narrative posture in the novel as one of "calculated coldness" or even "cruelty."[53] Such readings bear affinities with Gilles Deleuze's analysis in "Coldness and Cruelty" (1967), which dissociates masochism from sadism and then identifies humor as the properly masochistic and irony as the properly sadistic mode,[54] and affinities also with the rather formulaic cultural histories that celebrate the subversive free play of postmodernist humor over and against the repressive alliance of irony and power in modernism and/or the New Criticism.[55]

There is some validity to these associations of irony with the desire in modernist writing for stability and control. But we cannot really grasp modernist ironic practice such as Conrad's until we have also taken the measure of its destabilizing and masochistic dimensions. As Paul de Man suggests in a famous reading of Baudelaire's "De l'essence du rire," it requires no great effort of authorial control to carry irony through to the end; one merely yields passively to its onward pressure. For "irony possesses an inherent tendency to gain momentum and not to stop until it has run its full course."[56] It may start, says de Man, "as a casual bit of play with a stray loose end of the fabric, but before long the entire texture of the self is unraveled and comes apart. . . . Often starting as litotes or understatement, it contains within itself the power to become hyperbole. Baudelaire refers to this unsettling power as *"vertige de l'hyperbole."* This feeling of vertigo, of "unrelieved . . . dizziness,"

53. See Albert J. Guerard, *Conrad the Novelist* (Cambridge, Mass., 1958) 226, 229; Jeffrey Berman, *Joseph Conrad: Writing as Rescue* (New York, 1977) 128.

54. Gilles Deleuze, "Coldness and Cruelty" [1967], in Gilles Deleuze and Leopold von Sacher-Masoch, *Masochism*, trans. Jean McNeil (1971; Cambridge, 1989) 81–91.

55. The most stimulating and least reductive version of this argument is Candace D. Lang, *Irony/Humor: Critical Paradigms* (Baltimore, 1988). The ways in which irony continues to inform the anti-ironic discourse of postmodernism are traced by Alan Wilde, *Horizons of Assent: Modernism, Postmodernism, and the Ironic Imagination* (Baltimore, 1981) 127–65.

56. Paul de Man, "The Rhetoric of Temporality," in de Man, *Blindness and Insight*, 2d ed. (Minneapolis, 1983) 215.

betrays not only the uncontrollability of irony but the impossibility of achieving control through irony. The movement of irony puts into question the very "authenticity of our sense of being in the world" and may bring us even "to the point of madness." Thus, writes de Man, irony "is by no means a reassuring and serene process, despite the fact that it involves laughter."[57]

With its casual beginnings in "litotes or understatement" and its thematic culmination in "madness or despair" (*TSA* 252), *The Secret Agent* conforms in a general way to this description. Unquestionably, litotes is the dominant rhetorical figure of the novel. Characters, events, even inanimate objects are consistently described in terms of opposition to what they are not, or more precisely to the putative ideals they are furthest from embodying. Verloc, the slothful, machine-brained seller of propaganda and pornography, is not, we are told, "a well-read person" (151). In his family life, he is "not much of a psychologist" (190), not "prodigal of endearments and words" (208). Despite his "fat-pig" demeanor, he is "undisturbed by any sort of aesthetic doubt about his appearance" (18). His willfully shallow wife, Winnie, likewise is "not a well-informed woman" (219), cannot "pretend to . . . depths of insight" (146), does "not know too much" (144). Her whole philosophy consists "in not taking notice of the inside of facts" (133). Winnie's half-wit brother, Stevie, prone to stammering, is "no master of phrases" (146); his work as a dishwasher and blackboot at his mother's lodging house does "not amount to much either in the way of gain or prospects" (22). Even the most incidental characters are described in this way: Winnie's mother's low-rent boarders are gentlemen "not exactly of the fashionable kind" (19). The shady patrons of Verloc's stationery-cum-porno shop look as if "they were not in funds"; their filthy trousers appear to be "not very valuable" and "the legs inside them [do] not . . . seem of much account either" (18). Allowing for slight variations in form, this list could be extended indefinitely. "The visions of Mrs. Verloc lacked nobility and magnificence" (200); Stevie's "thoughts lacked clearness and precision" (146); "the mind of Mr. Verloc lacked profundity" (193). A maimed and decrepit cabman's "immortality" is "by no means assured" (142). A few pages before Winnie stabs her husband to death with a kitchen knife we are informed that "no system of conjugal relations is perfect" (203).

Descriptive rhetoric of this sort generates comic incongruities of the high/low variety along several axes—social, cultural, and moral. In social terms, the narrator's lofty, aristocratic vocabulary stands at odds with the

57. Ibid. 214.

language that actually circulates among London's petty bourgeoisie; Winnie Verloc would scarcely describe her marriage as an imperfect system of conjugal relations. In terms of prevailing cultural codes, the narrator seems to be simultaneously observing the highest standards of politeness (taking the circumlocutious high ground around his characters' failings) and stooping to every opportunity for mockery or insult. Most important, in moral terms, the ironic understatements produce tension between what is and what ought to be, between the actual state of affairs and the ideal state invoked by such terms as "magnificence" and "nobility," "precision" and "profundity," "well-informed" and "valuable."

One is thus tempted to say that these ironic negations depend for their comic success on settled hierarchies and stable norms or ideals. Considered as a social practice, litotes would seem to confirm subject and recipient in their superiority to the comic object by affirming their closer approximation to and identification with that which is powerful, proper, and good. But as most commentators on irony have recognized,[58] because the ironic text tends to "gain momentum . . . until it has run its full course," irony generates ironies that ironize even that which serves as a positive value for other ironies. In Friedrich Schlegel's phrase, the ironic process is a "permanent parabasis."[59]

The process is readily observable in *The Secret Agent.* Ideals invoked for ironic contrast at one moment in the novel are themselves ironically undone at other moments. M. Vladimir, for example, the Russian ambassador who conceives the whole inane bombing plot that leads to Stevie's destruction, serves as an ironic reflection on the supposed ideals of "masterful" phrase-turning and "fashionable" gentlemanly behavior. Though violently contemptuous of British institutions, Vladimir has managed through his "delivery of delicate witticisms" (41) to make himself a "favourite of the very highest society" (33) and a member in good standing at the elite Explorers' Club. The ironies of his position throw such phrases as "not a gentleman of the fashionable kind" or "no master of phrases" into a kind of awkward oscillation between positive and negative valence.

The presence of Michaelis, the "apostle of humanitarian hopes," intro-

---

58. A critic such as Wayne C. Booth (*A Rhetoric of Irony* [Chicago, 1974]), who valorizes irony as a "stable"—i.e., discrete, intentional, finite—rhetorical device, would be the exception here.

59. Friedrich Schlegel, "Fragment 668," *Kritische Ausgabe*, Band 18, *Philosophische Lehrjahre (1796–1806)*, ed. Ernst Behler (Paderborn, 1962) 85; quoted in de Man, "Rhetoric" 218.

duces ironic brackets in a similar way around the ideal of noble and magnificent visions. Michaelis speaks with the conviction of one who possesses an "intense" and noble "vision of truth," a utopian socialist (and essentially Kropotkinian) vision of community in which the principle of competition has been overturned, the strong no longer prey upon the weak, and the proletariat have at last come into their "lawful inheritance" (52). As the novel's "hermit of visions" (53), Michaelis provides a perfect counterpoint to Winnie Verloc, whose incapacity to see beyond the immediate givens of experience is so frequently ironized. (She is above all "a person untroubled by the problem of the distribution of wealth" [148].) Yet as we have already noted, Michaelis is scarcely an object of unalloyed sympathy and admiration. In addition to being the most grotesquely fat and inert of all the novel's fat and inert political agents, and in addition to being another "favourite of intelligent society women" (he and Vladimir frequent the same fashionable salon), Michaelis is incapable of sustaining even the briefest discussion. He is so absorbed in his visions of perfect unity that any hint of difference flusters him: "the mere fact of hearing another voice disconcert[s] him painfully, confusing his thoughts at once" (49). His efforts to express his noble communitarian creed in writing produce no better results: the long volume of meditations which he intends as "a book of Revelation in the history of mankind" is riddled with contradictions and stands mainly as a testament to "the zeal of his guileless vanity (first awakened by the offer of five hundred pounds from a publisher)" (107).

This ironization of values on which other ironies depend makes *The Secret Agent* a text that ultimately affirms everything and nothing. "The qualifications required by irony are present in abundance," writes Howe, "but it is difficult to determine *what* is being qualified, which standard of behavior is being singled out for attack or defense."[60] The effect is altogether different from that of a pre-Romantic ironic novel such as *Jonathan Wild* (whose irony consists entirely of "praising to blame"), and finds its true modern prototype in Flaubert's *Dictionnaire des idées reçues*, a text that manages to accommodate perfectly contrasting ideas within the same ironic compass. Conrad's irony continually draws the ladder up beneath it, moving farther and farther from any stable ground of value, indicating only, as de Man expresses it, "a discontinuity and a plurality of levels within a subject that comes to know itself by an increasing differentiation from what it is not."[61] Or, as Terry

60. Howe, *Politics and the Novel* 96.
61. De Man, "Rhetoric" 213.

Eagleton writes, "*The Secret Agent* is able to reveal the truth of itself only by that ceaseless process of 'self-detonation' which is irony," only by "the revolutionary act of negating its every proposition and reconstructing itself *ex nihilo*."[62]

Even the value of irony itself, and the presumed privilege of the ironist's smiling detachment, are ironized in the novel. Employing the characteristic trope, Conrad tells us that Winnie is "guiltless of all irony" (147), that "Chief Inspector Heat, though what is called a man, was not a laughing animal" (109). But it is not clear against what positive value an ironic gap might make itself felt in such utterances. Is ironic laughter privileged as the one legitimate response to a world in which every "serious" political project (whether an anarchist bombing plot or a Liberal fisheries bill) comes to resemble an "elaborate joke" (41)? Does Conrad hold irony to be "intrinsically essential, as a proper response to reality itself," as Eagleton argues?[63] Significantly, M. Vladimir, the object of some of the fiercest and most derisive ironies in the novel, is also the only character who might be described as a "laughing animal." He himself indulges in "enormous and derisive fit[s] of merriment" and has even supplemented his "humorous urbanity" (41) with "occasional excursions into the field of American humour" (35). By contrast, the Assistant Commissioner, who seems to enjoy a far greater share of authorial identification, is, like Winnie and the Chief Inspector, "not constitutionally inclined to levity" (130). Through such "self-detonations" as these, the ironic subject of the text differentiates itself even from the traits that would seem to define it: irony, levity, laughter.

As for the receiving subjects—Conrad's readers—de Man is no doubt right to emphasize that irony can be an unsettling process "despite the fact that it involves laughter."[64] Indeed, laughter comes into play precisely because the process is so unsettling. As D. H. Monro, Gregory Bateson and other reception-oriented humor theorists have argued—laughter does not consist in a single, discrete emotion but in an abrupt movement from one "emotional sphere" to another[65] or in the interval of affective "oscillation" that this movement effects.[66] A curious aspect of the critical literature on *The Secret Agent* is the presence, in roughly equal numbers, of readers who describe the novel's pathos in terms of "a fixed distance of amused scorn"

62. Terry Eagleton, *Criticism and Ideology* (London, 1978) 140.
63. Ibid.
64. De Man, "Rhetoric" 214.
65. Monro, *Argument of Laughter* 249.
66. Bateson, "Position of Humor" 6.

(presumably the effect corresponding to an ironic ethos of "coldness and cruelty"), as well as readers who insist on a closeness of identification with such characters as Winnie or Stevie.[67] Both views express retrospective solutions to what at the time of reading is an affective dilemma. Careful study of such scenes as that of the cab ride in chapter 8 (often cited in support of both "cold" and "warm" readings) discloses a ceaseless and at times quite jarring back-and-forth movement between mockery and compassion. Consider, for example, the famous passage in which Stevie's overwhelming sympathy for the maimed cabman and his "infirm" horse reaches the point of "a bizarre longing to take them to bed with him" (143). The text characteristically prevents us from merely laughing this off as lunacy ("For Stevie was not mad"), provoking instead a series of rapid affective reversals. Stevie's desire, says Conrad,

> was, as it were, a symbolic longing; and at the same time it was very distinct, because springing from experience, the mother of wisdom. Thus when as a child he cowered in a dark corner scared, wretched, sore and miserable with the black, black misery of the soul, his sister Winnie used to come along and carry him off to bed with her, as into a haven of consoling peace. Stevie, though apt to forget mere facts, such as his name and address for instance, had a faithful memory of sensations. To be taken into a bed of compassion was the supreme remedy, with the only one disadvantage of being difficult of application on a large scale.   (143)

The passage shows how impossible it is for the ironic text to sustain any particular affective response for long, be it serious compassion or amused scorn; as soon as it sutures us to a particular subjective position, effecting our identification with a character (in this case through the explanatory flashback to the battered child), the text begins to erode that position and disrupt that identification. With its constant qualifications and self-negations, its ceaseless negotiation of discontinuous levels, irony is precisely a way of moving between and among contradictory vantages, interchanging narrative distances that never can be "fixed." Just as for its speaking subject irony is a process of successive self-divisions, a process of disowning each particular unified self as it emerges, for its recipients it is experienced as inner conflict

67. The quotation comes from Guerard, *Conrad the Novelist* 226. The argument for Winnie as authentic Victorian heroine (a category that has no force in a work of absolute irony) has been made by U. C. Knoepflmacher, *Laughter and Despair* (Berkeley, 1971) 270–71, and Bruce Redwine, "Deception and Intention in *The Secret Agent*," *Conradiana* 11 (1979): 253–66.

and upheaval, a forced rejection of any singular, authentic response. A reader's laughter is an expression of this interruption of immediate affect.

Given the epistemological and affective disruptions of subjectivity which drive comic transactions of this kind, it is no easy matter to specify the ideological content of their joke-work. As I said, *The Secret Agent* is a text that affirms nothing. Even the idea of the organic working community, of solidarity achieved through close intervolvement and common struggle with nature, which has provided critics as diverse as Williams, Fleishman, Ian Watt, and Eagleton with a common ideological anchor for Conrad's work, is a casualty of "self-detonation" in *The Secret Agent*. Over and above the inevitable unworking of this idea, its witty manifestation of its own impossibility in the form of a fat-anarchist scapegoat, it is clearly implicated in the ironical treatment of Michaelis's flaccid communitarian dreams.

It will not help to look for positive, doctrinal values that Conrad has somehow snuck through the gates of irony. Rather, we must recognize irony itself as a thoroughly political practice and try to understand its appeal and its effectivity as a mode of cultural intervention in early twentieth-century Britain. This is not to deny that irony's great attraction for certain modernists was its ostensibly apolitical character, that promise of an escape from ideology which remains immanent to irony, necessary to its movement, even where the possibility of realizing any such purity has been ruled out in advance. The point is that with modernist texts the refusal of political content and function—a refusal that in any case was never absolute or unalloyed—must itself be regarded as a political gesture, and scrutinized as such. The hegemonic or New Critical reading of modernism was misleading not only because it overstated the (variable and intermittent) commitment to irony in the texts of modernist literature, but more significantly because it would not even pose the question of irony as politics.

Modernism's anxiety about an art that takes sides on the field of political struggle, which produces, even in novels as frankly political in their thematics as *The Secret Agent*, a claim to some higher order or heterocosm proper to art itself, can be understood as part of a broad cultural strategy by means of which difference may be denied or occluded or restructured as identity. It will perhaps seem unlikely that irony, an extreme practice of differentiation, should operate to these ends, but, after all, the Romantic theorists of irony recognized, as did Hegel more perfectly, that absolute difference becomes at a certain point indistinguishable from absolute identity. In any case, for Conrad as for other modernists irony is taken up as a way of fulfilling his artistic "duty" to overcome the "passion of his prejudices" and "narrowness of his outlook"[68]—that is, to transcend the exclusivity implicit in his historical position—yet the actual joke-work it performs, as part of a communitarian strategy deployed by an imperiled liberalism, belies this purpose.

Just what his "prejudices of . . . outlook" are, Conrad makes clear in his "Familiar Preface" to *A Personal Record*, the book of memoirs he began writing immediately after *The Secret Agent* (and published serially in 1908–9 under the title *Some Reminiscences*). This brief text, most of which constitutes a veiled defense of the ironic method he had employed in the novel, culminates in a jarring (because utterly unironic) denunciation of "the revolutionary spirit" and "the menace of fanaticism" (192). But at the very last Conrad retreats from this tone, acknowledging that the "philosophical" (i.e., ironical) attitude he has been endorsing "should be free" from such "scorn and anger" and that "one should smile at these things" (192). For, as he has already made clear, the ethos proper to art is that of "resignation," "the only one of our feelings for which it is impossible to become a sham" (191). Not surprisingly, this uniquely authentic attitude, resignation, is ultimately an achievement of *style*—indeed, of ironic style, which can effect an ambivalent and ultimately undecidable "mingling" of "the comic" with "pain" (189). "In this matter of life and art," writes Conrad, "it is not the Why that matters so much as the How . . . the manner. The manner in laughter, in tears, in irony" (192).

Though the commitment to ironic style guards the authentic work of art from the author's polemical outbursts against "the revolutionary spirit," the resignation or conscious political quietism it fosters constitutes no accommodation of radical politics. Despite the ironist's skepticism regarding all conservative agenda, and despite his or her resignation to the reality of social struggle, irony nevertheless "makes the bourgeois feel safe in Wapping," as William Empson was perceptive enough to realize even at the height of its New Critical valorization. "The fundamental impulse of irony," wrote Empson, "is to score off both the arguments that have been puzzling you, both sets of sympathies in your mind, both sorts of fools who will hear you; a plague on both of their houses."[69] But in this leveling process a certain advantage always accrues to the ruling estate, which, unlike the house of opposition, requires no acknowledgment of its moral or practical superiority. (In this sense a perfectly antihierarchical mode of representation is always counterrevolutionary.) Ironic transactions constitute an unending critique of

68. Conrad, "A Familiar Preface" 190.
69. William Empson, *Some Versions of Pastoral* (1935; New York, 1974) 7, 62.

bourgeois culture, but not an unconstrained critique, for they are incapable of achieving any very dangerous or impertinent repositionings of their subjects and objects. For all its ceaseless movement, irony does not permit much real "play" with established hierarchies (in the form of inversion, hybridization, etc.). It can only score off the arguments at top and bottom, establishing identical difference at both ends, collapsing the whole structure onto a single plane of value. And this collapse, as Empson says, "makes you willing to be ruled by your betters."[70]

Two major examples of this process in *The Secret Agent* are the ironizations of the diagnostic practices and of the policing practices that served to contain ostensible anarchist threats to community around the turn of the century. The first of these, which puts into ironic circulation the intertwined "scientific" discourses of eugenics, degeneration, and criminology, has as its primary locus Comrade Ossipon, "nicknamed the doctor, ex-medical student without a degree" (50). Ossipon is the author of a "quasi-medical study (in the form of a cheap pamphlet promptly seized by the police) entitled 'The Corroding Vices of the Middle Classes'" (50), and in this respect his scientific knowledge, such as it is, would seem to be in service of the anarchist cause. (Even porno-science can be useful revolutionary propaganda when it focuses widespread fears of social decay on the corrupt middle classes rather than on the "degenerate" underclass.) Yet, as already mentioned, Ossipon is a devotee of the famed Italian criminologist Cesare Lombroso (1836–1909), whose theories and typologies of degeneracy were perhaps the major source of scientific legitimacy for reactionary Edwardian eugenic analyses of the urban proletariat. Moreover, during the 1890s Lombroso had taken a particular interest in anarchism, devoting an entire study to this form of "hereditary criminal degeneracy" and tracing its origin to such factors as "great density of population" and "the crossing of races"[71]—notions that of course resonated deeply in a nation whose moral panics were coalescing upon London.

Ossipon's brand of science is thus a kind of joke, ironically undermining him at every turn, comically shadowing even his final words of the novel, "I am seriously ill"—which he "mutter[s] to himself with scientific insight" (252). Indeed, the text questions the value of all such insight, mocking the bogus certainties, the systematic falsehoods, of all science and of all men who carry the expression of "insufferable, hopelessly dense sufficiency

70. Ibid. 7.
71. Lombroso, *Crime* 227, 228.

which nothing but the frequentation of science can give to the dulness of common mortals" (50). And yet at the same time the narrative itself is at pains to present precisely the kind of physiognomic data on which the eugenic typologies of an Ossipon or a Lombroso rest. Conrad places as much emphasis on the "vacant droop of [Stevie's] lower lip" (21) as Ossipon does on "the lobes of his ears" (50). The "thick," "protruding" lips of Ossipon himself receive equally careful scrutiny (63); together with his "almond-shaped eyes," "high cheek-bones," and "flattened nose," the "protruding mouth" signals his conformity to the "rough mould of the negro type" (48). The "sickly face" of the Professor is likewise rendered in the language of degeneration studies: "His flat, large ears departed widely from the sides of his skull; . . . the dome of the forehead seemed to rest on the rim of the spectacles; the flat cheeks, of a greasy, unhealthy complexion, were merely smudged by the miserable poverty of a thin dark whisker" (62).

Such quasi-Lombrosan passages, by means of which "miserable poverty" is transposed onto a physiognomic/racial register, are not the only hints of scientism in this text that mocks science. For all its ironizing of science, the novel itself (as a number of contemporary reviewers noted) approximates the scientistic perspective of Zola and the Naturalists,[72] underscoring the often neglected linkages, visible since Flaubert, between the detachedly "scientific," seemingly humorless, and traditionally left-leaning or socialist vantage of naturalist fiction, and the elaborately ironic, confidently humorous, and generally reactionary vantage of the modernist art novel. As Bergson perceived (and Wyndham Lewis would in fact derive his entire "anti-Bergsonian" satiric practice from this Bergsonian insight), the most extreme scientism can be the most effective comic strategy.[73]

The point here is that the ironic transactions in *The Secret Agent* effect a collapsing of the subject-object hierarchy proper to a classificatory scientific discourse. The subjective position of Lombrosan science is shared out between an anarchist criminal "of the negro type" and a highly urbane modernist narrator who, according to Lombroso's most important disciple, should likewise be regarded as a degenerate type[74] and who in any case

72. Of course in an ironic novel this cannot be read as a *sincere* simulation. As Conrad wrote in a 1906 letter to Galsworthy (quoted in Watt's *Casebook*), his naturalism is a "beastly trick of style"; "it isn't even French really. It is Zola jargon simply" (*Casebook* 16).

73. Bergson, *Laughter* 143.

74. I refer to Max Nordau, whose extension of Lombroso's typology of degeneracy to include the artist opens another level of irony in Conrad's text. This point is discussed by Martin Ray, "Conrad, Nordau, and Other Degenerates: The Psychology of *The Secret Agent*," *Conradiana* 16 (1984): 125–40.

employs his scientism not only to identify degenerates but, at the same time, to mock the science of degeneracy. This "ironic method" neither affirms nor simply rejects the contemporary dividing practice whereby the proletariat and other perceived threats to England's racial and cultural vigor (such as anarchists) were eugenically separated from and placed in the way of the imagined community. It involves a valuable recognition that the diagnosticians of degeneracy were in some sense their own object—that, as Stedman Jones has written, what the degeneration panic provided was in part "a mental landscape within which the middle class could recognize and articulate their own anxieties about urban existence."[75] But such a method does not thereby grant any moral or ideological advantage to the proletarian "other" or to the champions of proletarian interests, who are ensnared in the same circular scientism as their bourgeois counterparts.

This process finds its most fully elaborated and totalizing manifestation in the collapse of moral distinction between rule makers and rule breakers, representatives of law and order and representatives of anarchy. It may be, as Eloise Knapp Hay has argued, that the novel's mockery of the former (Chief Inspector Heat and the Assistant Commissioner, the great Personage and Toodles, the wealthy lady patroness) is perceptibly "gentler" than its mockery of the anarchists and quasi-anarchists.[76] But the overriding pressure toward identity all but obliterates this mark of authorial prejudice. No theme in the novel is more heavily underscored than that of moral equivalence across the boundary of the law. Even Chief Inspector Heat, who is said to be "not insensible to the gravity of moral differences," finds his way to the troubling insight that the "mind and the instincts of a burglar are of the same kind as the mind and the instincts of a police officer," that they are simply twin "products of the same machine" (85). When checking up on his informant, Verloc, the Chief Inspector "maneuver[s] in a way which in a member of the criminal classes would [be] stigmatized as slinking" (169). On a similar errand, the Assistant Commissioner "lingers" carefully "out of sight" of an approaching policeman, as though he, too, "were a member of the criminal classes" (130). "Like to like," states the cynical Professor. "The terrorist and the policeman both come from the same basket. Revolution, legality—counter moves in the same game; forms of idleness at bottom identical" (68).

As Deleuze argues in "Coldness and Cruelty," we come to apprehend the law ironically because it is made to depend on an idea of the Good from which all actual practice is infinitely removed; the supposed moral difference be-

---

75. Stedman Jones, *Outcast London* 151.
76. Eloise Knapp Hay, *The Political Novels of Joseph Conrad* (Chicago, 1963) 243.

tween radical transgressor and policeman is folded into a whole system of ceaseless differentiation from the Good, and so engenders a great endgame of thought, of ironic move and countermove.[77] Considered ironically, the various political positions or stances in relation to the boundaries of law will thus indeed be found "at bottom identical." I have remarked that the novel contains the revolutionary commitment of its anarchists by disclosing an ironic gap between their professed ideals and the ignoble desire for domestic tranquillity and repose which actually motivates them. But precisely the same desire is shown to motivate the Assistant Commissioner's righteous activity on behalf of law and order. His unorthodox decision to take the Greenwich affair out of his Chief Inspector's hands is prompted by anxieties over his somewhat uneasy marriage. He realizes that Chief Inspector Heat is likely to pin the bombing on Michaelis, and that this move would greatly upset the esteemed lady patroness, who happens to be a "friend and patron" of his own wife as well as of Michaelis (99). When "that infernal Heat" (whose own interest in the case also has some "bearing upon his reputation, upon his comfort" [108]) first raises the question of Michaelis's involvement, the Assistant Commissioner can think of nothing but the potentially disastrous repercussions "at home" (101). The Assistant Commissioner's motives, as the text points out in its characteristic ironic mode, are "extremely unbecoming his official position without being really creditable to his humanity" (101).

It may be, as Terry Eagleton argues in an essay on "irony and commitment," that in this reduction to sameness through absolute differentiation one can observe the workings of "bourgeois *economy*: the leveling, equalizing, indifferent operations of the commodity form itself, which respects no unique identity, transgresses all frontiers, melts solidity into air, and profanes the holy."[78] Irony is, in any case, bourgeois *culture*'s primary expression of a radical skepticism that in other forms might have induced truly oppositional effects: it is a self-containing critique that allows the bourgeoisie in Wapping to feel safe even while it gives vent to anxieties over the increasingly manifest illegitimacy of their culture and the consequent erosion of their society and their own social position. For the English at the turn of the century it represented a conservatism far more seductive than any rhetoric of pure reaction, for it was marked by the liberal ideal of inclusiveness, by the promise of a supraprejudicial communitarianism, yet it required no concrete

77. Deleuze, "Coldness and Cruelty" 82.

78. Terry Eagleton, "Nationalism: Irony and Commitment," in Eagleton, Fredric Jameson, and Edward Said, *Nationalism, Colonialism, and Literature* (Minneapolis, 1990) 36.

display of solidarity, no movement building, no forging of new alliances. It enabled the dominant class to exercise their liberal belief that everyone is "at bottom identical" while remaining resigned to a system of rigorous exclusions and hierarchies.

Of course to speak this way about the social functions of irony is to speak unironically, as if one has managed to get one step ahead of the ironic movement itself. It is not really much of a critique, for it has always already been recognized in the ironic consciousness. As Jonathan Culler remarks, the ironist is acutely "aware of irony's vicious spiral, the sapping of confidence which it brings, the inability to act, except in roles, which it promotes."[79] And yet we need continually to remind ourselves of this vicious spiral, of this leveling that is also, in terms of praxis, a stalling. For irony, like the poor whose status outside or below the community it both exposes as a problem for liberalism and "manages" in the interests of continued liberal hegemony, is still very much with us. The identification of modernism with irony, always a misleading reduction as regards actual modernist literary practice, can mislead us about irony as well, which, unlike modernism, we cannot even begin to speak of in the past tense. For us, today, irony remains the form in which radical skepticism toward the bourgeois system of value most typically presents itself. In the work of many left-oriented literary and cultural critics, most of whom received their basic critical training in the era of New Critical hegemony, the role of the transgressor in assuring the continued existence of the law, and that of the police in assuring continued resistance to it, are unfolded not dialectically, as is usually supposed, but according to the familiar modernist logic of irony. Strategies of "subversion" and of "containment," the pursuit of anarchy and the defense of order, are thereby shown to be "at bottom identical," countermoves in the great game of power. Thus is Foucaultian cultural criticism filtered through a tenacious and politically disenabling modernist paradigm: Nietzsche meets Brooks and Warren, with predicatably tame results.

Unlike these contemporary ironists of power and transgression, Conrad never intended to be taken for a radical in the first place. But he did hope through irony to transcend the passion of his (reactionary) prejudices and achieve a comic practice at once more "artistic" and less "political" than satire. "I don't think that I've been satirizing the revolutionary world," wrote Conrad; "[*The Secret Agent*] has no social or philosophical intention."[80] Like

---

79. Jonathan Culler, *Flaubert: The Uses of Uncertainty* (Ithaca, 1974) 186.

80. Joseph Conrad, letters to R. B. Cunninghame Graham, 7 October 1907, and Algernon Methuen, 7 November 1906, *Collected Letters* 3: 491, 371.

those who institutionalized modernism in the forties and fifties, Conrad wants to deny the punitive and divisive social functions of modernist joke-work, to raise his (satiric) laughter to a higher (ironic) plane beyond the reach of ideology. What his text succeeds in doing, however, is something quite different: it deploys irony as the secret agent of reaction in a comic environment whose transactions might otherwise have opened the national community to its anarchic self-questioning.

Two

Imagining a Community of Men:
Black(shirt) Humor in *The Apes of God*

> And, very fascist this time, Blackshirt almost openly hurled his fascist curse at this female enemy of the liberties of the community of Freemen. He would have burnt her in effigy as a witch as soon as look at her.
>
> —Wyndham Lewis, *The Apes of God*

> We need to understand and combat fascism not because so many fell victim to it, not because it stands in the way of the triumph of socialism, not even because it might "return again," but primarily because as a form of reality production that is constantly present and possible under determinate conditions, it can, and does, become our production. The crudest examples of this are to be seen in . . . male-female relations, which are also relations of production.
>
> —Klaus Theweleit, *Male Fantasies*

The logic of *ressentiment*, as we have seen with *The Secret Agent*, takes the paradoxical form that Bateson and his associates claimed to be, in William Fry's words, "so involved in the architecture [of humor] as to constitute its very essence."[1] The subjects and objects of *ressentiment* undergo a strange and interminable oscillation, the weakness of the weak securing their power over the powerful, and this inversion immediately and inescapably calling forth its own reinversion. Fredric Jameson, whose path I will frequently be crossing again in this chapter (he is Wyndham Lewis's most searching critic), has rightly insisted that this particular logic, so prominent in late-nineteenth and early-twentieth-century political thought (from Nietzsche to Conrad), remains fundamental to the "culture critique" as practiced in the interwar

---

1. Fry, *Sweet Madness* 138.

period by José Ortega y Gasset, Julien Benda, Martin Heidegger, and by Lewis himself.[2] It is indeed part and parcel with what we call modernism.

But, as Jameson is aware, *ressentiment* does not perform the same work at every historical conjuncture. Lewis's novels of the twenties and thirties are stuffed with bourgeois revolutionaries and other paradoxical comic objects of the *Secret Agent* stripe. No writer was more obsessed with the "rich-man's gilded bolshevism,"[3] more convinced that revolutionism had become "palpably, dogmatically, wearisomely, and insolently 'top dog.'"[4] But in the interwar metropolis of the high modernist moment, *ressentiment* operates across, if not a wider sociosymbolic field, then certainly a very different one from that which faced Conrad in his "simple tale of the XIX century."[5] Scapegoats that had been discernible but not structurally necessary within the social imaginary of 1900 England—"the Jews," "the Negroes," "the Bolsheviks," "the feminists," "the homosexuals," "the young"—now played critical roles in the (still fundamental) ideological fantasy of British "degeneration."[6] In addition, new technologies, and in particular the technologies of mass culture, meant a proliferation of perceived soft spots or sites of cultural decay: to the "rosy," "optimistic" newspapers derided by Conrad (*TSA* 69), one could now add the cinema, the radio, the phonograph record. The consequent diffi-

2. Jameson, *Fables of Aggression* 128–32.

3. Wyndham Lewis, *The Apes of God* (1930; Santa Barbara, Calif., 1981) 565. Hereafter cited parenthetically as *Apes*.

4. Wyndham Lewis, *The Art of Being Ruled*, ed. Reed Way Dasenbrock (Santa Rosa, Calif., 1989) 32. Hereafter cited parenthetically as *ABR*.

5. Of course this phrase from Conrad's dedication of *The Secret Agent* to H. G. Wells, like everything else in the text, is ironic.

6. Just how decisively the war altered the way such groups functioned in discourses of England and Englishness is a subject of ongoing debate. Whether the differences between the pre- and postwar situations are better described in terms of an ideological break of some kind, or merely as an extension and intensification of existing ingroup/outgroup politics, is perhaps an arbitrary matter. To take anti-semitism, for example: It is certainly the case, as Kenneth Lunn argues in "Political Anti-Semitism before 1914: Fascism's Heritage?" (*British Fascism: Essays on the Radical Right in Inter-War Britain*, ed. Kenneth Lunn and Richard C. Thurlow [London, 1980] 20–40), that "we can identify important linkages between organisations, journals and individuals in the pre-1914 period and the activity of the inter-war years, suggesting a continuity of thought indicative of a tradition of British anti-semitism" (21); but this does not weaken G. C. Webber's argument in *The Ideology of the British Right, 1918–1939* (New York, 1986) that "the anti-semitism of [the interwar] period was subtly different both in substance and in tone from what had come before," for instance in becoming "more clearly political and more often identified with the Right than the Left" (17, 26).

culties involved in representing a healthy, working, and workable English community—never simply a positive, utopian project—are notoriously reflected in the literature of high modernism, which undertakes such a representation by almost entirely indirect or negative means.

The most nearly English of modernism's "Men of 1914"—born to an English father, educated at Rugby and the Slade, originator of the first specifically English movement of the historical avant-garde—Wyndham Lewis was also modernism's most ferocious and implacable critic of contemporary English society. From about 1914 to 1934 he was the self-declared "Enemy" of seemingly the whole sociocultural panorama; to a degree unusual even in modernism, his procedure was antagonistic, consisting of endless negations, refusals, impertinences, provocations—and sparing few of the shibboleths of the emergent modernist canon itself. His extreme application of the principle of refusal is undoubtedly a good part of the reason why, despite his major contributions to British culture—as one of England's earliest and most brilliant abstract painters, as the country's first radical critic of the new mass cultural apparatuses, as author of over a dozen controversial, experimentalist novels and collections of short fiction—Lewis has never been accorded a very prominent place in the pantheon of canonical modernism. No other white male cultural worker of the period has had his historical role so reduced and marginalized in official narratives of the modern, or is so little taught in today's classrooms.[7] And yet this apparently anomalous posi-

7. Hugh Kenner, who published a short book, *Wyndham Lewis*, in 1954 (Norfolk, Conn.), devotes considerable space to Lewis in *The Pound Era* (Berkeley, Calif., 1971), which I suppose is as close as one can get to an "official" narrative of modernism. But most studies of the high modernist period pass over Lewis with scarcely a glance, and even Kenner treats Lewis strictly as a Pound satellite. There are of course some books on Lewis, though not very many, and articles (mostly dealing with *Tarr* or *The Revenge for Love*) appear at the rate of about two or three a year. The indispensable studies are Jeffrey Meyers, *The Enemy: A Biography of Wyndham Lewis* (London, 1980), and Jameson, *Fables of Aggression*. One recent treatment of the "Men of 1914" which emphasizes Lewis's crucial role in the emergence of a consciously avant-gardiste literature in English is Dennis Brown's *Intertextual Dynamics within the Literary Group—Joyce, Lewis, Pound, and Eliot: The Men of 1914* (London, 1990); see especially pp. 60–67 on Lewis's 1914 Vorticist play, *Enemy of the Stars*. There is also Reed Way Dasenbrock's full-length study of Vorticism, *The Literary Vorticism of Ezra Pound and Wyndham Lewis: Towards the Condition of Painting* (Baltimore, 1985), which stresses the priority of painting among the arts during the modernist era and the importance of Lewis, as a cross-over figure, in effecting the modernist reorientation of writing toward the condition of painting. Undoubtedly the most significant event in Lewis studies has been the republication over the last decade of seventeen volumes of Lewis's work by Black Sparrow Press. These affordable scholarly

tion in fact confirms Lewis as a typical modernist writer, for it rests on a dialectic of insider and outsider which is fundamental to the literary production of the period. The adopted and canonized foreigners, the domestic writers who sought within England the vantage of an exile or émigré,[8] the women writers who by virtue of their class station enjoyed access to a cultural tradition that nonetheless was never really theirs—all are versions of this same archetypically modernist insider/outsider figure. As high modernism's excluded insider, Lewis is exemplary.

There is another (and in fact rigorously connected) reason for the eclipse of Lewis, and this of course is his fascism, most conspicuously on display in his 1931 book *Hitler*, which sports a large swastika on its cover and contains chapters with such titles as "Adolph Hitler a Man of Peace."[9] But here again, in spite of the notable peculiarities of Lewis's case, we are dealing with the typical rather than the anomalous. It is not simply that fascism "appealed," in the sense of an attractive political option, to a number of central figures in the modernist canon.[10] Rather, the professed or thinly veiled fascist sympathies of Yeats, Hulme, Eliot, Pound, Lawrence, Lewis and others must be read as a sign of the profound imbrication—the systematic overlapping—of fascism with what came to be the dominant or hegemonic strain of British modernism. The very construction of this modernism is wrapped up in the construction and dissemination of fascist ideology. So that, when we consider the operations (comic or otherwise) by means of which "community" is figured in the modernist text—the rearrangements of hierarchies, the scapegoatings and exclusions, the displacement or projection of impediments, the condensations of distinct social spaces, relations, and groups, and so on—we must be at all times attentive to the relation between these operations and those which produce the most extreme fantasy of community, the corporate state.

In pursuing this course of analysis, I focus on one of the most ambitious (and arguably the most intolerable) of all Lewis's novels, *The Apes of God* (1930). This text marks a culmination of the major project of Lewis's "Enemy" period, a monstrous transgeneric production that was to have been called *The Man of the World*, but that ultimately appeared more conven-

---

editions (of which four additional volumes are forthcoming) have laid the crucial groundwork for new considerations of Lewis.

8. See Terry Eagleton, *Exiles and Emigrés* (New York, 1970).

9. Wyndham Lewis, *Hitler* (London, 1931).

10. See Alistair Hamilton, *The Appeal of Fascism: A Study of Intellectuals and Fascism, 1919–1945* (London, 1971) 257–90.

tionally as two novels (the other being *The Childermass* [1928], the first volume of *The Human Age* trilogy) and two works of nonfiction, *The Art of Being Ruled* (1926) and *Time and Western Man* (1927). In these books, whose composition engaged him intermittently throughout the twenties (chapters of the *Apes*, for example, appeared in Eliot's *Criterion* in 1924), Lewis addresses himself to "the social decay of the insanitary trough between the two great wars,"[11] unfolding dialectically his sweeping culture critique. Proceeding through a series of negations, the Enemy attacks not merely factions (the Time cult, the Youth cult, the Health cult, the Homosexual cult, the Negro cult, the Dime-Novel and Cinema cults, Bloomsbury, the Sitwells, etc.) but whole arenas of opposition, what he calls the cultural "wars" (or "war-games") themselves: the "sex-war," the "class-war," the "race-war," the "nation-war," the "age-war" (or "child-parent war"). He attempts to propel himself by these negative means onto a Nietzschean cultural vantage point "beyond action and reaction" (*ABR 355*),[12] to clear the space for truly revolutionary social and aesthetic possibilities, and not, like so many of the self-declared revolutionaries and modernists around him, merely to toe the line of an increasingly respectable radicalism or to dress up Late Victorian platitudes in the guise of the New.

It would be a serious error to imagine that this revolutionary project can be understood, even on Lewis's own terms, as individualist or aestheticist: as a simple rejection (ostensibly typical of High Modernism) of the social and the political spheres. In his "Intellectual Autobiography," *Rude Assignment* (1950), Lewis wrote that the "peculiar note of solitary defiance" characteristic of his Enemy period derived not from "an exaggerated individualism" but from "the confidence of a herd—that was not there": "I felt it to be an accident—a disagreeable one—that I was straying around by myself. I was a group animal, behaving as one of the solitary breeds by chance" (212, 213). And like Pound and Eliot, Lewis understood perfectly well that the gathering or concretizing of this "herd that was not there," of this quite consciously

11. Wyndham Lewis, *Rude Assignment: An Intellectual Biography* (1950), ed. Toby Foshay (Santa Barbara, Calif., 1984) 214.

12. In this respect the "Man of the World" project is consistent with Lewis's prewar Vorticism. A crucial part of the second Vorticist Manifesto reads as follows: "1. Beyond Action and Reaction we would establish ourselves. 2. We start from opposite statements of a chosen world. Set up violent structure of adolescent clearness between two extremes. 3. We discharge ourselves on both sides. 4. We fight first on one side, then on the other, but always for the SAME cause, which is neither side or both sides and ours." Wyndham Lewis, ed., *Blast* 1 (1914; Santa Rosa, Calif., 1989) 30.

imagined community, could never be simply an aesthetic project. However centrally the new art figured in providing the "design" for a new "way of seeing," the task of preparing the cultural ground for an immanent community of "men who as yet were not there" was a thoroughly political one, necessitating "propaganda," "pamphleteering," an aggressive public role (*RA* 135). Moreover, as the transgeneric ambitions of *The Man of the World* attest (ambitions in some measure realized even in the four discrete texts), a major, if not always conscious, thrust of Lewis's work during this period was precisely to problematize any distinction between his art and his propaganda.[13]

Which is simply to say, once again and against those who lament Lewis's "lapses" into political error while praising his aesthetic achievements, that Lewis's modernism cannot in any way be bracketed from his fascism.[14] *Hitler* contains whole pages lifted directly from *The Art of Being Ruled*, the very text which *The Apes of God* systematically replays as fiction. It is not simply a matter, either, of aesthetic overreaching, of what Lewis's German contemporary Walter Benjamin saw as an essentially fascist drive to aestheticize the political (with modern warfare providing the aesthetic ideal or model). For Lewis is equally and simultaneously a politicizer of the aesthetic—as much the communist, on Benjamin's analysis, as the fascist. Indeed his work, which reminds us of the long and somewhat discomfiting history of radical-

13. This remains true even of Lewis's later aestheticist renunciations of politics, e.g., *The Writer and the Absolute* (London, 1952), which, no less than Julien Benda's *Trahison des clercs*, on which it seems to be based, is—in Jameson's words—"a tract against political *engagement* which is itself a political pamphlet" (*Fables of Aggression* 127). A few months earlier, Lewis had written a defense of his 1951 story collection *Rotting Hill* which stressed the necessarily political character of narrative fiction: "And those who would contradict me and assert that contemporary fiction can be otherwise than steeped in politics are those who would prefer that you would not have anything to do with books that cause you to use your rational faculty" ("A Cancelled Forward," *Rotting Hill*, ed. Paul Edwards, [Santa Barbara, Calif., 1986] 345–46).

14. It is not surprising that, among those who insist on maintaining such a separation, we can count Oswald Mosley himself, the founder of the British Union of Fascists. Writing of Lewis and Roy Campbell (the South African writer, a close friend of Lewis's, on whom Zulu Blades is modeled in *The Apes of God*), Mosley remarks: "These men will undoubtedly get the recognition they deserve when their opinions cease to be unpopular. How contemptible it is to denounce any work of art on account of the artist's political beliefs, and how often has history held up the mirror of ridicule to the perpetrators of this philistine absurdity." *My Life* (London, 1968) 226.

left/radical-right cross-pollination, effectively collapses Benjamin's famous but inadequate distinction between these two aesthetico-political articulations.[15]

We approach *The Apes of God*, therefore, as a political novel, and moreover as one whose political energies express themselves most characteristically in the joke mode. "*Life justified as joke.* Imagine that principle," says the novel's garrulous Blackshirt (503). In imagining and interrogating this principle, in seeking some handle with which to grasp the logic of Lewis's unrelenting and sometimes brutal black(shirt) humor, I will stress the centrality of gender and sexuality to the novel's comic transactions. For, as we will see, it is through gender relations that Lewis's savage indictment of liberal democratic society in its degenerative phase articulates all the other relations or "wars" constitutive of that society. Lewis's jokes bring us to the feminist thesis provocatively elaborated in Klaus Theweleit's *Male Fantasies*, that "a specific male-female (patriarchal) relation might belong at the center of our examination of fascism,"[16] and hence offer us an opportunity to extend into the British context an important line of thought about the psychological structure and strategic intention of fascism, which has been largely focused on the German case. A consideration of Lewis's jokes along these lines also provides points of departure for the next chapter, in which I attempt to relocate the post-modernist British novel as an emergent phenomenon of the late thirties, and to understand it in terms of a specifically feminist response to the perceived culpability not only of "male" modernism but of feminist modernism as well, in both organized and inchoate forms of fascism. To forestall objections here I should add that I try to trace out as fully as possible the problematic implications of Lewis's (and, in the next chapter, of Virginia Woolf's) joke-work, and on no account would I wish to effect a reduction of the whole text of interwar British fiction to a corrective fable featuring morally reprehensible male writers and their "good" female antagonists. Such a narrative would certainly be inaccurate, and in any case praise and blame on this level can be of no possible interest to students of cultural history. What matters, rather, is that we come to see how any discussion of modernism, fascism, or feminism in connection with the interwar years is unavoidably a discussion of

15. Walter Benjamin, "The Work of Art in the Age of Mechanical Reproduction" (1936), in Benjamin, *Illuminations*, ed. Hannah Arendt, trans. Harry Zohn (New York, 1969) 241–42.

16. Klaus Theweleit, *Male Fantasies, 1. Women, Floods, Bodies, History*, trans. Stephen Conway (Minneapolis, 1987) 227.

all three, that these terms, and the historical movements to which they refer, are mutually implicated in ways we must learn better to understand.

"The Peterpaniest Family": From Satire to Psychodrama

> Peter Pan mounts on the reversal of values established by nature and proven by history.
>
> —Sir Oswald Mosley, *My Life*

Under the category of satire Lewis included *The Apes of God*, but also *Hamlet*; in his usage the term "satirist" was "so extended as to mean all artists not specifically beauty-doctors."[17] Though he understood satire to involve laughter, Lewis placed largely negative value on such terms as "humor," "fun," and "play." Satire for him meant an artistic practice that amounted almost to a natural science of human appearance and social behavior, an essentially visual practice that remained detachedly "upon the surface of existence" (*Apes* 451). To a certain extent the term as Lewis uses it may be folded into the broader neoclassicist discourse of the modernist period, whose high priest was T. E. Hulme and whose legacies can be traced through high modernism in the valorization by Pound, Eliot, and others of impersonality, intellection, coldness, hardness, concreteness, stasis, order, and related antiromanticist principles. (That this classicism was also a *political* discourse, involving, as Lewis put it, "something of the same order as the principle of dictatorship" [*MWA* 156], is evident not only from its eventual appearance in Pound's wartime radio broadcasts but, at the very outset, from the alliance and interleaving of Hulme's aesthetics with the protofascist Action Française.)[18] At any rate, while Lewis is not in practice perfectly faithful to this neoclassicist doctrine, or even to his own theory of satire, his

17. Wyndham Lewis, "The Greatest Satire Is Non-Moral," in Lewis, *Men without Art*, ed. Seamus Cooney (Santa Barbara, Calif., 1987) 85; the reference to *Hamlet* appears on p. 93. Subsequent references to *Men without Art* will be included parenthetically, with the title abbreviated *MWA*.

18. On Pound's broadcasts, see Robert Casillo, *The Genealogy of Demons: Anti-Semitism, Fascism, and the Myths of Ezra Pound* (Evanston, Ill., 1988) 91. As Casillo points out, Pound's appeal in these broadcasts to the classical/fascist value of "hardness" derives "from his reaction to that 'fluidity' and 'undertow' . . . which characterizes not merely usury, *contra naturam*, but chthonic, unregulated, feminine Nature" (91). On Hulme's importance for Anglo-American literary modernism, see Michael H. Levenson, "Hulme: The Progress of Reaction," in *A Genealogy of Modernism* (Cambridge, 1984) 80–102.

novels of the Enemy period are quite striking in their repudiation of what might be called humanist habits of reading—and, for that matter, of laughing. One of the characters in *The Apes of God*, paraphrasing William Hazlitt, declares that "true satire must be vicious" (450), and judged by this standard the novel has few rivals. Reading it one may be put in mind less of Waugh or even Swift than of Sade: it is an interminable and unflinchingly cruel puppet show that plays out on the field of human sexuality and with almost mathematical rigor the extreme consequences of a certain cultural logic.

In form the novel is essentially picaresque, propelled by the familiar device (also favored by Sade) of pedagogy, or initiation. A nineteen-year-old naif named Dan Boleyn has been taken up as a sort of disciple by the notorious practical joker and repressed homosexual Horace Zagreus, who proposes to educate him in the ways of London's art-Apes—wealthy, pseudo-bohemian poetasters and dabblers clearly modeled after the Bloomsbury and Sitwell circles. The trusting and perfectly witless Dan, whom Zagreus presents to these society types as a "bio-chemist" or a "young man of genius" (248), is thus thrust helplessly into an escalating series of Ape-gatherings, undergoing in each episode some adventure highly degrading both to himself and to the Apes involved.

Let us consider a representative and more or less unremarkable passage. Richard and Jenny (recognizably Edward Wadsworth, a cosigner of Lewis's 1914 Vorticist manifestos, and his wife Fanny),[19] flush with Richard's recent inheritance, have taken their new Bugatti out to visit Dick Whittingdon (the wealthy amateur painter Richard Wyndham), at his mansion, March Park— also recently inherited. While Dan as usual looks on in bewildered silence, Dick displays his latest painting to the sycophantic Richard and Jenny:

> "Damn good Dick! Damn good!" . . .
> "I should call that a jolly good day's work Dick. . . ."
> The studio echoed with their delighted Dicking, as the pair took it in turn to Dick this rich coveted amateur, so haughtily 'county' (just the thing for their imperfect brand-new social-life), conscious of all the Tomming Dicking and Halling that their class-war-profiteered factory-wealth but lately-inherited, made possible—proud of the presence of such as the noted lesbian (of Gossip-column calibre) squatted in their rear—with whom they would soon with luck be Bloggie and Jennie, shaken up like a cocktail in the bowels of the Bugatti. Marvelous

---

19. For the Vorticist manifesto, see *Blast* 43. Wadsworth also contributed five illustrations and some translated extracts, with brief commentary, from Kandinsky's *Considering the Spiritual in Art* (1912) to this inaugural "Review of the Great English Vortex."

money that turns everything into a pet-or-nick-name or a Dick-like something! (180)

When, however, the "preposterous Jenny," who "*would* lay down the law about pictures because she had once played a piano in a Cinema for a living" (181), goes so far as to suggest that this new picture is an improvement over Dick's previous effort (in which the house, she says, was "too red"), Dick takes offense. "Everything else might be fair game for Jenny the law-giver, but for painting she had not a mandate" (181). Here is a representative excerpt from the six pages of quarreling that follow:

> "I don't care" jauntily cries the wilful old Jenny, squaring her jaw: it was clamped down upon the stem of the cigarette-holder, caught between the only two teeth that had started life in her head and not in another's, and she smiled most aggressive, with the glittering false residue. "I think it's still too red. It's far too red!"
>
> "I'm sorry you think I'm wrong Jenny!" lightly and loftily and fiercely sneered Dick, throwing up his head with eyes almost closed to shut out this absurdity.
>
> "Well Dick let's have them out side by side!" the undaunted voice of old Jenny rang out. [. . .]
>
> "There you are Dick what did I say!" the attractively self-willed little Jenny is heard to exclaim, as she flings herself over heavily in front of the picture [. . . .]
>
> "What did I say? You see—the red house spoils it. You must admit Dick that the red house spoils it."
>
> "I don't admit anything of the sort!"
>
> "I maintain that it could not be that red!"
>
> "How do you mean Jenny—'*could* not be' that red! What does it matter whether it *could* be or not! Dick peevishly pumps out his argument, in spasms of rich-toned complaint.
>
> "No Dick you can't have I maintain in a realistic picture——."
>
> "But it isn't realistic!"
>
> "*Yes it is !*"
>
> "Really Jenny I don't think you."
>
> "No Dick. I still maintain it's the wrong red, I'm sorry!"
>
> "Jenny is *maintaining* again Richard!"
>
> "Oh I know!" brother Richard laughed helplessly to brother Dick.
>
> The kindergarten was all alive with the dispute over the big boy's oil-picture, with the Noah's Ark H for House that they all knew he had squeezed out of the tube of vermilion, when left to himself, just to be clever and steal a march, but only the little old girl dared to speak up, and it was a ticklish moment. A thrill went down the spine of Dan. Here if anywhere was the authentic Ape-feeling to be encountered in the very atmosphere. (183)

One sees in this passage both the appeal of the *Apes* (which, as Hugh Kenner points out, lies precisely *not* in the rigorous visual method for which Lewis tirelessly propagandized but in his remarkable skill as a verbal mimic) and also the possibility of finding it, as even Jameson does, "virtually unreadable for any sustained period of time."[20] At over six hundred pages, the book presents us with enough of this almost absurdist empty dialogue to raise what Lewis half-acknowledged to be a problem with "*the poor quality* of his enemies."[21]

Certainly this is a problem if we view Lewis's enemies as simply bad, pseudomodernists with the means to exercise their meager talents. Lewis *did* resent such practicing "amateurs," whose proper role in his view was patronage rather than participation. (A number of his Apes, including Richard and Dick, are based on valuable patrons who, as a consequence of Lewis's extreme rudeness and ingratitude, withdrew their patronage in the mid-twenties.)[22] Lewis saw the practicing amateur as in effect usurping the limited social space for art in interwar England, squeezing out the truly professional artist. Dick, for example, rents not one but ten studios, thereby consigning ten more genuine but less well-heeled artists to "small ill-lit rooms while he sat on all these valuable workshops in solitary egotistic state" (189). Following the classic logic of *ressentiment*, Lewis's bitter resentment of these moneyed Apes is reproduced in their supposed resentment of the true artist-gods. The slavelike Apes are both "insolent and vindictive where their betters are concerned" and formidably "damaging, in their influence, to every form of creative thought" (*Apes* 121); that is, they are simultaneously the cultural underclass or rabble and the official arbiters of taste.

Even if we could accept the terms and implications of this critique—the distinction, for example, between authentic and inauthentic artist (with members of the Bloomsbury and Sitwell sets attached to the latter category as it were automatically, as much by virtue of their economic and social

20. Kenner, *Wyndham Lewis* 103; Jameson, *Fables of Aggression* 5.

21. *Wyndham Lewis on Art: Collected Writings, 1913–1956*, ed. C. J. Fox and Walter Michael (New York, 1969) 267.

22. On the patronage of Edward Wadsworth and Dick Wyndham, see Meyers, *The Enemy* 103, 112–13, 178–79. Meyers reports an incident in early 1924 which nicely captures Lewis's relation with these sponsors (who, along with the painter Anne Estelle Rice and her husband Raymond Drey, were providing him at that time with a sixteen-pound monthly allowance): "When one monthly installment failed to arrive on time Lewis sent Fanny Wadsworth, who doled out the money, a postcard that demanded: 'Where's the fucking stipend?'" (113).

standing as of their particular aesthetic programs or achievements)—we cannot take Lewis's lengthy and savage denunciations of the bourgeois bohemian at face value without experiencing *The Apes of God* as a work of colossal overkill. Rich painters of "bad" pictures are not worth so much trouble, no matter what real or imagined obstacles they may have thrown on the paths of Lewis and other penniless interwar artists. (And it is only fair to say that Lewis's ability to earn a living wage as a painter was systematically undermined by Roger Fry and the Bloomsbury set.)[23] As always, to unpack these sorts of comic transactions we need first to address ourselves to the displacements and condensations in the comic object. The "authentic Ape-feeling . . . in the very atmosphere" of Dick's mansion marks a complex congregation of elements whose ostensibly noxious character has less than we might think to do with questions of aesthetic practice and the institution of art. More fundamental to the joke-work involved in this scene are its imbecilic "kindergarten" quality (Dick's aesthetic procedures—the "Noah's Ark H for house"—are not just amateurish, they are juvenile), the emphasis it places on Jenny as "law-giver," and the presence throughout of a "noted lesbian (of Gossip-column calibre)." To understand the joke-work of *The Apes of God* we need to investigate a fluid but rigorously constrained system of articulation whose negative terms include the idiot, the child, the homosexual, and the gossip-column or salon society, and whose nodal point or ideological linch pin is not, as is usually assumed, art, but sex.

We can enter this system most readily through the portals of the "age-war." Infantilization is a familiar enough comic strategy; it effects a bathetic reduction in the object. For Lewis, however, satire was less a matter of comic distortion than of brutally accurate observation, and infantilization was an important real-world phenomenon of interwar England. As he saw it, the catastrophic experience of the Great War had turned the younger generation against its Victorian Fathers and produced a profound legitimation crisis in English society. The symptoms of this crisis included widespread refusal of the patriarchal role and a concomitant valorization of the eternal child and the principle of play (under which art was often, though in Lewis's view, unjustifiably, subsumed). The cult of the child, wrote Lewis in *The Art of Being Ruled*, "is perhaps the most characteristic and central peculiarity of our time" (388). He warned that the bourgeois bohemians—the "*precieuses ridicules*" for whom art was a playful leisure activity rather than a matter of professional commitment—would soon be pitching their salon "next door to the nursery"; "then gradually the connecting door will become a large

23. At least this is the impression one gets from Meyers, *The Enemy* 39–51.

folding-door; and then at length all septum of any sort will disappear. The *precieuses ridicules*, dressed in baby frocks, will be on the floor with their dolls, or riding rocking-horses in Greek draperies" (*ABR* 216). This dystopian fantasy of the "pan-nursery," which *The Apes of God* so unrelentingly dramatizes, is not without some empirical justification. The *Sonnenkinder* cult was indeed a powerful cultural force in the twenties—so much so that Martin Green can say of those who refused to accept the Children-of-the-Sun style that they simply "ceased to be contemporary, whatever their birth date."[24]

This last phrase in particular resonates with Lewis, whose emphasis is not on youth itself, youth *as* youth, but on a "peterpanism" of the middle-aged.[25] It is typical that in the scene at Dick's mansion attention is called to such incongruities as the false teeth of "little Jenny." Later in the novel reference is made to a group called the CBY, the Communion of British Youth. This is a sort of "boy-scout religion" led by a man "of fifty bright young summers" whose chief difficulty is getting "any genuine *youths* to join up—for what *youth* in his senses wants to go about shouting—'Oh look—I am a youth!'" (564). Lewis acknowledges, in the *Apes* and elsewhere, that actual young people did participate in this elite subculture. But at the same time he throws doubt on the very category of "genuine youth," seeing youthful behavior as at root a kind of act or impersonation, and youth itself as a fantasy constructed and disseminated by the decadent middle-aged. According to Lewis, not only was the youth cult originally "confined to grown-up and elderly people," but even when it caught on with the younger generation it remained a form of collective artifice: "real children also played at being 'children,' even outdoing their most skilful adult imitators" (*ABR* 164).

Quasi-rebellious cults of this kind (the youth cult being "associated with others of the same blood with itself") are not, in other words, spontaneous but rather "highly organized" social phenomena, systematically propagated and elaborated through the culture industry (*ABR* 164). "I know a hard-working middle-aged journalist," says a character in the *Apes*, "[who] keeps a wife and large hungry family in considerable style on sucking-up to the Young. His Youth-stuff he calls it—in papers and magazines. 'Youth at the Helm!' or 'Bravo Twenty-Five!' or 'When Youth Can—When Old Age Does Not Know' are the sort of headings he gives his articles, you know the sort of thing, there's money in it" (276–77). The point is that what the young take to be rebellious

24. Martin Green, *Children of the Sun: A Narrative of 'Decadence' in England after 1918* (New York, 1980) xvii.

25. The term was in widespread use throughout Lewis's career. J. M. Barrie's famous play had first been published in book form in 1911.

self-celebration is in fact passive conformity to a cynically and profitably manufactured image of themselves. This journalist's hugely successful articles declaring everyone past thirty to be "worn-out," implicitly "criminal," and deserving of "the electric chair or the Tarpeian Rock" are quite conscious extensions from Shaw's "Every man over forty is a scoundrel" (277): the twenties' youth cult, as Lewis never tires of insisting, is merely the same old cant recycled through more powerful and insidious cultural instruments. And as such it is scarcely uncontaminated by the Fathers.

In Lewis's suppressed 1930s novel *The Roaring Queen*, an eleven-and-a-half-year-old author called "little Nancy Cozens"—very much the child playing at being a child—manages to sell 25,000 copies of her novel *Bursting Ripe* on the day of publication. But she achieves this stunningly premature "culmination of her career" only because the great father of the book-review racket and chief stooge of the publishing industry, Samuel Shodbutt (Arnold Bennett), has enthusiastically promoted the book, even urging his readers to buy multiple copies.[26] It is this emphasis on the mass-produced character of ostensibly "popular" culture, on the orchestration from above of contemporary cultural phenomena (including threats to the Culture of the Father), which made Lewis an important figure for Marshall McLuhan and led a recent critic to call him (in a doubly unlikely but nonetheless telling phrase) "a one-man Frankfurt School of the right."[27]

But jokes like the one about little Nancy Cozens have more than one cutting edge. Certainly one object of attack is the capital-controlling class in back of the "bookselling factory" (*RQ* 156), for whom culture is an industry used to construct the society's desires in accordance with the profoundly antisocial requirements of capital. Lewis's suspicion and contempt could scarcely run deeper in this direction. Indeed, in his insistence that not only "*What the Public Wants*" but what it is capable of saying and thinking at any given time are functions of the "businesslike organization of its desire" by "some superior will which is seldom explicit" (*ABR* 364, 363), Lewis anticipates the profound pessimism of Theodor Adorno and Max Horkheimer's mass culture theory, as well as the closed economy of Louis Althusser's theory of ideological reproduction and the quasi-conspiratorial aspect of Foucault's clinic and prison period.[28] But such a totalizing critique of mass

26. Wyndham Lewis, *The Roaring Queen*, ed. Walter Allen (New York, 1973) 155. Libel threats delayed publication of this roman à clef (written in 1936 and set in 1930) for thirty-seven years. Subsequent references are cited parenthetically as *RQ*.

27. Dasenbrock, "Afterword," in Lewis, *Art of Being Ruled* 441.

28. While Lewis's understanding of agency and power is less nuanced than that of Foucault, he is not, anymore than Foucault is, a naive conspiracy theorist. The "superior

culture also involves, as has often been said of the Frankfurt School, a certain contempt for the masses themselves as well as an automatic and unreflective denigration of all cultural workers and works that draw a non-elite audience. The *Bursting Ripe* joke is directed in part at Nancy Cozens's readership, which is to say at the mass audience for literature, members of "the American Book of the Month Club . . . and the Novel League of Great Britain" (*RQ* 157), who are content to have their desires organized in businesslike fashion by the likes of Arnold Bennett. This audience was largely composed of women, and as Andreas Huyssen has written, "the fear of the masses" which runs through modernism, providing a point of unlikely convergence for, say, Adorno and Eliot, "is always also a fear of woman, a fear of nature out of control, a fear of the unconscious, of sexuality."[29] Hostilities toward the mass readership of little Nancy Cozens cannot be cleanly separated from hostilities toward the "girl writer" herself and toward her feminine product, the title of which (*Bursting Ripe*) clearly promises something in the sensuo-emotive line, a work of nature unbridled by intellect. In short, the joke of the child author not only manages the fears and hostilities connected with the capitalists behind the scenes—those figures of power and authority whose will "is seldom explicit"—but also the fears connected with a mass cultural realm, already feminine, whose complete feminization it is in the interests of capitalism's "superior will" to secure.

It is therefore significant that the "master-stroke" of Lewis's manipulative journalist in *The Apes of God* is "to have taken women up into his system" (278). This middle-aged man behind the scenes hesitates to treat women "on the same radical footing" by means of which he had "stabilize[d] scoundrelism at the thirty milestone" for men (277). "And yet [women] were not *all* young. That was the great difficulty" (278).[30] He overcomes this problem through an ingenious modification of a fundamental piece of Ape-wisdom,

---

will" to which he refers in somewhat paranoid tones is clearly on the order of a systemic tendency or cultural logic (the logic of capitalism), and not of a conscious intention or plot. D. G. Bridson's reading of *The Art of Being Ruled* as a work that tends toward "conspiratorial theory," particularly in its analysis of feminism as an advanced elaboration of liberal-capitalist hegemony, seems to me misleading in this respect. See Bridson, *The Filibuster: A Study of the Political Ideas of Wyndham Lewis* (London, 1972) 35.

29. Andreas Huyssen, "Mass Culture as Woman: Modernism's Other," in *Studies in Entertainment: Critical Approaches to Mass Culture*, ed. Tania Modleski (Bloomington, Ind., 1986) 196.

30. The joke that "all women are young" is a variation on the joke that "all women are innocent," which Theweleit identifies specifically as a key to the fascist practice of violence against women. See *Male Fantasies*, vol. 1, 180–81.

namely that "all artists should . . . be recognized as noble." This bit of prevailing dogma (which, by establishing equivalence on the level of production, threatens to collapse the hierarchical distinctions among cultural products—debasing genuine works of art by ennobling Apish endeavors) provides the journalist with just the "cue" he needs:

> "This was enough for him! . . . Now he saw his way out.—Why should not all women (for *artist* he substituted *woman*), be recognized as *young!*"
> "I think that's a marvellous idea!" said Mrs. Keith.
> "Not bad is it?" said Kalman.
> "Your friend is a genius!" said Sadofsky. . . .
> "For *noble* he substituted *young!*" Kalman said.   (278)

The "genius" of the media is to elaborate the obsession with youth through a series of equations and substitutions, whereby the bohemian salon set can conceive of all its men (the painting and scribbling "Dicks") as virtual nobility, and all its women as fashionably young; this nicely glamorizes things for the gossip columns. But the step in this elaboration which is here underscored as the masterstroke is the substitution of "woman" for "artist." To understand the genius of this cultural system we must see that the accordance of special privilege to youth is part and parcel with the feminization of culture.

It would seem that one cannot specify an exact line of priority to these steps and substitutions. They form, as Lewis puts it in *The Art of Being Ruled*, a "vicious circle" of causes and effects: a mass-cultural "revolution in favour of standards unfriendly to the intellect" means elevation of "the passions, intuitions, all the features of the emotive [i.e., feminine] life"; this leads to widespread recognition of the woman as supreme human creator, the baby as the "supreme 'creation,'" and babyhood as the "supreme condition of perfection"—which in turn guarantees continued "war on the intellect" (*ABR* 216). Jokes of course flourish in this kind of fluid environment, with its loose logic of displacement and overdetermination. But a vicious circle is precisely not open, not free: it arises out of the insistence on a center and the need to contain. That the center which secures this fatal cultural logic is woman—as we might expect of a culture critique produced during the most productive years of the suffragette movement and at a time when women outnumbered men in the population by record margins[31]—is made clear at numerous points in *The Art of Being Ruled*.

31. According to A. J. P. Taylor, *English History, 1914–1945* (New York, 1965) 166, the 1921 census shows the preponderance of women over men at an all-time high.

Of particular interest is a discarded early chapter in which the seeming "Trinity" whose "Dramatis Personae" are "the Woman," "the Child," and "Man" is found to be a disguised "Duality" whose true terms are simply "Man . . . and all the forces in subjection or opposition to his pride and authority with the great material figure of Nature at their back, the great Mother." Thus "the role of THE CHILD . . . merges in that of *the woman*," with the latter being itself no more than a counterrole or foil, the role of "anti-Man" or un-Man.[32] And not surprisingly, the homosexual role, the role of shaman (as we will see in the second part of this chapter, there is always with Lewis an emphasis on roles, socially constructed and manipulated subjectivities, which problematizes his discourse of essences),[33] merges with the great unmanning forces as well: the "male invert" is, precisely, the "*child* of the 'suffragette'" (*ABR* 218, my emphasis). His unmanning role is in part that of an "unconscious propagandist of feminism": "the modes and incentives of his obsessional life supply the propaganda picture of a feminized universe" (*ABR* 242).

This articulation of the woman with the homosexual through the figure of the child means that such scenes as the kindergarten quarrel over Dick's painted house, which on one level are part of an elaborately coded comic restaging of specific struggles within the London art world—struggles centering on the institution of art (on modernism, realism, romanticism, primitivism, provincialism, patronage, etc.)—must also be read as scenes in a psychodrama (still, however, a "satire" in Lewis's terms) whose only dramatis personae are Man and his Other. Moreover, this condensation occurs quite explicitly and consciously in the text: Lewis's strategy is not merely to expose Dick Wyndham or Bloomsbury or the rest of the interwar Apes to the unsparing laughter he associated with true satire, but to direct that laughter at Woman and all that "merges" with her in her opposition to the "pride and authority" of Man. The misogyny of *The Apes of God*, in other words, is not hidden, however extensively it is elaborated. This is a novel whose patriarchal character it requires no interpretive effort whatsoever to demonstrate. Indeed, the chief interpretive difficulty arises from what can seem even to a contemporary feminist cultural critic an excessive investment in the category of gender—in this instance a conscious need to articulate every social rela-

32. Untitled chapter 4, rejected draft (*ABR* 394). The phrase "anti-man" is from p. 199: "All orthodox opinion—that is, today, 'revolutionary' opinion either of the pure or the impure variety—is *anti-man*."

33. For example: "The present widespread invert fashion . . . is much more a political phenomenon than anything else" (*ABR* 239).

tion, every manifestation of social struggle, in terms of a grand opposition between Man and unmanning Woman.[34]

Even the "Jewish question," on which Lewis has much to say in the *Apes* and elsewhere, must be posed in terms of gender. It is not "quite true," writes Lewis in *Hitler*, that "the Jews govern England": "for if indeed, wearing the trousers, the Jew is the brilliant and bossy Hausfrau of this stolid english hubby, the latter has at least, in his quiet way, succeeded in influencing her, decidedly for the good. In short, upon that hypothesis, is not the Jew here, from the Hitler standpoint, disinfected and anglicized[?]" (*Hitler* 40–41). This peculiarly lighthearted and backhanded defense of England's Jews, who despite their irritating bossiness are really not so noxious to the community as the Nazis believe ("the Hitlerite," Lewis goes on to say, simply "takes the Jew too seriously" [41]), is doubly revealing. First, apart from the matter of race, we observe that the problem of rule or governance—of social power—is here framed in terms of gender rather than economics. What is constantly thematized in Lewis, as in Pound and Eliot, is the question of the ruling gender rather than of the ruling class, and in this respect he calls to mind Theweleit's observation that "one of the primary traits of fascists is assigning greater importance to the battle of the sexes than to the class struggle, even in their *conscious* thinking" (1:169). Just as important here, though, is the fact that this initial subordination of class to gender is what makes possible its further occlusion behind race and nation, the other terms that organize the fascist critique of liberal rule. The English community is a household whose proper and indigenous authority is masculine, and to which the Jew specifically, and by implication any alien or immigrant group, poses a threat not so much of miscegenation as of petticoat rule.[35] England

34. Jameson says of Lewis's "obsessive sexism and misogyny": "I wonder if I will be understood when I suggest that Lewis's expression of this particular *idée fixe* is so extreme as to be virtually beyond sexism" (*Fables of Aggression* 20). Perhaps in my case Jameson has *not* been understood, but in any event I am trying to suggest that the proper site of the "modernist as fascist" is precisely *not* "beyond sexism."

35. Lewis's one sustained meditation on the question of race is *Paleface: The Philosophy of the "Melting Pot,"* published in book form in 1929 (London). The polemical intention of the essay is to defend Western civilization and, especially, Western culture against the decadent cult of "primitivism." The book manifests a clear refusal to treat with respect the cultural achievements of non-Western peoples; it would be absurd to argue that this is not a racist tract (as Lewis's apologist D. G. Bridson does in *The Filibuster* 75). But along with his dismissive attacks on Native American art, African American music, and so forth, Lewis condemns such diverse Western figures as Bergson, Spengler, Lawrence, and Sherwood Anderson as major propagandists for the new primitivism. And in discussing

and Englishness can be preserved only to the extent that the father, despite the apparent eclipse of his power in (inter)marriage, manages "in his quiet way" to continue to exercise a dominant influence. For it is in subjecting the Jew/Woman to his stolid masculine influence that the Man of England effectively "anglicizes" her (though, as Homi Bhabha has remarked, "to be anglicized is *emphatically* not to be English";[36] the anglicized Jew is simply marked by a *different* difference).

The passage from *Hitler* is, of course, a singularly uncompelling analysis of the "Jewish question," lacking even the pretention to historical or "scientific" rigor of contemporaneous British fascist tracts such as those of Arnold Leese and the Imperial Fascist League.[37] But it is precisely the jocular, throw-away quality that makes the passage so arresting, for it suggests a minimal investment in the Jewish question as such and an appeal to patterns of association and condensation which have become virtually automatic and at the same time extraordinarily fluid, readily adaptable to new circumstances. This situation may help us to account for the strangely belated place of anti-semitism within the main current of British fascism. Oswald Mosley and the British Union of Fascists in some sense clearly inherited the Jewish question from Germany; it played no visible role in their doctrine until British Jews and other antifascists, rightly stressing the similarities between the BUF and the Nazis, forced the issue. But it also seems clear that, at that moment in 1934, the BUF was fully prepared, in both senses of the word, to launch an anti-semitic campaign.

Prepared, first of all, to use the Jew as a way of explaining away the sites of resistance within British society to the fascist project, the fascist community. As I mentioned in the introduction, Slavoj Žižek has spoken to just this

---

these men Lewis makes the characteristic turn from race to gender. For it turns out that the role being played by primitive or non-Western culture is precisely that of unmanning or feminizing the West. The true project behind primitivism turns out to be "glorification of the feminine principle"; its motto might be "Back to the Womb" (*Paleface* 184, 183).

36. Homi Bhabha, "Of Mimicry and Man," *October* 28 (Spring 1984): 128.

37. In 1930–31 Mosley had not yet founded the British Union of Fascists, and the BUF's attacks on the Jews would not begin until 1934. But anti-semitism was from the beginning a cornerstone of the doctrine of the IFL, which Leese had founded in 1928. Indeed, by early 1931 Leese was proposing, in the IFL organ *The Fascist*, either "compulsory segregation" or "extermination" as the only workable solutions to the problem of the "Jewish menace." See John Morrell, "Arnold Leese and the Imperial Fascist League: The Impact of Racial Fascism," in *British Fascism: Essays on the Radical Right in Inter-War Britain*, ed. Kenneth Lunn and Richard Thurlow (London, 1980) 57–75; quotations taken from pp. 68–69.

point. The Jew, remarks Žižek, is how fascism "simultaneously denies and embodies the structural impossibilities" in its corporatist vision of society; only a scapegoat, "a foreign body introducing corruption into the sound social fabric," can account for "the distance between this corporatist vision and the factual society split by antagonistic struggles."[38] But British fascism was prepared to scapegoat the Jew in another sense as well. The mechanisms required by this scapegoating process, the systematic associations by means of which both "the sound social fabric" and its "corruption" by the Other could be imagined, are already in place at the moment when continuing (and theoretically "unaccountable") English resistance to an ostensibly organic English community focuses fascist attention on the Jew. The psychic groundwork of scapegoating has already been done before the Jew even begins to appear, and this work (which, Freud says, is bound to be witty, is bound to take the form of joke-work) consists in a rigorously gendered system of articulation—the association of community with household, leadership with fatherhood; the displacement of social struggle onto the struggle of marriage and child rearing, and so forth—which is more fundamental to fascism's impossible vision of society than any particular scapegoat, even the racial scapegoat, the Jew. What we see in Lewis, in other words, is not only that the scapegoating of the Jew becomes necessary to fascism (even in England, where this polluting element has been more or less "disinfected"), but that the Jew is necessarily to be scapegoated *as Woman*.

Something approaching a third of the characters in *The Apes of God* are marked as Jewish. The implication, of course, is that the Ape milieu is *too* Jewish, both disproportionately and disagreeably so. In this regard, the novel is consistent with the fear, so visible in National Socialist and IFL literature, that the Jews have taken control of and are degrading (effeminizing) the cultural apparatus at both ends: "high" (as key players in the emergence of European modernism) and "low" (as major financiers of the cinema and recording industries).[39] But in the *Apes*, as in *Hitler*, Lewis is prepared to downplay the alien or external character of the Jew. What is constantly stressed is the homogeneity of the Ape world; the Jew, though internally "split" or "divided" by the demands of assimilation, fits into this world quite well. The trouble is that it is the inverted world of petticoat rule, a feminized universe unrelieved in this case by the influences of any "stolid hubby."

The novel's exemplary Jew, Julius Ratner, "Joo"—sometimes spelled "Jew" as "a joke" (143)—is also, like virtually all the Jewish characters, an

---

38. Žižek, *The Sublime Object of Ideology* 126.
39. See Morrell, "Arnold Leese and the Imperial Fascist League" 67.

exemplary denizen of Bloomsbury ("No. 50 Great Eustace Street"). He is unmarried, childless, a "great big baby," and a wealthy amateur novelist resentfully aware of the Apish quality of his own work, with its "clichés of the epileptic schools . . . those thrilling words in isolation, of high-brow melodrama, and the rest of the 'sickening' traits of the least ambitious, sham-experimental, second-rate literary cabotinage" (155, 163, 160). What matters most is not his Jewishness as such but his participation, as the cultural *hausfrau* of the moment, in the feminization of English society and culture. Woolf, whom Lewis regarded as having "presided over this process in the first post-war decade," and whose Apishly "exact and puerile copies" of Joycean effects he held to be symptomatic (*MWA* 140, 138), is clearly a target of the parodic excerpts from Ratner's work-in-progress:

> A cloud threatened the tail of the serpent. A little child picked a forget-me-not. She lifted a chalice. It was there. *Epiphany*. There were three distinct vibrations. (156)

This is not the writing of a Jew, except insofar as the Jew may be said to write *as a woman* and thereby to have contributed to "the part that the feminine mind has played—and minds as well, deeply feminized, not technically on the distaff side—in the erection of our present criteria" (*MWA* 140).

Everything in *The Apes of God* leads us back to this horror of feminization. The joke-work of Lewis's monstrous satire is work on and through sexual material, the material of sexual relations. It is a resolutely anti-psychological text (the psychological novel representing for Lewis the "distaff side" of modernism) which cries out for psychoanalysis—even while the "black-bearded" "Jewish witch-doctor" is one of its early comic targets (81). This is a distinctly fascist pattern: on the one hand the notorious aversion to any form of psychoanalysis (which, as Žižek argues, could expose the pleasurable dimension, the "obscene enjoyment" at work in fascist ideology);[40] on the other hand a vision of community explicitly (and even to some degree consciously) constructed in terms of the family drama, and animated above all by a terror at the thought of fatherlessness, of the father's castration or inversion or removal.[41] What I want to examine in the second half of the chapter, however, is the way in which Lewis's version of this drama, conceived as

40. Žižek, *Sublime Object of Ideology* 82. Consider, for example, Mosley's insistence, at the outset of his autobiography, that "few things are more overrated than the effect of childish experiences on later life" (*My Life* 7).

41. It may be relevant to remark here that Lewis's father abandoned the family in 1893, when Percy was eleven, and ceased to support them financially after 1900. See Meyers, *The Enemy* 3–6.

revolutionary satire, somehow *over*works the joke of England as "God's own Peterpaniest family" (*Apes* 498), exacerbating inconsistencies in the fascist idea of community as Fatherland ("the aryan Family-idea" [*Apes* 531]) and carrying them to the point of ideological crisis. Like a number of prominent fascist or protofascist writers, Lewis is a dangerous writer even for fascism; it is not for nothing that his *Hitler* was banned by the Nazis.[42]

Female Impersonation as the Comic Entertainment of Fascism

> The Sitwells were giving a private dance
> But Wyndham Lewis disguised as the maid
> Was putting cascara in the still lemonade.
>> —W. H. Auden, "A Happy New Year"

> We definitely prefer "women who are women, and men who are men."
>> —A. Raven Thomson, Deputy Director of Policy, British
>> Union of Fascists

In *The Inoperative Community*, Jean-Luc Nancy "start[s] out from the idea" that "the thinking of community as essence . . . is in effect the closure of the political" (xxxviii): "The community that becomes *a single* thing (body, mind, fatherland, Leader . . .) necessarily loses the *in* of being-*in*-common. Or, it loses the *with* or the *together* that defines it. It yields its being-together to a being *of* togetherness. The truth of community, on the contrary, resides in the retreat of such a being" (xxxix). "Nothing," he goes on, "indicates more clearly what the logic of this being of togetherness can imply than the role of *Gemeinschaft*, of community, in Nazi ideology" (xxxix).

One of the qualities which makes *The Apes of God* such a treacherous and difficult book is that it seems to be committed both to a communitarian ideology of (masculine) essence and to the deconstruction of this ideology. It both yearns for an authentic fatherland, a masculine *Gemeinschaft* in place of the country of women which England has become, and exposes the fatuity of this yearning. The novel's essentialism is evident in its supposition of time-less masculine and feminine principles, a supposition Lewis shared not only

---

42. See Meyers, *The Enemy* 190. Lewis claims in *The Hitler Cult* (London, 1939), his retraction of the pro-Nazi sentiments in *Hitler*, that the German edition of the latter was confiscated and pulped on the orders of Goebbels. This has not been confirmed.

with male modernists such as Pound but with most of the women writers of
the modernist period as well. This gender essentialism, which informs his
entire thought on culture and society, is the justification for his constant
displacement in the *Apes* of diverse and historically specific social struggles
onto the singular struggle between man and woman, father and mother,
husband and wife. But at the same time a rejection of essence, an insistence
that "classification by gender" is a "pigeon-hole" logic that can produce only
"illusory" distinctions (*MWA* 131)—and indeed a desire to move beyond the
"sex-war" altogether, onto a social field unregulated by the binary logic of
patriarchy—can be traced through the innumerable and potentially destabilizing comic transactions in the novel involving impersonation, mimicry,
role playing, and divided or multiple subjectivity. In satirizing a (shattered)
community that has forsaken its essential masculine features—above all, its
Father/Leader—Lewis exposes the very mechanisms of identity construction which we would expect patriarchal essentialism to obscure.

We have already seen that "youth," for Lewis, is a construction: "a piece
of political machinery" (*ABR* 253) and, more specifically, a marketing strategy. Even the young must learn their youthful behavior, a process of imitation
through which, at least in the twenties, "the *aged* mind . . . is reproduced"
(*ABR* 270, my emphasis). Asked if the work of his young protegé is written in
free verse, Zagreus is indignant:

> "Not at all—it is in a quite traditional metre. Absolutely the *youngest* genera-
> tion, sir, do not write in free verse—they have gone back to *quite* traditional
> forms."
> "Have they? That is very interesting."
> "Yes quite the youngest generation! It is only, you will find, the thirties and the
> forties that believe in violent experiment—*the very youngest generation*" Mr.
> Zagreus thundered, his eyes flashing "are super-victorian now, if you like—are
> classical *to a man!*" (40)

The *Apes* is full of inversions along these lines, the effect of which is to install
youth so firmly as a category of the fashion system that it is effectively
disabled or neutralized as a category of essense.

Other ostensibly fundamental categories—race, nationality, sexuality,
even gender itself—are similarly dislodged from the field of essence and
permitted to circulate as mere cultural contrivances. When Archie Margolin,
the "child-height," boyish East-End Jew who succeeds Dan Boleyn in
Zagreus's affections (42), pays a visit to Dick Whittingdon at March Park, he
quite consciously plays the Jew for his racist host, striking "the popular note,

of what all of his race ought to be, the Dickens-Jew of *Our Mutual Friend*, a myth he freely hated . . . [but one which] had a strong appeal for [Dick's] historic sense" (46). Dick meanwhile makes sure to act before the Jew the part of the True English Gentleman at his Country Manor:

> Dick flung his feet out this way and that—he stamped up and down upon the swagger carpet of this *Rittergut* to show his East End visitor how *he*, the jew-boy from the slum, would have behaved, if he had been absolutely at home, as was Dick, and had he trodden these exclusive mansions from the cradle up.   (44)

Thus race is accentuated but at the same time reduced to artifice. "Englishness" as much as "Jewishness" becomes a matter of performance. Racial stereotypes seem not to be grounded in essence but in "popular . . . myth"—which leaves them free to be transposed from one group to another without becoming any less (or any more) "true." Dick's uncle, Sir James, is said to have developed a hatred of the "whole Scottish nation" (31):

> He became convinced that the Scottish People were aiming at a new world-hegemony, of an oppressive character that beggared description, with the noble welstadt of Glasgow as its capital and main port, that was his persuasion, the fruit of a great deal of obscure and I fear not very creditable meditation. In every land they are to be found, he argued, in positions of the highest trust: England, he would doggedly affirm, is run by Scots—that of course was why it was going to the dogs—and he predicted freely that the day would come when all nations of the earth would eat porridge and worship in a kirk. . . .
>
> It was in vain that I protested that half of the Scotch were now Irish . . . owing don't you know to irish immigration, and that Glasgow was more irish than scottish—that was absolutely no use at all! He would reply that the more mixed they were the worse they became, and indeed the more *scotch*!   (31–32)

Of course the joke here depends on one's perception of an incongruous substitution of Scots where, in the twenties, Jews *ought to be*; old Sir James has confusedly latched onto the wrong scapegoat. But such a substitution, even while it indirectly rehearses the main narrative of interwar anti-semitism,[43] tends to expose the shaky or "not very creditable" grounds on which the whole scapegoating process rests. Sir James's plainly absurd hypotheses regarding the Scottish world conspiracy make a mockery of his faith in the especial persistence of the Other's racial essence ("the more

---

43. That is, the "Hidden Hand" narrative embodied in the bogus *Protocols of the Elders of Zion*. See Gisela C. Lebzelter, *Political Anti-Semitism in England, 1918–1939* (London, 1978).

mixed . . . the more *scotch*")—a faith that exactly reproduces that of Henry Hamilton Beamish and other British anti-semitic propagandists of the twenties.[44]

Sexuality and gender in the *Apes* are similarly submitted to the kind of joke-work which unsettles, even while it appeals to, essentialist conceptions of identity. Virtually all the male characters in the novel are marked homosexual, though most, like Boleyn and Zagreus, do not self-identify as such. Indeed the nonpracticing or "repressed homosexual" (172) is the archetypal male Ape: his Apishness is not a question of sexual practice but of cultural orientation. The homosexual is defined as a man who *acts like a woman* in his relation to the culture at large—and this performance may often entail "girlish . . . sexual modesty" and "bashfulness" carried to the point of total repression (*ABR* 266).

This identification of homosexuality with the feminine (and lesbianism with the masculine) is a familiar piece of essentialist doctrine, by means of which the assumption of a stable sexual binarism (man and woman) is continually reconfirmed through a reductive logic of inversion. Moreover, the attachment of the label "homosexual" to men who do not practice sexual relations with other men suggests an essentialist appeal to grounds of sexual identity more fundamental than sexual practice itself. But the grounds to which Lewis appeals may actually be less rather than more fundamental. By emphasizing the cultural dimension of homosexuality Lewis represents it as a social and external phenomenon rather than something private, internal, natural. Sexuality becomes, like race, a matter of performance, of "acquired or affected" rather than inborn traits (*ABR* 271); it becomes indeed, a matter of "political" practice, part of "a *politics*," as the Blackshirt observes to Dan in the *Apes*, "*of revolt*" (530).

Furthermore, in his zeal to represent the "Homo" as "child of the 'suffragette'"—as the "anti-man" or "shaman" of interwar culture and enemy of "the aryan Family-idea"—Lewis deploys a chaotic comedy of cross-dressing and female impersonation which is impossible fully to reconcile

44. Sir James's belief that the "essence" of the feared and hated race is somehow more powerful than that of other races, so that miscegenation extends without diluting the noxious element, reproduces the pathology of Beamish's group, the Britons, who in 1920 denied membership to "Aryans" who could not "show that their ancestry is free from Jewish taint," arguing that intermarriage caused "a deep degradation and defilement of our stock" while doing nothing to improve or anglicize the stock of the Jews. See Lebzelter, "Henry Hamilton Beamish and the Britons: Champions of Anti-Semitism," in Lunn and Thurlow, eds., *British Fascism* 41–56; quotations from 43, 50.

with a discourse of essences. The most extended episode of this kind runs through the novel's 150-page penultimate chapter, "Lord Osmund's Lenten Party," a sprawling but fierce treatment of the Sitwell family circle (here the "Finnian Shaws"). Dan, whose humiliations in the novel often involve nudity, and particularly the exposure of his "girlish" buttocks to menacing "manly" women (he is threatened with spanking or flagellation by such women on three occasions), manages early on in this all-night costume party to catch fire to the lower portion of his outfit. With only a codpiece remaining in front and "no codpiece in back," Dan is brought before Zagreus, "droop[ing] and blush[ing] and tugging at his hose in a deep girlish fidget, of virginal concern" (424). Whereupon Zagreus, announcing that "for the rest of the evening you'll have to be a girl," sends him up to the formidable Mrs. Bosun in the servants' quarters to effect the transformation.

The cross-dressing is so successful that Dan becomes the focal point of male desire at the party, "a lovely tall young lady . . . of a most droopy and dreamy presence" (455). Pursued by an aging film star and "notorious expert in *public seduction*" named Harry Caldicott, Dan can only stammer and blush in embarrassment, thereby augmenting his "feminine" appeal and intensifying Caldicott's ardor. Even when Zagreus dispatches the Blackshirt to act as "protector of [Dan's] youth" and ward off these "deceitful advances," the "transformation of his sex" continues unabated (468, 469). Dan soon becomes drunk, collapses into the arms of his blackshirted "deliverer" (who refers to him as "she" and whom Dan judges to be even "more passionate" than the old movie actor), and begins in effect to think like a woman: "ah these men (he smiled) they're all the same!"; or, later, "he would not like to be married to a man like this" (574, 578). Indeed, at this point "it was just as if he *were* a girl" (583), and when, after he has fallen from a tree, been buffeted about by the Blackshirt, been pressed into a small closet during one of Zagreus's magic tricks (ruined by Dan's ill-timed nosebleed), and undergone all manner of degrading incidents, he at last changes back into a man's clothes, he finds that this re-cross-dressing makes him feel "shy . . . at first and just like a girl"—that is, like a girl pretending to be a boy (602).

The corporeal humiliation of the feminine/homosexual art-Ape—his public debagging, forcible cross-dressing, and general rough handling—can be readily accounted for in terms of the fascist imaginary delineated in Theweleit's *Male Fantasies*, in terms of the "peculiarly damaged ego," as Hal Foster puts it, "that seeks a sense of corporeal stability in the very act of aggression against other bodies somehow deemed feminine by this subject

(Jews, Communists, homosexuals, 'the masses')."[45] But the very fluidity of this system, in which *any* body, in theory, may be "deemed feminine," would seem to open up other possibilities, contesting the gender categories themselves at least as forcefully as Woolf's *Orlando* (1928) or Djuna Barnes's *Nightwood* (1937)—two contemporaneous texts whose representations of transsexuality we would be hard pressed to attribute to the damaged male ego. While Lewis was clearly antagonistic to the interwar feminist movement, positioning it along the "vicious circle" of resentment which was weakening the Aryan family/community, his recognition that the whole burden of femininity *can* be shifted from women to men, that the feminine ideal is a matter of social construction and imposition, is consistent with more recent lines of feminist argument. The real significance of Dan's transformation, according to one passage in the *Apes*, is that the feminine ideal that "has not been the lot of girls since the first sombre circles of Bluestockings assembled" has come to be "embodied" in male art-Apes (455). Dan's perfect translation across the gender boundary is a way of saying:

> "You must come to poor defeated Man if you desire to find what was once the Eternal Feminine—alas only in Man is now to be found the true-blue Ladyhood or Girlishness—by man invented, by Man never betrayed!" That is what those sad and melting eyes, with a shrinking modesty, proclaimed. (455)

Men invented "woman," and when women finally organized to reject the terms of the invention, men simply took it upon themselves—they became their own women. This is a reactionary joke, a transparent instance of *ressentiment* (which exaggerates to the point of absurdity the actual gains that had been made against patriarchy by the late 1920s), but one that depends on a certain free play of subjects and objects on the field of gender. And this play across the supposed boundaries of identity, the parodic *performance* of gender that exposes the performative character of gender itself, has been promoted by Judith Butler and other recent feminist theorists as the key move of a truly subversive feminism, a feminism prepared to "destabilize and render in their phantasmatic dimension" the most fundamental categories of the patriarchal imaginary, the categories of man and woman.[46]

45. Hal Foster, "Armor Fou," *October* 56 (Spring 1991): 65. Throughout this fine essay, Foster is working with Theweleit's terms of analysis.

46. Judith Butler, *Gender Trouble: Feminism and the Subversion of Identity* (New York, 1990) 147.

Yet, as Theweleit points out, the fascists of Germany loved this sort of entertainment. Dramatic performances featuring soldiers in the women's parts, costume parties at which officers (including, on at least one occasion, Hermann Göring) would appear in drag, "with powdered face, red painted lips, and red varnished fingernails," and other parodic repetitions of "woman" were common forms of amusement among the Nazis (2:330). The dependence of so many of Lewis's comic transactions on parody-women, women performed by men, is thus not inconsistent with actual fascist entertainment practices or with the quite serious entertainment of fascist notions of community. But does this dependency necessarily preclude the transactions' subversiveness, their effectivity as destabilizing comic practice? Does it make sense to say that there are certain symptomatic moments within fascism, certain moments within the economy of fascist joke-work, which are somehow subversive of fascism itself?

These questions point to a problem with the whole idea of gender parody as subversion. As Butler's work demonstrates, this orientation produces an analysis that will always stall at the point of deciding whether a particular parodic repetition, a particular instance of cross-dressing or impersonation, is "effectively disruptive, truly troubling," or rather has "become domesticated and recirculated as [an] instrument of cultural hegemony." "There must be a way," says Butler, to decide such questions. But she can get no further in this direction than to remark that, in general, subversive effects must be gauged with reference to social context, "for parodic displacement, indeed, parodic laughter, depends on a context and reception in which subversive confusions can be fostered."[47]

Butler must stop short of actually indicating how, in the particular instance, we might specify this context and this reception. But Theweleit's discussion of fascist cross-dressing suggests something of the difficulties involved. Theweleit acknowledges that there is something "playful [and] apparently transgressive" about the practice of female impersonation among fascist men. But ultimately, he says, these activities are mere "flirtations," "strictly regulated" by the context of their occurrence (2:327). Precisely because they *are* performances, received by an orderly assemblage of spectators, they pose no real threat: "the social context makes a more general homosexualization of the situation impossible. The public serves as a dam against any possible intrusion by sexuality" (2:330). Of course, under this

47. Ibid. 139.

analysis virtually all parodic performance of gender is contained by its immediate context; the very performativity to which we would ascribe its subversive effects also defines a social context that will assure that those effects are
neutralized. (Curiously, however, this same analysis leaves room for the genuinely transgressive force of the fascist novel, whose parodic transactions
involving gender and identity cannot be regulated by the public forum of
reception. By Theweleit's reasoning, the very bourgeois character of the
novel, its asocial and individualist context of reception, might ultimately
redeem it, even in its most reactionary moment, as a subversive practice.)

One could, certainly, produce a more nuanced or refined analysis of
context than Theweleit's. But, as I try more fully to suggest in Chapter 5, the
analysis inevitably collapses into some sort of paradox or stalemate when
events are identified with subversion and *contexts* with containment. Context
must be seen as constitutive of event—as enabling events and rendering
them intelligible as events—not as an external system of territorial boundaries which sets limits on an event's political effectivity. And that political
effectivity must be seen not only as multiaccentual but as multidimensional,
not only as irreducible to a purely subversive (or hegemonically contained)
set of effects, but as unmappable on any planar model of social space.

In the absence of better maps or models, we can say only that the "ficti-
tious transsexuality" that runs through Lewis's text, the various conscious
and unconscious, willing and unwilling parodies of women by men in the
novel, are both consistent with what may be called fascist joke-work and,
as such, revealing of inconsistencies in the fascist imaginary. The *Witz* of
fascism lies in its determination to "play with," indeed to *enjoy*, the terrifying
knowledge that a man *can* act as woman by constantly invoking just such a
figure as its scapegoat, turning up cross-dressed she-men or "shamen"
at every turn along the path (back) to the utopia of essentially masculine
community. The boundaries of the male body, and of the community conceived as a male body, are thus asserted and maintained by a process of
victimage which projects all fear of dissolution onto the victim, effecting
what Theweleit calls "the victim's loss of contours," the aggressive unbound-
ing of his/her body, his/her corporeal, sexual identity (2:305). Yet this very
process puts on display the precarious nature of male identity and the phantasmatic character of the fascist community. As Lewis himself remarks in *The
Wild Body*, laughter is what protects the "Self" from its debasement and
dissolution to "the conditions of an insect communism." But he also notes
that laughter "occasionally takes on the dangerous form of absolute revela-

tion";[48] it protects the self, but also reveals the self as a desperate and unstable construction.

Indeed, for Lewis identity as such is always a kind of joke, a more or less witty, more or less laughable performance. Zagreus, the Ape who most often (re)states the pronouncements of Lewis himself, is merely a mouthpiece for the supposedly brilliant but always absent character Pierpoint, a shadowy authority figure in the background of the novel. The lengthy speeches with which Zagreus regales everyone around him are in fact "broadcasts" of Pierpoint's speeches. When someone suggests he speak as Zagreus for a change, he broadcasts Pierpoint's dismissive reply to this absurd request. Another avowed Pierpointian is the Blackshirt, who claims to be wearing the fascist uniform only for the sake of the costume party (and who, like Mosley, denies its special symbolic significance, accounting for the choice of a black shirt simply on the basis of its inexpensiveness and availability),[49] but who nonetheless delivers, often in the form of Pierpointian broadcasts, perfectly fascist pronouncements. What happens to the question of identity in this secret society of men whose members all think the thoughts and speak the words of their charismatic leader? Is this the space in which the essence of community—Leader, Father, the Masculine principle of unity—is being preserved or prepared for its triumphant return? Or is it merely the Ape version of that space, not essence but the Aping of essence, not the fascism that could revitalize and revirilize society, but its mock-performance on the (feminine) plane of "Society"? Perhaps what *The Apes of God* has to tell us is that there is finally no difference between the one and the other, that fascism is its own parodic twin; it is worth bearing in mind that Oswald Mosley himself was a *Sonnenkind* of the Sitwell (Finnian-Shaw) stripe, a Society regular who, Martin Green notes, "apparently modelled himself on Ferdinand Lasalle, the brilliant dandy . . . of the German socialist movement."[50]

In any case, we must recognize that the effective nodal point of Lewis's politics—sexual identity—is always caught up in the processes of comic transaction. As in many of the texts of male modernism (those of Ford,

48. Wyndham Lewis, *The Complete Wild Body*, ed. Bernard Lafourcade (Santa Barbara, Calif., 1982) 158.

49. Mosley, *My Life* 290. Mosley expresses a certain regret here at any "resemblance to foreign parties" conveyed by the uniform (291).

50. Green, *Children of the Sun* 50. The Sitwells, who brought dandyism to Bloomsbury, are credited by Green—as by Lewis, Lawrence, and many others—with being the supreme "leaders of Youth," the ones who, in Lawrence's phrase, "taught Young England how to be Young" (81, 78).

Lawrence, Pound, Eliot), a determination to bolster and protect the principle of maleness, the masculine style, the stable male ego, the hard male body, the solid(ary) male social corpus, cannot be untangled from a certain compulsion to play across the supposed boundaries of gender identity, to *perform* gender from different sides and on different registers.[51] The fascist vision of community as solid (masculine) body, as corporate state, apparently cannot emerge from the very modernist texts that assist in its production unless the terms that constitute it undergo a kind of elaborate comic interrogation. I recognize that for some readers this fact reaffirms the power of modernist art to achieve a distanciation of fascist ideology and thereby to redeem itself. But I am trying to suggest that we take from it a different lesson, one more in line with Žižek's argument about ideology in general. What a text such as *The Apes of God* has to tell us is that ideology's task is not the one that ideology critique has always indicated, the task of veiling its inherent contradictions or impossibilities, but rather that of displaying its contradictions as symptoms, projecting them onto the social field in objectified form and making them available for *enjoyment*. It is thus not merely the heterodox or subversive or otherwise exceptional fascist texts that make an entertainment of fascism's built-in failures, but precisely the most typical ones. This is not to say that the texts of high modernism are altogether unexceptional in their attitudes toward fascism, or that every gesture of critique or subversion must necessarily collapse back into ideology. Indeed, as I begin to argue in the next chapter, it is from the modernist tendency to organize comic transactions around the instabilities of the fascist imaginary that a form of (self-)critique begins to emerge which we might call a postmodernist as well as a postfascist writing. But let us not, through an eagerness to celebrate the subversive power of comic transactions, lose sight of what is undoubtedly more than an analogical relation between modernist joke-work and fascist violence toward "bodies deemed feminine."

51. For a wealth of examples, see Sandra M. Gilbert and Susan Gubar, *Sexchanges*, vol. 2 of *No Man's Land: The Place of the Woman Writer in the Twentieth Century* (New Haven, 1989).

Three

Broken English: Disarticulated Community in *Between the Acts*

> A community is held together by two things: the compelling force of violence and the emotional ties (identifications is the technical name) between its members. If one of the factors is absent, the community may possibly be held together by the other.
>
> —Sigmund Freud, "Why War?" (1933)
>
> We will in the end succeed in putting down war—by force if necessary.
>
> —Julian Bell, *We Did Not Fight* (1935)
>
> We must attack Hitler in England.
>
> —Virginia Woolf, *Diary*, May 1938

Even in the early twenties the British were far from convinced that the Great War had brought an end to all wars. And it is safe to say that by the early thirties the interwar period was actually being experienced by the vast majority of people in England *as* an interwar period. The more or less continual public discussion of means for avoiding war, which saw many leading literary figures engage the task of pacifist pamphleteering; the unprecedented 1933 Oxford Union resolution *not* to fight for king and country; the tremendous growth around mid-decade of the national pacifist movements (the Peace Ballot initiative and the Peace Pledge Union)—these must be read as signs not of a confident antiwar consensus but of anxiety and desperation in the face of seemingly irreversible historical tendencies toward ever more destructive and global warfare.

Like other social feminists (particularly Evelyn Sharp and Helena Swanwick) who attempted between the wars to draw out fundamental connections between the peace movement and the women's movement, Virginia Woolf had been a pacifist during World War I. Indeed, her career in antiwar agitation began even before that, and in characteristic fashion, with the comic impertinence of the famous 1910 *Dreadnought* hoax. Woolf and five others, including Horace de Vere Cole, the notorious practical joker whom Lewis later used as a model for Horace Zagreus in *The Apes of God*,[1] dressed up as the emperor of Abyssinia and his entourage and managed to get themselves officially received aboard H.M.S. *Dreadnought*, in terms of design the most advanced warship in the British navy. The officers of the *Dreadnought* not only welcomed these Bloomsbury impostors (whose "Abyssinian" language consisted of mispronounced recitations from the fourth book of the *Aeneid*) but offered them a complete tour of the ship, assembled a guard of honor for their inspection, and saluted them with twenty-one guns.[2] Coming as it did in the midst of the prewar armaments buildup and nationalist propaganda campaign, this antimilitarist prank caused a major stir when it reached the papers. It was, after all, more than simply a protest against current policies; it was a matter of laughing at the very symbols of a phallocentric social order, refusing to take the great muscle-flexing rituals and the gleaming machinery of power *seriously*.

Thirty years later, with London experiencing nightly bombardment and the body count across Europe mounting once again into the millions, Woolf had taken her early amusement at militarist pomp through some complex thinking on the question of war and pacifism. But she still chose to use the carnivalesque *Dreadnought* incident as the centerpiece of a public talk in July 1940.[3] As her final novel, *Between the Acts* (1941), attests, impertinent mockery remained fundamental to Woolf's strategy as an antiwar writer. And I would argue that, despite its significant limitations, this commitment to comedy, to the explosive or deflationary potential of the incongruous, of paradox, of play-acting and masquerade, drives the work to its most radical insights. For what can be read in Woolf's last novel is not only her anger at being entrapped for two decades between wars, simply waiting for "the killing machine . . . to be set in action" once again (*Diary* 5:235), but also a new willingness to confront and elaborate through joke-work certain incongruities or paradoxes of "society" and of "peace" itself—paradoxes whose

1. Paul Edwards, "Afterword," *Apes of God* 635.

2. Adrian Stephen, *The Dreadnought Hoax* (London, 1983) 40–51. The identification of Zagreus comes from Edwards's "Afterword" to *Apes of God* (635).

3. This was an address to the Rodmell Women's Institute on 23 July, mentioned in the *Diary of Virginia Woolf*, ed. Anne Oliver Bell with Andrew McNellie, 5 vols. (New York, 1984) 5:303. Hereafter cited parenthetically as *Diary*. Fragments of the talk are gathered in vol. 1, app. E, of Quentin Bell, *Virginia Woolf: A Biography*, 2 vols. (London, 1972).

denial or stitching over seemed to implicate even the major feminist-pacifist strains of modernism in the logic of fascism and the violence of war.

In describing the abiding utopian impulse behind Woolf's pacifism, Alex Zwerdling usefully quotes Wilhelm Mühlmann: "The thought of a general peace," observes Mühlmann, "presupposes a change of consciousness that would make the concept of unitary humanity possible."[4] This is the ideal, says Zwerdling, toward which all Woolf's novels strain—all, that is, until *Between the Acts*, the novel of Woolf's disillusionment and "crisis of belief," the novel in which "the secular faith in community that had sustained her" has come to "seem no more reliable than the Christianity she could never take seriously."[5]

Zwerdling is right about this—right not to accept the utopian reading of *Between the Acts* as a novel "of the whole community" in which a happy feminist-communitarian *we* (an authentic "collective voice" that is "subversive . . . without being coercive") at last and unproblematically supplants an ostensibly male-modernist *I*.[6] But it seems to me that what drives Woolf's

4. Alex Zwerdling, *Virginia Woolf and the Real World* (Berkeley, 1986) 278.

5. Ibid. 290.

6. Woolf herself suggested, in a well-known passage in the diaries (*Diary* 5:135), that her aim in the novel was to replace the auctorial "I" with a collective "We," and many critics have seized on this formulation. To my mind the subtlest and most useful reading of the novel as achieved "art of the whole community" is Melba Cuddy-Keane, "The Politics of Comic Modes in Virginia Woolf's *Between the Acts*," *PMLA* 105 (March 1990): 273–85, from which I take my quotations (283, 276). Cuddy-Keane recognizes that "unity," "centre," and so forth are not simply positive values in the novel and that Woolf is not invoking community as a binary alternative to the fragmentation and heterogeneity of modern society. When Cuddy-Keane remarks that Woolf's "comedy ultimately undermines all definitions of a group as a centered, unified identity and rewrites the concept of community as a fragmented, questioning, contradictory, but fully collective voice" (280), and especially that the novel sketches "a model of community as the dynamic inhabiting of mutual space" (284), she may seem to be rendering my own arguments redundant. But apart from the fact that I try to situate this comic rewriting historically in relation to the complex interleaving of modernism, feminism, and fascism between the wars, I differ from Cuddy-Keane in seeing certain problems and limitations in Woolf's text. Cuddy-Keane says hers is not a "utopian" reading (283), but in fact she credits the novel with perfectly achieving a "subversive" and "collective" vision of "politics" without "power" (283, 284). As I elaborate further on, this vision is neither subversive nor wholly endorsed by the novel. And to the extent that the novel does tend toward this liberal utopia of a collective space the other side of power, it calls for critique rather than enthusiastic applause.

Earlier discussions of the novel in connection with the idea of community include Avrom Fleishman, who argues in *Virginia Woolf: A Critical Reading* (Baltimore, 1975) that Woolf's last novel moves from "individual voices" to a "collective voice" suggestive of "a

discourse of community to a point of crisis (to the point where, like Christianity, it cannot be "taken seriously") is more than simply her sense that, as Zwerdling puts it, "individualism" had by the late thirties succeeded in achieving a decisive "triumph . . . over communal identity."[7] The ideals of "unitary humanity" and "communal identity" are scarcely peculiar to Woolf or to the socialist, feminist, and pacifist traditions that her writings seek to articulate together. The rejection of bourgeois individualism, the attempt to bring about (in significant measure, through art) the radical "change in consciousness" necessary to realize the underlying accord, the immanent or essential community that bourgeois modes of production and of consciousness unhappily impede: this is not simply the social feminist project Woolf shared with such women modernists as Dorothy Richardson and H.D. Broadly conceived, it is the (male) high modernist project of 1914, the project of Lewis, Pound, Eliot, and of Lawrence. And it is also the fascist project, the project that ultimately puts its impossibility on display in the objective or symptomatic form of the Jew-as-woman. This troubling convergence of various specific ideologies and aesthetics around the idea of an

---

growing identification with the historical community," and that this identification "is then widened and gives signs of encompassing the entire race" (210). To the extent that this is in fact Woolf's aim in the novel, one would have to agree with Phyllis Rose, who argues in *Woman of Letters: A Life of Virginia Woolf* (New York, 1978), that "like much of Woolf's fiction, her last novel is inspired by a kind of nostalgia, an effort to rescue or resurrect a world which is passing or past . . . a communal past, the life of rural England" (237). But even if Woolf could not altogether overcome a tendency to conceive of community in the faulty terms of nostalgia, I would argue that the danger and thinness of this appeal to "a communal past" are nonetheless vividly exposed in *Between the Acts*. A reading of E. M. Forster's contemporaneous village pageant, *England's Pleasant Land* (London, 1940), can serve to underscore how relatively troubled and equivocal are the standard evocations of rustic (feudal) harmony in Woolf's novel.

Jane Marcus is one of several critics who have stressed the feminist implications of Woolf's increasing commitment to an art of the "we" rather than the "I." In "Thinking Back through Our Mothers," in Marcus, *Art and Anger* (Columbus, Ohio, 1988), Marcus credits Woolf with achieving in her last two novels a specifically feminist collectivism: "the 'egotistical sublime' of the patriarchy has been replaced by a democratic feminist 'collective sublime'" (82). Aside from the problem that, as so often in Woolf criticism, Woolf herself remains always the stable subject and heroine of this familiar emancipatory narrative, there are two assumptions here that *Between the Acts* would seem to disrupt: that appeals to the community, the collective, and so forth are anathema to "the patriarchy" and that the "we" of the "feminist collective" is already given, immanent, ready to be called forth and embodied in feminist art.

7. Zwerdling, *Virginia Woolf and the Real World* 320.

immanent community accessible through art is what *Between the Acts* begins to bring into view. It does so through the special (and finally unsupportable) pressure it brings to bear on the "we" of a certain village-community version of English nationalism and, not least, through its determination to submit the notion of the social matrix as a "unified whole" with a specifiable "centre" to an encounter with, as Woolf puts it, "little incongruous living humour" (*Diary* 5:135).

"Outsiders' Societies": Modernism, Feminism, Fascism

> For fifteen years . . . I have felt very much a fish out of water, very alien to all the standards that I saw being built up around me. I have . . . found myself in a peculiarly isolated position.
> —Wyndham Lewis, "Virginia Woolf"

> I often think . . . [a]bout being an outsider. About my defiance of professional decency.
> —Virginia Woolf, *Diary* (5: 251)

> The community of the old black house . . . was more complete because we were banded together by . . . the savage animosity of the old world towards us.
> —Oswald Mosley, *My Life*

What does it mean for a pacifist woman to tell a pacifist man, as Woolf famously does in *Three Guineas*, that she and her sisters constitute an Outsiders' Society, "outside your society but in co-operation with its ends"?[8] What sorts of borders and claims of possession are being staked in this discourse of the inside and the outside? Where is *my* exclusion from *your* society mandated, inside your society or inside mine? Does "your society" have any existence outside the society of "its" outsiders, the outsiders I claim as my fellow insiders? And what form of "co-operation" is it that takes place across the border separating this inside from this outside of this society?

We have here another specific (feminist) form of the modernist insider/outsider problematic, which made the ambiguous, and indeed reversible badge of outsider virtually obligatory for the serious artist. "If one's an outsider, be an outsider," Woolf wrote in her diary, "only dont for God's sake attitudinise & take up the striking the becoming attitude" (5:245). Yet she knew this was hardly an option in the interwar years, when the endless

---

8. Virginia Woolf, *Three Guineas* (1938; New York, 1966) 106. Hereafter cited parenthetically as *TG*.

castings and recastings of the whole problematic forced her into any number of attitudes, saw her positioned, by herself and others, in various relations of interiority and exteriority to putative social and cultural centers. To Lewis, no member of the Stephen family could speak convincingly of her membership in an outsiders' society; the Bloomsbury circle, he never tired of pointing out, "consisted of monied middleclass descendants of victorian literary splendour" whose "rather scandalous shabbiness" and other "bohemian" affectations were a confirmation and indulgence of sociocultural privilege rather than a sign of marginality or oppositionality (*Apes* 123). Bloomsbury, as Lewis framed it (and so, to differing degrees, did Pound, Lawrence, and the Leavises), *was* the center, the center of a soft and "deeply feminized" culture that had effectively saturated the social field and deprived genuine (masculine) art of its proper *lebensraum*. Indeed, for Lewis, Virginia Woolf was the central or presiding figure of this feminine hegemony in the late twenties and early thirties.[9]

Woolf herself sometimes assumed just this position of social insider in her smug attacks on Lewis and the other 1914 modernists (excepting Eliot), joining in the salon-society view of them (expressed also by Edith Sitwell) as underbred and, more to the point, "provincial" writers—that is, as outsiders. But given the logic of modernism, Woolf's quite pronounced class snobbery and elitism did not prevent her from identifying with "commoners and outsiders" herself[10] or from taking the fact of "being an outsider" as funda-

9. In 1934 Lewis wrote of the "aesthetic movement" being "presided over in the first post-war decade by Mrs. Woolf and Miss Sitwell," but added that "Miss Sitwell has recently been rather overshadowed by Mrs. Woolf" (*Men without Art* 140).

10. From Virginia Woolf, "The Leaning Tower," an address to the Worker's Educational Association, Brighton, in May 1940, collected in *"The Moment" and Other Essays*, ed. Leonard Woolf (New York, 1948) 154. One wonders, though, how Woolf's working-class audience would have responded to these somewhat strained gestures of solidarity. It is not easy for someone of Woolf's plainly aristocratic breeding to speak convincingly in the first-person plural about "commoners and outsiders like ourselves" who "get our accents wrong" (154). As Phyllis Rose has pointed out, Woolf's diary entries at this time are far from professing solidarity with Brighton's working class. To Woolf, the local working-class women were parasites of the rich, "fat white slugs . . . vampires. Leeches. Anyone with 500 a year and an education is at once sucked by the leeches" (quoted in *Woman of Letters* 239). Woolf's long attachment to the idea that writers were somehow entitled to "500 a year" in itself shows how little connection there was between her and the women of the working class. In 1937, something approaching half of all working women were earning below Rountree's "human needs" standard of 30/9d, many earning less than a pound a week. See Jane Lewis, *Women in England, 1870–1950: Sexual Divisions and Social Change* (Bloomington, Ind., 1984) 165–68. A writer enjoying, unearned, six or eight times the income of an average working-class woman (and Woolf's own income in the late thirties

mental to her condition as a feminist writer (*Diary* 5:251). She flatly rejected the image of Bloomsbury as a mere continuation in shabbier guise of "victorian literary splendour," feeling that she, at any rate, *had* rebelled against the Stephen heritage in adopting more or less orthodox bohemian unorthodoxies. Woolf at times acknowledged Bloomsbury's hegemonic role in postwar British culture, but never equated the male homosexual ethos of the Bloomsbury group with femininity or a feminine milieu; on the contrary, she stressed the extent of her exclusion, as a woman, from both the male-dominated Bloomsbury circle and the received tradition of British and Western culture.

This logic whereby Woolf identifies as both an outsider and a guardian against provincial incursions is fundamental to the cultural polemics of modernism. The accusations of provincialism which crop up so frequently throughout this period always seem to operate in both directions. Thus, asserting the properly internationalist character of modernism, Lewis and other ostensibly provincial enemies of Bloomsbury could turn the center-margin figure inside out and label Bloomsbury itself an insular backwater, a place so hopelessly out of touch with Vienna and the Left Bank that it imagined Duncan Grant to be a major modernist painter. As the transient continental expatriot becomes the central figure of modernism's self-construction—which is to say, as the modernist problematic of inside/outside is increasingly cast in national and geographical terms—the "domestic" artist comes to be associated with the bourgeois culture of a feminine and moribund Society rather than with the authentic Culture of a new society in the making. The resultant positioning of Woolf inside Society and hence outside modernism survived, by way of Hugh Kenner and *The Pound Era*, well into the 1970s.

As with Lewis and all other Anglo-American modernists, Woolf's insistence on calling herself an outsider was always to some degree simply a matter of asserting distance between herself, as an authentic artist, and the everyday material world of political struggle and "raw fact."[11] She could insist, for example, over and against the Auden generation, that the use of art "to propagate political opinions" was debasing, that art is properly distinct

---

was considerably larger than this) is scarcely in a position to complain of the parasitism of the workers. In fairness to Woolf, however, she always called attention to her class position and the limitations it imposed on her. As she wrote in "The Niece of an Earl," "there is no animosity, perhaps, but there is no communication. We are enclosed, and separate, and cut off" (*Collected Essays of Virginia Woolf*, ed. Leonard Woolf [New York, 1967] 1:219).

11. Virginia Woolf, "A Letter to a Young Poet," in Woolf, *"Death of the Moth" and Other Essays*, ed. Leonard Woolf (New York, 1970) 219.

from, and nobler than, propaganda (*TG* 170).[12] She never actually joined the Communist party or any of the major pacifist groups whose goals she supported, never signed their petitions or manifestos.[13] But this aestheticism and aloofness from politics are no more definitive in Woolf's case than in Lewis's or Pound's. Her mockery of the Art for Art's Sake school, particularly in *Orlando* (1928), is as emphatic and as funny as Lewis's. Like the other modernists she was a thoroughly politicized writer; she made no apologies for "taking up journalism" in the thirties (*Diary* 5:241) and gained a reputation (with *A Room of One's Own* [1929] and *Three Guineas* [1938]) as one of England's most spirited political pamphleteers.[14] The true aesthete of cartoon-history modernism, devout believer in a discrete cultural heterocosm, would not have remarked, as Woolf characteristically did during the Spanish Civil War, that "there is a very close connection between culture . . . and those photographs of dead bodies" (*TG* 97).

All of this is simply to say that, with Woolf as with the other figures of Anglo-American modernism, the question of social position, of where the artist or cultural worker stands in relation to society, is a complex and open one. We cannot say simply and in advance that Woolf writes from this or that subjective standpoint, from this or that place within, on the margins of, or outside British "society." Even to say, what seems obvious, that Woolf writes from the position of a woman in a society and a culture dominated by men is to ignore the very difficulties of categorization and articulation which drive her extended, troubled, and increasingly obscure meditation on the artist and community.

In *Between the Acts*, as elsewhere, this meditation takes the form, or follows the logic, of joke-work. As I discuss in the second part of the chapter, the

12. Woolf's fullest discussion of the Auden generation is her 1940 lecture "The Leaning Tower," cited above. Here again Woolf's attachment to the idea of artistic transcendence is foregrounded, as she uses a contrast between Wordsworth and Spender to secure privilege for the "poet's poetry," the poetry of "solitude," over and against the "politician's poetry," the poetry of the "group" ("Leaning Tower" 146). And yet in this very lecture Woolf appeals to her working-class audience to engage literature as a social practice: "Let us trespass at once. Literature is no one's private ground; literature is common ground" (154). For what is still one of the best discussions of Woolf's politicized aestheticism, see Jane Marcus, " 'No More Horses': Virginia Woolf on Art and Propaganda," *Women's Studies* 4 (1977): 265–90.

13. See Zwerdling, *Virginia Woolf and the Real World* 274. Woolf was, however, a member of several feminist organizations that contributed strenuously to the causes of pacifism and internationalism. See Naomi Black, "Virginia Woolf and the Woman's Movement," in *Virginia Woolf: A Feminist Slant*, ed. Jane Marcus (Lincoln, Nebr., 1983) 180–97.

14. Woolf notes in her diary of 1938 that "the Lit Sup says I'm the most brilliant pamphleteer in England" (*Diary* 5:148).

strategic intention of the novel's humor seems to be to expose the tensions and contradictions of subjectivity, the multiple fissures across language and society, rather than to secure stable positions for the joking author and her targets. That is, Woolf makes no effort to resist the (more or less unavoidable) failure of her novel as satire, the slippage or dissolution of both subjects and objects of the satiric text. Nevertheless, I want to begin here by considering the artist Miss La Trobe—herself the ostensive subject, the impertinent "laughing bird" (183), of the comedic village pageant that is the novel's central event or occasion—as a satiric target of a rather complicated sort. Along with Lucy Swithin, the "batty" believer in transcendent unity, and Mrs. Manresa, the self-celebrating embodiment of patriarchy's notion of the feminine, Miss La Trobe seems to me to be the character most consistently positioned as an object of laughter. This is not to deny that she is also a character with whom Woolf herself must be closely identified. On the contrary, it is precisely her overlaps with Woolf—as modernist, as feminist, as a consciously antifascist writer—which make La Trobe's satiric positioning of such crucial importance.

An absolutely unhidden duplicity of presentation marks La Trobe as modernist: an artist at once inside and outside the society that is her material, her means, and her audience. La Trobe is both the legitimate presiding artist, the authorized voice of Culture, the "tyrant" and "commander" of the village's cultural ship (187, 62); and a hopeless "outcast" (211), not "pure English" (57), a "failure" and a "slave" (209, 211), an object of everyday snubs and jokes among the villagers.[15] This positioning of the artist character directs us, first of all, to read La Trobe's comic pageant as a modernist work: a "very up to date" production (183) whose partial and somewhat anxious distanciation within Woolf's novel can be said to signal the emergence, here, in the late thirties, of a postmodernist British fiction. With its far-flung, quasi-scholarly allusiveness and recycled Elizabethan ethos, its presentation of the contemporary situation by means of fragmentary cultural pastiche[16]—scattered bits of the English Literary Tradition rendered in

15. In "Virginia Woolf and the Concept of Community: The Elizabethan Playhouse," *Women's Studies* 4 (1977): 291–98, Brenda R. Silver argues that Miss La Trobe's double position as both an "outsider . . . without social acceptance in the community" and an "acknowledged" voice of culture "who can embody the communal self" marks her not as a modernist but as a throwback to "her Elizabethan predecessor[s]" (298). But this argument depends on an opposition between the modernist aesthete "on his tower of privilege" and the Elizabethan artist "down on the ground" (298) which is itself eminently a product of modernist ideology.

16. As I argue in Chapter 5, the problem of distinguishing parody from pastiche is

uncertainly valenced imitative forms—and its indirectly articulated commitment to a deeper and redeeming social unity that might be accessed through art, the pageant may well remind us of Eliot's *Waste Land*.

It is important, though, that the lesbian La Trobe is also a feminist artist and that the cultural "orts, scraps and fragments" she assembles (188) indicate patriarchal relations as a major continuity across this otherwise disjointed, disintegrative culture. (Indeed, as Judith Johnston has pointed out, the Shakespearean phrase "orts, scraps and fragments" itself alludes to the violently proprietary and misogynist discourse of romantic love).[17] This feminist emphasis is sustained throughout the play. The first performer on stage—little Phyllis Jones, who pipes, "England am I," and then forgets the rest of her lines (77)—marks the ideologically powerful equation of nation with idealized, desexualized woman (the virgin girl or White Mother), which the pageant later traces in broadly satiric fashion to the concern for national "purity" and "respectability" under "the White Queen Victoria" (162). Even in the final scene, in which the work turns itself outward onto the audience, satire continues to operate at the expense of patriarchal equations—here, the equation of woman with nature. A confrontational display of mirrors finds only Mrs. Manresa, the self-declared "wild child of nature," able to fit comfortably into "the present time" as framed by the pageant. Because Mrs. Manresa has internalized as "natural" her training in properly feminine behavior, she is ideally adapted to the present-day patriarchal order. While the rest of the audience is jolted by the mirrors into feeling the falseness of their roles or positions, the underlying tensions and contradictions of identity, Mrs. Manresa hilariously uses these mirrors to fix her make-up, smooth-

---

fundamental to language production as such and, *pace* Jameson, is by no means a strictly postmodern development. It is true, however, that the thematization of this problem as a politically paralyzing crisis of language marks an important moment of *self-conscious* postmodernity for the political left, a moment that occurs in Britain some two decades later than the emergence (in the thirties) of a postmodernist literature.

17. See Judith L. Johnston, "The Remediable Flaw: Revisioning Cultural History in *Between the Acts*," in *Virginia Woolf and Bloomsbury: A Centenary Celebration*, ed. Jane Marcus (London, 1987) 253–77. Johnston traces the phrase to a passage in *Troilus and Cressida* in which Troilus contemptuously denounces Cressida, whose alleged promiscuity has consumed all but the "orts of her love, / The fragments, scraps, the bits and greasy relics / Of her o'er-eaten faith" (5.2.158–60). According to Johnston, La Trobe pointedly borrows the term from Shakespeare's play, which, "unlike Chaucer's version . . . is built on the misogynist assumption of women's fickleness" (267). I suspect that Woolf may have read Shakespeare's cynical farce rather differently, as purposefully disruptive of a chivalric organization of desire which is itself far more misogynist than the assumption that women's desire is as divided and changing as men's.

ing over any slight cracks that La Trobe's interventions might have induced in the mask of her "natural" femininity. And as if anticipating this moment in its reception, the pageant then has an anonymous "megaphonic" voice call out from the bushes to assert, among other things, a connection between patriarchal violence ("the gun slayers, bomb droppers here or there") and a woman's "lipstick and blood-red nails" (187).

Yet one could make the same point about *The Waste Land*—that patriarchal relations, and the violence inherent in them, are its theme, the key strain of continuity which runs through its fragments. That is, we cannot really set La Trobe's pageant in opposition to the dominant modernist project simply on the basis of its bitterly comic engagement with the operations of patriarchy. To be sure, there is a question of intention or critical consciousness here; Eliot himself seems to have been more concerned with the social costs of increasing effeminization or gender confusion than with those of an entrenched and authorized misogyny.[18] But as we have seen even in the extreme case of Wyndham Lewis, it is a mistake to assume that representations of gender in the more or less masculinist texts of male modernism are blind to the insupportability of patriarchal categories. These texts are constantly, aggressively exposing the very problems whose thematization we might expect to find only in feminist art. One might argue, perhaps, that the real masculinism of *The Waste Land*—and its most telling point of contrast with La Trobe's amusingly plot-indifferent pageant—is rather to be located in its overriding commitment to narrative, that is, to an organization of desire in terms of quest, whereby the "sadistic" logic of patriarchy is salvaged from any critical interrogation it may have undergone (consciously or not) at the level of thematics.[19] Certainly *Between the Acts* calls attention to the function of "plot" in effecting a powerful and all too familiar convergence of "love . . . and hate" (90). But the reading of Eliot's text as patriarchal quest seems to me a singularly reductive and uninteresting one—even if it was authorized by Eliot himself—and in any event we would be hard pressed to establish the commitment to narrative as a hallmark of (male) high modernism. Indeed, in British literature it has really been the staunch antimodernists, many important women writers among them, who have sustained the narrative tradition in the twentieth century.

18. This is how, for example, Gilbert and Gubar read Eliot's intentions in *Sexchanges*, vol. 2 of *No Man's Land* 339–40.

19. I am thinking here of Teresa De Lauretis's well-known discussion of narrative and sadism, "Desire in Narrative," in De Lauretis, *Alice Doesn't* (Bloomington, Ind., 1984) 103–57.

In form and theme, then, the pageant can be described as feminist without a denial of its essential affinities with the high modernist project. The same is true in its use of the author function. Like Woolf herself, La Trobe displays a characteristically modernist ambivalence as regards the value of artistic impersonality and disinterestedness. As an ambitious artist with didactic tendencies, she insists on controlling the processes of production and reception down to their minutest particulars, on achieving and communicating precisely "*her* vision" (98). But to succeed in this she believes she must in the end become "invisible" (191): she refuses to present herself as the specially gifted individual responsible for the work of art; she "wishes it seems to remain anonymous" (194). This is a doubly familiar ambivalence. One of the more striking contradictions running through modernist polemic, from Pound's and Lewis's vorticist manifestos to the mature critical writings of Eliot, is the coexistence of the neoclassicist discourse of impersonality and intertextuality with continued investment in the romantic categories of individual "genius," individual poetic "vision"—and, indeed, with particularly energetic forms of self-promotion. Women writers have tended, whatever their specific relation to high modernism, to reproduce this contradiction. On the one hand it is a commonplace that, as Marsha Rowe once put it in an anthology of feminist writings, "Feminism in the arts" has meant an effort to "demystify the concept of the individual artist [as someone] . . . thrown up out of nowhere by the moving spirit of 'his' own genius."[20] On the other hand, as is equally apparent, and as nothing illustrates better than the feminist reception of Woolf herself, feminism has its own special investment in the figure of the brilliant individual artist deserving of full credit for her achieved "greatness."[21]

On several levels, then, we are invited to regard Miss La Trobe's production as both modernist and feminist, to recognize its feminist dimension without thereby denying its modernism. The playwright is in some sense Woolf's satiric double, a figure through which Woolf can frame a critique of her own major aesthetic project—her feminist modernism—as its inadequacies were brought into relief by historical events in the thirties. There is no question that this feminist modernism, as practiced by La Trobe, is intended in part as a form of resistance to fascism. In mocking the identifica-

---

20. *Spare Rib Reader*, ed. Marsha Rowe (Harmondsworth, 1982) 260.

21. "It is up to us to see that the academy gives its little silver cups to those who deserve them. We must ourselves forge a great big golden bowl in honor of Virginia Woolf." Marcus, *Art and Anger* 154.

tion of nation with "pure" woman, for example, or the equation of Woman with Nature, the pageant strikes at crucial points in the elaboration of fascist hegemony under both Mussolini and Hitler.[22] Nonetheless, the novel makes use of the pageant to begin to expose complicities between even this feminist modernism and the fascism it meant to resist, a fascism that was offering itself with increasing confidence as the most radical and practicable alternative to the moribund individualism of liberal democracy.

This is perhaps not saying anything very new: a number of critics have drawn out connections between Woolf's final artist figure and the modernist-as-fascist. But arguments along these lines have typically centered on La Trobe's tyrannical relation to her material, her players, and her audience. Patricia Joplin puts this case very clearly. Insofar as the novel satirizes La Trobe's authorial will to power, Joplin argues, it stands as "a meditation on the proximity of artist to dictator—of author to authoritarian ruler."[23] I want to revise or supplement this reading of Woolf's "meditation" and to suggest that the novel traces a rather different sort of connection between La Trobe's feminist modernist appropriation of the village pageant and the logic of fascism. But I don't want to deny the importance of Joplin's point. La Trobe is most memorable for her outbursts and tirades in the backstage bushes. The mere occurrence of a half-hour Interval for tea sends her into paroxysms of fury: "'Curse! Blast! Damn 'em!' Miss La Trobe in her rage stubbed her toe against a root. Here was her downfall; here was the Interval. Writing this skimble-skamble stuff in her cottage, she had agreed to cut the play here; a slave to her audience—to Mrs. Sands' grumble—about tea; about dinner—she had gashed the scene here. Just as she had brewed emotion, she spilt it" (94). La Trobe becomes at such moments the cartoon dictator suggested by her nickname in the village: "Bossy" (63). Her aesthetic purpose is to slide an ideological "noose" around the necks of her audience, to

22. On the connection between idealized woman and fascist nationalism see Maria-Antonietta Macciocchi, "Female Sexuality in Fascist Ideology," *Feminist Review* 1 (1979): 67–82; and Theweleit, *Male Fantasies* 1: 3–228. The ways in which the pageant works to unmask Mrs. Manresa and disrupt the equation of woman with nature can also be read as indicating resistance to fascism. Elizabeth Abel, *Virginia Woolf and the Fictions of Psychoanalysis* (Chicago, 1989) 120–27, reads the "wild child of nature" jokes as implicitly antifascist. Mrs. Manresa, she says, is a parodic version of the "fascist mother" (126) who "ultimately (through Woolf's manipulation) parodies fantasies of woman as nature. Despite her minor infractions of social codes, she plays out the equation 'nature = woman = mother' that, as fascism insisted, is axiomatic to patriarchy" (120).

23. Patricia Klindienst Joplin, "The Authority of Illusion: Feminism and Fascism in Virginia Woolf's *Between the Acts*," *South Central Review* 6 (Summer 1989): 89.

"[hold] them together" and "[make] them see," *make* them share "her vi-sion" (98). But though she insists on directing the pageant like "an Admiral on his quarter-deck" (62), "bark[ing] out" orders in "gutteral accents" (63), the audience keeps blithely "slip[ping] the noose, split[ting] up into scraps and fragments," leaving her stomping her feet, "gnash[ing] her teeth," and crushing her manuscript in frustration (122).

In this comedy of the teeth-gnashing, toe-stubbing drama director there is certainly a meditation, as Joplin says, on the authoritarian and hence patri-archal tendencies of authorship. The petty (and often ineffectual) tyrant had always been a key figure in Woolf's critique of patriarchal culture—Mr. Ramsay being the archetype—and when she extended this critique to fascism in *Three Guineas* she clearly saw in the Führer an extreme manifestation of the petty-tyrannical father.[24] Her subsequent reading, late in 1939, of Freud's *Group Psychology and the Analysis of the Ego* (as noted in the *Diary* 5:252) would have supported this line of thinking (as well as her tendency to overextend it, to see too many fathers, and too few brothers, in the militarized, or protofascist, society).[25] In the relation between Miss La Trobe and her performers we first of all see the idea, which Freud carries over from Gustave Le Bon, that group formations, of which the army is an exemplary instance, involve an automatic, contagious, and "extreme passion for authority" (*GPAE* 59): the village players who would resist being "ordered about singly" begin to crave a "leader" as soon as they are arranged "in little troops" (63). But the more important, and more specifically Freudian, insight that this leader of the troupe or troop holds

24. For a full discussion of the tyrannical father figure in Woolf's novels see Beverly Ann Schlack, "Fathers in General: The Patriarchy in Virginia Woolf's Fiction," in Marcus, ed., *Virginia Woolf: A Feminist Slant* 52–77.

25. For Woolf, the whole culture of masculine power consists in "fathers in public, massed together in societies, in professions" (*TG* 138). Like Freud, she tends to collapse the military officer together with the dictator as father figures in the psychological struc-ture of fascism. Theweleit opposes Freud on this point, arguing that the authority of father and of military officer derive from entirely different mechanisms of legitimation. The father's authority is absolute, "axiomatic," unsurpassable; the clearly limited and ulti-mately surpassable power of the officer, by contrast, must always be "made to appear legitimate by his capacity, and willingness, to do what he demands of others." Freud's analysis of military organization, says Theweleit, is theoretically consistent but empirically unsound, based not on research or case studies but on a "wish-fulfillment army [pulled] out of a hat" (*Male Fantasies* 2:175–76). The argument, it seems to me, can be generalized insofar as it is relationships of brotherhood (with consequent glorification of the mother and exclusion of the sister) which predominate in patriarchal social arrangements, even where those arrangements are clearly hierarchical.

the libidinal place of the "primal father" is evident also (*GPAE* 59), in the unrelentingly masculinizing language Woolf uses to describe La Trobe in her role as cultural commander (62).

If we are comfortable with a critique of the modernist as tyrannical father, we may be less so when the modernist in question is, like Miss La Trobe and Woolf herself, a woman and a feminist. But the point is that whoever sets out to lead or dictate to the group may be assimilated to the father's role. And Woolf was keenly aware that feminism was not beyond susceptibility to leadership on the military model. Even Sylvia Pankhurst, who had been far more willing than Woolf to pursue the course of feminist militancy, observed in 1931 that such a course could and sometimes did mean organizing "like an army" and indulging a "glorification of autocracy."[26]

I think we should be careful, though, not to be overly impressed by this critique of (feminist-modernist) artistic tyranny, which is amusingly but not, I would say, particularly fruitfully elaborated in the novel. La Trobe's problem isn't simply her desire to lead or her connection in this capacity with the primal father—any more than the problem with the politics of (male) modernism is simply that the modernist writes as a tyrant. To be in complicity with Hitler an author need not be a rival Hitler. To be sure, a hectoring, bullying auctorial mode would dovetail too snugly with the norms of patriarchal discourse to be of strategic value to Woolf's pacifist, feminist Society of Outsiders. Unlike the suffragette Pankhursts, who came rather late to the view that the autocratic impulse ought in principle to have been held more "remote . . . from the struggle we were waging,"[27] Woolf had always rejected the notion that a charismatic, dictatorial style of leadership might assist the cause of feminism. This rejection is one reason that even in her two powerful feminist pamphlets Woolf eschews a confrontational or conventionally militant style, preferring an indirect melange of jokes, anecdotes, quotations, and increasingly complicated staged dialogues with imagined interlocutors. But while *Between the Acts*, like *The Years* before it, shares this concern with styles of leadership and with the autocratic effect of the "voice assert[ing] itself" (*BA* 186),[28] it also pursues on a more fundamental level the

26. E. Sylvia Pankhurst, *The Suffragette Movement: An Intimate Account of Persons and Ideals* (London, 1931) 517. Sylvia was the daughter of Emmeline and younger sister of Christabel Pankhurst, founders of the Women's Social and Political Union (WSPU), the most militant of the suffragette organizations.

27. Ibid. 517.

28. For a reading of *The Years* as an "anti-fascist novel" that dialogically frustrates its readers' desire for a didactic, loudspeaker-style authorial voice and charismatic central

paradoxical and mutually constructing logics that bind "leadership" to "community."

The two most obvious and symmetrical paradoxes of leadership are firmly underscored in the novel, as they are in Le Bon and Freud: that of the masses' self-enslavement and that of the tyrant's slavelike dependence on the masses. ("*A tyrant, remember, is half a slave,*" says Miss La Trobe's didactic megaphone [187].) But there is a more profound paradox of the Community Leader. The very idea of organic community on which the authorization of the Leader is founded (the leader can represent the will of the community because there is, *essentially*, a community with a common will), this idea which in fact always tends toward the authorization of a leader, is itself contradicted by the leader's appearance. This is the paradox underscored by one of Isa Oliver's quasi-poetical musings at the pageant's midpoint: "Hear not the cries of the leaders who in that they seek to lead desert us" (156). The leader, in leading, ceases to be numbered with the community. He becomes, as Bataille argued in "The Psychological Structure of Fascism," a "*heterogeneous* element," an element that "immediately stand[s] out as something *other* . . . a force that disrupts the regular course of things, the peaceful but fastidious homogeneity" of the prefascist society.[29] The very appearance of the leader-as-Other marks an absolute fissure in the community whose essential (though impeded) unity was assumed to justify and legitimate the leader.

The thinking of community in terms of an underlying homogeneity (even

---

figure, see Margaret Comstock, "The Loudspeaker and the Human Voice: Politics and the Form of *The Years*," *Bulletin of the New York Public Library* 80 (Winter 1977): 252–75. As Comstock points out, Woolf herself regarded *The Years* as a sort of companion volume to her "anti-Fascist pamphlet," *Three Guineas*, referring to them "together as one book" (273–74; quotations from the *Diary*). But it seems to me that what *The Years* opposes to fascism is still a vision of immanent social unity or essential identity which, by the time of *Between the Acts*, Woolf has begun to perceive as the problem rather than the solution to the European crisis. Even humor in *The Years* is thematized (in characteristic modernist fashion) as a possible point of access to the authentic human community rather than as a marker of that community's "impossibility." Consider, for example, the "strange effect" of Peggy's laughter: "It had relaxed her, enlarged her. She felt, or rather she saw, not a place, but a state of being, in which there was real laughter, real happiness, and this fractured world was whole; whole, vast, and free" (390). This is far indeed from the "cacophon[ous]" laughter of *Between the Acts*, which tends rather to "shiver into splinters the old vision [of] . . . what was whole" (183).

29. Georges Bataille, "The Psychological Structure of Fascism" (1933), in *Visions of Excess* 143.

that of "humanity"), productive as it is of the very heterogeneity it denies, is fraught with political danger—or rather with the danger of foreclosing the political altogether. Belief in something organic, unifying, already there at the "center," ultimately justifies the more or less violent removal of those symptomatic elements responsible, as someone must be, for the failure of this immanent unity to have realized itself. This act of exclusion or removal, by means of which the community can achieve its realization, is of course carried out by authority of the community, by the authority whose supposed authorization *by* the community always precedes the actual achievement *of* community.

As I said, the fascist or protofascist author would not necessarily be at all intent on rivaling or simulating this premature authority. If we read Miss La Trobe as a satiric figure, what is satirized is not simply a modernist-fascist impulse, shared by certain militant feminisms, toward authorized tyranny (and her assimilation in this respect to the primal father), but, behind or within that impulse, an insistence more fundamental to modernism, to fascism, and to feminism, on corporative unity, on community as the submerged reality and proper teleology of the social field. The "vision" that La Trobe means to "impart," to make them see, is a vision of perfect social unity: in her view the sole criterion of the play's success is the extent to which it has "held them together" as one (98). Her artistic and political goal, as Sallie Sears has written, is to stir the audience's "sense of oneness; that Dionysiac rapture in which, as Nietzsche puts it, 'the individual forgets himself completely . . . expresses himself through song and dance as the member of a higher community.'"[30]

This vision of a disintegrative society held together by culture, or at least by the working of art on an ostensibly common "structure of feeling,"[31] is, as I have said, not only constitutive of high modernism and of the fascist theory of art. It also informs, in different ways but just as crucially, much writing in the social feminist tradition. In their efforts to draw out fundamental connections between the women's movement and the antiwar movement, feminists of the interwar period tended to treat social unity as the precondition (or at any rate the condition) of achieved pacifism and to represent the

---

30. Sallie Sears, "Theater of War: Virginia Woolf's *Between the Acts*," in Marcus, ed., *Virginia Woolf: A Feminist Slant* 224. Sears's reference is to Friedrich Nietzsche, *The Birth of Tragedy and the Genealogy of Morals*, trans. Francis Golffing (New York, 1956) 22–23.

31. I mean to suggest by using Raymond Williams's famous term here that, like the companion phrase "whole way of life," it is of a piece with the aspirations of Anglo-American modernism and cannot be effectively deployed as a critical alternative.

woman as a born unifier, possessed of a special capacity for synthetic vision. As is well known, it was this strain of feminist thought which held most appeal for Woolf and for other feminist modernists such as H.D. and Dorothy Richardson; and it held out to them a special and uniquely promising role in the modernist project of finding a new cohesion and community through a new art. "The fact of woman," as Richardson put it, is that "she is relatively to man, *synthetic*. Relatively to man she sees life whole and harmonious. . . . She can solve and reconcile, revealing the points of unity between a number of conflicting males."[32] It is this vision of "life whole and harmonious," of achieved social unity, this politically dangerous vision that drives the work of both the men and the women modernists, and of which Woolf herself had been (particularly with *To the Lighthouse* [1927] and *The Waves* [1931]) a major exponent, that the joke-work of *Between the Acts* begins to unravel.

"Who's '*We*'?": The Comic as Crisis of Articulation

> The very word "society" sets tolling in memory the dismal bells of a harsh music.
> —Virginia Woolf, *Three Guineas*

> To return to the meaning—Are machines the devil, or do they introduce a discord . . . Ding dong, ding . . . by means of which we reach the final . . . Ding dong. . . . Here's the car with the monkey . . . Hop in . . .
> —Virginia Woolf, *Between the Acts* (ellipses in original)

Humor theory often invokes such semantic categories as "irrelevance" or "inappropriateness" to explain certain comic effects. Misunderstandings, awkward interruptions, miscommunications of various kinds, open out a field of multiple and contradictory narratives, logics, or discursive "universes"— and this is the social-semiotic field on which joke-work takes place.[33] Here lies the connection between the comic and the dialogic. *Between the Acts* can rightly be called, as it often has been, a dialogic novel in the Bakhtinian sense, precisely because it undermines or disallows the illusion of dialogue in the narrower sense of orderly and "successful" communication. It is not a novel in which multiple voices are skillfully, harmoniously orchestrated from

32. Dorothy Richardson, "The Reality of Feminism" (1917), in *The Gender of Modernism*, ed. Bonnie Kime Scott (Bloomington, Ind., 1990) 404, 405.

33. See, for example, Monro, *Argument of Laughter*, or Raskin, *Semantic Mechanisms*.

above (this would be Miss La Trobe's model), but rather one of interruptions and inappropriatenesses, a novel in which remarks like "marriages with cousins can't be good for the teeth" can occur in a discussion of fresh fish (30); a novel in which the characters' "common effort[s] to bring a common meaning to birth" succeed only in a common failure (152).

The dialogic effect is most pronounced in the dispersal scene after the pageant, in which the voices of the audience comically interrupt and clash with one another across ellipses-strewn pages:

> Then those voices from the bushes. . . . Oracles? You're referring to the Greeks? We're [*sic*] the oracles, if I'm not being irreverent, a foretaste of our own religion? Which is what? . . . Crepe soles? that's so sensible . . . They last much longer and protect the feet. . . . (198)

But this comic strategy of intruding different discursive universes upon one another (usually with calculated bathetic effect: our own religion is crepe soles) is firmly established long before the scene of dispersal. Indeed, it is evident in the novel's first sentence, in which a garden setting on an idyllic summer's night is intruded upon by talk "about the cesspool." And it is a matter not only of semantic incongruities, narrowly defined, but of social ones. The awkward inappropriatenesses of language, the little crises of communication, expose the crisis points of "community": the novel's broken English bespeaks a breakdown in the dominant idea of Englishness.

A telling if not particularly funny instance of this conversational awkwardness is a stalled exchange between Isa's handsome but "surly" husband Giles (93) and Mrs. Parker, a woman unknown to him, who has come to the pageant with her neighbor Mrs. Elmhurst from a village ten miles away. The conventional and unworldly Mrs. Parker complains of "how creepy" it made her feel to watch Albert, the "village idiot," playing himself in the pageant's Elizabethan scenes. William Dodge, a more cosmopolitan (and somehow discernibly homosexual) visitor, reminds her that this use of the idiot as spectacle is justified historically: "he's in the tradition" (111). But for Mrs. Parker what was fitting in the sixteenth century is by no means acceptable fare for a modern audience. She turns to Giles:

> "Surely, Mr. Oliver, we're more civilized?"
> "*We?*" said Giles. "*We?*" He looked, once, at William. He knew not his name; but . . . it was a bit of luck—that he could despise him, not himself. Also Mrs. Parker. But not Isa—not his wife.
> "Surely," said Mrs. Parker, looking from one to the other. "Surely we are?" (111, ellipsis added)

There is always something potentially comic in rudeness, and Giles's jar-ringly rude (though perhaps unspoken) "*We?*"—which reiterates not only Mrs. Parker's utterance but Miss La Trobe's, since "we" is the final word of the Elizabethan act and of the pageant as a whole—this particular interroga-tive repetition appears as the punch line in any number of contemporary jokes. Its most familiar appearance in American culture (as I believe another Woolf critic has already remarked) may be the joke in which the Lone Ranger and Tonto have been surrounded, after a long chase, by hostile Indians. "What do we do now?" whispers the Lone Ranger. To which Tonto disdainfully replies, "Who's '*we*,' white man?"

Every instance of such a joke marks the fundamental instability and per-manent negotiability of "we," the social fact of being always only condi-tionally and differently together. And this crisis of "we," as I am arguing, is the point of access, in *Between the Acts*, to the problem of ideology *in general*, the problem of subjectivity and identification, which is just another way of putting the problem of "community." But one must also recognize that each instance of such a joke performs work within and upon *specific* ideologies and that on this more local level, too, it intervenes in the politics of community. Taking the canned joke about the Lone Ranger as a conveniently bare example, we can say that insofar as it abruptly reopens a chasm that liberal personal-friendship "solutions" to the problem of race seek to cover over, and insofar as it interrupts the colonial fantasy of the Native Who Loves Me despite Everything, the joke can serve progressive purposes. But it can also be a transaction in colonial suspicion and double-bind, a way of confirming that the colonized person will betray you in the end, that his most impressive displays of loyalty and solidarity merely index the depth of his deception: in short, that falseness is the truth of the subaltern.³⁴

In the denser context evoked by Woolf's novel, the joke of "we" inserts itself even more problematically into the matrix of social relations. Mrs. Parker's initially proposed "we," her "more civilized" modern community, is already marked by an ambiguous line of inclusion/exclusion. Evidently we should *exclude* the "idiot" from our village pageants on the ground that our community is more *inclusive*, more tolerant, than that of the Elizabethans. It is because the idiot has been *included* as a legitimate member of the commu-nity, as one of "us" that he must be *excluded* from community activities that would put his difference from "us" on display. The liberal logic encoded in the word "civilization" seeks to deny or erase the very differences of which

34. I have in mind here some remarks made by Homi Bhabha in the course of his Richard Wright Memorial Lectures at the University of Pennsylvania in April 1991.

an increasing tolerance is its whole promise and appeal. One suspects that Woolf, who tended rather to idealize the more differential model of community implicit in the Elizabethan drama,[35] is as skeptical as Giles about Mrs. Parker's "more civilized" *we*, though for entirely different reasons. For Giles the question is not one of the idiot's relation to the village community but of Mrs. Parker's. He refuses to acknowledge her communitarian claim of solidarity with him because, on the one hand, she is altogether too provincial, and on the other hand she has an insufficiently organic connection with his own (provincial) village.

The contradiction here, Giles's hesitation between the postures of cosmopolitanism and of ultra-narrow village-communitarianism, is more important than may at first appear. As the novel's key figure of official culture and authority, it matters where he situates himself in Britain's symbolic matrix of borders and gateways. And it seems to me revealingly symptomatic that Giles's rejection of Mrs. Parker's "we" leads him immediately both to an exclusionist, scapegoating impulse and to what may be read as a pastoralizing, mythologizing one. Giles cannot accept Mrs. Parker's invocation of civilized society, either on its own (presumably too provincial) terms, or from the vantage of a more cosmopolitan sense of civilization. For in either case his own proper community would have to include and tolerate the (notably cosmopolitan and by no means uncivilized) homosexual artist William Dodge, the "toady" and "lickspittle" whose exclusion and denigration are the "luck[y]" means of Giles's own ego maintenance. But any alternative "we" that effects this exclusion of the homosexual Other must have its own fundamental principle of unity to take the place of "civilization," the liberal principle of increasing tolerance for decreasing differences within a generalized "humanity." With a certain hesitation (understandable given the fact that he and Isa are for the moment barely on speaking terms), but with sure instinct, Giles invokes "his wife," the mother of his children, as the nodal point by means of which he can manage these contradictions and identify himself with a specially adapted, communifying image of the great country house and the small country village.

It is a familiar enough ideological move, and one that resonates profoundly within the Condition of England tradition that Woolf's novel both extends and disrupts. A stockbroker in the City, Giles is acutely conscious of the nonproductive and parasitic character of his work. His Aunt Lucy, whom he always feels to be "mocking him, . . . laughing" (109), infuriates him with her professed "amazement, her amusement, at men who spent their lives,

35. See Silver, "Virginia Woolf and the Concept of Community."

buying and selling—ploughs? glass beads was it? or stocks and shares?—to savages who wished most oddly—for were they not beautiful naked?—to dress and live like the English" (47). Her "frivolous . . . malignant statement" of his situation obviously angers him because it resonates with his own feelings of social, or indeed, national unworthiness. These feelings are symptomatic of the fundamental contradiction mentioned in my Chapter 1, in terms of which the world's most industrialized nation was able to harbor in its social imaginary an image of itself as *essentially* rural.[36] "Given his choice," Giles absurdly believes, "he would have chosen to farm" (47). And like other urban "farmers" forced by an externalized "conglomeration of things" (whose partial coextension with their own desires and interests is conveniently passed over) to spend their days reaping the fruits of empire and industry in the City (47), Giles reproduces his split identifications in the structure of his everyday life. Pointz Hall, a City man's weekend retreat, so provincial it seems insulated even from the urgent news, in June 1939, of what is occurring "just over there, across the gulf" (46)—this exasperatingly peripheral site is also the true center of the community to which Giles the urbanized farmer most authentically belongs.

This strange but characteristic mapping of England, which by fixing the provincial countryside as imaginary center of the urban life makes possible a centered remoteness, a "remote village in the very heart of England" (16), is more imbricated than one might think with patriarchal habits of mind—specifically, with the pastoral conception of woman. It is the pastoralized woman who maintains a linkage between the family idea and the mythical country-village England at a time when actual English families are overwhelmingly and increasingly crowded into the major metropolitan areas. For as wife and mother, rooted in the home, woman can represent the nurturing community of the rustic village in contradistinction to the brutality or indifference of modern urban society. As a result, Giles needs only to invoke "his wife" to affirm his belonging in an authentic national community despite his inauthentic social function as a cosmopolitan trader in stocks and bonds.

This pastoral idea of community, of a community essentially familial, nurturing, peaceful, orderly, free of industrial machinery, as remote as possible from where English people actually live and work and yet somehow "in the very heart" of England—this idea circulates so busily and playfully through *Between the Acts* that one cannot hope to assign it a simple positive or negative value. But whatever traces the novel may carry of a "nostalgia," as

---

36. As I noted in Chapter 1, the important discussions are Wiener, *English Culture*, and Williams, *The Country and the City*.

both Elizabeth Rose and Alex Zwerdling have put it,[37] for the preindustrial village community of authentic England (and I don't deny that such nostalgic nationalism or regressive utopianism informs Woolf's writing to the very last), they are crossed by other traces (such as that initial intrusion of the cesspool) which mark the pressure of a more skeptical thinking. Giles's abortive exchange with Mrs. Parker underscores the connection between his need to anchor the "we" of the national village community to wife and family and his violent homophobia. The homosexual "fingerer of sensations," as Giles interestingly puts it, the cosmopolitan artist who cannot "have straight-forward love for a woman" (60), represents too great a strain on the pastoral family paradigm. As Iris Marion Young has argued, a communitarianism that represses the material fact of modern urbanization also closes itself to the deviant, to the circulation of "unassimilated otherness" which city life ideally enables.[38] And the failure to accommodate the deviant, the homosexual artist—the urban bohemian type, indeed the very type of Bloomsbury—had to have been a sign, in Woolf's eyes, of crippling limitations in the village-community idea and the nationalism to which it was attached. Woolf did recognize the complicities between male homosexuality and dominant culture in the postwar period (a dominant culture that, however, as I remarked earlier, she never makes the mistake of calling "feminine"). William Dodge arrives at Pointz Hall in the company of Mrs. Manresa, the docile participant in patriarchal constructions of femininity ("she preferred men, obviously" [39]); and both of them quickly fasten their desire on "the muscular, the hirsute, the virile" Giles (106), "the very type of all that [they] adored" (47). But Woolf also takes care, in this novel as elsewhere, to acknowledge the continued denegration and exclusion of the male homosexual during the interwar years. Giles's refusal to consider Dodge "one of us" is consistent with a still rigidly masculinist social structure that ensures the man whose desire is not "straightforward" enough will be tortured at school (the other boys held Dodge's head "under a bucket of water" [73]) and forced to secrete his unspeakable sexuality (as Dodge has done) behind the screen of a convenient marriage and a bastard child. The "family values" that provide the linkage between the lived experience of the modern metropolis and the

---

37. Rose, *Woman of Letters* 237; Zwerdling, *Virginia Woolf and the Real World* 308.

38. Young, "Ideal of Community" 317–19. One can accept Young's critique of the pastoral community without necessarily accepting her alternative utopia of the "unoppressive city" (319), which seems to exaggerate the emancipatory potential of eating in ethnic restaurants. But the whole critique of communitarianisms (including feminist ones) which Young offers in this essay is of considerable relevance to my reading of *Between the Acts* as a work of emergent postmodernism.

compensatory nationalist fantasy of village pastoral are thus seen to be maintained through violence, and the pastoral communitarian fantasy itself is exposed as a coercive and exclusionary social mechanism.

But if we agree that *Between the Acts* is largely intent on satirizing this pastoral or deurbanized vision of the Englishman's authentic community, with its concomitant pastoralization of woman and exclusion of the womanly man, we must also recognize that the object of critique is by no means restricted to the minds of retrograde patriarchs such as Giles. It is true that in the right-wing, antisuffrage propaganda of the interwar years (which does not abate with the passage of the Act of 1928) one finds the pastoral vision of community interwoven with the separate-spheres idea of woman's natural domesticity. The linch pin of this rhetoric is woman's assumed exteriority to industry, which simultaneously justifies her exclusion from much of the workforce and her identification with a domestic space at once "remote" from industry and at "the very heart of England." The British Union of Fascists, which made extensive use of the rustic England myth, left no doubt about where woman's place would be in the new order. "In theory women would be eligible for all posts within the Fascist state," observed a BUF official in 1934, "but in practice a natural and inevitable differentiation of function would appear, women filling those posts for which they are best fitted. . . . We definitely prefer 'women who are women, and men who are men.'"[39] But what was driving this rhetoric, most immediately, was the shortage of jobs which arose when men returned from the war, a shortage that became acute during the years of economic depression. And this shortage meant that, where women and industry were concerned, the labor movement and others on the left were speaking the same language as the conservatives and fascists. (And as Doris Lessing was one of the first to observe, the pastoral figure of the nurturing "Mum" in her properly domestic setting continued to hold a key place in leftist thinking about community throughout the postwar period and even in the years of New Left dissidence.)

Even more significantly for Woolf, this situating of woman in a maternal sphere outside industry, and "in the very heart" of an immanent English community that has been impeded by industry and cosmopolitan business, runs through both major streams of postsuffrage social feminism. On the one hand, the New Feminists, led by Eleanor Rathbone and the National Union of Societies for Equal Citizenship (a postwar formation out of Millicent Garrett Fawcett's National Union of Women's Suffrage Societies), fo-

---

39. A. Raven Thomson, BUF deputy director of policy, quoted by Brian Harrison, *Separate Spheres: The Opposition to Women's Suffrage in Britain* (London, 1978) 231.

cused their attention on "women's issues" in the narrow sense, fighting for the "endowment of motherhood" or, as it later became known, the "mothers' allowance," a government subsidy of motherhood inspired by the separation allowances paid to wives and children of military men during WWI.[40] On the other hand were social feminists such as those with whom Woolf herself associated in the Women's Co-operative Guild, who tended to emphasize the less specifically domestic issues of pacifism, internationalism, anticolonialism, and antifascism.[41] But as Naomi Black has shown in her study of social feminism, this latter stream, which became increasingly dominant in the thirties, in fact rests on the same maternalist ideology of difference which the New Feminism (and patriarchy itself) does. In both cases there is little or no room for conceiving of woman except as good mother, nurturer, embodiment of nature over and against the "masculine" world of the machine and the workings of capital. And this conception is one important reason why Black can say of such feminism that, whatever the appeal of its specific goals, one must beware of its ideological bedfellows: "its wicked stepsister is the reactionary Nazi Woman; her companions are the Total Woman, the Superwoman, the Mother of Twenty."[42]

Between the Acts, it seems to me, marshals a critique rather similar to Black's insofar as it refuses to allow this pastoral and maternalist conception of community to gather any real force, refuses to make its realization the great mission of the woman artist. It is, again, a postmodernist critique, which problematizes the terms of much feminist modernism, the system of associations which informs the writings of, for example, H.D., in which man is one with "the great overwhelming mechanical demon, the devil of machinery" and woman must draw upon her deep interconnectedness with nature to build the new, noncoercive community remote from industry.[43]

Both the pastoral idealization of Woman and a postmodernist resistance to such idealization are constitutive of the context of Giles's awkward exchange

40. For one recent account of the NUWSS, its postwar splinter groups, and the debate over family endowment, see David Rubenstein, *A Different World for Women: The Life of Millicent Garrett Fawcett* (New York, 1991) 269–74.

41. See Black, "Virginia Woolf and the Woman's Movement," in Marcus, ed., *Virginia Woolf: A Feminist Slant* 183–88.

42. Naomi Black, *Social Feminism* (Ithaca, 1989) 354.

43. H. D., "Responsibilities," in Scott, ed., *Gender of Modernism* 128. In her remarkable book *Landscape for a Good Woman: A Story of Two Lives* (New Brunswick, N.J., 1987), Carolyn Kay Steedman considers some of the ways this pastoralization of woman, and especially of the mother, has continued in the postwar years to color the work of both men and women writers of the left.

with Mrs. Parker, the context that ensures that this and other such exchanges *will* be awkward. The rudeness or antagonism produced by the fact that Giles's "'we'" has no rapport with Mrs. Parker's, the fact that they cannot even really begin to "communicate," this inarticulateness of individuals is also a symptom of inarticulated community, of a community that is always being thought under the law of unity rather than that of articulation. Failure of communication thus defines not just the comic ethos but the political stakes of the novel. For 1939–40 is a year that places special urgency on the question of who *we* are, on achieving a certain closure to this question which *Between the Acts* seems always to be reopening between double quotation marks.

There is some question, though, just how far a text—a dialogic, an impertinent, a mocking text—can evade or disrupt the constraints that have always been imposed in advance on the utterance of "we." For all its dialogic play on and around the "we" of nationalism, does the novel ever really free itself from the national-community idea? How can La Trobe's pageant (in 1939), how can Woolf's novel (in 1941), *not* be about the Condition of England, about the community of the English? And how can England, English, be invoked at all in these years without effecting a certain resonance with the "we" of the patriot? If one accepts Bruce King's description of (English) nationalism as "an urban movement which identifies with the rural areas as a source of authenticity, finding in the 'folk' the attitudes, beliefs, customs and language to create a sense of national unity among people who have other loyalties,"[44] is it not misleading to say that *Between the Acts* is *simply* a work of antinationalist burlesque?

We know that Woolf was no fan of nationalism. "I don't like any of the feelings war breeds: patriotism, communal &c, all sentimental & emotional parodies of our real feelings" (*Diary* 5:302). The trouble is that in a world that has always already hailed you as a nationalized subject, as "English" or "German," nationalism is less a matter of conscious outlook than an inescapable effect of language. Where declarations of war are part of the speech situation, you cannot simply refuse your interpellation in a system of national differences. One does not solve the crisis of 1939 by denying that one is English, by claiming, as Woolf does at one point in *Three Guineas*, to "have no country" (109). But given this difficulty, how can an English subject, writing about England at the very verge of wartime, interfere in the process whereby "we," despite its illimitable negotiability, comes to anchor itself in the com-

44. Bruce King, *The New English Literatures* (London, 1980) 42, quoted in Timothy Brennan, "The National Longing for Form," in Bhabha, ed., *Nation and Narration* 53.

mon struggle, the cooperative war effort? Can joke-work in such circumstances be harnessed unproblematically to the ideological project of pacifist internationalism?

One place the question arises in *Between the Acts* is at the end of the interval between the pageant's Restoration and Victorian acts, when Colonel Mayhew, seated in the audience, examines the program. The colonel does not dispute "the producer's right to skip two hundred years in less than fifteen minutes. But the choice of scenes baffle[s] him. 'Why leave out the British Army? What's history without the Army, eh?'" (157). These objections—in which we hear the specifically nationalist "we," the "we" of King and Country—are soon quieted by Mrs. Mayhew, who suggests with touching optimism that "very likely there would be a Grand Ensemble, round the Union Jack, to end with" (157).

What makes Mrs. Mayhew's suggestion comical, of course, is that the pageant not only makes a point of leaving out the very elements the Colonel views as essential, but consistently mocks the whole idea of the English community as a Grand Ensemble with the flag as its center and the army along its borders. La Trobe, the double outsider, the feminist modernist, fully shares Woolf's hostility to patriotism. But we should also recognize that Mrs. Mayhew's suggestion, and the Colonel's ready acceptance of it, mark the unreliability, and indeed in this case the failure, of mockery as a disruptive political strategy. La Trobe attempts at several points parodically to appropriate nationalist material, but her parodistic intentions do not in fact neutralize the nationalist effect. When she plays some snatches of particularly inane and "pompous" marching music, for example ("Bold and blatant / Firm elatant / See the warriors—here they come"), it rallies the restive audience and puts them in "good humor" (79). Indeed, Mrs. Manresa, the "fascist mother," as one critic has called her,[45] becomes at this moment the effective "Queen of the festival" (79).

Of course it is a truism that imitative modes such as parody and travesty are parasitic of what they criticize; they are immersed in the very repertoire of images and dependent on the very range of effects they aim to repudiate. But in this case the problem goes beyond the parasitism of parody. Even a straightforwardly polemical critique of nationalism and the literature that sustains it had to contend, in 1939–40, with a repertoire of images and a range of effects which were extraordinarily difficult to evade. From Woolf's vantage, the suffragettes had erred in 1914 not by turning patriot but by accepting the link between patriotism and cooperation in the war effort; she

---

45. Abel, *Virginia Woolf and the Fictions of Psychoanalysis* 126.

and the women of the Women's Co-operative Guild were determined not to make the same mistake in 1939.[46] But feminist-pacifist patriotism tended all too easily to rely on the very system of images which had been held out to the troops of the first war as reminders of what "England" truly meant: the pastoralized, virtually depopulated southern village, remote from industry,[47] with its hedgerows and church spires, and usually, at the heart of that village, an idealized home where Mum is perpetually caring for her little ones.

This reliance on the discursive repertoire of nationalism is the danger with which both La Trobe's play and Woolf's novel are constantly flirting. Their design leads them constantly to recycle (and it may not help to say "parodically") the very images and associations by means of which, as Sir Arthur Quiller-Couch observed approvingly in 1918, English literature had managed to stimulate patriotic feeling during the first war: the country setting in a "green nook . . . where there is seed-time and harvest," the "spirit of 'Merry England' sustained in poetry, folk and popular song from Chaucer onwards," and the invocation of "home" as center of the whole social matrix.[48] There is clearly an effort in *Between the Acts* (as there is not in, for example, E. M. Forster's contemporaneous village pageant, *England's Pleasant Land* [1940]) to offer resistance, rather than merely further incitement, to such a patriotic structure of feeling. The myth is not permitted to recirculate unhampered: a cesspool is indicated in the idyllic green nook; the spirit of Merry England is dampened by a willingness to read the literature from Chaucer onwards as at least partly a record of barbarism and misogyny; "home" is identified as the originary site or training ground for the violence that occurs between nations. But Mrs. Mayhew's comic misreading of the pageant as one through which a nationalist "we" may be secured and fortified is perhaps a joke that can replay itself more ominously on the level of the novel's readership.

46. Indeed, according to Black, "Virginia Woolf and the Woman's Movement," the WCG passed a resolution against rearmament in summer 1938, and "as late as March 1939 the WCG was calling for repeal of the Conscription Bill" (187).

47. There is perhaps more than a hint of this rustic, depopulated landscape in Woolf's statement of her own patriotism, which seems to mention people almost as an afterthought: "Of course I'm 'patriotic': that is English, the language, farms, dogs, people" (quoted in Zwerdling, *Virginia Woolf and the Real World* 276). Again, in *Three Guineas*, having expressed women's proper "indifference" to a country that has never been theirs, Woolf leaves room for "some love of England dropped into a child's ears by the cawing of rooks in an elm tree, by the splash of waves on a beach" (109).

48. Q [Arthur Thomas Quiller-Couch], "Patriotism in Literature" (1918), quoted in Brooker and Widdowson, "A Literature for England," in Colls and Dodd, eds., *Englishness* 117.

In any case, *Between the Acts* recognizes the tremendous risks involved in any talk of "we," in any talk where "we" may be heard—risks that go well beyond the possibility of conversational awkwardness, embarrassment, humiliation. The problem of language (the "communication" problem), which is a prime opportunity for jokes, is also an opportunity for violence to unleash itself on a global scale. It would be tempting—several critics have been tempted—to read Woolf's last novel as offering a solution to this problem of communication and of community. But such a temptation leads us only to tendencies in the novel which need to be resisted emphatically: the tendency to keep alive a certain dream of perfect unity, for example (even if it is unity arrived at through disunity, a "discord . . . by means of which we reach the final . . . " [201 ellipses in original]), or the tendency to gesture toward a consensual or dialogic politics beyond power, a politics free of coercion.[49] These are the traces of a way of thinking about community and communication from which Woolf never very cleanly or consciously detached herself, but which one can none-theless learn, from *Between the Acts*, not to take quite seriously.

We must accept in any event that the problem this novel attacks and which, as a new (postmodernist) sort of culture critique, it traces within and among the communitarian critiques that had gone under the rubrics of modernism, fascism, and feminism—this problem is not of the sort that allows of solution. The best such a critique can do is to interrupt attempts at political closure, including those attempts which—whether through the no-tion of immanent community or that of ideal communication, or through some other means—hold out the liberal promise of perfect cooperation, consensus, persuasion without power. When the Rev. Mr. Streatfield stands at the end of the pageant to suggest that "one spirit animates the whole——" he is interrupted just there by the warplanes overhead. This is a comic interruption, a bit of bathos or "descending incongruity" which draws us from the reverend's hopeful idealism to the realities of the historical situa-tion. But joke-work always involves the possibility of a resolution to the incongruity, and in *Between the Acts* it becomes necessary to think the logical and historical connections between this idea of a unifying essence—of a common animating spirit that can transform the many fragments into a single whole—and the violence of war. The "whole" society, the society

49. This is how I interpret Cuddy-Keane's argument that the novel "substitut[es], for the definition of politics as the exercise of power, a model of community as the dynamic inhabiting of mutual space" ("The Politics of Comic Modes" 284). The problem is that community, even thought in these terms, is not something that can obviate, or substitute for, the exercise of power.

defined by the immanence and the intimacy of a lost or somehow impeded communion, is in fact realized and fulfilled in, not interrupted or obstructed by, war. The "whole" society is, as Jean-Luc Nancy has argued, precisely an imaginary community prepared for war, a nation for which the people are prepared to die.[50]

The novel doesn't think these connections for us, doesn't announce that the reverend and the warplanes are, incongruously, speaking the same language. And perhaps in its final sentences, where the possiblity emerges of "another life" the other side of fighting, the novel too is speaking this language. Perhaps in the end Woolf's resistance to the dominant discourses of communion and community simply folds back onto a familiar communitarianism itself, onto a pacifist conception of "the good society as a telos," which, as Iris Marion Young has written, is always also a conception of community as totality, community that has "no ontological exterior, since it realizes the unity of general will and individual subjectivity," and "no historical exterior, for there is no further stage to travel."[51] We need not claim *Between the Acts* as a work of absolute or perfectly sustained critique to see it as a remarkable intervention in the problematic of community: an intervention that marks the end of modernism along the frayed edges of a discursive system whose organizing principle is wholeness but whose actual telos is death. It would take twenty some years for the unworking of this system to begin to make itself felt as a general and conscious effort within British culture. After the war, as I argue in the next chapter, cultural rebellion once again attaches itself firmly to the project of realizing an immanent and solidary order; literary humor, even where its ostensible target is modernism, is more than ever counted on to perform the work of community-as-exclusion. It would require, as I argue further on, the combined and at times mutually interfering pressures of a resurgent women's movement, an intensified colonial struggle, and a new configuration of the left—a combination that arises vividly in the case of Doris Lessing—for the postmodernist moment of the late thirties to acquire broader and deeper cultural resonance. But it is nonetheless a key moment for cultural historians, the moment when a specifically *feminist* modernism perceives its complicities in the logic of fascism and begins, not so much to declare a new and more radical dissidence as to identify its own finished work as the proper object of a new laughter.

50. Nancy, *Inoperative Community* 13.
51. Young, "Ideal of Community" 308.

Four

Barbarism as Culturism:
Lucky Jim and the Politics of the
Campus Novel

> Even in a decent country like England, rebellion becomes
> necessary.
>
> —Kingsley Amis, *Lucky Jim's Politics*

Ever since commentators on the left began systematically to reflect on the
first phase of Britain's postwar history, to isolate roughly the years 1945–65
as an intelligible period of historical analysis, a recurring question has been
whether this period of the political "settlement," of the great "compromise,"
created an opening for progressive social and cultural change which was, as a
result of various strategic errors and defeats, subsequently clamped shut, or
whether the settlement in itself constituted a kind of political foreclosure
which virtually assured the emergence of a rightist hegemony. By conceding
the legitimacy of a capitalist mode of production, did Labour widen or
narrow the scope for democratic and socialist initiatives? Is it more important
to emphasize the changes that occurred during this period or rather to
illuminate the stable framework of oppression underpinning them?

On the one hand, the formation of the welfare state undeniably entailed
major institutional overhauls in the areas of health, education, housing, and
the arts, as well as aggressive flattening of both pre- and, especially, aftertax
income curves. Jobs-creation programs combined with a rapidly enlarging
system of government benefits and entitlements to provide a social safety net
of unprecedented breadth. Culturally, moreover, these years saw a widespread repudiation of the leisure-class arts establishment, and of the arid,
art-as-autonomy version of modernism it favored, by an emergent generation
of less-privileged, less-cosmopolitan artists and writers announcing a new
concern for the social: "We saw that the Thirties Novel, the Experimental

Novel, had got to be brushed out of the way," wrote William Cooper, fairly typically, in 1959. "The Experimental Novel was about Man-Alone; we meant to write novels about Man-in-Society as well."[1]

But on the other hand, even the earliest commentators questioned the depth of these socioeconomic and cultural transformations, stressing the underlying continuity or even stasis of British society. Beginning in 1961 with Michael Shanks's *Stagnant Society*, hand-wringing bestsellers began to appear which saw the fifties and early sixties as mainly a period of false transformations and pseudo-rebellions.[2] The truth about postwar Britain, said John Holloway in a series of *Third Programme* talks in 1967, is that it managed transformations of only "a limited and in a sense decorous kind." Postwar society was so constituted, he said, as to preclude any possibility of real social change: "Almost every aspect of our culture, and most of our amenities and our strengths, invite us to any measures, and to any spirit, save that radical one we need."[3] Recent historians, particularly those on the left, have tended to agree. The welfare state, Elizabeth Wilson has written, was an utterly fraudulent socialism, "the socialism at which Marx and Engels had sneered long ago . . . an illusion of socialism achieved by contriving to make all classes *appear* 'middle-class.'" Britain in the fifties was not a society in process of radicalizing (or even radically reforming) itself, but rather "a conservative society described in the rhetoric of a radical ideology. This held out in one hand the image of social revolution achieved, a political achievement, while with the other it demolished politics as a valid activity. . . . Socialism was vilified, yet somehow, simultaneously, Britain *was* socialist."[4]

This sheep-in-wolf's-clothing interpretation is frequently extended to the literary culture as well. It is pointed out that the "rebellious" young writers of this period, the Movement writers and the Angries,[5] showed up increasingly

1. William Cooper, "Reflections on Some Aspects of the Experimental Novel," quoted in Malcolm Bradbury, "The Novel," in *The Twentieth-Century Mind: History, Ideas, and Literature in Britain*, vol. 3: 1945–1965, ed. C. B. Cox and A. E. Dyson (London, 1972) 338.

2. See Arthur Marwick, *British Society since 1945* (Harmondsworth, 1982) 126.

3. John Holloway, "English Culture and the Feat of Transformation," *The Listener* 77 (1967): 132.

4. Elizabeth Wilson, *Only Halfway to Paradise: Women in Postwar Britain, 1945–1968* (London, 1980) 6.

5. I use these terms, "Movement" and "Angry [Young Man]," more or less interchangeably in connection with Amis, who was frequently linked to both groupings. The term "Movement" was coined in the mid-fifties to comprise the young, mostly lower-middle-class poets who had by then gained recognition for their stripped-down, anti-modernist, anti-Romantic verse and for several comic *bildungsroman* of lower-middle-class

at the rightward end of the political spectrum as the years went by and that their rebellions against certain modernist gestures and aesthetic practices never amounted to a genuine politicization of literary production or an effective challenge to the elitist institution of art itself.[6] Indeed, even on the level of aesthetic practice these writers were less at odds with the dominant culture than they claimed to be. Their *anti*modernism was in many respects perfectly consistent with the version of modernism which achieved its ascendancy in the forties and fifties under the impetus of F. R. Leavis. For what the Movement objected to in modernism were precisely those aspects which Leavis's journal *Scrutiny* had downplayed or circumvented in its (highly selective) promotion of a modernist canon: the "alien" symbolist inheritance; the narrative and formal experimentalism; the stance of transcendent exile.

Of course one will always find, in retrospect, the continuities that compromise an ostensible revolution. And while one can argue that the relative speed with which Margaret Thatcher's government dismantled the welfare state betrays the latter's true nature and tendency, the new social order of the eighties and nineties should also caution against too cavalierly dismissing what *was* achieved, however provisionally, in the fifties and sixties. Nevertheless, it seems fair to say that the first two postwar decades frame a period of rather special ideological ambivalence, such that the very forces or tendencies that appear most radically innovative can be seen on many fronts as preparing the ground for the Thatcherite hegemony of more recent years.

One such ideological front, and not merely one among others, is education. At no time in British history has education occupied such a privileged place in political discourse, or carried such a burden of societal hopes and expectations, as during the fifties and sixties. The view perhaps most closely associated with Leavis, that educational reform was the key to a postwar social transformation—and in particular that the "humane centre" of the new "national community," its sense of "unity" and "cohesion," ultimately rested on the institution of a certain "idea of the University"[7]—can be traced

---

scholarship boys. "Angry Young Men" appeared several years later as a term to describe the emerging group of impertinent, mostly working-class young novelists and playwrights which included William Cooper, Alan Sillitoe, John Osborne, and sometimes Amis himself. In general, the Movement is seen in aesthetic terms, as leading an attack against modernism, the Angries in class terms, as leading an assault on middle-class values. But the distinction is obviously not a secure one.

6. See, for example, Blake Morrison, *The Movement: English Poetry and Fiction of the 1950s* (London, 1986).

7. F. R. Leavis, *Education and the University* (New York, 1948) 24–27.

across the whole postwar political spectrum. Though versions of this thinking had been circulating ever since the late nineteenth century, when the idea
of a national system of education emerged,[8] the view of the university as a
specially privileged site of community-building gathered considerable momentum in the immediate postwar years. Suddenly, it seemed, everyone was
interested in education, especially in higher education and the wider dissemination of "culture." Detailed criticisms and proposals proliferated on all
sides; bold projects, entailing vast expenditure, were undertaken by Labour
and Conservative governments alike. These educational initiatives were perceived as nothing less than the linch pin of the entire quasi-socialist (or
state-capitalist) postwar project; this was the cultural work on which the
communitarian overcoming of class oppression and social divisiveness would
ultimately depend. And the special status accorded educational reforms was,
if anything, reinforced by the fact that they served as the principal target of
conservative reaction when Thatcher, first as shadow education minister and
then as Edward Heath's secretary of state for education and science, began
taking the initial steps toward a social and cultural counterrevolution in
1969–72.[9]

At the same time, and as is characteristic of the period, these seemingly
radical rearrangements of the postwar educational system have struck many
historians as themselves performing the work of social conservatism. As
Frank Parkin pointed out in 1972, while the sheer numbers of university
students from all classes had increased dramatically by the late sixties, the
relative educational advantage of upper classes over lower remained perfectly
consistent with prewar ratios.[10] Though there "may have seemed to be truly
democratic [effects]," writes Roy Lowe, "the reality was otherwise. Between
1945 and 1964 the English education system developed in ways which were
to confirm the deep social cleavages which only became fully apparent during
the 1980s."[11]

The emergent postwar literary culture offers a wide avenue into these

---

8. See Philip Dodd, "Englishness and the National Culture," in Colls and Dodd, eds.,
Englishness 1–28. To give just one example, Dodd cites a 1921 *Report of the Committee to
Enquire into the Position of the Classics* in which "the political, social and moral welfare of the
community" is said to "depend mainly on the development of a national system of education" (23n).

9. For a justifiably bitter account of Thatcher's role as education minister, see Brian
Simon, *Education and the Social Order, 1940–1990* (London, 1991) 405–30.

10. Frank Parkin, *Class Inequality and Political Order* (London, 1972) 55–56.

11. Roy Lowe, *Education in the Post-War Years: A Social History* (London, 1988) 202.

questions of education and hegemony, since literature was from the start deeply implicated in the education debates. "English studies"—the development of an intellectually earnest, socially responsible, and finely discriminating sensibility through the critical reading of English literature—was after all to have been the central discipline, the key to a communitarian cultural practice, in Leavis's model university. It continued to hold this place at the "core" of the new, interdisciplinary curriculums that evolved in Keele, Essex, and other new universities in the sixties (though not always in ways consistent with the Leavisite agenda), and it serves even today as the main object of education and "culture" controversies on both sides of the Atlantic.[12]

The writers of the postwar generation incorporated these controversies, as it were, generically. Whereas there existed already a tradition of novels about, or partly about, student life—a tradition associated with Oxford dandyism and including Max Beerbohm's *Zuleika Dobson* (1911), Compton Mackenzie's *Sinister Street* (1913–14), Beverley Nichols's *Patchwork* (1920), and Evelyn Waugh's *Brideshead Revisited* (1945)[13]—the postwar generation, who were far more likely than their predecessors to have found employment in the university system, created the quite distinct genre of "campus novel," the satire not of undergraduate life but of the academic life, of faculty mores and professional practices. Kingsley Amis broke the ground with *Lucky Jim* (1954), still the best-known campus novel and the one with which I will be most closely concerned here, and later added *One Fat Englishman* (1963), the first of many campus novels to address the increasingly trans-Atlantic context of higher educational developments in Britain. Between these two novels of Amis's, Malcolm Bradbury published *Eating People Is Wrong* (1959), and he went on to specialize in the genre, with *Stepping Westward* (1965), *The History Man* (1975), and *Rates of Exchange* (1983). Bradbury's contemporary and epigone David Lodge has carried the genre through the Thatcher years with his popular Rummidge trilogy: *Changing Places* (1975), *Small World* (1984), and *Nice Work* (1988).

From the standpoint of the present study, these novels are among the most interesting texts of the welfare state and its aftermath. They are funny books, at times outrageously so, but it is not easy to say what exactly they are making one laugh at, what positions exactly they are offering in the complex network of hostilities and alliances which constitutes the academic situation

12. See John Sutherland, "The Politics of English Studies in the British University, 1960–1984," in *Historical Studies and Literary Criticism*, ed. Jerome J. McGann (Madison, Wisc., 1985) 126–40.

13. This line of novels is discussed by Martin Green in *Children of the Sun* 151–97.

of postwar Britain. It is not only that the joke-work performed by these novels resists any simple characterization as subversive or conservative—that is the case with all manner of joking. What draws us to the humor of the campus novel is that the marked tensions between subversive and conservative impulses are in this instance symptomatic of particularly fundamental and persistent contradictions in the postwar social order and in England's attempted rethinking of the national community.

The Movement from Left to Right

> It was a perfect title, in that it crystallized the article's niggling mindlessness, its funereal parade of yawn-enforcing facts, the pseudo-light it threw upon non-problems. Dixon had read, or begun to read, dozens like it, but his own seemed worse than most in its air of being convinced of its own usefulness and significance.
>
> —Kingsley Amis, *Lucky Jim*

> *Academic.* 1) (Pejorative) Used of knowledge difficult to master, irrelevant to contemporary reality and deriving from dead or elderly "authorities."
>
> —Kingsley Amis and Robert Conquest,
> "A Short Educational Dictionary"

These two jokes might seem to depend for their comic effect on essentially the same skepticism as regards the value and relevance of the academy. The mock lexicographers of the latter text appear to share with Jim Dixon, the author-identified protagonist of the former, the view of academic knowledge as a mere "funereal parade of yawn-enforcing facts." But as anyone remotely familiar with Amis's career will know, the irony of the "Dictionary" is meant to work quite the opposite way. By 1971, when he and Robert Conquest contributed this mock glossary to the collected *Black Papers on Education*, Amis had become a prominent figure in the conservative backlash against the "irresponsible expansionism" and "rampant progressivism" that had marked higher education in the fities and sixties and that he held responsible for filling the universities with "students who do not understand what study is about, and who are painfully bewildered by the whole business and purpose of university life."[14] These "academically-unfit" students, and the progressivist teachers who supported them, were the ones for whom "academic" was a

14. Kingsley Amis, "Pernicious Participation," in *Black Papers on Education*, ed. C. B. Cox and A. E. Dyson (London, 1971).

pejorative term connoting pointlessly difficult and irrelevant knowledge; and it was this "pernicious" view that Amis and Conquest, together with all the other *Black Paper* contributors, wished to disparage. In "looking for relevance," Amis commented, such students were really just "looking for vocational training." And while this was "a harmless desire in itself," it was fundamentally "antiacademic and therefore not to be indulged at a university." Indeed, "any teacher who want[ed] to import" such an anti-academic attitude into the university could properly be regarded as "an enemy of culture."[15]

Thus Amis, whose 1954 novel had notoriously and hilariously framed the university as a place of "niggling mindlessness," had by 1971 (and indeed much earlier than that) set himself on the staunchly traditionalist pro-academy side of the higher education debates. The "anti-art, anti-knowledge, anti-tradition" University Wit who had outraged England's cultural establishment with cracks about "filthy Mozart" was now using his jokes to defend the bastions of higher learning against "anti-academic" barbarians and "enem[ies] of culture."[16]

15. Ibid. 171.

16. "Filthy Mozart" is from *Lucky Jim* (1954; London, 1961) 63. Hereafter cited parenthetically as *LJ*. Hilary Corke's review of *That Uncertain Feeling* in *Encounter*, 5 October 1955, 87–88, offers a typical example of the cultural establishment's attitude toward the early Amis, calling him "anti-art, anti-knowledge, anti-tradition, anti-manners —opposed, in fact, on principle, to 'the best that is known or thought' or enjoyed or done" (quoted in Dale Salwak, *Kingsley Amis: A Reference Guide* [Boston, 1978] 6). In a pattern that has been frequently repeated in contemporary debates on culture and the academy, Corke, the self-appointed guardian of art, knowledge, and tradition, here shows himself far less conversant in the texts of the canon than the "philistine" he is attacking. While Corke is incapable even of correctly quoting the definition of culture from Arnold's *Culture and Anarchy* (the single most important text for postwar defenses of "civilization"), Amis and his supposedly barbaric protagonist display an impressive command of the very texts they deride. Thus, for example, although Dixon hates classical music, he recognizes Mozart as the "filthy" composer of the "skein of untiring facetiousness" he is hearing (63), and he identifies another snippet as the "'rondo' of some boring piano concerto" (87). This curious reversal of roles, whereby precisely those who are lacking in cultural capital become the guardians of culture, is everywhere evident in the recent spate of attacks on the Humanities faculties of American universities. The Milton scholar Stanley Fish, for example, is immeasurably more learned in the classics of English literature than are Roger Kimball (*Tenured Radicals: How Politics Has Corrupted Our Higher Education* [New York, 1990]) and Dinesh D'Souza (*Illiberal Education: The Politics of Race and Sex on Campus* [New York, 1991]), both of whom presume to attack him from the cultural high ground; David Lehman, another neoconservative journalist who has taken it upon himself to defend the "great tradition" against the new barbarians (in *Signs of the Times: Deconstruction and the Fall of Paul de Man* [New York, 1991]), is likewise conspicuously lacking in the kind

In part, one can attribute this changed cultural role to a genuine rightward shift in Amis's generation of writers, many of whom discarded their (rather tepid) commitment to socialism after the 1956 Hungary crackdown and then dropped even their stance of supposed neutrality when confronted with the Campaign for Nuclear Disarmament (CND) and student rebellions of the sixties. (Asked about his "disilliusionment with the Left and the Socialists," Amis replied, "It was protest in a way; protest, that . . . finally put me off.")[17] There is also something here of the inevitable slide into reaction of

---

of cultural capital that his deconstructionist adversaries, whatever their shortcomings, have ready to hand.

17. Amis was still describing himself as having "left-wing sympathies" in his 1957 Fabian tract, *Socialism and the Intellectuals* (London) 1, though already he saw himself as having moved to the right after an early flirtation with Marxism. The key documents of Amis's conversion to conservatism are his article "Why Lucky Jim Turned Right: Confessions of an Ex-Radical," *Sunday Telegraph*, 2 July 1967, and his 1968 Conservative Political Centre Pamphlet, *Lucky Jim's Politics* (from which the quotation about "protest" is drawn, p. 16). A comparative reading of the 1957 and 1968 political pamphlets is instructive, in that it discovers many points of overlap in the arguments and rhetoric of the "left-wing" and the avowedly "conservative" Amis. Even in the former, Amis often sounds dismissive and hostile toward left intellectuals who are more committed than he is. Like other Movement and Angry writers, Amis sees "apathy" as a more appropriate response to the political situation in 1957 than "romantic" activism, for there are "very few" legitimate political battles left to be fought: "No more millions out of work, no more hunger-marches, no more strikes" (*Socialism and the Intellectuals* 9). This commitment to decommitment, which practically defines the dominant political ethos among the fifties generation of British writers, already anticipates Amis's later "grudging toleration" of the Conservative party, which he was "driven into" in the mid-sixties because he had "lost the need to be political" and he saw the Conservative party as "the party of non-politics, of resistance to politics" (*Lucky Jim's Politics* 9). Again in the earlier pamphlet Amis's professed sympathy with the left wing is oddly combined with the familiar counterrevolutionary device of containing specific instances of political activism by means of a grand psychologizing narrative. Discussing Auden and his contemporaries, Amis avers that they, like virtually all radical intellectuals, were "only conducting in public a personal vendetta against their parents." "The notion of political writing and other activity as a kind of self-administered therapy for personal difficulties rather than as a contribution towards the reform of society," writes Amis, may be "an important key to the whole intellectual approach to politics, not just to that of the Thirties" (4). This insistence that left intellectuals are motivated only by "personal vendettas" of the oedipal variety—or by "shift[s] of fashion" in the academic world, as Amis also remarks (4)—is reproduced almost exactly in the later CPC pamphlet (*Lucky Jim's Politics* 8). It is also, one might add, an ideological staple of the postwar campus novels, most conspicuously perhaps in David Lodge's *Small World* (Harmondsworth, 1984), where the political stances and practices of prominent literary intellectuals always turn out to be comical reflections of personal (and usually sexual) needs or preoccupations.

the first generation of successful lower-middle-class meritocrats, whose investment in a competition-centered model of social relations initially secured their opposition to entrenched (and ostensibly unworthy) prewar elites but later turned this oppositional stance toward their new (and again "unworthy") challengers from below. The real motor of meritocratic ideology is not, after all, a desire to level the playing field but a desire to prove one's own superior worth. What I would like to emphasize here, however, is that a certain slippage between rebellious, academy-bashing "barbarism" and the reactionary defense of High Culture and Traditional Standards is already observable in the comic transactions of *Lucky Jim*, and that the tendency of these seemingly antagonistic positions to collapse on one another is in fact fundamental both to the genre of the campus novel and to other arenas of postwar debate over the proper relation of the academy to the larger community.

A good point of entry to these concerns is the relation of Amis's first campus novel to the perceived modernist cultural hegemony of the postwar years. This relation is articulated along a number of axes, of which I will focus on just three: gender, class, and geography. Like other campus novels and other works of fiction and poetry produced by the so-called Movement writers (Amis, Conquest, John Wain, Philip Larkin, Donald Davie, D. J. Enright, Thom Gunn), *Lucky Jim* sets out to repudiate the aesthetic practices of what was by the late forties a widely disseminated and thoroughly institutionalized modernism—practices that were regarded by many writers of the younger generation as the decadent vestiges of a bankrupt romanticism.[18] Formally, the novel reaches back to the earlier (i.e., pre-Romantic) comic and picaresque traditions—the domain of Amis's favorite writer, Fielding—from which it also borrows an ethos of robust "masculinity" and a thematic preoccupation with manliness.

The modernists had tended to reproduce, albeit in highly problematic ways, the nineteenth-century opposition between a masculine high culture and a feminine mass culture.[19] Wyndham Lewis may have attacked the Sitwell and Bloomsbury circles as effeminate, but he did so in the name of a more authentic high-cultural modernism that would refuse Bloomsbury's complicities in a pacifying (i.e., effeminizing) mass culture industry. Rhonda

18. See Morrison's chapter "Against Romanticism," in Morrison, *The Movement* 145–91. For a broader discussion of the often rather confused circulation of the terms "romanticism," "realism," and "modernism" in postwar literary and art criticism, see Robert Hewison, *In Anger: British Culture in the Cold War, 1945–60* (New York, 1981) 85–126.

19. See Huyssen, "Mass Culture as Woman."

Hyman, the Virginia Woolf character in Lewis's *Roaring Queen*, for example, is firmly placed in the effeminized milieu of the bestseller/book-of-the-month racket. The Movement writers also included Bloomsbury and the Sitwells among their most favored targets, but in contrast to Lewis they tended to represent modernism in general—everything from Henry James to Dylan Thomas, including the whole Pound-Eliot-Joyce-Lewis experimentalist moment—as essentially feminine, while stressing their own ties to a working- or lower-middle-class mass culture that they reinscribed within the sphere of the masculine. Amis's vigorous championing of the James Bond novels (along with science fiction and jazz) is understandable in this light as an attempt to deploy a popular genre against dominant high-cultural standards without in any way privileging the feminine—the spy novel serving as masculine counterpart of the manifestly feminine romance genre with which modernism, from *Madame Bovary* on, had identified mass culture.[20]

In adapting the picaresque to the purposes of campus satire, *Lucky Jim* was thus participating in and extending a thoroughly gendered discourse of antimodernist rebellion characteristic of Movement and other emergent postwar writing. The novel's protagonist, Jim Dixon, junior lecturer in history at a provincial university, embodies the same putatively ideal qualities that constitute the robustly masculine heroes of Fielding: qualities such as instinctive candor, lack of pretension, a "healthy" sexual appetite, a strong attachment to "common sense," and an inherent notion of "decency" which marks the authentic English gentleman (of whatever class background) and overrides all local rules of manners or propriety. What makes the university environment so insufferable to Dixon, and such a fine arena of comic opportunities, is that it functions to undermine precisely this masculine-rationalist ideal. University life is seen as fundamentally effeminizing: its denizens are highly evasive and indirect; they are pretentiously arty, narcissistic, and self-

---

20. See Amis, *The James Bond Dossier* (London, 1965). Amis observes at one point that the (male) audience for this kind of popular fiction expects the author to avoid demonstrating any interest in or "acquaintance with the female heart," since "only highbrow authors are allowed to do that" (59)—but he also attempts, not at all persuasively, to make the case for Ian Fleming as feminist. As always, Amis's investment in the popular over and against high culture is difficult to weigh up in this study. He never mentions the fact that the Bond books achieved success as a fad among intellectuals before they gained their vast bestseller audience. And he seems unable to decide whether his aim in the *Dossier* is to applaud Fleming for "that huge virtue of never stooping to pretentiousness, of never going in for any kind of arty or symbolical flannel" (141) or rather to demonstrate that, contrary to appearance and reputation, the Bond novels are "just as complex and . . . have just as much in them as more ambitious kinds of fiction" (9).

dramatizing; their sexuality is threateningly complex or ambiguous; they are wildly irrational and impractical; and their behavior toward one another is frequently catty and cruel. These traits, all coded as effeminate (and thus suggesting, as Alan Sinfield's recent study of postwar British culture makes clear, "homosexual" as well as "female"),[21] are what unite the two main representatives of academic types in the novel, Neddy Welch and Margaret Peel. Despite their many differences, the absent-minded department head and the bright young lecturer both threaten a conception of male identity in which the Movement writers were deeply invested.

The misogyny for which Amis was later to become notorious (a notoriety culminating in the controversy surrounding the American publication of *Stanley and the Women* in 1984–85)[22] is already plainly evident in the portrait of Margaret, his first female character. A classic stereotype of the female intellectual, she is repeatedly labeled "hysterical," "difficult," and "neurotic." Described as "one of those people—they're usually women—who feed on emotional tension," she is said to create "rows about nothing" and groundlessly to accuse men of "hurting her" and "trying to humiliate her" (235–36). Yet as long as he remains at the college Dixon seems incapable of extricating himself from "the Margaret problem" and its attendant horrors (234). Though several rational (i.e., nonacademic) people advise him to "let dear Margaret stew in her own juice" (121), he has no power to act. The neurotic woman, whose empowerment is somehow secured by the neurotic "situation" of academe, has inexplicably rendered him passive, deprived him of his presumed masculine autonomy and will, so that his actions and even his words seem to be "directed by something outside himself" (186). The authentic, active Dixon is visible only in the parenthetical silent outbursts—the stage-whisper howls and groans—which set the comic rhythm of the novel:

> Still looking at him, she shook her head slowly, like a doctor indicating that there is no hope. Her face had a yellowish tinge, and her nostrils seemed pinched. She remained standing and not saying anything.
> "Well, how are things?" Dixon said, tugging a smile on to his mouth.

21. See Alan Sinfield, *Literature, Politics, and Culture in Postwar Britain* (Berkeley, 1989) 62–84. Sinfield argues convincingly that "the repellent misogyny of much Movement and Angry [Young Man] writing" was "part of the attempt to repudiate the perceived [homosexual] ethos of the literary establishment." For "male hostility towards women often goes with hostility towards homosexuality" (81). Thus Sinfield sees the "masculine/feminine dichotomy in the construction of literary intellectuals" during the late forties and fifties as being "overlaid with another: masculine/homosexual" (65).

22. See D. A. N. Jones, "Kingsley Amis," *Grand Street* 4 (Spring 1985): 206–14.

She shook her head again, a little more slowly, and sat down on the arm of the chair, which creaked sharply. . . . "Do you hate me, James?" she said.

Dixon wanted to rush at her and tip her backwards in the chair, to make a deafening rude noise in her face, to push a bead up her nose. "How do you mean?" he asked. (156)

Only a series of dramatic (and improbable) interventions from beyond the walls of the university rescues Dixon from this comedy of paralysis and frustration. And once the suppressed or parenthetical Dixon, whom Margaret has reduced to furtive fantasies of violence and rape, is restored to his role as active subject of the narrative, he launches forth in pursuit of the proper object of his desire, the ideally beautiful Christine Callaghan.

Christine is less an independent character than the necessary mirror-image or counterpart to the "unmanning" academic woman (11); her fetching "simplicity" and "normal[cy]" (she describes herself as "the sort of person you soon get to the end of" [149]) stand in perfect contrast with Margaret's complex "neuroses," just as her fabulous beauty contrasts with Margaret's much remarked "sexual unattractive[ness]" (242). Christine represents a perfectly congenial (and hence imaginary, autoerotic) model of the "feminine" which serves to maintain rather than to threaten the male ego. With "the blonde and busty Callaghan piece" at his side (91), Dixon experiences a resurgence of the masculine "excitement and pride" Margaret has drained from him. Suddenly he feels like a real man again: "a special agent, a picaroon, a Chicago war-lord, a hidalgo, an oil baron, a mohock" (113). Once he replaces Margaret with "the more normal, i.e., less unworkable" Christine (242), the provincial lecturer of history can identify himself unproblematically with the street-smart urban tough guy—the "intellectual tough, or tough intellectual" that Walter Allen identified as the Movement ideal.[23] Any guilt Dixon might feel about Margaret is ultimately swept aside with the observations that Christine is after all "nicer and prettier," and—one of Amis's characteristic tautological quips—that "nice things are nicer than nasty ones" (243). Such a view, Amis has told an interviewer, appeals "to common sense"; "it's nice to have a pretty girl with large breasts rather than some fearful woman who's going to talk to you about Ezra Pound and hasn't got large breasts and probably doesn't wash much."[24]

The fact that the frightening, dirty, and insufficiently large-breasted woman Amis invokes here wants to "talk to you" about literary modernism is

23. Walter Allen, *New Statesman*, 30 January 1954, quoted by John McDermott, *Kingsley Amis: An English Moralist* (New York, 1989) 25.

24. Dale Salwak, "An Interview with Kingsley Amis," *Contemporary Literature* 16 (Winter 1975): 8.

not incidental. Most readers of Amis are struck by his fundamental reliance on such categories as "nice" or "nasty," "sexually attractive" or "sexually unattractive" (243) to organize and motivate his narratives; the first thing to be got straight about a woman character in an Amis novel is always whether she's "on the right side of the line dividing the attractive from the rest."[25] But while this conventional reduction of women to objects or nonobjects of heterosexual desire has drawn comment over the years, it has not always been recognized as integral to the gendered discourse of British culture and the arts which organizes much postwar writing. It is not merely a certain type of woman but a certain type of culture—conceived as an effeminate modernism that has taken up residence in the universities—that we find fearfully represented in a comic figure like Margaret Peel. Margaret's unmanning unattractiveness is not simply a matter of appearance; it is in some sense a matter of language. What makes the (academic) woman so "difficult" and enraging is that she always wants "to talk to you," to subject you to "questions and confessions" (11): like Ezra Pound (or like Freud, that other brunt of Movement derision) the university/woman turns language into an obstacle and a trap for the man of common sense.

This is why it is worth stressing that Dixon's male identity can be threatened just as pointedly, and through precisely the same mechanisms, by his witless and seemingly benign department head, Professor Welch, as it is by his "hysterical" female colleague. Like Margaret, Welch always has a great deal of indirect or seemingly irrelevant things to say; to be with him is to be trapped in the "misfiring vehicle of his conversation" (9). Irrational, impractical, yet a skilled master of "evasion-technique" (194), Welch in fact often succeeds even better than Margaret in disarming and entrapping the straightforward Dixon, forcing him to "give apologies at the very times when he ought to be demanding them" (174). A passive-aggressive manipulator on campus and pathetically hen-pecked husband at home, father of an affected artist named Bertrand and an "effeminate" writer named Michel, devoted to such pastimes as "homemade pottery" and "recorder-playing" (227), Welch is a character scrupulously deprived of any "masculine" traits or achievements. He is another version (essentially the homosexual version) of that female Other whose unfamiliar and unmanning logic reduces the hero to paroxysms of impotent rage and violent fantasies of (vaguely sexual) revenge: just as Dixon wants to "tip [Margaret] backwards in her chair, . . . to push a bead up her nose," he wants "to tie Welch up in his chair and beat him about the head and shoulders

25. Kingsley Amis, *That Uncertain Feeling* (London, 1955) 9.

with a bottle" (85). Unfortunately, the university is not a place where battles can be won with physical violence; in this way, too, it deprives the masculine hero of a key mode of action. The closest Dixon can get to beating up an academic is punching out Welch's (sexually suspect) artist son, Bertrand— and it is made quite clear even before he does so that the hero can be certain of "winning any such encounter with an artist" (42).[26]

This rather crude gender framework that is imposed on academic and intellectual life by Amis and other campus novelists (up to and including the Lodge of *Small World* and *Nice Work*)[27] is more than simply the incidental infection by patriarchy of an otherwise subversive or at least countercultural discourse.[28] It is important to recognize not only that the campus-novel attack on *haut-bourgeois* culture was framed in terms fully as patriarchal as those of the cultural establishment it sought to displace, but also that this misogyny fundamentally compromised whatever democratic tendencies the campus novel might have had in respect to postwar educational reform. For while the ostensible democratization of access to higher education in the fifties and sixties did not in fact enlarge the working-class portion of the educational pie, it did partially, and to some extent inadvertently, ameliorate the relative educational disadvantage of women.[29] The creation of local direct-grant schools, for example, turned out to open a predominantly female track from the provinces into Oxbridge.[30] Consequently, the specific

26. Sinfield makes the same point in calling attention to the lingering doubts about Bertrand's heterosexuality (*Literature, Politics, and Culture* 80).

27. In *Nice Work* (Harmondsworth, 1988), for example, the heroine's poststructuralist, literary-critic boyfriend, Charles, is a suspiciously feline type who favors sex without intercourse. As Lodge describes him in one of several very similar comic passages, "Charles was not an imperious lover. Calm and svelte, stealthy as a cat in his movements, he seemed to approach sex as a form of research, favouring techniques of foreplay so subtle and prolonged that Robyn occasionally dozed off in the middle of them, and would wake with a guilty start to find him still crouched studiously over her body, fingering it like a box of index cards" (57). The connection between academic or intellectual practices and insufficiently robust heterosexuality could scarcely be made more explicit.

28. One still finds Jim Dixon's attitudes described as "subversive" in, for example, the entry for Amis in the *Oxford Companion to English Literature*, 5th edition, ed. Margaret Drabble (Oxford, 1985) 24.

29. But although the proportion of women students in the universities rose steadily by about a half percent a year, it remained below 30 percent as late as 1970. And, as Simon points out, even "at this stage a much smaller proportion of young women with A levels went to university than was the case with young men—44 per cent compared with 67 per cent" (*Education and the Social Order* 261).

30. Lowe, *Education in the Post-War Years* 156.

terms in which the still overwhelmingly male university of the early fifties was derided in *Lucky Jim* would, with their perpetuation in later campus novels and other cultural arenas, tend to intensify rather than moderate that derision as expansion proceeded. As long as the attack on irrelevance, pretension, and elitism at the university cast its object as female, any embrace of the postwar democratic reforms, the most genuinely democratizing effect of which was an enlargment of educational opportunities for women, would be difficult to negotiate. The University Wits of the fifties would perforce find themselves on the reactionary side of the education controversies of the sixties.

Moreover, this whole gender framework was all too conveniently available for transposition onto other unmanageable institutions that emerged under welfare-state capitalism, particularly in such areas as primary schooling and health care, where associations with the feminine were already firmly established. One characteristic of Amis's more recent novels, for example, is that, as a reviewer of *Stanley and the Women* observed, they encourage us to think of modern hospitals and welfare institutions as working "in a 'female' way."[31] Such thinking is simply a logical extension of the masculinist framework within which the Movement worked out its opposition to academic-modernist cultural hegemony.

That oppositional stance has other aspects besides the persistent fear of effeminacy and effeminizing institutions, however. Even Sinfield, for whom homophobia holds the key to the literary culture debates of the fifties, recognizes that masculinism is only one piece of the complex paradigm that structures Movement and Angry thinking on the relation between literary culture and the community.[32] In particular, the notions of masculine and

31. Jones, "Kingsley Amis" 214.
32. Sinfield offers this schematic representation of "the paradigm within which literary culture was constructed" in the immediate postwar period (*Literature, Politics, and Culture* 66):

dominant	the state	working class	'masculinity'
literary	the personal	leisure class	'femininity'

Connections or alliances obtain horizontally on this scheme, while oppositions obtain both vertically and diagonally. Sinfield is right to see the project of the Movement as involving the construction of a new space for the "literary" which would be allied with the state, the working class, and the masculine, over and against the personal, the leisure class, and the feminine. But I am not convinced by Sinfield's argument that the confusions and insta-

feminine are charged in this context with significant intra- and interclass tensions. In *Lucky Jim* Dixon is constantly straining to escape from the effeminizing world of the "gown" into the main masculine arena of the "town": the pub. But this is also, of course, an escape from the pretentious entertainments of the upper-middle class (university soirées and arty week-ends at the Welches) to the more mundane and relaxed diversions of the lower-middle or working classes.[33] Richard Hoggart observed in *The Uses of Literacy* (1957) that a cultural institution such as the Arts Council would typically be depicted in the press as "a 'fiddle' by a lot of 'cissies' who despise the amusements of the plain Englishman," and Sinfield has described the work of the Movement as in part an attempt "to change this story" about "civilization and the 'effeminate.'"[34] But as the case of *Lucky Jim* makes clear, the story of high culture's effeminacy is rewritten by the Movement only insofar as the Movement writer attempts to maneuver himself person-ally out of the cissie camp into solidarity with the plain Englishman without relinquishing any of the prerogatives of the "serious" writer, the privileges of

---

bilities of this paradigm were primarily a consequence of the missing or "concealed term lurking behind the ideal of the feminine: homosexuality." According to Sinfield it was this which "problematized the class divide in the paradigm, because homosexuals often chose their partners across it (as Oscar Wilde had done), producing connections where the model envisages oppositions" (66). Here it seems to me that Sinfield privileges homosexu-ality arbitrarily within the system. It is clear that each of the oppositions involved is highly vulnerable and unstable both in its own right and in relation to all the others, so that connections will *always* be produced "where the model envisages oppositions." Even if we put aside the Movement's problematic notions of masculinity and femininity we can see deep ambivalence in its class commitments, as also in its putative privileging of the "state" over the "personal." This is not to say that such ambivalences are unrelated to the matter of sexuality, only that no one term in the paradigm provides the exclusive key to all the others.

33. It is interesting to note Amis's outrage when bourgeois pretensions began to manifest themselves in English pubs in the early seventies (a development roughly parallel with the emergence of "fern bars" in the United States). The new pubs, Amis said, were "fast becoming uninhabitable. The interior of today's pub has got to look like a television commercial, with all the glossy horror that implies. Repulsive 'themes' are introduced: the British-battles pub, ocean-liner pub, Gay Nineties pub. . . ." The pub, in short, had been overwhelmed by mass culture. Comments such as these are consistent with the stratifica-tion and gendering of mass culture which characterize Movement writing. As a traditional lower-middle and working-class institution, the pub is "masculine"; but when it attempts to make itself chic according to the middle-class fashion code, it is soon emasculated. In general, mass cultural phenomena are seen as more feminine the more they answer to demands of fashion rather than tradition. See Amis, *On Drink* (New York, 1973) 13.

34. Richard Hoggart, *The Uses of Literacy: Changing Patterns in English Mass Culture* (London, 1957) 152; the line is quoted by Sinfield (*Literature, Politics, and Culture* 64).

being Civilized. Such an operation, which casts the Movement writer as a paradoxically privileged outsider and underdog, does more to reinforce than to disrupt the association of the literary/artistic/academic spheres with effeminacy and of the popular cultural strata with robust masculinity.

But while Dixon clearly prefers the town to the gown, and is himself a lower-middle-class, grammar-school-educated Northerner, it would be incorrect to conclude that the traditional masculine values he represents are identified simply or exclusively with the lower classes. The other important character who shares with Dixon the positive traits of the masculine hero— his blunt common sense and plain, unaffected way of dealing, as well as his manly enthusiasm for alcohol—is Gore-Urquhart, a millionaire Scot and the closest thing the novel offers to a full-fledged aristocrat.

Gore-Urquhart is a prominent and much admired "devotee of the arts" whose life seems to consist entirely in locating the cultural institutions and projects most worthy of his patronage, and in having "persons of distinction" come to stay at his country house (47). We might well expect Dixon to be repulsed by all this. It is after all Dixon who argues for the aggressive redistribution of wealth, while Bertrand, caricature of the phony and talentless bohemian artist, mouths reactionary clichés about the "essential role" of the rich as guardians of England's "beautiful things" (51, 52). Yet Dixon joins eagerly in the general groveling before this figure of benign wealth and power, actually blushing with pleasure when, after being introduced, he finds that Gore-Urquhart has "caught his name" (110). Nor, when Gore-Urquhart finally steps forth to rescue him from the effeminizing world of the academy, does Dixon suffer any pangs of a guilty conscience; the possibility that earning five hundred a year as Gore-Urquhart's private secretary might involve some sort of moral or political compromise is never entertained.[35]

---

35. This problem of the novel's ending—i.e., of the novel's refusal or inability to see its ending as a problem, as a moral dilemma for the protagonist—is discussed in Morrison, *The Movement* 71–72. Morrison quotes the 1955 letter to *Encounter* in which John Wain identified the "main butt" of *Lucky Jim* and other Movement satires as "the aping of upper-class culture by the provincial bourgeoisie" and not, as most readers then saw it, upper-class culture itself. Morrison appears not to "accept this reading in its entirety," but he nonetheless sees clearly the "ambivalence" in Amis's fiction "which allows 'old' values—social inequality, 'elitist' culture, metropolitan patronizing of the provinces—to be preserved while seeming to be under attack" (72). Though my own argument frames this ambivalence rather differently, I am indebted to Morrison's study, the best full-length work on the Movement.

A similarly troublesome ending can be found in Lodge's *Nice Work*. The protagonist, Robyn Penrose, is said to be a committed Marxist feminist and an uncompromising

The upper-class world of Gore-Urquhart, no less than the lower-class world of the pub,[36] is represented as fundamentally compatible with the hero's manly—in fact, as it turns out *gentle*manly—system of values.

The novel's comic strategy, buttressed by a calculated distribution of masculinity, is thus to attack the sociocultural middle while valorizing (and asserting the common interests of) the upper elites and the ordinary working-class Englishman. Indeed, this strategy is apparent in the construction of Gore-Urquhart himself, who is not only socially and culturally superior to the university crowd but also more down to earth, more "a man of the people," as Amis put it in an interview.[37] At the college's annual ball, Gore-Urquhart is less elegantly turned out than many of the other guests, and pronounces himself happy to stay in the bar among "the rabble" (109). With his heavy Lowland accent and Scottish nationalist sympathies he quickly wins over the surly bartender Maconochie, who (to Dixon's amazement and delight) makes an exception to the college's "halves-only" rule and smuggles full pints of beer to Gore-Urquhart's table. The appearance of these manly, pub-sized beers amid all the womanly, college-sized half-pints marks Gore-Urquhart as a true man of the people, while at the same moment his seemingly casual aside to Jim—"You're in luck, Dixon"—marks him as the comic novel's requisite wealthy benefactor, its intervener from *above*.

Christine, who is Gore-Urquhart's niece, reflects this same ideal melding of common and aristocratic elements. On the one hand, she is so clearly above "the huge class . . . destined to provide [Dixon's] own womenfolk" that at first meeting the very "sight of her seemed an irresistible attack on his habits, standards, and ambitions: something designed to put him in his place

---

opponent of Thatcher's market capitalism. Yet when at the end of the novel she suddenly inherits two hundred thousand pounds, she uses it to achieve a happy reconciliation with the male antagonist, whose thoroughly capitalist (and traditionally sexist) industrial venture she agrees to bankroll without so much as a glance toward the political compromises this decision entails. Like Amis, Lodge does not take the intellectual's opposition to the established social order seriously enough to let it interfere with his comic ending.

36. It is probably more accurate to say that Gore-Urquhart belongs to the very upper tier of the middle class, while the pub life to which Dixon escapes from the college represents the lower tier. Strictly speaking, the novel offers no real working-class or upper-class characters. Nonetheless, its effect is to draw connections between "upper" and "lower" while excluding the "middle," and there is no basis for supposing that a different pattern of inclusion would emerge if one extended beyond Gore-Urquhart (or "below" the pub crowd) on the social scale.

37. "Gore-Urquhart, who is Jim's eventual savior and benefactor, is certainly a man of the people who has made his way . . . " (Salwak, "Interview" 8).

for good" (39). Indeed, "the notion that women like this were never on view except as the property of men like Bertrand" is so ingrained in Dixon that when Christine later permits him to dance with her he finds it hard to believe that "the men near them wouldn't spontaneously intervene to prevent him" (39, 113). The conflation of sexual desire with class ambition is made perfectly explicit here, as it is in Larkin's *Jill* (1946), John Wain's *Hurry on Down* (1953), John Braine's *Room at the Top* (1957), and other Movement and Angry novels. Dixon makes no bones about the fact that beautiful women are a form of "property" signifying special privilege and that ultimately the "possession of the signs of sexual privilege is the important thing, not the quality nor the enjoyment of them" (108).

Critics such as Elizabeth Wilson and Jonathan Dollimore have ably examined the compromises and limitations that such a view entails for the Movement and Angry attacks on existing class relations,[38] but it is worth noting some compromises in the way the class lines themselves are drawn here as well. Though Christine is clearly valuable property, she does not dress the part of privilege. In fact, she wears the same plum-colored corduroy skirt and unornamented white blouse on so many occasions that Dixon begins to wonder if she has any other outfits. Nor has she taken the trouble to straighten her "sightly irregular" front teeth (71), to correct her "rather unmusical" laugh and the "faint cockney intonation about her voice" (70, 202), or to suppress her slightly unladylike enthusiasm for food (67). And these "loopholes of . . . vulgarity" in her "refined façade" make Christine emphatically more, rather than less attractive to Dixon (141). The irregular teeth, for example, prove "more disturbing to his equanimity than regularity could possibly have been" (71). For it is one of the organizing principles of *Lucky Jim* that the "common touch" counts among the signs of deserved privilege, separating the truly "U" from the "non-U,"[39] the worthy elite from the vulgar pretenders.

38. Wilson, *Only Halfway to Paradise* 154; Jonathan Dollimore, "The Challenge of Sexuality," in *Society and Literature, 1945–1970*, ed. Alan Sinfield (London, 1983) 64–71.

39. The U/Non-U controversy, sparked by Nancy Mitford's article "The English Aristocracy," *Encounter*, July 1955, and fueled by Evelyn Waugh's response, "An Open Letter to the Honble Mrs Peter Rodd" *Encounter*, December 1955, received attention for several years in the English newspapers and culture magazines. The sudden heightening of concern with precise gradations of class can be read as a symptom of (1) unease within the established middle class resulting from real and imagined leveling effects of the postwar welfare state, and (2) unease within the lower classes who were now being encouraged to think of themselves as part of the "bourgeoisie without a proletariat" which postwar England had supposedly become. My point is that Amis's seemingly contemptu-

Of course "vulgarity" is a middle-class category: the middle class invokes it to make distinctions that operate only within the middle class, for whom alone such distinctions are socially necessary. Thus too pronounced a concern with vulgarity may itself be regarded as a form of vulgarity, a sign that one is too preoccupied with and defensive about one's class status to be regarded as altogether U (which perhaps accounts for Nancy Mitford's and Evelyn Waugh's embarrassed discomfort when they found themselves at the center of seemingly endless U/non-U debates).[40] Conversely, a selective flaunting of vulgarity, an apparent enjoyment of vulgarity, can be (in addition to its value as a "masculine" indicator) a middle-class way of simulating lofty-aristocratic as well as bedrock-commoner indifference to this whole arena of middle-class negotiation.

At any rate, the much celebrated "vulgarity" of *Lucky Jim* is perhaps best understood in terms of this lofty disdain for the cultured middle classes. Amis's quite limited and strategic vulgarities (the emphasis on drinking and vomiting; the occasional rude insults directed at monuments of high culture) signal an alliance with the upper classes—represented by Gore-Urquhart and Christine—fully as important as that with the pub crowd. For the old-maidish (i.e., effeminate), middle-class, Bloomsburyish posture of militant antivulgarity is ultimately represented as more egregiously vulgar than that which it seeks to proscribe. This is why Amis could say about his notorious allusion to "some skein of untiring facetiousness by filthy Mozart" (63) that the point was "to annoy Mozart lovers, not denigrate Mozart."[41] The joke strikes not at high culture as such (the work of Mozart) but at the expanding middle-class culture clacques, whose very sensitivity to such gibes, and whose devotion to taste tests ("tests," as Dixon puts it, of one's "reactions to

---

ous detachment from the concerns of Waugh and Mitford should be recognized as a strategy for negotiating precisely the structure of differentiated class positions that the U/Non-U controversy was all about. The Mitford piece is reprinted in *A Talent to Annoy*, ed. Charlotte Mosley (London, 1986) 92–105; the Waugh in *The Essays, Articles and Reviews of Evelyn Waugh*, ed. Donat Gallagher (Boston, 1983) 494–502.

40. I am thinking, for example, of Mitford's increasing insistence, as the "U" affair wore on, that her original article had been just a "joke." To take seriously the class implications of saying "note paper" rather than "writing paper," as thousands of middle-class *Encounter* readers clearly did, would itself be quite conspicuously non-U. Thus while Mitford initially described the piece as "full of teases" but "very fair" and accurate in its analysis, a year later she wrote with some exasperation to Waugh: "Can you get over them going *on* with U? I mean really we've had enough—even I have & you know how one loves ones own jokes" (*Talent to Annoy* 92).

41. Quoted in Morrison, *The Movement* 75.

culture" [24]), betrays their specifically middle-class preoccupations. Under scrutiny, however, such a joke appears curiously self-canceling, for it requires that the joker make a display of his cultural capital (Dixon knows *Mozart's* facetiousness when he hears it) in order to establish his philistine credentials. The impulse of the joke is a kind of competitive one-upsmanship disguised as a refusal to play the middle-class culture game; the vulgarity it asserts is a condescending vulgarity.

The point is simply that a novel whose ostensible philistinism scandalized reviewers at *Encounter* or the *Sunday Times* is not necessarily antielitist. Despite the fact that the novel's two explicit political dialogues both favor a Labour line (and Amis, we should remind ourselves, was still voting Labour until 1965)[42] its satire rests as heavily on a Flaubertian as on a proletarian hostility toward the bourgeoisie.[43] If the hero's professed socialism carried any weight, there would be obvious problems with the heroine Amis has prepared for him, for Christine not only declares herself opposed to progressive taxation and the welfare state but appears to find political discussion in general "a bit irritat[ing]" and urges Dixon not to "talk in that strain, if you don't mind" (52). But since manners and taste (or strategic lack of manners and taste) always supersede doctrine as indicators of value in this kind of novel, it doesn't matter that Christine is a Tory provided she isn't boring about it; and her dislike of political talk makes clear that she won't be boring about it. Her family's wealth, which we might have expected to be a liability in Dixon's eyes, is on the contrary a crucial asset, part of what makes her so undeniably superior to the whole middle-class crowd that hovers sycophantically around her uncle. Though her class superiority is represented indirectly, and very traditionally, in terms of extraordinary physical beauty, we know that it ultimately rests on a system of financial privilege which neither Dixon nor Amis seems at all anxious to disrupt.

42. "In 1964 I voted Labour for the last time, . . . and voted Conservative for the first time in the 1967 GLC elections" (*Lucky Jim's Politics* 5).

43. Amis levels this same charge at leftist writers of the thirties "like Auden, Spender, Day Lewis": "Even in a comparatively straightforward political play like *The Dog beneath the Skin* the actual political content, even the anti-fascist content, is very small. It is jostled by a whole lot of other interests, in which the desire to shock the *bourgeoisie* was very important. And that *bourgeoisie* which Auden and his friends were so interested in ridiculing and denouncing was the *bourgeoisie* of Flaubert rather than that of Marx, from whom they merely borrowed a few technical-sounding terms to use about it" (*Socialism and the Intellectuals* 4). To my mind this description suits Amis's own early writing much better than it does Auden's work in the thirties.

Class, then, maps on to the novel's gendered discourse of culture in a way that exploits overlaps between working-class and elitist contempt for bourgeoisified academic and cultural institutions. In this respect the campus novel begins to run in an ideological direction exactly counter to the New Left of the later fifties and sixties. For the New Left, as Sinfield has provocatively argued, was basically a dissident "middle-class subculture" that "defined itself against both high culture and working-class culture," aiming at something both less elitist than the former and less frivolous, conformist, and commercial than the latter.[44] It is not altogether clear that this pattern of class identifications is in itself more radical or progressive than that which structured the Movement outlook on culture: both vantages are problematic. But one can see that, insofar as the campus novel had its roots in Movement rather than New Left ideology, it would tend, in the sixties at least, to find its effective cultural "position"—its most congenial locale on the cultural map—among those who rejected the aims of leftist activism.

Another key concern of the Movement, the relative cultural significance of London versus the provinces, manifests itself in *Lucky Jim* in a somewhat similar way. Many commentators have followed Donald Davie, who in 1957 located the sociological importance of the Movement in the challenge it posed, as "a more or less coherent group" of provincial writers, to "the monopoly of British culture sustained for generations in the London haut-bourgeois."[45] To Davie, the Movement was important both as a symptom and as an instrument of the decline in London's cultural hegemony, and implicitly in the hypercosmopolitan, antiprovincial orientation associated (somewhat misleadingly) with the modernists. But as Blake Morrison has pointed out, "this picture of an exodus from London is . . . a belying of what [actually] happens in movement texts"; the narrative trajectory in *Lucky Jim*, as in other Movement novels, is not "out of and away from London but into and towards it."[46]

To a certain extent the novel does stake out a position of authentic Englishness in the provinces, mocking the London artists and intellectuals not only for being unmanly and tiresomely bourgeois in their dutiful consumption of "good" culture, but also for being un-English, affecting inauthentic continental lifestyles. The bearded, beret-wearing Bertrand, arriving from London for the Welches' arty weekend, is ridiculously condescending, declaring himself

44. Sinfield, *Literature, Politics, and Culture* 260, 265.
45. Quoted in McDermott, *Kingsley Amis* 25.
46. Morrison, *The Movement* 64.

pleased "to come down here and know that the torch of culture is still in a state of combustion in the provinces" (40). His brother, "the effeminate writing Michel," is so determined to be cosmopolitan that he makes himself sick eating "filthy foreign food . . . cooked in olive oil" (i.e., "coagulated flour-and-water and peasant's butter-substitute") and is obliged to come out to the provinces to recuperate on some less pretentious "English fare" (178).

But in ridiculing the "indefatigably Gallic" Welch brothers, the novel is not really satirizing the London cultural establishment. We should keep in mind that the Welch brothers' cosmopolitanism is partly a veneer on their own semiprovincial background; they are no more born and bred Londoners than Dixon is. Indeed, in many respects, Dixon's attitude toward London and the cultural elite is identical to theirs. He is ruled by the same powerful "desire to leave the provinces for London" (26), and when he arrives there (having most recently fled the same provincial town that they did) he will hold the very job within the London art world that Bertrand had hoped for, and be attached to Bertrand's former girlfriend. If Dixon represents a greater challenge to the London cultural establishment than does Bertrand, whose fawning attachment to "rich people" and "beautiful things" is continually mocked, it is only because of his superior temperament, his inherent "decency." Dixon, it is supposed, will bring his down-to-earth, pubgoing attitudes with him to London; like his revered boss Gore-Urquhart, he will traffic in the London art world without losing his masculine identity or his common touch. Like the modernist he takes for his antagonist, the Movement writer wants to maintain some kind of connection with the "true" but remote center of England (the smaller, more rustic community) even while he struggles for position in the largest of large cities.

This familiarly ambivalent geographics enables *Lucky Jim* to have it both ways, making Little Englandism as much the object of its humor as cosmopolitanism. It is characteristic that Michel's making himself sick on pretentious continental cuisine is only half the joke; the "final stroke" that draws a laugh out of Dixon is Michel's hope of recuperating on the abominable provincial diet at his parents' (178). Indeed, in their extreme forms, beret-wearing cosmopolitanism and recorder-playing traditionalism appear to be natural counterparts, interchangeable "aspects" of the ghastly world view that all the Welches embody—a world view clearly meant to typify the effeminized bourgeoisie. "My own interests," Professor Welch explains to Dixon,

"have turned more towards this English tradition in the last few years. Whereas my wife's are . . . I always sum her up as a Western European first and an English-woman second. With her, you see, with her sort of Continental way of looking at things, almost Gallic you might say she is in some things, well, the things that are so important to me, the English social and cultural scene, with a kind of backward-looking bias in a sense, popular crafts and so on, traditional pastimes and that, well, to her that's an aspect in a way, you see, just an aspect—a very interesting aspect, of course, but no more than an aspect," and here he hestitated as if choosing the accurate term, "a sort of aspect of the development of Western European culture, you might say. You can see it most clearly, really, in her attitude towards the Welfare State, and it's a great advantage to be able to view that problem in what you might describe as a wider perspective. She argues, you see, that if people have everything done for them . . . " (176, ellipses in original)

The "sort of Continental way of looking at things" comes off as rather the more despicable vantage here; forced to choose, Dixon says at one point, he would defend even Neddy Welch against his horrible wife. The choice seems to suggest some slight preference for the banal, little-village-idea romantic socialism of Neddy over the authoriatarian leanings of Mrs. Welch, with her "attitude towards 'so-called freedom in education,' her advocacy of retributive punishment," and so forth (176). But Neddy's investment in popular English traditions, with its "kind of backward-looking bias," is itself pointedly parodied in the cynical closing lines that Dixon prepares (but in the event can't quite bring himself to read out loud) for his public lecture on Merrie England:

Each of us can resolve to do something, every day, to resist the application of manufactured standards, to protest against ugly articles of furniture and tableware, to speak out against sham architecture, . . . to say one word against the Yellow Press, against the best-seller, against the theatre-organ, to say one word for the instinctive culture of the integrated village-type community. In that way we shall be saying a word, however small in its individual effect, for our native tradition, for our common heritage, in short, for what we once had and may, some day, have again—Merrie England. (205, my ellipsis)

Indeed, this kind of native traditionalism and glorification of the preindustrial provincial way of life is an even more common object of the novel's ridicule than the affected continentalism of Mrs. Welch and her sons. It is this sort of thing—"the home-made pottery crowd, the organic husbandry crowd, the recorder-playing crowd" (227)—that Dixon is most desperate to escape. And it is by publicly denouncing the "conjectural, nugatory, deluded, tedious rubbish" of the Merrie England crowd at the very climax of his drunken-lecture fiasco that Dixon wins the support of Gore-Urquhart and thereby does manage to escape the provinces and take up a place in the (presumably cosmopolitan) London art world.

Ultimately, then, the novel is not much concerned to discriminate between the admirers of the Continent and the traditional-English-village types, casting them as merely two of the more common varieties of culturist bore. What is interesting is that these ostensibly boring and commonplace culturists are ridiculed precisely for deviating from the common, for spurning the ordinary cultural pursuits and pastimes in favor of more exotic or remote ones. Whether this remoteness is geographical like that of the Continent or chronological like that of Merrie England and the integrated village community is of no great moment; either can be made to seem comic by foregrounding its discontinuites with the actual scene of contemporary lived experience.

There is a valuable, a potentially progressive, edge to this antiexoticism, at least insofar as it resists the tendency of high-minded culturists in the fifties (on the left as well as the right) to disseminate the "correct" kind of culture as antidote to such inauthentic popular forms as American movies, televised football, and Tin Pan Alley pop tunes. *Lucky Jim* makes available a standpoint from which F. R. Leavis, Richard Hoggart, Raymond Williams, E. P. Thompson, Perry Anderson, David Daiches, and most of the other major players in the culture and education debates can all be seen as reaching much too far afield (or much too far into a romanticized past) for a "good" culture to supplant the actual cultural practices of ordinary working people. But, at the same time, this fear and loathing of the exotic are part and parcel with the misogynist anti-intellectualism, the hostility toward all "female" counterlogics or obstructions to reason and "common sense," which is continually expressing itself in the jokes of the novel. Ultimately, as I argue below, what makes the campus novel work, what has sustained the genre, is not its attachment to actually existing popular culture—an attachment that, however tentative or intermittent, seems to me mostly laudable—but rather its confluence with a protean and powerful current of British anti-intellectualism. For it is this ideological confluence that effects, in the campus novel as elsewhere in postwar culture, a harnessing of popular energies to the narrow communitarian agenda of the cultural elite.

English at the Center

> These are the fifties, not the twenties. . . . What good is it being an intellectual? This is the time of the common man. You miss everything if you are an intellectual.
> —Malcolm Bradbury, *Eating People Is Wrong*

In *Education and the University* (1948) Leavis invoked English as a central, "non-specialist" discipline around which all the other disciplines might be brought into coherent interrelation. What were at that time the more arcane or remote aspects of the discipline—the Germanic-philological component, the emphasis on Anglo-Saxon[47]—Leavis was anxious to jettison in order to bolster the appeal of English and its legitimacy as a sort of intellectual commons or meetingplace. English, for Leavis, was to provide a "humane centre" for the diverse fields of higher education, a shared point of unity for England's "Educated Class." The Educated Class would then in its turn effect a kind of unification of the entire society, supplying a sense of "common enterprise" and cultural centeredness for the national community as a whole.[48]

Four decades later this view of English as a discipline which occupies and secures the center of the center of the community, and which ought therefore to be "non-specialist"—even, Leavis was willing to accept the term, "amateur[ish]"[49]—continues to inform the culture and education debates. Though participants in these debates seem to accept the presence in other disciplines of highly technical vocabularies, new theoretical or conceptual apparatuses, and extensive interchange with continental schools of thought, they frequently draw a unique line around English, whose practitioners, despite their highly developed literary critical skills, are still expected to conform in some fundamental way to the ideal of the home-grown, resolutely common-sensical "amateur." I want to argue that the appeal of the campus novel rests, in more ways than one, on the persistence of this hostility to specialization where English is concerned, and on the particular thinking of culture and community which gives rise to it. Amis's treatment of "flatulent" medievalist research in *Lucky Jim* (he also published a 1957 piece in the *Spectator* called "Anglo-Saxon Platitudes" rudely denouncing *Beowulf, Piers Plowman,* and other "boring" long poems in Old English)[50] is to be understood as an early moment in a postwar discourse of antispecialism which is in fact directed against intellectualism as such and which may be traced to the antijargon and antitheory jokes of the more recent campus novels.

A typical instance of the latter can be found in Lodge's *Nice Work,* whose heroine, Robyn, is taken aback to find her boyfriend Charles reading a book on investment banking. Though Charles, like Robyn, is an aspiring literary critic, he has lately developed a fascination for "what's going on in the City" (219). When pressed by Robyn, who wouldn't have believed he "could ever

47. See *Education and the University,* where Leavis calls for an "emancipation from Anglo-Saxon" in English studies, with all its "associated encumbrances" (40).

48. Ibid. 24, 27, 28.

49. Ibid. 59.

50. Kingsley Amis, "Anglo-Saxon Platitudes," *Spectator,* 5 April 1957.

get interested in business," Charles explains: "This isn't business. . . . It's not about buying and selling real commodities. It's all on paper, or computer screens. It's abstract. It has its own rather seductive jargon—arbitrageur, deferred futures, floating rate. It's like literary theory" (219). Someone is certainly being put down here, but it is not immediately clear just who. Investment bankers? Literary theorists? The idealistic Robyn, who thinks literary critics are somehow above the world of business? The cynical or deluded Charles, who is prepared to overlook the difference between oppositional and hegemonic uses of abstraction?

Indeed, the value of this sort of joke for the campus novel is precisely its ability to organize and exploit a considerable range of social antagonisms. Such jokes appeal, first of all, to a generalized British hostility toward intellectuals, experts, and ivory-tower elites of any stripe. This resentment of intellectuals is by no means monolithic or univocal, but jokes like Lodge's can effectively bring together its various strains. Consider, for example, two possible nonacademic (and more or less typically anti-intellectual) readers of *Nice Work*: a Labour-voting small businesswoman struggling through hard times in the North and a thriving young Tory financial consultant in London. While the latter could be expected to identify with the denizens of the City, the former would more likely regard them as the virtual standard of loathsome 1980s parasitism. But in either case the joke functions effectively as a vehicle for anti-intellectual suspicion and hostility. For the reader who detests investment bankers, Charles's analogy is a straightforward and pleasurable insult to academic and arty types, whose activities she is prepared to regard as something less than "real work." But the young financier can enjoy the joke here as well, since the incongruous equation of arbitrageur with literary theorist can be read as an effective counterattack on the latter's infuriating moral arrogance, a way of reducing the lefty intellectuals to the same moral plane as the capitalists they're always running down.

At the same time, these kinds of jokes make an appeal to the academic insider; the campus novel is, after all, particularly popular on campuses. The jokes can appeal to the established academic expert's more or less indiscriminate hostility to emergent forms of expertise—whether literary theory or technologies of the body—since new and incomprehensible specialties imply a dynamism in the academic sector which can eventually render one's own special competences obsolete. The jokes can also provoke the more focused hostilities of a specialist whose own orientation runs counter to that of the particular specialism at issue. Some Marxist-feminist critics, for example, though by no means hostile to literary theory in general, might find the equation of a certain brand of ambitious young male theoretician with the investment banker a telling conceit. (Lodge's joke would, however, depend in this case on a distinction that the text does little elsewhere to reinforce, between Robyn's concretely historical Marxist-feminist literary theory and the more arid or formalist literary theory of her politically suspect lover.) Finally, there are places in this comic transaction for academic insiders of the vehemently "non-specialist" variety. Leavisite literary *critics* can experience their sudden glory at the expense of literary *theorists*—Marxist-feminists and deconstructionists alike, along with all other scholars who pursue a "specialist" line too far from the generalist or "amateur" ideal of English studies. For in asserting a similarity between the literary theorist and the corporate takeover artist, the joke suggests that all this higher froggy and yank nonsense is merely a short-term, opportunistic phenomenon, a rather discreditable 1980s fad, which, once over with, will have left the timeless core of the discipline untouched.

What the antispecialist joke can accomplish, in short, is a spurious fusion or alignment of quite diverse antagonisms on the field of culture and education. The justifiably resentful working-class outsider and the complacent tenured professor, the Thatcherite bureaucrat who wishes to dismantle the universities and the Leavisite academic who wishes to elevate them to primary and central status in the community—all can be made to share a laugh and an apparent object of disdain through this form of comic transaction. One cannot say of such jokes that their true orientation is left-populist rather than right-elitist, or vice versa. The whole point is that these orientations will tend to converge and infuse one another, obscuring the real contradictions and social stakes involved, wherever anti-intellectualism is comically deployed. When we read the jokes of the campus novel it does not settle anything to point out that, say, David Lodge was himself a disseminator of continental literary theory in the early eighties[51] or that the *Black Paper* project to which Amis contributed his proto-Thatcherite denunciations of progressive education was initially conceived in pro-Labour terms.[52] The lifeblood of campus satire is a ubiquitous and homogenizing anti-

51. David Lodge, *Working with Structuralism: Essays and Reviews on Nineteenth- and Twentieth-Century Literature* (Boston, 1981).

52. Cox and Dyson report their surprise at being branded Tory reactionaries, since they were still loyally supporting Labour at the time of the first *Black Paper*'s appearance in 1969. Moreover, as the coeditors of *Critical Quarterly*, they had frequently published Raymond Williams's work in the early sixties and had urged that the Leavisite traditional canon for English studies be enlarged to include such "current classics" as Williams's *Culture and Society* and Hoggart's *Uses of Literacy*. See Stuart Laing, "The Production of Literature," in Sinfield, *Society and Literature* 148–49.

intellectualism that obscures contradictions and encourages impossible alliances at every level of the discourse on culture and education.

Perhaps the most fundamental of these contradictions reveals itself in a characteristic remark of Leavis's. English studies, said Leavis, should be the university's "special—but not specialist—discipline"—the discipline, that is, whose special task would be the training of "a non-specialist intelligence."[53] What Leavis nearly comes out with here is that this most special of disciplines, with all the special training it entails, unavoidably amounts to another specialism. The only difference is that a crucial part of the specialized training goes in this case toward the veiling of the discipline's specialist character. A certain group of very specially trained intellectuals, whose training constitutes a formidable barrier of exclusion, can thus describe all other specialisms as marginal, cliquish, centrifugal in their cultural effect, while claiming for themselves an open, inclusive, and unifying position at the center of the community.

Leavis knew very well he was defending an elite, as did the university English teachers who launched the *Black Paper* movement. But it is an elite whose elitist character is constantly being slipped out of view by means of metaphors of the "centre" and by vehement exclusion of anything deviant from or marginal to this axiomatic common cultural ground. Always at the center of a preexisting but imperiled "community," never atop a pyramid of negotiable power relations, this special class of "ordinary Englishmen" has continually to signal its rejection of anything too exotic, too foreign, too fancy, too female, too remote in time, or otherwise too divergent from traditional "community" standards. For by this means the specially trained anti-specialist elite—not "tough intellectuals" but anti-intellectual intellectuals—effects a crucial alliance with the excluded and properly resentful majority, in perpetuating barriers of exclusion and preserving positions of privilege.

As we know, Amis had by the mid-sixties made his own antidemocratic sentiments clear. Fully as devoted to the categorical distinction between "bright" students and "thicks" as to that between "nice"-looking women and "nasty" ones, he anticipated a major emphasis in the *Black Paper* movement on the value of intelligence testing and privileged educational streams.[54] For Amis and other Movement meritocrats, the postwar community could not

53. Leavis, *Education and the University* 43.

54. This emphasis, like that on "declining standards," was apparently based on the bogus research and fraudulent data of Cyril Burt, who wrote the lead article for *Black Paper Two*. See Simon, *Education and the Social Order* 398–99. Amis's comments about "bright" students versus "thicks" are found in *Lucky Jim's Politics* 7.

afford to dilute its bright stream with thicks, or to extend the thick stream beyond the secondary educational level. Describing himself as "frightfully reactionary," he told an audience of conservative educators and students that "more has meant worse" and that "there must be an elite, and there can't be equality."[55] The warm reception of such remarks at Oxford in 1967 reminds us that Thatcher—who was to replace Sir Edward Boyle as shadow minister of education within two years—would not be seen by everyone in the higher educational establishment as an implacable foe. But conscious supporters of this *Black Paper* elitism were undoubtedly in the minority. Far more pivotal in the rise and eventual triumph of educational conservatism has been the interleaving of its assumptions with populist rebellion against the university establishment—the stance of rebellion which finds its most characteristic expression in the campus novel. With its wide appeal among Labour-voting liberal culturists, the campus novel has never tended simply to embrace or reproduce unproblematically the cultural ideology of the right. One need only consider Somerset Maugham's bewildered and splenetic description of Jim Dixon in the *Sunday Times* to see how little Amis's hero accorded with the sensibilities of the cultural ruling class. (Though it is also true that Maugham, whose class assumptions led him notoriously to misread the novel as an *haut-bourgeois* attack on uncultured "scum" like Dixon, was actually closer to the mark than subsequent commentators have recognized).[56] But

55. Amis, *Lucky Jim's Politics* 17.

56. Maugham's summary of the novel appears in his contribution to the "Books of the Year" feature, *Sunday Times*, 25 December 1955, 4. His comments are often cited as an attack on *Lucky Jim*, but in fact he praised it as a timely, and indeed "ominous" indictment of vulgar young people like Dixon, who "do not go to the university to acquire culture, but to get a job, . . . [who] have no manners, and are woefully unable to deal with any social predicament. Their idea of a celebration is to go to a public house and drink six beers. They are mean, malicious, and envious. . . . They are scum." It is worth noting that what Maugham objected to in the young men of the fifties, that "they do not go to the university to acquire culture, but to get a job," is precisely what Amis objected to in the students of the sixties (who were looking for "vocational training"). It is in this respect that Maugham's reading of *Lucky Jim* seems to me more acute than is usually supposed. For there does appear to be in the novel a certain doubt whether even a bright provincial scholarship student like Dixon should really have gone to university in the first place—whether the university isn't already, in 1954, opening its doors too wide. After all, Dixon seems to have taken nothing from his university experience other than a job for which he is manifestly ill suited. The key difference, though, between Dixon and the sixties students who, Amis said, "do not understand . . . [the] purpose of university life" is that for all his philistinism Dixon has, in fact, acquired considerable cultural capital at university, though strictly of the nonspecialist, "amateur" variety. And as an ordinary bloke who carries his cultural capital

the point is that even the most "barbaric" satires of the institutions of higher learning are dependent on ways of thinking about culture and community which preclude any effective challenge to the prerogatives of a cultural and academic elite. There is a symptomatic tendency in *Lucky Jim* to remove from the satiric field some of the most obvious potential targets. Oxford and Cambridge, for example, are mentioned only once, and then merely to point up the contrast between "the way history might be talked about" on those glorious quadrangles and the sorry way it is talked about between red-brick walls in the provinces (8).

Moreover, in setting against the feminized, foreign-inflected, bourgeoisified cultural establishment a masculine sensibility ostensibly shared by the "decent" millionaire and the plain Englishman, by the powerful patron of the arts and the provincial pubgoer, the text ultimately appeals to a "higher" cultural standard rather than a more democratic one. *Lucky Jim* throws down no challenge to the most crucial assumption of neo-Arnoldian and Leavisite defenses of culture: that objective determinations of cultural value can be and have been made, that the greatness of a work of art resides in the work itself and not merely in the institutional mechanisms of its selection and privilege. Though Welch's and Bertrand's vacuous clichés about neoprimitivism and so forth are held up for scorn, there is no question that an urbane and upper-class "devotee of the arts" like Gore-Urquhart "knows what he's talking about" (112). It is essential to the final triumph of Dixon, who has been tormented by the thought that his rival Bertrand might actually "be a good painter" (112), that Gore-Urquhart pronounces Bertrand's pictures "no good" as soon as he sets eyes on them (234).

In *Lucky Jim* as in other campus novels, the real, material question of "community"—the question of cultural inclusion and exclusion, of what groups of people finally belong in the apparatuses of culture and may properly share in their operation—this question is addressed in primarily negative and narrowing ways. *Lucky Jim* can tell us who does *not* properly belong, who should *not* contribute to determinations of cultural value: not the arty and effeminate types, the vestiges of Bloomsbury, the neoromantics and neodecadents, the subjectivists, the dandies, the women; not the cosmopolitan avant-gardistes and high modernists after the letter, with their émigré chic and their passion for all things foreign; certainly not the ghastly provincial types, the bores of red-brick common rooms, the pretentious middle-class

---

lightly, Dixon is an ideal candidate for the reconfigured (defeminized, debourgeoisified) cultural apparatus Amis imagines for postwar England.

poetasters and enthusiasts of Merrie England. Even the good ordinary blokes like Jim Dixon aren't really "fit for university life" (the demonstration of this point is what Maugham took to be the novel's main intention). Only a tiny elite of Oxbridge dons and wealthy patrons is finally credited with "knowing what they're talking about." Everyone else, apparently, belongs to that "more" that means "worse."

Here, as in so many instances of postwar discourse on education and culture, an investment in the "ordinary" citizen, in the "common" structures of knowing and feeling, in the idea of culture as that which sustains the bonds of "community"—this potentially inclusionary disposition exhausts itself in a series of exclusionary gestures. Drawing, both for its comic efficacy and for its continuing market power, on the popular suspicion of and hostility toward intellectual and high-cultural elites, the campus novel works this suspicion and hostility less into a desire for greater openness, for a more democratic and broadly based cultural apparatus, than for its opposite: a smaller and more tightly sealed elite. Through the joke-work of these texts a potentially radical energy resulting from quite justified feelings of exclusion and resentment is provoked into expression, but it is also managed in such a way as to reinforce the very walls of exclusion.

Five

Actually Existing Postmodernism:
The Comedy of Disorganization
in *The Golden Notebook*

> And you're even laughing, at this awful, pitiful mess.
> —Doris Lessing, *The Golden Notebook*

Near the beginning of Doris Lessing's 1960 novel *In Pursuit of the English*, the autobiographical narrator, a young *engagé* novelist from colonial Africa, observes that "the English" are like "the Working Class": "a platonic image, a grail, a quintessence."[1] As a middle-class Marxist, this narrator has spent most of her life in pursuit of the working class, striving to achieve a correct working-class viewpoint from which to produce her writing. In Africa, where she lived and labored for twenty-five years "in the closest contact with the black people, who are workers if nothing else," she began to think she had acquired "some knowledge, or intimation, or initiation by osmosis" into the working-class experience. But an indignant comrade explains to her that "the Africans in this country are not working-class *in the true sense*. They are semi-urbanized peasants" (13). After moving to England, where she lives on little money "in a household crammed to the roof with people who [work] with their hands," she begins once again to think she has served her "apprenticeship." But a member of the local watch committee remarks that "these are not the real working-class. They are the lumpen proletariat, tainted by petty bourgeois ideology" (13). When she argues that many of the working-class people with whom she has been most intimate, in Africa as well as in England, have been her comrades in the party, she is told that these are not the genuine article, either: "The Communist Party is the vanguard of the working-class and obviously *not typical*" (14). She decides to make a

1. Doris Lessing, *In Pursuit of the English* (New York, 1961) 13.

pilgrimage to a mining village, where she lives among mining families for a time and makes herself familiar with their way of life. But when she arrives back in London it is explained to her that miners "are members of a very specialized, traditionalized trade; mining is already (if you take the long view) obsolete. The modes of being, mores and manners of a mining community have nothing whatsoever to do with the working-class as a whole" (14). So she makes a second pilgrimage, this time to one of the New Towns, where there can be no question of the community's class complexion: everyone she meets is "a trade unionist, a member of the Labour party," or in possession of some "other evidence of authenticity." But at this point the futility of her quest is at last spelled out to her: "The entire working-class of Britain," she is told, "has become tainted by capitalism or has lost its teeth. It is petit bourgeois to a man. If you really want to understand the militant working-class, you have to live in a community in France. . . . Or better still, why don't you take a trip to Africa where the black masses are not yet corrupted by industrialism" (14).

This joke appears in a hundred guises throughout the first phase of Lessing's work: a man from Newcastle is "not English, not properly speaking," because "they're different from us, up in places like that" (*Pursuit* 64); an American producer of TV films wants to use the actual music of central African natives for an upcoming production until she learns that, at the time the story is set, the predominant music among central Africans was "jazz from America"—the "organic" forms emerged somewhat later.[2] We are used to thinking of such jokes in terms of the paradoxes of authenticity, the contradictions of a category that invokes both ideal and empirical frames of reference. But we should also think of these jokes in terms of ideological narratives (narratives of emancipation, narratives of belonging) that presuppose impossible communities, communities whose subjects are uncompromised, undivided, inexcessive, and bound to one another by a simple and natural logic of identity. The potential comedy of these ideological narratives is not only that of a society whose defining law or principle of selection, whose quintessence, excludes its own actual members, but that of a field of action on which the would-be political subject can never be in the right place at the right time. One is always too late or too early, too near or too far away, from the moment and the site of achieved community.

Lessing became entangled in the logic of these jokes somewhat earlier

2. Doris Lessing, *The Golden Notebook* (New York, 1973) 293. Hereafter cited parenthetically as *TGN*.

than did other members of the postwar intelligentsia because her multinational and multiaccentual background in leftist politics had thrown into unusually sharp relief the *disorganized* character of her own political identity and of oppositional British politics in general. Few figures are more difficult to situate firmly as political subjects on a cultural map of postwar England. There is, to begin with, the question of her generational position. Arriving in England from Southern Rhodesia in 1949, Lessing began publishing sexually "frank" stories and novels featuring rebellious young protagonists, which were in certain respects consonant with the work of the Movement and the Angry Young Men (e.g., formally, in their straightforward representationalism and resolutely metonymic language, and, thematically, in their use of robust male heterosexuality to mark healthy pockets of resistance in a pacified/effeminized postwar English society).[3] Edward Thompson, who welcomed Lessing onto the board of the *New Reasoner* in 1957, recalls thinking of her as someone who could help the journal (which carried a markedly "older" political ambience than did the other post-1956 journal of dissident communism, *Universities and Left Review*) reach out "to new and younger ('angry') constituencies."[4] But while other emergent writers were celebrating these youthful constituencies, Lessing was vehemently denouncing them. Her 1956 novel *Retreat to Innocence* is as thorough an indictment as the period has to offer of the bootlessly Angry postwar generation, with its apparent determination to rebel mainly against political rebellion itself. Julia Barr, the pretty but petulant university student who represents this generation in the novel (and who, typically, regards the intellectual work of the university as tedious nonsense), is basically a more interesting and nuanced version of Amis's beautiful young heroines: she is much like Christine Callaghan, who becomes irritated whenever people talk to her about politics (*Lucky Jim* 52); and she is much like Jenny Bunn in Amis's *Take a Girl like You* (1960), who clings to a set of good, old-fashioned values (romantic love, preservation of virginity, church-marriage, motherhood), opposing these to the messed-up

3. As Jonathan Dollimore points out in "The Challenge of Sexuality," this tendency to draw connections between heterosexual vigor and the good society carries over into Lessing's later writings. As regards *The Golden Notebook*, for example, Dollimore remarks that while the novel at various moments "contradicts almost all normative statements about sexuality," it also highlights uncritically Anna's insistence on vaginal orgasm, her horror of homosexuality, and her fear that (in her words) England is "a country full of men who are little boys and homosexuals and half-homosexuals . . . [with only] a few real men left" (72).

4. E. P. Thompson, "Preface," to Malcolm MacEwen, *The Greening of a Red* (Concord, Mass., 1991) x.

"modern" and cosmopolitan values of the previous generation. But this characteristic "retreat to innocence," this fear of politics and intellectualism, and this nostalgia for a society in which the simple moral ideas of the "Bible-class" have not yet (as Amis puts it in *Take a Girl like You* "taken a knocking" at the hands of sexual or intellectual sophistication,[5] are treated in Lessing with the quasi-sociological detachment of a worldly outsider, and never with the Movement or Angry writer's apparent self-investment. The author's main object of identification in the novel clearly is not Julia, in whom the rebelliousness of youth takes a symptomatically counterrevolutionary form, but rather Jan Brod, an aging and somewhat battered Jewish émigré from central Europe, a communist intellectual whose old-world wisdom and sexual savoir-faire nearly but don't quite succeed in rescuing Julia from the postwar slide into false consciousness.[6]

The point is that Lessing's political identifications in her adopted country were not those of "her" generation. When she arrived in England at the age of thirty she was contemporaneous with everyone and no one. Chronologically, she was contemporaneous with practically the entire first wave of postwar poets and novelists (Amis, Larkin, Braine, Wain, Enright, Burgess, Spark, and Murdoch were all born within five years of her) as well as with the young intellectuals who were to have the greatest impact on the "first" New Left: John Saville was then thirty-three, Richard Hoggart was thirty-one, Raymond Williams was twenty-eight, Edward Thompson was twenty-six. But she brought with her a long and intimate history of involvement in Communist-International politics which she shared with none of her fellow writers and not even, beyond a point, with the left intelligentsia. Thompson may have identified with the 1930s generation, but he was not formed within that generation to the extent that Lessing was; only Saville's background at the London School of Economics (where the Harold Laski circle gathered Britain's communist students together with opposition leaders from India and the African colonies) was remotely comparable.[7] To Thompson, it was

---

5. Kingsley Amis, *Take a Girl like You* (Harmondsworth, 1960) 317.

6. Doris Lessing, *Retreat to Innocence* (London, 1956).

7. Stuart Hall discusses political generations in his piece "The 'First' New Left: Life and Times," in *Out of Apathy: Voices of the New Left Thirty Years On*, ed. Robin Archer et al. (London, 1989) 11–38. As Hall sees it, the *New Left Review* represented the "coming together" not only of two leftist journals but of "two different political traditions" (21). The *Reasoner* group was "organically rooted in a provincial [i.e. northern] political culture" (23) and "belonged to a political generation formed by the politics of the Popular Front and the anti-Fascist movements of the thirties" (22). The *Universities and Left Review* contingent

Lessing's presumed solidarity with "new and younger ('angry') constituencies" which freed her from the static quarrels and recriminations of the Communist party's old guard and enabled her to become a "founder of the New Left."[8] But one could more accurately say it was Lessing's intensive and prolonged involvement in those party quarrels, and her consequent inability to see the crisis of belonging and belief in the old left, its ideological disorganization, as something completed and bygone, which set her apart both from the Angries and from many of her associates in the New Left.

What the left meant to Lessing, what was at stake in this period of its self-critique and attempted self-renewal, was not just the emancipation of the workers but also that of colonized peoples and of women. As a participant in Communist efforts to lead the anticolonial struggles in central and southern Africa, Lessing had been forced to reckon with Western Marxism's manifest failure to provide either the kind of analysis of the colonial situation or the practical tools of rebellion which were needed in the colonized lands. There were of course problems of racism within the colonial labor unions and even within the (mostly informal and illegal) colonial Communist groups.[9] Problems also arose from the extremely centralized organization of the Third Communist International, which bound anticolonial Communists to a remote,

was more "cosmopolitan," comprising a number of "exiles and migrants" (19), and the political formation of this group "was irrevocably 'post-war'" (22). This analysis differs somewhat from my own and makes Lessing's prewar political formation seem less of a sticking point as regards the *Reasoner* group. But since Lessing's cosmopolitanism and non-"organic" situation do not map onto the expected tendency here, this scheme by no means ameliorates the difficulties involved in situating her within the (increasingly fragmented and contradictory) postwar left. My point in indicating these problems is not to isolate Doris Lessing as a special case but to suggest reasons why she might have been more than usually aware of the inadequacy of the available categories of political identity: left/right, organic/inorganic, provincial/cosmopolitan, prewar/postwar, etc.

8. Thompson, "Preface" x.

9. A brief account of these problems can be found in Peter Weiler, *British Labour and the Cold War* (Stanford, Calif., 1988) 27–52. On the particular situation in Southern Rhodesia during Lessing's years there, see Eve Bertelsen, *"The Golden Notebook*: The African Background," in *Approaches to Teaching Lessing's "The Golden Notebook,"* ed. Carey Kaplan and Ellen Cronan Rose (New York, 1989) 30–36; and Murray Steele, "Doris Lessing's Rhodesia," in *Doris Lessing*, ed. Eve Bertelsen (Johannesburg, 1985) 44–54. Bertelsen notes that blacks in Southern Rhodesia were prohibited from participating in all forms of organization, including trade unions, and she suggests that this exclusion was the main obstacle to the development of an indigenous "revolutionary consciousness" (32), not the inappropriateness of Marxist doctrine—though she goes on to say that the doctrine was poorly adapted to the colonial situation (34).

high-handed, incompetent, and seemingly indifferent body of authority. (This is not even to mention the deplorable abuses of power which the autocratic structure made possible, abuses whose continued condonation by the various post-Comintern national CPs—including that of Great Britain —were obviously instrumental in the steady decline of memberships.)[10] But what Lessing and other colonial Communists began to perceive in the late thirties and forties were also the inherent problems in any attempt to understand and resist colonial hegemony by means of a political thinking that treats racism as a "secondary contradiction." As Communists, they were only secondarily and selectively concerned with the "colour bar"; as committed anticolonialists, they were only secondarily and selectively concerned with Africa's "working class." In Lessing's *Ripple from the Storm* (1958), the one black member in attendance at a meeting of the Zambesian (i.e., Rhodesian) Communist group dutifully rehearses the group's party line: "the Communists say racial prejudice is created by capitalism." But the very way he expresses this view of his situation marks an "uncomfortable" gap and failure of identification: "He had said 'the Communists' as if he wasn't one of them."[11]

In part because of her colonial background Lessing brought to England a far greater awareness of and concern with this problem of identity and solidarity than was normal in the emergent New Left (despite the fact that the "New" fraction was itself a symptom of this very problem). Other dissident Communists may have been "alert to the fragmentation and the emergence of new lifestyles" in postwar British society, but, as Raphael Samuel puts it, "we nevertheless took a two-camp [i.e., class] view of society as axiomatic."[12] This two-camp paradigm, with its orientation toward the idea of "working-class community" (everywhere visible in the early productions of the New Left),[13] was further strained in Lessing's case by the question of

10. Membership in the British CP peaked in December 1942 at about 56,000. Between then and 1975 membership declined in twenty-three of the thirty-three years, to about 33,000. Not surprisingly, the sharpest drop occurred in response to the events of 1956; by 1958 a third of the 1955 membership had abandoned the party, either to join Labour or, in smaller numbers, to assist in inaugurating the "new" communism. These numbers are taken from Peter Shipley, *Revolutionaries in Modern Britain* (London, 1976) 33.

11. Doris Lessing, *A Ripple from the Storm* (1958; New York, 1970) 116.

12. Raphael Samuel, "Born-Again Socialism," in Archer, ed., *Out of Apathy* 55.

13. What Samuel calls "our preoccupation with 'community'" ("Born-Again Socialism" 56) can be seen in the work of Richard Hoggart, Jeremy Seabrook, and Raymond Williams throughout the 1950s, as well as in that of the Institute for Community Studies, founded in 1954. In connection with the two-camp paradigm, see in particular chapter 3 of Hoggart's *Uses of Literacy*, "'Them' and 'Us.'"

gender. In this regard, too, the shortcomings of the party could seem at times to be simply a matter of a compromised or infected membership; the fact that misogyny is as pervasive among Communist men as elsewhere is thematized throughout the *Children of Violence* novels. Martha Quest, the heroine of those novels, remarks at one point that her male working-class comrades all "have this damned sentimental thing about [their] mothers," which leads them to present women with a laughable vision of the socialist community: "We'll abolish poverty, and give women freedom and then they'll simmer and boil, sacrificing themselves for everyone—like my mother" (*Ripple* 94). But while such misogynist distortions were by no means easily surmounted (even by the declaration of a "new" communism; Lessing's mockery here is directed not only at her wartime comrades but also at the idealizations of motherhood in the work of Hoggart and other New Leftists),[14] the more fundamental difficulty was plainly that posed by the Marxist reliance on community as the telos, and class as the category, of final analysis.

Of course, as Lessing was very much aware, while feminism could expose this as a problem in Marxism, it also reproduced the problem in a form of its own. Just as Marxism's investment in class causes race and gender to withdraw themselves to a secondary level in the analysis, so does the discourse of gender liberation effect a troubling occlusion of the other terms. Marie du Preez, the most outspoken feminist in the Zambesian Communist group, tells a gathering of mostly black men that in the last instance they are no different from their misogynist oppressors: "If there's one thing that teaches me there's no such thing as colour [it] is that men are men, black and white" (*Ripple* 186). Another woman in the group shares Martha's sense that the promised workers' paradise is scarcely worth fighting for since, from a feminist standpoint, it will leave power relations essentially unaltered. "As far as I can see," she tells Martha, "when we get socialism we'll [just] have to fight another revolution against men" (*Ripple* 247). It is always a matter of one ideological narrative superseding or overtaking another, never of their being

14. See the section "Mother" in Hoggart, *Uses of Literacy* 38–45. One should probably note Williams as an exception here, since his writing on community (in, for example, *Culture and Society* [London, 1958] 313–19) is far more complex and critical than that of most of his New Left comrades. As Jenny Bourne Taylor has argued, Williams's communitarianism was not organized, as Richard Hoggart's and Jeremy Seabrook's was, around the thought of a lost home where the idealized "good mother" of the working class is perpetually toiling. See Jenny Bourne Taylor, "Raymond Williams: Gender and Generation," in *British Feminist Thought: A Reader*, ed. Terry Lovell (London, 1990) 296–308, especially 301.

effectively articulated together. And indeed no such articulation is possible, for in each case society, both as a given state of affairs and as an ideally imagined community, is thought in terms of a single essence. Lessing's Martha Quest understands, as a Marxist, that the relations of production are the essential social relations; but as a feminist what she observes is that the "fabric of society" is "essentially male" (*Ripple* 19). Her difficulty, Lessing's, and that of the "leftist" in general (a term that in this period begins to acquire scare quotes), is that of being constituted as a political subject by various discourses of social essence whose closure to one another amounts to a foreclosure of the political itself.

Retreat to Innocence, A Ripple from the Storm, In Pursuit of the English, and many of Lessing's other early novels and stories thematize this crisis of closure for the fragmented and hopelessly disorganized political subject. In *The Golden Notebook* (1962) the crisis is embodied as well as thematized; it informs the structure and the language of the entire text. (And as I tried to suggest in Chapter 3, this more or less conscious playing out of the crisis of communitarianism may be regarded as one of the markers of a *postmodernist* literary practice.) The fact that this novel, which Lessing described as her major artistic engagement with the historical failure of Marxism, was hailed by many of its readers as a bold manifesto of the reemergent Women's Movement, tells us more about the book than either the Marxist or feminist vantage alone can do. To read Lessing as a late-sixties feminist *avant la lettre* is undoubtedly to miss the point and to erase the historical contradictions out of which her work was produced. But by the same token one must be wary of Lessing's dogmatic insistence (in her notorious 1971 Introduction) that the novel was simply "about" Marxism, a broad tracing across the mid-century of the "movements of various kinds of socialism, or Marxism, in advance, containment, or retreat" (xi). The point of such a description was not really to restore Marxism to a proper position at the center of the text but to force at least some consideration of the catastrophic political failures the novel is concerned to explore, and thereby to obstruct its overly optimistic appropriation or subsumption within any narrative of emancipation and belonging. Lessing did not want her novel to be read as a solution, a bible of the Women's Movement, but as a provocative illustration of a problem, or set of problems, in which feminism—along with all other available discourses of freedom and community—was implicated. And no one who read the novel as a tracking of "Marxism, in advance, containment, or retreat" could make the mistake of seeing it as a triumphant manifesto, for it clearly carries Lessing's sense that this most powerful and privileged narrative of emancipation was "finished as a force" by the early fifties (xi): there is retreat here, and containment, but no discernible advance. In short, the single-minded emphasis on Marxism in the 1971 Introduction is not so much a disavowal of feminism—even of the predominantly white and middle-class consciousness-raising feminism that Lessing was all too inclined to dismiss as a "small and quaint" project (xi)—as it is a disavowal of any premature circumvention of the problems *The Golden Notebook* was meant to embody.

But why should a novel that foregrounds the paralysis of the divided and disorganized political subject invite optimistic appropriations from feminist readers any more than from readers on the nonfeminist left? One reason is that *The Golden Notebook* seems to involve its readers in two different sorts of comic transaction, one attaching to a Marxist and the other to a feminist agenda. Marxist practice, as represented in the novel, is largely a play with orthodoxies. Language and behavior within the Communist party are subject to certain codes and rules whose increasingly inadequate or dysfunctional status is signalized without their ever actually being flouted. Lessing's paradoxically disillusioned-but-committed Marxists do not reject the normative codes of the old left, but they find themselves reproducing them ironically, or "parasitically," according to a joke-logic of cynical reason which ultimately discloses the inauthentic, self-parodic character of even the most "sincere" acts or statements of adherence. By contrast, feminist practice in the novel consists in quite boisterous transgressions, gay refusals to play by the rules of the patriarchal order. This practice, too, operates according to a kind of joke-logic, the logic of the carnival—but its comedy possesses a markedly different ethos from that of the cynic or the parasite.

In effect, then, the novel provokes and thematizes two distinct laughters: a (self-)parodic laughter that questions the authenticity of the utterance and is linked thematically with the struggle to maintain a Marxist political identity in a condition of subjective excess or fragmentation; and a transgressive laughter that questions the legitimacy of the law and is linked thematically with the struggle to make cultural space for a community of "free" women. It is not surprising that readers looked to this second laughter, and this second field of struggle, for a site of celebration. The comedy of transgression has exercised a wide appeal over the last thirty years, and feminists in particular have taken it to be more closely allied to a liberating politics than is the comedy of provocative parasitism. Insofar as *The Golden Notebook* marked not only the comic force of women's transgressions but the transgressive force of women's comic pleasure—and thus the possibility that a woman's laughter might serve as a strategic transgression or tactic of resistance—it anticipated a recurring and optimistic emphasis within feminist thought.[15] Just as recent feminist theory and performance art have done, *The Golden Notebook* seemed to aim toward the formation of a specifically feminist "cult of comedy,"[16] a new community of laughing women.

And yet, as I will try to show, the novel ultimately pursues the logic of transgression to a rather dispiriting inconclusiveness, insisting not so much on the limited effectivity of transgressive laughter as political practice, as on the inadequacy of the analytical framework within which that effectivity can be asserted. Moreover, in elaborating these problems in the logic of (feminist) transgression, the novel draws the whole problematic of women's freedom into an entanglement with the logic of (Marxist) (self-)parody. Ineluctable connections between these two inadequate political logics, which are also two modes of contemporary comic transaction, are drawn out both formally and thematically. The connections amount to a map of postmoder-

15. This interest became especially prominent in the French essentialist feminism of the seventies, which saw in women's laughter the possibility of a specifically "feminine syntax" outside of phallogocentricism. See, for example, Hélène Cixous, "The Laugh of the Medusa," and Annie Leclerc, *Woman's Word*, both excerpted in *New French Feminisms: An Anthology*, ed. Elaine Marks and Isabelle de Courtivron (Amherst, Mass., 1980). The topic has been pursued in a more concrete and somewhat less utopian way by American cultural feminists including Patricia Mellencamp, "Situation Comedy, Feminism, and Freud: Discourses of Gracie and Lucy," in *Studies in Entertainment*, ed. Tania Modleski 80–98, and Modleski herself, in "Rape vs. Mans/Laughter: Hitchcock's *Blackmail* and Feminist Interpretation," *PMLA* 102 (May 1987): 305 and *passim*. Much literary criticism deals with the feminist potential in "comedy" (usually conceived in generic terms); a range of this writing is collected in two recent volumes edited by Regina Barreca: *Last Laughs: Perspectives on Women and Comedy* (New York, 1988), and *New Perspectives on Women and Comedy* (New York, 1992). The important full-length literary/cultural studies are Judy Little, *Comedy and the Woman Writer* (Lincoln, Neb., 1983); Nancy Walker, *A Very Serious Thing: Women's Humor and American Culture* (Minneapolis, 1988); and Barreca's *They Used to Call Me Snow White . . . But I Drifted* (New York, 1991). A somewhat different, though no less optimistic, estimate of women's laughter is found in anthropological writings on symbolic inversion, for example Ivan Karp, "Laughter at Marriage: Subversion in Performance," in *Transformations of African Marriage*, ed. David Parkin and David Nyamwaya (Manchester, 1987), 137–54. A recent conference devoted entirely to women and laughter ("Tickled Pink," University of Colorado, Boulder, 16–18 March 1990) indicates continued academic concern with this topic. The proliferation of popular anthologies and collections, such as *Titters*, ed. Anne Beatts and Deanne Stillman (New York, 1976), and *Spare Ribs*, ed. Collier and Beckett, demonstrates strong interest outside the academy as well.

16. The phrase is here transported into a feminist context from Kenneth Burke, who frequently expresses a "conviction that *man's* only hope is a cult of comedy" (my emphasis). *Language as Symbolic Action: Essays on Life, Literature, and Method* (Berkeley, 1966) 20n.

nity which—precisely because it is so local and so unexhilarating, so fixed on the particulars of a crisis (that of failed articulation between and among Marxism, feminism, black nationalism, and other oppositional political formations)—manages very usefully to supplement the grander maps that have guided recent postmodernism debates. These debates have shared the novel's preoccupation with "the jokes people make," with the "new laughter" of the postmodern subject (68), but *The Golden Notebook* stands apart in linking both this laughter and its felt "newness," its frequent invocation as a marker of postmodernity, to a concrete set of problems which arose out of the old left's ideas of identity and community and persisted stubbornly in the attempted rethinkings of the New Left and the new social movements.

Women's Laughter and "Freedom" in *Free Women*

> A feminine text cannot fail to be subversive . . . to blow up the law, to break up the truth with laughter.
> —Hélène Cixous, "The Laugh of the Medusa"

As I have suggested, the commercial success of *The Golden Notebook*—which was not immediate but rather a phenomenon of the late sixties and seventies—can be attributed to readers for whom the novel was first and foremost a "feminine" text, a "subversive" text, a text with the power to "break up" the patriarchal law and liberate women from the (phallogocentric) "truth." I will argue that such readings entail a circumvention or denial of the very problem of oppositional politics, and of the oppositional political subject, whose relentless elaboration makes this novel an early and important text of literary postmodernity. But I should acknowledge at the outset that to the extent that such readings follow from a perception of women's laughter as a transgressive practice,[17] the novel offers them abundant support.

Throughout *The Golden Notebook* men monopolize humor, assuming it to be a properly male discourse—an assumption that continues even today to underwrite putatively scientific demonstrations of the inferiority of the fe-

---

17. That is, to use the definition Stallybrass and White borrow from Barbara Babcock, a practice "which inverts, contradicts, abrogates, or in some fashion presents an alternative to commonly held cultural codes, values and norms be they linguistic, literary or artistic, religious, social and political." Barbara Babcock, in *The Reversible World*, ed. Babcock (Ithaca, 1978) 14, quoted in Peter Stallybrass and Allon White, *The Politics and Poetics of Transgression* (Ithaca, 1986) 16.

male brain in processing "objectively humorous stimuli."[18] Of course what such laboratory data, as also the data of the novel, indicate is not essential difference but rather the existence of social prohibitions against women's joking and laughter. Men, for whom joke-work routinely serves the purposes of symbolic sexual violence and masculine ego maintenance,[19] are inclined to perceive women's laughter not only as a potential challenge to their social position but as a sexual threat, a castration threat. (As comedienne Anne Beatts has expressed it, a man "hears our laughter," regardless of its manifest object, as "bedroom laughter," laughter "at the size of his sexual apparatus.")[20] The result is that men intervene in various ways to discourage such laughter (except, as anthropologists have observed, among very young, old, or "ugly" women—women who fall outside the normative compass of male heterosexual desire),[21] and then they profess bewilderment at the humorlessness of the women they become involved with. "You never find anything humorous," Paul Blackenhurst tells Maryrose, his object of desire in the Black Notebook, the notebook of the culture industry. "You never laugh. . . . Whereas I laugh continuously" (428). "You don't laugh enough," complains Saul Green to Anna Wulf in the Golden Notebook, the notebook of ostensible artistic breakthrough. "Girls laugh. Old women laugh. Women of your age don't laugh" (638). The fact is that both Maryrose and Anna *do* laugh; the novel is much concerned with their jokes, particularly those about sexuality and sexual difference.[22] But in the company of men, and especially in

18. Jerry Suls discusses this research, which attributes women's lesser ability to recognize "objectively" comic stimuli to their reliance on the right hemisphere of the brain, in McGhee and Goldstein, eds., *Handbook of Humor Research* 2: 50. (McGhee also summarizes the relevant studies in *Handbook* 1: 23–24.) It should be added here that, even if this sort of "scientific" research took into account the social constraints on women's laughter, it would still be fatally compromised by a formalistic and idealized notion of the comic object. Humor is a social process, not a formally distinct class of *énoncé*. There is no standard or universal joke the "appreciation" of whose comic properties can stand as an index of one's "objective [humor-]processing" capability. The researcher's hypothesis of essential lack (i.e., women lack a sense of humor) thus amounts to no more than this: "'They' (the women under study) do not always respond enthusiastically to texts, situations, events, that 'we' (men like me) regard as 'humorous.'"

19. Of course the classic account of this normative joke situation is Freud's analysis of the "obscene" joke in *Jokes and Their Relation to the Unconscious* 96–101.

20. Anne Beatts interview, in Collier and Beckett, eds., *Spare Ribs* 28.

21. An overview of these studies can be found in chapter 2 of Apte, *Humor and Laughter*. The classic study is A. R. Radcliffe-Brown, "On Joking Relationships," in Radcliffe-Brown, *Structure and Function in Primitive Society* (New York, 1965) 90–104.

22. For example, Maryrose and Anna "burst into helpless fits of laughter" watching

traditionally male discursive realms (which the novel conveniently compart-
mentalizes in the Black Notebook and the Red Notebook, the notebook of
the Communist party), the women largely accede to the suppression of their
humor.

Not always, however. The normative arrangement breaks down in *Free
Women*, the mock novel that frames and periodically interrupts the other
fragments of *The Golden Notebook*. *Free Women* is a work of domestic melodrama in which two single mothers, Anna and Molly, try to cope with Molly's
disruptive late-adolescent son, Tommy. Making their job more difficult are
the frequent visits of Molly's former husband Richard, Tommy's father, who
attributes his son's brooding manner and indecision regarding a career to his
formative contact with this pair of loose, lefty women. Richard is the perfect
conventional bourgeois male, domineering, anti-intellectual, filled with a
sense of his own importance. In the course of the novel he tries to seduce
Anna, to commit his unhappy alcoholic second wife to an asylum so as to
install a young secretary as his new trophy-mate, and to free Tommy from
the snares of Anna and Molly's socialist propaganda and set him up with a
good corporate job.

Now although Molly and Anna are not particularly lighthearted people,
Richard's visits seem invariably to provoke them into "fits of laughter" (27).
To Molly, who has no interest at all in her former husband's professional life,
Richard's air of "worldly importance" has always been a joke, as incongruous
as the sporty "country" clothes he insists on wearing around central London
every Sunday. And it is a joke even for Anna, who unlike Molly has actually
visited Richard's downtown offices and seen firsthand the spectacular evidence of his authority. (Richard, we are told, is "in fact one of the financial
powers of the country" [23].)

That the women can treat as a mere figure of fun a man who holds such
vast power and authority in the City strikes Richard as a sign of their typically
feminine naiveté and ignorance of the world:

---

the teenage Jane Boothby, whose almost palpable aura of sexual desire (which passes
unnoticed by the men) provokes their "recognition and amused pity" (96); but they take
care to "stop" laughing as soon as the men look their way (98). When Saul accuses Anna of
never laughing, she has in fact been laughing violently just the previous night—at Saul's
"guilty" and "boyish" manner of love-making: "[He] came into me, very big but like a
schoolboy, making love to his first woman, too quick, full of shame and heat. . . . And
[after he left] I laughed and I laughed. Then I slept and woke laughing" (630). Of course
Saul would rather believe that women "don't laugh" than have this covert laughter brought
to his attention.

"You two are so extraordinarily naive."

"About business?" said Molly, with her loud jolly laugh.

"About big business. . . . Very big business," said Anna laughing. . . . "You've been putting Richard across to everyone for years as a sort of—well, an enterprising little businessman, like a jumped-up grocer. . . . And it turns out that all the time he's a tycoon. But really. A big shot. One of the people we have to hate—on principle," Anna added laughing.

"Really?" said Molly, interested, regarding her former husband with mild surprise that this ordinary and—as far as she was concerned—not very intelligent man could be anything at all.

Anna recognized the look—it was what she felt—and laughed.

"Good God," said Richard, "talking to you two, it's like talking to a couple of savages." (24)

In this, as in other similar scenes, the women's laughter—which expresses the incommensurability of their system of value with that which secures Richard's "importance"—unites them; they face Richard as "a laughing unit of condemnation" (26). Their laughter is precisely what the French writer Annie Leclerc has in mind when she says that "man's value has no value. My best proof: the laughter that takes hold of me when I observe him in those very areas where he wishes to be distinguished."[23] Like the way Molly "stop[s] Richard talking simply by making fun of him with [her] hands," mimicking "the gesture of a child waiting for a lesson," the women's laughter is an unanswerable "impertinence" (25). It stops Richard talking by placing him in a double bind. Its paradoxical message is: you will be judged ridiculous in just those areas, and to just that degree, that you claim not to be.

As Hélène Cixous has suggested, the fact that such laughter is spontaneous does not prevent it from being strategic; the women can't help their laughter, but it helps them refuse the lessons that men are determined to teach. Like the king's wives set to study the code of battle in a parable Cixous recounts from Sun Tse, Anna and Molly use "a certain kind of laughter" (the laughter of "feminine disorder") to make themselves momentarily *un-teachable.*[24] By means of impertinent sounds and parodic gestures they produce an alternative syntactic flow that drowns out the lectures about patriarchal battle codes and the importance of "very big business."

23. Leclerc, *Woman's Word* 79.

24. Hélène Cixous, "Castration or Decapitation?" in *Out There: Marginalization and Contemporary Cultures*, ed. Russell Ferguson et al. (New York and Cambridge, 1990) 346.

Of course the areas in which the teacher wishes to claim his greatest importance and expertise are those that have been most thoroughly colonized by the phallic regime. And in taking up the role of mocking "savages" (or impertinent "monkeys" as Richard also refers to them [24]) the women are in effect directing laughter at what Cixous used to call the "little pocket signifier."[25] This is made explicit enough in several scenes of the novel. There is Richard's virtually mechanical, can't-help-myself attempt to seduce Anna (44–45), which, like so many of Lessing's seduction scenes,[26] goes farcically awry when the woman refuses to respect the established frame of the heroic seduction quest and repeatedly transgresses the rules and codes that constitute it. Anna's "unacceptable" remarks in this scene (and the "unacceptable" was one of Freud's terms for the punch line) effect a Bergsonian deflation of her seducer by calling attention to his tedious predictability—achieving what Bergson calls his "momentary transformation . . . into a thing" (*Laughter* 97). Like Martha Quest in several seduction scenes of the *Children of Violence* novels, Anna is a comedic "frame-breaker" in Umberto Eco's sense.[27] By breaking the frame of the seduction scenario she permits the narrative to be retold as comedy, with the putative hero or subject of desire recast as comic object. When she later provides just such a retelling for Molly, complete with her own spontaneous, carnival-like disruptions and Richard's dazed responses ("But Anna, I'm a very virile man"), the two women "double over" with laughter (46).

Richard speaks again of his virility when he asks Anna and Molly for advice on his rapidly disintegrating second marriage. "I'm sure you two emancipated females will take this in your stride," he tells them, "but I just can't make it with [her]. . . . I [can't] get a hard on with Marion. Is that clear enough for you? . . . There's one problem you haven't got—it's a purely physical one. How to get an erection with a woman you've been married to fifteen years" (30–31). Richard brings this out with a great show of male candor, the shocking confession of a "very virile man." He is trying his best ("and it hasn't been easy mind you") "to talk frankly about sex with women"

25. Quoted in Marks and De Courtivron, eds., *New French Feminisms* 36.

26. A particularly telling and well-elaborated example is the story "One off the Short List," in Lessing, *A Man and Two Women* (New York, 1963). A condensed version of this story appears in Anna's Yellow Notebook (*TGN* 450–51).

27. Umberto Eco, "The Frames of Comic 'Freedom,'" in *Carnival!* ed. Thomas Sebeok (New York, 1984) 1–10. For a feminist reading of Eco's piece see Regenia Gagnier, "Between Women: A Cross-Cultural Analysis of Status and Anarchic Humor," in Barreca, ed., *Last Laughs* 135–48.

(31). But this turns out to be even more difficult than he expects, for the women respond to his frank remarks with great "peals of laughter."

What strikes them as funny is not so much Richard's "problem"—though they do not for a moment share his concern over getting it up—as the way he defines it, and the "club-man's act" he puts on in order to talk about it with women (31). Richard insists the problem is a "purely physical one," thus setting aside his wife's chronic depression, her alcohol dependency, and his own neglect of her and their children to focus on the exalted question of genital blood flow. Though it angers them, Anna and Molly can't help laughing at this unabashedly phallocentric view of human relationships. "At least," says Anna, "we've got more sense than to use words like physical and emotional as if they didn't connect" (31). His air of profound gravity strikes them as equally preposterous, another sign that for Richard the problem of "how to get an erection" (the male problem, the problem women "haven't got") has assumed biblical proportions. "You bring out all this stuff," Anna tells him, laughing again, "as if it were the last revelation from some kind of oracle." "You're . . . such a pompous ass" (32).

The scene is typical of many in which the patriarchal figure, the man who represents at once big business and virility, economic power and symbolic power, is ridiculed by Lessing's "free women." As numerous studies of feminism point out, the key transgressive gesture is to "poke fun at the male erection, the male preoccupation with getting it up, keeping it up, and the ways in which the life and death of the penis are projected into other aspects of culture."[28] It should be stressed that other men besides Richard provoke this kind of laughter—no special degree of idiocy or pomposity attaches to him. What takes place in *Free Women* is not simply burlesque, the exposure of foolishness in high places, for Richard is really not a buffoon. What is being exposed and mocked is the whole phallocentric discursive order in which, for example, the "physical" may be opposed to the "emotional." Because it expresses women's resistance to this order, the women's laughter in *Free Women* constitutes a gesture less toward the "correction" of errant men than toward their own self-liberation. Its satiric (prohibitive) aspect is subsumed within a predominantly carnivalesque (transgressive) ethos.

But how effective is this transgressive gesture in securing *actual* freedom for women? In terms of the strategic goals of women fighting against domination by patriarchal institutions, what kinds of work can and cannot be

---

28. Marks and de Courtivron, "Introduction III: Contexts of the New French Feminisms," in *New French Feminisms*, ed. Marks and de Courtivron, 36.

accomplished through this sort of comic practice? Around these questions the novel projects various and irreconcilable frames of reference. First of all, the continued availability throughout *Free Women* of Marxist and anticolonial perspectives tends to impede a reading of even this quite resolutely domestic novel in terms of a strictly domestic social context. At home, the women mock Richard's offers to "place" Tommy in a good position, his "stubborn confidence in the quality of what he [is] going to offer his son" (23), but even they are aware of the sound basis for this self-confidence. Richard can arrange for Tommy to do whatever he likes, not just "share-pushing or promoting or money-making," as Molly puts it, but work for the United Nations or UNESCO or other welfare work in the colonies (23). When Tommy insists that the first thing he would do in such a position is to "start organising revolutionary groups among the workers," Richard simply remarks that revolutions are "a primary risk of big business these days" and that he will "be careful to take out an insurance policy" against the revolution Tommy will stir up (263).

This remark, as Tommy points out, is Richard's own joke about big business (263), a joke whose paradoxical logic is that of what Eco calls the "authorized transgression":[29] the revolutionary gesture that has already been taken into account and tacitly legitimized by the very power it would disrupt. By means of this paradox Richard claims to supersede the women's laughter at home with the laughter of men-at-work. He is confident that the (patriarchal, but also capitalist and imperial) social order that accords him his importance can accommodate women who laugh in their kitchens as long as it's still men who are laughing in the board rooms. A later scene in his enormous, plush office, where he manages quite easily to reimpose the normative patriarchal frame around his attempted seduction of Anna, reducing her to the "awkward and flustered" object of his conquering desire (388), reinforces the point: even from Anna's vantage Richard's continued power in this world of "very big business" weighs in heavily against the carnivalesque inversions of power which take place in his former wife's apartment. After all, while Anna and Molly have been practicing their laughter of "liberation," Richard has steadily extended his dominion over the means of production, quadrupling the holdings and profits of his empire (387).

But *Free Women* does not simply credit Richard with the last laugh, either. While it sets the women's feminist transgressions in a Marxist frame that encompasses the corporate realm, it doesn't privilege that realm to the point

29. Eco, "Frames of Comic 'Freedom'" 6.

where domestic disturbances can be seen only as always-already-contained events. One of the reasons this novel struck a chord with progressive women readers in 1962 (and even more resonantly a decade later) was its recognition that the "personal" was indeed "political," in that the field of domestic relations offered prime sites for contestation of the existing symbolic order.[30] The novel accurately foresaw that the men of business would more readily, though still reluctantly, authorize a "sexual revolution" of the workplace, even conceding a few chairs in the board room, than relinquish their place of domestic-symbolic authority, their big chair in the living room. The new corporate woman, who perforce shares "man's value" and confirms his importance, perhaps poses less of a threat to the determined patriarch than do laughing women closer to home. In this light, Anna and Molly's willingness to be seen as "unimportant" and "ignorant as monkeys" about big business is precisely an index of their resistance—a sign that, as Molly puts it, "we haven't given in" (25).

Free Women itself thus negotiates the space between home and marketplace, personal and public spheres, in a way that offers irreconcilable (feminist, Marxist) frames for assessing the effectivity of Anna and Molly's laughter. When we return *Free Women* to its place(s) within the larger text of *The Golden Notebook*, this matter of framing becomes still more uncertain. On the one hand, it is the larger text, and in particular the Black and Red notebooks, which makes clear just how disruptive of gender norms this sort of laughter really was in early-fifties Britain. Only in a context in which humor is designated a male discursive domain, and in which all business, all official culture, all political and ideological struggle are conceived in terms of men's competing for power with other men, can the women's hilarity over Richard's erection troubles be properly felt as a transgression of consequence. On the other hand, while Anna and Molly's comic impertinence does enable them to resist certain lessons on the value of big business and virility, their virtual paralysis at key political junctures in the larger narrative shows how little it assists them in constructing the linkages of a broader

30. Sheila Benson describes the considerable impact of *The Golden Notebook* on progressive women readers of 1962 in "Experiences in the London New Left," in Archer, ed., *Out of Apathy* 107–10. But Benson points out that for many such readers the dominant assumptions about what constituted the *political* impeded the reception of Lessing's text for some years. (*The Golden Notebook* had to wait until the early seventies to find its larger readership.) In 1962, says Benson, British women were so little prepared for a work in which "the deeply personal" dimensions of their experience were treated as "political" problems that a kind of "time-delay" occurred in the novel's reception (109).

oppositionality. In this regard, as I elaborate further on, the laughter of cynical (self-)parody which dominates the Notebooks subsumes the seemingly happier laughter of *Free Women*. The title "Free Women" after all refers us to a self-lacerating joke of Anna's (it is, as Lessing remarks in the Introduction, "an ironic title" [viii]), and the novel ends with Molly about to marry a wealthy businessman who "salve[s] his conscience by giving money to . . . progressive causes" (664) and with Anna making grim jokes about achieving integration with British life "at its roots" (665). Indeed, the whole narrative is framed by the mother text as a self-parody of Doris Lessing, who in 1962 no longer saw her conventional realist novels of domestic crisis and resolution as anything more than exercises in bad faith. Viewed in this light, the idea that *Free Women* might offer keys to a genuinely emancipatory comic practice must itself seem a kind of joke.

But if *The Golden Notebook* frames *Free Women* in a way that calls attention to its symptomatic 1950s aesthetic conformism and its lack of avant-gardiste credentials, the larger text can itself be framed in a way that (in line with some recent feminist theory)[31] would shift our concern from the aesthetics of form to the aesthetics of reception. That is to say, we can consider the text as a transgressive social *event*. As with other discursive practices, literature traditionally has not supported a place for the laughter of women-among-themselves. The conception of humor as a properly male discourse is at work in the whole canon of our literature and is only perpetuated by the commonplace of "exceptionally witty" female characters (or women authors) who can beat men at "their own" game. Literary jokes about sex in particular have followed the normative pattern sketched by Freud, with woman consigned to the position of passive object between two men (author-speaker and listener-reader) who contest or divide between them the active role of subject.[32] *The Golden Notebook* rewrites this old story of reading by offering comic transac-

31. For example, Teresa De Lauretis, *Technologies of Gender* (Bloomington, Ind., 1987), traces a recent "shift in women's cinema from an aesthetic centered on the text . . . to what may be called an aesthetic of reception, where the spectator is the film's primary concern" (137).

32. As I mention in my Introduction, Samuel Weber makes this arrangement clear in "The Shaggy Dog" chapter of his *Legend of Freud* (100–117). For Freud the recipient of the joke is an active participant in the transaction and can even claim a certain priority, insofar as his reply (laughter or nonlaughter) alone determines the status of the utterance (joke or nonjoke). The speaker is not the subject of a joke until the recipient has acted to make him one. For a feminist attempt to invert the gendering of subjects and object in Freud's theory of the (obscene) joke see Mellencamp, "Situation Comedy, Feminism, and Freud."

tions that can take place entirely between women, requiring for their completion no response or reply whatever from a male reader. Its humor, often sexual in content, is directed at rather than to men, and in this regard the novel uses humor to perform a feminist task analogous to that which Teresa De Lauretis has indicated for women's cinema: *it addresses its reader as female*.[33]

But here again, even if many male (or male-identified) readers have been effectively marginalized by the patterns of reception which form around women's laughter in the novel, they might still invoke, in the manner of Richard, a laughter "beyond" the women's which inscribes all such "literary" transgression within a zone of virtual inconsequence. Theirs would be a comic perspective on the novel which converges with a perspective staged within the novel by Anna herself. The joke is on women who think they advance the cause of "freedom" by participating (either as authors or as readers) in a thoroughly ideological communicative situation (i.e., "Literature") that substitutes the pleasures of a reified pseudo-community for the difficult work of building actual links of articulation between women. From this perspective it is as laughable to imagine the (woman) reader, as reader, an effective agent of emancipation as it is to imagine the (woman) writer, as writer, a cultural worker of real consequence in postmodern society. It is from this perspective that Anna laughs at the very idea of writing a novel that calls itself *Free Women* (638).

In short, whether we concern ourselves with its thematics or with its Chinese-box formal construction—indeed, whether we approach it as a *text* in the narrow sense or as an *event* on the social field called literature—we find *The Golden Notebook* referring all questions about the strategic value of women's laughter to an unending succession of irreconcilable contextual frames. No absolute priority is assigned to the various feminist frames (thematic, aesthetic-receptive, etc.) within which such laughter may be perceived as liberating. In this way the novel enacts a problem in the articulation of transgression with radical politics which most of its readers have preferred to overlook and which continues today to be dodged or denied in various discourses of liberation. Because the context of an event is given in the analysis and not empirically, the size of the contextual frame is always an open question. Generally speaking, as we construct larger and larger, but in themselves equally valid, frames around an event, its capacity to produce effects will appear less and less pronounced; from a sufficiently remote and

33. De Lauretis, *Technologies of Gender* 143.

encompassing standpoint (a standpoint too often adopted by grand strate-
gists of emancipation) nothing makes much difference.

The study of transgression is particularly vulnerable to this process of
scaling-up to the vanishing point, since what is at issue is precisely a stepping
across or beyond some limit or boundary. Actually, to remark a transgression
is always to assert at least two boundaries: there is the boundary crossed, and
there is a further, uncrossed boundary that is the boundary or frame of the
analysis and that makes possible the appearance of the other, inner boundary
(the boundary whose *far side* is still *inside* the analysis). Hence, as *The Golden
Notebook* suggests, it is a very simple matter to reframe one (limited) analysis
with another (limited) analysis so as to indicate this "second" boundary as
the true, unviolated limit of the event. And when the general field under
consideration is, as in the case of "power," "ideology," or "patriarchy," coextensive with the social field itself, there is obviously no final limit, no absolute
beyond or outside, "no 'margins,'" as Foucault has put it, "for those who
break with the system to gambol in."[34]

The laughter of *Free Women* is thus subject to a kind of infinite regress;
these comic transactions cannot be described, on the novel's own terms,
as a political solution. Indeed, the narrative of freedom in terms of which
they could be so described is itself one important object of ridicule here.
This is not to say that with a different logic than that of transgression-and-
containment, and a different conception of the political event and its contextual frame, one could not somehow salvage women's laughter as an act of
resistance. The work of Foucault aims (though not in the name of feminism)
at precisely this kind of enabling reconceptualization. But there is ample
evidence in the cultural criticism of the last decade, and even in some of
Foucault's own most influential formulations, that we are far from having
achieved this new thinking.[35] Critics' continued willingness to speak of *The

34. Michel Foucault, "Powers and Strategies," written interview, trans. Colin Gordon
et al., in Foucault, *Power/Knowledge: Selected Interviews and Other Writings*, ed. Colin Gordon (New York, 1980) 141.

35. Part of the problem is that the antitotalizing notions to which Foucault appeals as
means of improving on the law-and-transgression model of power relations—such notions
as the "local struggle" and the "specific intellectual"—are themselves caught up in the
binary logic of inside/outside, with its tendency to scale up toward totality or infinity. The
border between local and global, specific and general, can always be redrawn a little
further from the site of struggle. The frame of analysis within which one might "prove that
these local, specific struggles haven't been a mistake and haven't led to a dead end," as
Foucault wants to do, can itself serve as the dead end, the containing limit, within a second
analysis that "proves" just the opposite. Thus in enumerating the strategic "obstacles and
... dangers" with which the "specific intellectual" is faced, Foucault seems in spite of

Golden Notebook in terms of subversion, emancipation, and a natural community of women signalizes the persistence of the very narratives whose necessary abandonment the book marked and enacted thirty years ago.

The (Self-)Parody of Politics: "Enlightened False Consciousness"

> What is really disturbing . . . is the underlying belief in the liberating, anti-totalitarian force of laughter, of ironic distance. Our thesis here is almost the exact opposite of this: . . . in contemporary societies, democratic or totalitarian, that cynical distance, laughter, irony, are so to speak, part of the game. The ruling ideology is not meant to be taken seriously or literally.
>
> —Slavoj Žižek, *Sublime Object of Ideology*

> Well, no one's a communist these days—except the Communists.
>
> —Doris Lessing, *Retreat to Innocence*

This failure of an ideological narrative that one has not yet learned how not to tell plays itself out in other ways and on other registers throughout *The Golden Notebook*. And even where the carnivalesque laughter of women, and the claims that might be made for it, are no longer at issue, jokes of some kind continue to occupy a decisive place in the text's symptomatology of the postmodern. The novel is dominated, formally and thematically, by a certain joke-logic that is set in concrete relation to the historical crisis of Marxism, or of the Marxist political subject. This Marxist dimension, the political

---

himself to fall back on the "meager logic" of inside/outside. The intellectual undertaking local resistance, says Foucault, faces "the danger of remaining at the level of conjunctural struggles, pressing demands restricted to particular sectors. The risk of letting himself [*sic*] be manipulated by the political parties or trade union apparatuses which control these local struggles. Above all, the risk of being unable to develop these struggles for lack of a global strategy or outside support." That is to say, the struggle either remains "restricted to particular sectors," or it crosses over onto a wider, presumably non-conjunctural field; it is either contained and neutralized by the "apparatuses which control these local struggles," or it breaks free of this control, finds "outside" support, and achieves a "global" character. The events of struggle may be genuinely transgressive of established limits, or they may be taking place on the side of the law after all. Such alternatives, at this stage, can only lead us back to the familiar gridlock. (Quotations taken from "Truth and Power," interview, in Gordon, ed., *Power/Knowledge* 130.)

background of the text's own production, is recorded in two main compartments: the Black Notebook, in which Anna has reconstructed her experiences as a Communist in colonial Africa, and the Red Notebook, in which she traces her involvements with the Communist party of Great Britain. As is the case throughout *The Golden Notebook*, these compartments inevitably bleed through or infect one another; they are never as pure as Anna would like them to be. But in this case the notion of a kind of disease or "cancer" that spreads outward from the Black Notebook is insistently attached to "the jokes people make" in the southern African communist group (68).

The term Anna uses most frequently to define this form of joking is "cynicism"—a term I consider in some detail toward the end of this section—and the primary locus of the cynicism is clearly indicated as Paul Blackenhurst. Paul is the "real" RAF pilot of the Black Notebook[36] and the model for the fictional hero Peter Carey in Anna's best-selling first novel, *Frontiers of War*. Though as "dashing" and "brilliant" as his fictional counterpart, Paul is scarcely the figure of naive idealism Anna presented in Peter Carey (57). She has in fact modeled her "gallant young hero" (75) not on Paul but on Paul's favorite role, the stock character he most enjoys playing. Paul's "cynicism" is above all a matter of multiple and broken identifications. He is addicted to what Anna later calls "pastiching about" (437). He confronts everyone he meets "with an intensely serious, politely enquiring, positively deferential bright-blue beam from his eyes, even stooping slightly in his attempt to convey his earnest appreciation" (75). Exploiting the ideological blind spot that neutralizes parody for precisely those who are parodied, he echoes back at people an at first imperceptibly but then more and more plainly exaggerated version of their own discourse, keeping his voice to a "low charming deferential murmur" even when his disingenuousness becomes apparent: "It took most people a long time to discover that he was

---

36. Just how closely the supposedly "objective" account (153) of "the materials that made *Frontiers of War*" (152) is meant to reflect Anna's actual experiences in southern Africa is open to question. In the Blue Notebook Anna admits that she has consciously fictionalized characters in the Black Notebook: the portrait of Willi, for instance, is loosely based on Anna's former husband Max Wulf (230, 233). This practice would suggest that Paul Blackenhurst, too, may be a fictional creation rather than a straight portrait of the "real" pilot Anna knew in Mashopi. But there is another problem. The entry in the Blue Notebook in which Anna confesses to having written fiction in the Black Notebook is dated 1950; the relevant entries of the Black Notebook itself are dated 1954. That is, Anna admits in the Blue Notebook to having fictionalized an account she has not yet written. Problems of this kind do not finally sort out in *The Golden Notebook*; in the last analysis the text simply does not make chronological or narrative sense.

mocking them. I've seen women, and even men, when the meaning of one of his cruelly quiet drawling statements came home to them, go literally pale with the shock of it; and stare at him incredulous that such open-faced candour could go with such deliberate rudeness" (75). Paul amuses himself in this way continually, even with those who are sufficiently used to him not to be shocked. His enjoyment of the game is not dependent on any particular response from those with whom he plays it; he is precisely *not* bound by the field of "communication." He is content simply to leave a local farmer's daughter ("about sixteen, pretty, pudgy, wearing a flounced flowered muslin dress") "hypnotised" and "blushing" at his impersonation of the young gallant: "I've been wanting to tell you ever since I came into this bar, that I haven't seen a dress like yours since I was at Ascot three years ago" (87). With equal pleasure he mimics and exaggerates the idiolect of colonialism to the local colonials, of patriotic militarism to the other pilots, of Marxism to the Marxists who make up his circle of friends. Arrogant, well educated and well placed, indifferent master of every political language, Paul is at once the most narcissistic and the most fragmented character in the novel.

The effect of Paul's constant mimicry within the Communist group is gradually to undermine the notion—one they consider vital to their collective political identity—of an "authentic," a "sincere" voice with which to articulate the necessity for revolution in colonial Africa. Under the direction of the pedantic German theoretician Willi (a recurrent type in Lessing's fiction), the group applies itself to what Anna describes as "logic-chopping" and "endless analytical discussion" (72). They are concerned to get their theoretical apparatus in good order, to make certain that their "line" is "correct," before proceeding to praxis (64).

This rigorous devotion to theory makes the group especially vulnerable to the kind of discursive subversion Paul's humor effects. His game of speaking always in a borrowed language, at one moment mouthing elitist clichés about his place of privilege within "the family," "the City," or "the system" (76), the next moment passionately reciting the tenets of a radical socialism whose future he cannot intelligibly be said to "believe in" (78), infects and ultimately paralyzes the entire group. Paul can be a conservative young Englishman without any "fancy ideas about the kaffirs": "You mustn't let [your black servants] take advantage of you. . . . Because if you do, they lose all respect" (100). Or a model bureaucrat of the revolution: "So all we have to do is persuade them towards a correct understanding of their class position, and we'll have the whole district in a revolutionary uproar" (111). Or a capitalist spy and "future lieutenant" of industry: "I'm using my time usefully, wouldn't you say? By observing the comrades? I'll have a flying start over my rival lieutenants, won't I? Yes, I'll understand the enemy" (76). Caught up in this comedy of citation, Anna and the others find that they are no longer able to communicate effectively on political issues; uncertainties regarding authority and intention lead them to suspect that every utterance is in a sense nonserious.

This communication breakdown results from certain discursive paradoxes that Paul's humor brings to attention. His joking exploits the masks, the roles that language forces upon a speaker, the disappearance of a speaking subject's "true" intention within the labyrinth of iteration. It is the (normally suppressed) humor of language that has been channeled by citation into new contexts, the potential humor of all "parasitic" speech acts (the speech acts of actors)—and indeed, of all utterances without exception, once their "parasitic" or "non-serious" character is allowed to appear.[37] According to the rules of Paul's game, every instance of discourse shall be read as precisely a speech *act*: a pretending or ironic recontextualization.

Through Paul's "pastiching about," the boundary between the serious and the nonserious, the authentic and the parasitic, is dissolved. Lessing is certainly aware that this dissolution of categories could be enabling: a breaking-down in her novels can always lead to a breaking-through, and there is no question that the Communist group's orthodoxies are in need of deconstruction. Indeed, it is because the group's discourse of emancipation is reliant on insupportable conceptions of identity and subjectivity that the *pasticheur* crops up in their midst: Paul Blackenhurst is not the cancer, he is its symptom. But Marxism has not equipped the group to formulate a sufficiently radical cure. Neither their attempted affirmations of group solidarity and a common positive agenda nor their rigorous self-applications of ideology critique can effect a remission of the new laughter.

The "affirmative" cure—the appeal to a common political identity and purpose—is blocked by the group's insertion, through the comic transactions

37. A provocative elaboration of this humor is Jacques Derrida's "Limited Inc.," trans. Samuel Weber, *Glyph* 2 (1977): 162–254. In this response to John Searle, a "gay and lightheaded" Derrida draws out the absurdities and paradoxes of the oppositional logic by which speech act theory distinguishes between "normal" and "parasitic" utterances. The serious side to Derrida's humor in the article lies in his suggestion that "something like a relation" exists between the speech act theorist's exclusion of parasitism and the notions of normality and responsibility manipulated by repressive state apparatuses (251). Paul Blackenhurst's potentially positive function in Mashopi can be summed up by this statement from "Limited Inc.": "The parasite parasites the limits that guarantee the purity of rules and of intentions, and this is not devoid of import for law, politics, economics, ethics" (242).

Paul orchestrates, into a fluid economy of subject positions or roles. Like the group of Americans whose party Anna attends years later, members of the group are caught up in "the wild, painful, laughing dance . . . [of] parody, and urging all the other members of the group to keep up the parody, for their dear lives' sake" (493). "For the purposes of such jokes," writes Anna, "Willi and I were Colonials" (84). "For the purposes of jokes like these, Ted, Jimmy and Paul despised the Colony so much they knew nothing about it" (84). It is especially revealing that Willi, the most committed and lugubrious member of the group, eventually joins in the game, "parodying the Colonial clichés" in order to help Paul "make fools of people" (100–101).

In a sense the group does maintain its solidarity in these games, but what keeps them together is a common sense of their coming apart, or rather of the coming apart of the Marxist/anticolonial political nexus. As white Marxists they find themselves on the wrong side of the color bar, leading a privileged and typically decadent life, cut off from the black masses. As anticolonial activists they find themselves frequently forced to modify or reject the "correct" Marxist line. Their group identity continues to be defined by a core narrative—the narrative of revolution and socialist community in southern Africa—but it is a narrative that can now only repeat itself as farce. In his role as revolutionary strategist and visionary, Paul elaboratates various scenarios concerning "the two-men-and-a-half," a parodic (Dostoevskian) revolutionary committee that aims at "deciding the whole fate of the African continent 'without, of course, any reference to the Africans themselves'" (111):

> "The two-men-and-a-half" . . . worked for twenty years to bring the local savages to a realisation of their position as a vanguard. Suddenly a half-educated demagogue who had spent six months at the London School of Economics created a mass movement overnight, on the slogan: "Out with the Whites." (92)
>
> . . . And now Paul described how the two-men-and-a-half would go about "guiding Mashopi towards a correct line of action."
>
> "I would say that the hotel would be a convenient place to start, wouldn't you, Ted?"
>
> "Near the bar, Paul, all modern conveniences" . . .
>
> "The trouble is, that it's not exactly a centre of the developing industrial proletariat. Of course, one could, and in fact we probably should, say the same about the whole country?"
>
> "Very true, Paul. But on the other hand the district is plentifully equipped with backward and half-starving farm labourers."
>
> "Who only need a guiding hand from the said proletariat if only they existed."
> (111)

It is important that Ted is here playing straight man for Paul, for Ted had initially been a source of resistance to such self-parody. Like George Hownslow and Anna herself, he has regarded such joking as a form of "treachery"—especially when, as here, it is practiced in the presence of outsiders and potential recruits. But by this time the notion of a treacherous discourse has lost its force within the group. They have all capitulated to "the new tone of disbelief and mockery" (110); "wild helpless fits of laughing often took members of the group, singly, in couples, or collectively" (424). It is underscored that the phenomenon is experienced both individually and collectively; what has occurred is a group process, a Marxist version of the "laughing disease" or laughing hysteria observed by anthropologists,[38] but it plays itself out intra- as well as intersubjectively. It is on the one hand an index of the group's increasing fragmentation and mutual isolation (which is ocurring along gender lines as well), and on the other hand a confirmation of their continued entanglement with one another. At times Anna describes the new laughter as the group's undoing, at other times she presents it as the only thing that held them together. "The reason I stayed in the Colony long after there was any need," she says, "was because such places allow opportunities for this type of enjoyment. Paul was inviting us all to be amused" (105).

The affirmative cure for this laughing disease—the tightening of the group's bonds of solidarity and the rehearsal of its key objectives—thus merely feeds the process of comic transaction, of politics as its own self-parody. The alternative, negative cure—the application of rigorous ideology critique—proves similarly ineffectual. As should be clear by now, comic transactions pose, or rather expose, considerable problems for the critique of ideology. Since a joke can never be reduced to a simple or terminable utterance, the practice of "pastiching about" cannot be arrested at any specifiable ideological position. When Paul speaks as an elitist ("The Lord gives, The Lord takes. In my case he has given" [424]) or as a colonial ("Of course, there's centuries of evolution between them and us, they're nothing but

---

38. We could also say that what occurs in the Mashopi group is a curious merging of this collective "laughing hysteria" with the individual psychic disorder known as *Witzelsucht*, a compulsive and elaborately nuanced practice of self-parody which only the sufferer seems to find amusing, and which has been said to mark the sufferer's profound *disconnection* from his or her social context. In Lessing's Black Notebook, *Witzelsucht* is experienced collectively, as a social phenomenon. See Michael S. Duchowny, "Pathological Disorders of Laughter," in McGhee and Goldstein, eds., *Handbook of Humor Research* 2: 92.

baboons really" [100]), Anna and the others cannot be certain that he "means" the opposite of what he says; the irony could be used to mask a genuine sense of class or racial superiority. For Paul is thought to be a man whose "snobbishness is expressed indirectly, in jokes" (105). By the same token, when he speaks as a "good comrade," his friends cannot be sure that he "really" means to express contempt for communism; the mockery may itself be a mask or a pretense. For they believe that he is at bottom a "frustrated idealis[t]" (93), not an apologist for the colonial order.

By initiating this paradoxical movement, this ceaseless vacillation, Paul's ideological pastiche performs the work Freud attributes to a special, "fourth and rarest class" of tendentious jokes: the "skeptical" (*JRU* 115). Though effecting joke-work similar to that of Freud's third class, the "cynical" jokes that direct "blasphemous" or "rebellious" criticism against some "collective person . . . in whom the subject has a share" (113), Paul's humor is "skeptical" insofar as it raises what Freud calls "the problem of what determines the truth" (115). According to Freud, skeptical humor foregrounds this problem by focusing on the unavailability of intention, typically on the difficulties opened up by deceptive honesty or "representation by the opposite" (115). The classic example (somewhat modified here) is as follows: Leaving the house one evening a man smilingly tells his wife, "Well, I'm off to visit my mistress." "Oh, sure!" cries the wife. "You just say you're visiting your mistress so I'll think you're going to the office. But I bet you really are going to visit your mistress—you liar!" Paul's humor puts Anna and the others in this wife's position. Even when they believe him to be speaking from his "true" ideological position, they still sense a deception. Honesty becomes dishonesty, and yet, as Vincent Descombes has said in connection with the regress of deconstruction: "there is no *hypocritical mask*, for the face covered by the mask is itself a mask, and any mask is thus the mask of a mask."[39]

But this is a general rather than a specific statement of the problem Paul Blackenhurst's joking poses for ideology critique. It is not merely a "fourth and rarest class" of jokes which raises the question of the truth, but all jokes, all utterances that might be laughed at. The great usefulness of jokes is that they impede the normal process whereby intention or purpose is attributed, enabling a thing to be said without anyone's "meaning" it. What affords the ideological *pasticheur* his rather special immunity to ideology critique is not

---

39. Vincent Descombes, *Modern French Philosophy*, trans. L. Scott-Fox and J. M. Harding (Cambridge, 1980) 182. Descombes is here paraphrasing Pierre Klossowski, "Nietzsche, le polythéisme et la parodie," in Klossowski, *Un si funeste désir* (Paris, 1963).

so much his skepticism as his cynicism. As I noted above, this is the term the text affixes most insistently to the kind of joking Paul practices; and the term is employed, I think, in something like the sense in which Peter Sloterdijk uses it in his *Critique of Cynical Reason*.[40] The cynic is the name given to the counterrevolutionary political subject who has already assimilated whatever critique you might offer of his or her position and made a habit of reproducing the terms both of the critique and of the position itself in "non-serious" form.

Sloterdijk shares Lessing's view of this "modern, self-reflexive cynicism" as a "universal" and "diffuse" social phenomenon (3), which is nonetheless "lived as a private disposition" (7): "Modern cynics are integrated, asocial characters" (5). Most important, the contemporary cynic is in no sense politically naive, he or she is not a happily unenlightened dupe of advanced capitalism:

> Psychologically, present-day cynics can be understood as borderline melancholics, who keep their symptoms of depression under control and can remain more or less able to do work. . . . A certain chic bitterness provides an undertone to [their] activity. . . . For cynics are not dumb, and . . . they certainly see the nothingness to which everything leads. . . . Thus we come to our first definition: Cynicism is *enlightened false consciousness*. It is that modernized, unhappy consciousness, on which Enlightenment has labored both successfully and in vain. . . . Well-off and miserable at the same time, this consciousness no longer feels affected by any critique of ideology; its falseness is already buffered. (5)

Though Paul Blackenhurst puts his cynicism on display, "draws attention to it" in a way that Sloterdijk's analysis does not anticipate (*Critique* 7), he fits this description quite closely in all other respects. He is a melancholic who describes his "view of life" as "morbid, and increasingly morbid with every passing minute" (428). Though he laughs "continuously," it is a miserable laughter; he has "never laughed because [he was] happy" (428). But for all his melancholia Paul is believable when he says, "I'll be a captain of industry. I have intelligence and the education and the background" (76). There is no doubt he is capable of performing work within the system that he derides with such clear-headed bitterness, a system about whose oppressive violence he has no illusions. Paul is enlightened, he sees clearly the need for social change, yet his consciousness is still "false"; *and he recognizes this.* In Sloterdijk's terms, his condition transcends the three generally acknowledged

40. Peter Sloterdijk, *Critique of Cynical Reason*, trans. Michael Eldred (Minneapolis, 1987).

forms of false consciousness: lie, error, and ideology. Enlightened, self-reflexive cynicism constitutes a "fourth configuration" (8). Paul does not lie about "the system"; he makes no naive errors in judging his conditions of existence; he does have a critical purchase on the dominant ideology. But his cynical consciousness has negotiated a reconciliation with the system nonetheless: a parodic reconciliation that leaves him divided and unhappy, but not dysfunctional or self-deceived.

Of course, as Sloterdijk points out, "logically," we are dealing with "a paradox, for how could enlightened consciousness still be false?" (5). But this, he remarks, is "precisely the issue." The "actual state of affairs" which obtains for the cynic is that which "is regarded in logic as a paradox and in literature as a joke" (6). The cynic himself is not troubled by the idea of an objective reality constructed in terms of joke-logic. Paul takes the greatest "intellectual pleasure in paradox" (77); for him the sole attraction of history is that it provides opportunities to indulge this "ruling passion," this profound "enjoyment of incongruity" (105). It is, rather, the critic of false consciousness who finds such a state of affairs confounding, for as Sloterdijk puts it, to marshal a critique of this *enlightened* false consciousness requires "a new attitude of consciousness toward 'objectivity'" (6). One must deal with the fact that, as Anna reluctantly acknowledges, it is the cynic in his "spirit of angry parody" who actually comes "near[est] the truth" of the political situation (93).[41]

What *The Golden Notebook* makes clearer than *The Critique of Cynical Reason* is that cynicism is a crisis for the left not only because it defeats the project of ideology critique but also because it serves within Marxism itself to perpetuate a set of assumptions and practices (including those of traditional ideology critique) whose inadequacy, like that of the "system" they oppose, has been fully recognized. What Slavoj Žižek says (in the epigraph to this section) about "cynical distance, laughter, irony" having become "part of the game" of a ruling ideology that "is not meant to be taken seriously or literally" speaks to the situation of Marxist ideology as well. The paradoxical form of "enlightened false consciousness" means that it can flip-flop across the supposed boundary separating left from right. But while the crisis thus appears more universal in Lessing's text than in Sloterkijk's, she is no less

---

41. There are echoes here, as also in Sloterdijk's formulations, of Nietzsche's affirmative remarks on cynicism in *Beyond Good and Evil: Prelude to a Philosophy of the Future*, trans. Walter Kaufmann (Harmondsworth, 1979). "Cynicism," writes Nietzsche, "is the only form in which common souls come close to honesty" (40).

determined to historicize it, and to do so from the standpoint of a fully implicated present. Sloterdijk writes of Marxism's failure to construct a new hegemony in western Europe in the twenties and early thirties; Lessing of its failure to do so in colonial Great Britain during and immediately after the war. But she writes unmistakably in the aftermath of 1956 as he does in the aftermath of 1968. Both are responding to a collapse into cynicism as contemporary as it is widespread, to a disorder on the left which tends to fill up the historical time of earlier moments of crisis precisely because it has assumed for the present the character of a postmodern condition. Both, too, treat this condition as a kind of disease, and both suggest that with the traditional affirmations and negations of leftist thought effectively disabled, the cure for the disease must be homeopathic.

But while Sloterdijk offers the beginnings of such a formula for the future,[42] Lessing—at least on my reading—is concerned only with the symptomatology.[43] Rather than pursue a cure for the postmodern disease of "bad laughter" (56), *The Golden Notebook* patiently traces its symptoms onto every level of contemporary political and cultural practice—including, inevitably, that of the novel's own production.

The Politics of (Self-)Parody

The novel's particular form of engagement with this "bad laughter" (the laughter of the cynical *pasticheur*) is the key to its postmodernism and distin-

---

42. Sloterdijk calls for a reawakening of the radical potential in cynicism itself; he proposes combating the essentially quietist, paralyzing cynicism of the modern "schizophrenic" with the vital, rebellious cynicism of the fully integrated *Kyniker* of classical times (whose model, for Sloterdijk, is Diogenes of Sinope). See in this connection Leslie A. Adelson, "Against the Enlightenment: A Theory with Teeth for the 1980s," *German Quarterly* 57 (Fall 1984): 625–31.

43. While early critics of the novel often claimed for it some ultimately synthesizing or transcendent power, recent criticism has tended to reject a utopian reading. "Despite the rhetoric of wholeness that informs [*The Golden Notebook*]," writes Molly Hite, the novel "turn[s] away from realist conventions and especially the convention of coherence, which like all conventions emerges as at root an ideological construct" ("Subverting the Ideology of Coherence: *The Golden Notebook* and *The Four-Gated City*" in *Doris Lessing: The Alchemy of Survival*, ed. Carey Kaplan and Ellen Cronan Rose, [Athens, Ohio, 1988] 62). There are still some critics, however, who insist on a "strange and unexpected image of wholeness that lies at the center of [Lessing's] writing," as Katherine Fishburn does in "*The Golden Notebook*: A Challenge to the Teaching Establishment," in Kaplan and Rose, eds., *Approaches* 131.

guishes it from other, seemingly cogeneric postwar novels. *The Golden Notebook*, after all, takes its place on a long shelf of postwar abyssal or Chinese-box novels: the novels about novelists writing novels about novelists. But such texts, most of which have been produced within the American university by male writer-professors such as William Gass (Washington University), John Hawkes (Brown), John Barth (Johns Hopkins), and Gilbert Sorrentino (Stanford), are generally instances of a persisting modernist/avant-garde experimentalism emptied of its political content. Though invariably disruptive of certain nineteenth-century novelistic conventions these works are usually quite sanguine and reassuring about the condition of the novel as such. They seem to want to say about themselves what Mary McCarthy said about Nabokov's *Pale Fire* (the other now "classic" metafiction of 1962): that a creation of such "perfect beauty, symmetry . . . [and] originality" proves the continued viability of "the modern novel," which "everyone thought dead" but "was only playing possum."[44] In the celebration of their "originality" these novels fairly burst with nostalgia for the triumphs of the twenties. They are playful books, half in love with themselves, buoyed up by the conviction that they are once again making it new, that the Modernist Idea still holds great possibilities for the writer great enough to grasp them.

The Golden Notebook, whose departures from the bourgeois novel are equally radical and disconcerting, shares none of the high spirits of these other metafictions. It does not take pleasure in itself as a great achievement of experimentalism. The difference is not primarily transatlantic; it is the difference between a political and an apolitical conception of literary production, and hence between a political and an apolitical reading of modernism. Much of the fiction that first gained the label "postmodernist"—the work of Nabokov et al.—undertook simply to continue what (under the tutelage of the New Criticism) it took to be a purely aesthetic project of formal innovation. But there was already another, neglected body of work, stretching back at least to the late novels of Woolf, whose postmodernity lay precisely in its problematic contestation of a modernist project whose formidable social and political dimensions had been recognized—problematic, because such work does not aspire, in orthodox 1914 fashion, to a condition of radical newness, but situates itself within the very discursive and institutional structures it means to resist.

It is to this body of work, in which the problem of parody (or of pastiche) which has played so prominently in recent theorizations of the postmodern is

44. Mary McCarthy, "A Bolt from the Blue," *New Republic*, June 1962: 27.

already theorized as a problem, and, indeed, as a political problem, that *The Golden Notebook* makes its contribution. What I want to argue in this closing section of the chapter is first of all that the problems the novel raises on the level of narrative form (and which preclude its optimistic appropriation as a narrative of synthesis and emancipation) are elaborations of the political impasse I have called the "(self-)parody of politics" or the comedy of "enlightened false consciousness." And I will argue, moreover, that in thus elaborating a particular laughter of the (fragmented) left, the novel anticipates, and can help us both to situate and to critique, one of the dominant theories of postmodern and I will argue, aesthetics—a theory that is prefigured here even in its errors.

A good place to take up these arguments is with the synopsis for the film *Forbidden Love*, one of the many interior or embedded texts within *The Golden Notebook*. This text is itself embedded within another interior text, the Black Notebook, which, since it is written by Anna Wulf, is in a sense embedded in yet another interior text, the novel of which Anna is protagonist, *Free Women*. The Black Notebook, in turn, is devoted to Anna's reflections and commentaries on her own novel *Frontiers of War*; and it is on this latter novel—a novel written by, and partially reconstructed in the notebook of, a novelist in a novel-within-a-novel—that the proposed film *Forbidden Love* is based.

Readers of contemporary fiction have grown accustomed to such dizzying patterns of subordination and interrelation, which are of course intrinsic to the Chinese box novels mentioned above. But only a few such novels (Burroughs's *Naked Lunch*, Sorrentino's *Mulligan Stew*) incorporate the vast and heterogeneous assortment of imitative and "found" documents which Lessing's does. *The Golden Notebook* is full of letters, book reviews, newspaper clippings, scenes from films and plays, diaries, stories, and many dozens of less easily classified fragments. It is a text comprised quite explicitly of imitations and borrowings, whose function is not to elaborate the author's splendid hidden design but rather to mock the seeker of such designs and indeed the whole idea of an "artistic creation of perfect beauty, symmetry, and originality."

Forbidden Love marks the novel's first abyssal movement, its first step outside the "conventional short novel" *Free Women* (vii) and into this labyrinthine sequence of colored notebooks and subsidiary fragments. It is also the first of the many parodic imitations in the novel (or rather the first that is immediately recognizable as such; the fact that *Free Women* is itself a parody is for many pages concealed), imitations that carry forth in different contexts and on different registers the joke-work of leftist disorganization which Paul Blackenhust initiates in Mashopi.

A bracketed interruption of the Black Notebook informs us in advance that the *Forbidden Love* synopsis has been written by Anna "with her tongue in her cheek" (57). Such an explicit marking of the synopsis as parody hardly seems necessary, even here, where we have not yet learned of Anna's infectious contact with the laughter of compulsive mimicry. *Forbidden Love* transforms Anna's *Frontiers of War*, an engaged political novel about racism in colonial Africa during World War II, into a clichéd wartime melodrama concerning "dashing young Peter Carey . . . of the R.A.F." and his doomed love affair with a "dark young . . . beauty" he meets in Africa. The entire description is written in the cloying, breathless style of the promotional blurb:

> Idealistic and inflammable, young Peter is shocked by the go-getting, colour-ridden small-town society he finds, falls in with the local group of high-living lefts, who exploit his naive young radicalism. During the week they clamour about the injustices meted out to the blacks; weekends they live it up in a lush out-of-town hotel run by John-Bull-type landlord Boothby and his comely wife, whose pretty teen-age daughter falls in love with Peter. . . . [Peter] falls in love with the cook's young wife, neglected by her politics-mad husband, but this love defies the taboos and mores of the white settler society. . . . Heart-broken Peter, all his illusions in shreds, spends his last night in the Colony drunk, and by chance encounters his dark love in some shabby shebeen. They spend their last night together in each other's arms, in the only place where white and black may meet, in the brothel by the sullied waters of the town's river. Their innocent and pure love, broken by the harsh inhuman laws of this country and by the jealousies of the corrupt, will know no future. (57–58)

The critical ethos of this imitation would seem to be plain enough, and any clumsy or cynical film adaptation of a serious political novel may be understood as the target text. Anna's radical novel "'about' a colour problem" (63), "about the colour bar" (284), becomes a movie about "pure love"; the politics of race is represented mainly as an obstacle to romantic fulfillment, as in the line about the "politics-mad" cook who neglects his wife. "Radicalism" in the racist colonial state is either a form of madness, a sham (as with the "high-living lefts"), or, in the case of our "naive young" hero, a harmless and rather endearing form of misguided idealism. Ironic distance from these views is mainly signaled in the language of the synopsis, by Anna's relentless adjectival overkill, a comically exaggerated version of the hyphenating tendency in synopses and promotional literature of the entertainment media.

Forbidden Love is, from this vantage, a conventional and unproblematic parody, employing traditional devices of style (rhetorical inflation and exaggeration) and aiming at a familiar and easy target. Similar critical imitations appear throughout Anna's notebooks, and they form one of the important comic sequences in the novel. Anna likes to "amuse" herself (434) by submitting this kind of parodic manuscript to film people and literary editors who request her work, mocking their ideas through mimicry. She and James Schafter, an American writer who has been amusing himself in similar fashion, collaborate on a pair of mock journals, one imitating the language of a young American novelist touring the Continent, "living on an allowance from his father, who works in insurance" (434), the other that of "Anna Wulf" herself, recast as a "lady author who [has] spent some years in an African colony, and [is] afflicted with sensibility" (437). In addition, James composes a mock-lyrical, pseudo-modernist African story titled "Blood on the Banana Leaves" (440).

The irony of these imitations is, like that of *Forbidden Love*, laid on "a bit thick" (439), so that one finds little difficulty in identifying its targets. The young American on allowance hesitates to admit Tolstoy to his literary "pantheon" but deems his own pornographic paperback, *Loins*, "good" and "true" (435). Reflecting detachedly on the "troubles" and "problems" of various women he has abandoned, he justifies any pain he may have caused with the meaningless declaration that "a writer is, must be, the Machievelli of the soul's kitchen" (434). When a prostitute offers him "one of her nights for free" he records the event with tears in his eyes: "No greater compliment has been paid me" (435). The "Anna" of the other mock journal wonders if a play based on *Frontiers of War* might succeed in capturing "the essential tragedy of the colonial situation, the tragedy of the whites"; she contrasts "*pedestrian* degradations" such as homelessness and malnutrition to "the reality, the human reality of the white dilemma" (438). James's story about a young African woman raped by a white trader is narrated by the woman's vengeful husband. It begins, "Frrrrr, frrr, frrr, say the banana trees ghosting the age-tired moon of Africa, sifting the wind. Ghosts. Ghosts of time and of my pain" (440), and ends in a bathetic swoon of italics: "*oh red is my pain, crimson my twining pain, oh red and crimson are dripping the moon-echoing leaves of my hate*" (443).

Insofar as these parodies can be said to share with *Forbidden Love* a common target, it is the diminishment or displacement of mere "pedestrian degradations" in pursuit of loftier, more literary sentiments. In each case a gap is felt between the emotions properly belonging to the situation (the pain of real victims of war, racism, or sexual violence) and the emotions evoked in the text (the angst, the nostalgia, the pride, the excitement, the aesthetic *frisson* of the writer). The texts are comically, painfully bad because they so willingly falsify the experience of pain. Their only ambition is to translate this experience into one of conventional readerly pleasure. Lessing's target is thus the "obscene" text in Adorno's sense: the text that seeks "to wring aesthetic pleasure out of . . . naked bodily pain."[45]

This much seems obvious to any reader of *The Golden Notebook*. One must note here, however, an important distinction between Lessing's readers and Anna's. Within the novel the laughable displacements of emotion, the falsifying self-concern of these parodies, go unnoticed. However obviously parodic they may seem to Anna and James or to us, the imitations are all accepted as genuine by the film people and literary editors who read them. The two mock journals and James's "Blood on the Banana Leaves" are "gratefully" received at the *Pomegranate Review* and *Xenith*. The film producer who reads *Forbidden Love* not only declares himself quite pleased with it initially but persists in regarding it as a "perfectly good synopsis" even after Anna explains that she has "written it in parody" (59). As James remarks about such people, nothing one might submit to them "can be more incredible than they would be prepared to [write] themselves, and so they never know whether [one] is laughing at them or not" (436).

It is this circumstance that leads Anna to conclude that "something has happened in the world which [makes] parody impossible" (440). Considerable thematic stress is laid on this statement, and it resounds periodically through both the Black and the Red notebooks. One entry of the Red Notebook is said to have "gummed in" to it the manuscript of a short story by "Comrade Ted," mailed to Anna at her office in the local branch of the British CP. Comrade Ted's blundering narrative (which switches unawares from third to first person and makes even more copious use of the exclamation mark than the young American's journal) recounts a trip to the Soviet Union during which Ted is summoned to the Kremlin by kindly, "twinkling-eyed" Father Stalin to help set right party policy toward Britain:

> Comrade Stalin sat behind an ordinary desk, that showed much signs of hard use, smoking his pipe, in his shirt-sleeves. . . . He passed his rough worker's hand across his brow. Now I saw the marks of fatigue and strain—working for us! For the world! "I have disturbed you so late, comrade, because I have need of your advice. . . ." Like a real Communist leader, he is prepared to take advice from even rank and file party cadres like myself! . . . I spoke for about three hours

45. Theodor W. Adorno, quoted in Janet Malcolm, "Graven Images," *New Yorker*, 8 June 1987: 102.

. . . [while] Comrade Stalin nodded and smoked his pipe . . . . When I had finished, he said simply: "Thank you Comrade. I see now I have been very badly advised" . . . We exchanged a wordless smile. I know my eyes were full—I shall be proud of those tears till I die!" (304–5)

Anna thinks at first that this narrative must be "an exercise in irony" or "a very skilful parody" of "a certain attitude" prevalent in the party (302). In 1952, four years before the Twentieth Congress and the revelations of Nikita Khruschev, Anna and others in the party are still half-persuaded of a naive conception of power which supposes that the leader of the worker's party must himself be a worker: the Stalin of their official myth is perpetually laboring in his shirt-sleeves alongside rank and file cadres. (In another parody the same "burly figure" stops at the roadside to help a couple of workers get their tractor started [306].)[46] After a second or third reading of the letter, however, it suddenly occurs to Anna that Comrade Ted's story may in fact be "serious."

Other party members display a similar uncertainty of response; when Anna reads the story aloud at a CP meeting her comrades hesitate between condemning it as a subversive parody of the correct attitude toward Father Stalin and praising it as "good honest basic stuff" (305). And this uncertainty, the fact that it can "be read as parody, irony, or seriously," is precisely what seems "important" to Anna about the Comrade Ted manuscript: "It seems to me this fact is another expression of the fragmentation of everything, the painful disintegration of something that is linked with what I feel to be true about language, the thinning of language" (302). Again the implication is that "something [has] happened in the world which [makes] parody impossible." A certain "thinning" of language, which Anna links with a process of general social and cultural disintegration, with the disorganization of the social field into isolated groups and fragmentary specialisms, is said to have made parodic, ironic, and serious discourses effectively interchangeable.

For Anna, the postmodern lifeworld is essentially schizophrenic: the "fragmented society" has produced a "fragmented consciousness. . . . Human beings are divided, are becoming more and more divided, *and more subdivided in themselves*, reflecting the world" (61). And this schizophrenia, this fragmentation simultaneously of language, society, and the individual

46. In *Modern French Philosophy* Descombes remarks that prior to 1968 this naive conception of power had "dominated the politics of intellectuals for more than thirty years" and that it remains "highly conspicuous" in Althusser and his disciples. Of the various Stalin-as-Laborer fables, Descombes comments: "[It is] as if the famous *Caesar fecit pontem* were to be taken literally. Julius Caesar is imagined in shirt sleeves, hauling stones one by one, to construct the pillars of the bridge" (132).

subject, blocks any appeal to a normative language or aesthetic code: one is no longer able to distinguish standard from substandard, acceptable from unacceptable texts. The critical function of parody is thereby disabled, and the act of parodic imitation becomes identical with that of reiteration, quotation, or pastiche. The writer's relation to society thus collapses with that of the enlightened cynic, the political *pasticheur*: the writer is a mimic in an age of postmockery.

These heavily thematized views on parody and schizophrenia are not to be accepted without reservation: there are problems with the way Anna unfolds the problems. But her analysis, which is central to the novel's thematization of its own postmodernity, clearly anticipates the terms of more recent leftist diagnoses. The yielding of parody to pastiche (understood as a shift in the ethos of imitative art from critical to neutral) and the reflection within this movement of a kind of collective schizophrenia (understood as essentially a disorder of language, a breakdown or coming-apart of the signifying chain under the contradictory pressures of late capitalism) are among the most frequently cited features of postmodern art. Adorno wrote from a modernist standpoint that "parody entails the use of forms in the epoch of their impossibility";[47] more recent critical theorists have defined postmodernity as the epoch of the impossibility of parodic form itself.

Some of the examples critics have pointed to include the fictions of Jorge Luis Borges and Donald Barthelme, the paintings and collages of Andy Warhol and Robert Rauschenburg, the musical compositions of Karlheinz Stockhausen and Lukas Foss, the films of George Lucas and Brian de Palma, and the architectural designs of Robert Venturi and Philip Johnson. All share what appears to be a postmodern compulsion to borrow from and mimic other works, other genres, other artists. But a critical intention has been difficult to infer from most of these productions; they seem rather to involve a kind of pure "play-giarism."[48] Though often creating humor through startling acts of transcontextualization (a Rubens nude sharing the canvas with army helicopters and a Coca-Cola sign in Rauschenburg's *Tracer*, for instance), the postmodern does not by most accounts provoke critical laughter, the laughter of derision and correction.[49] There is incongruity, but

47. Theodor W. Adorno, "Towards an Understanding of *Endgame*," in *Twentieth-Century Interpretations of "Endgame,"* ed. Gale Chevigny (Englewood Cliffs, N.J., 1969).

48. See David Bennett, "Parody, Postmodernism, and the Politics of Reading," in *Comic Relations: Studies in the Comic, Satire, and Parody*, ed. Pavel Petr, David Roberts, and Philip Thomson (New York, 1985) 193–210.

49. The term "transcontextualization" is from Linda Hutcheon, *A Theory of Parody: The Teachings of Twentieth-Century Art Forms* (New York, 1985).

it is the sort of open, undirected incongruity that for Freud, and for some critics of postmodernism, is merely "idiocy masquerading as a joke" (*JRU* 138n). The incongruity is between artistic modes or aesthetic systems of equal status, not between a normative or ideal mode and a deviant or false one. And most critics have followed Herbert Spencer in believing that an incongruity that does not *descend* will "fail to cause laughter."[50]

The major statement of this argument is Fredric Jameson's, as presented in a 1984 *New Left Review* article and elsewhere. Attempting to identify the two most basic features of postmodernism, Jameson seizes on "pastiche" and "schizophrenia." In an analysis not too different from Anna Wulf's, he suggests that the loss of the critical function in imitative texts may be a consequence of the "immense fragmentation . . . [of] social life as a whole" under the conditions of late capitalism. With each artistic school or social group "coming to speak in a curious private language of its own, each profession developing its own private code or idiolect . . . the very possibility of any linguistic norm in terms of which one could ridicule private languages" has vanished. And this is precisely "the moment at which pastiche appears and parody has become impossible": "parody finds itself without a vocation . . . and that strange new thing pastiche slowly comes to take its place."[51]

It is not really surprising that this conception of postmodernist culture is so thoroughly prepared for in Lessing's 1962 novel—or, to put it differently, that we find Jameson still elaborating Lessing's thematics twenty-five or thirty years later. The distinction between parody and pastiche, and the insistence on the former's historical impossibility, derives from a distinctly postwar Marxist sense of ideological disorganization and paralysis—a sense of crisis which has never been fully shared on the right, where the process of constituting and articulating political subjects as a hegemonic bloc, as well as that of maintaining (nationalist, racialist, culturalist) myths of belonging and community, have been managed with far greater success. The impossibility of parody is, for Jameson as for Lessing, essentially a "political phenomenon"; it is the impossibility of "any great collective project," of any grand

50. Spencer, "The Physiology of Laughter" 1: 206.

51. The shortest and apparently earliest version of this argument is Fredric Jameson, "Postmodernism and Consumer Society," in *The Anti-Aesthetic*, ed. Hal Foster (Port Townsend, Wash., 1983) 111–25; the more expansive statement is "Postmodernism; or, The Cultural Logic of Late Capitalism," *New Left Review* 146 (July-August 1984): 59–92, rpt. in *Postmodernism; or, The Cultural Logic of Late Capitalism* (Durham, N.C., 1991) 1–54. Quotations from "Postmodernism and Consumer Society" 114, 118, 114; *Postmodernism* 17.

narrative of belonging, in the face of a "stupendous proliferation" on the level of "micropolitics," a proliferation of the languages of "ethnic, gender, race, religious, and class-factional adhesion" (*Postmodernism* 17).

Of course this continuity in the thinking of the left-in-crisis does not guarantee its diagnostic accuracy or usefulness. We need to inquire whether parody *has* in fact become impossible, for Doris Lessing, for postwar literature, or for late-capitalist culture as a whole. If nothing else, the fact that imitation still retains the power to excite laughter, and the suspicion that even postmodern laughter is unlikely to be always and completely free of critical or hostile purposes ("amputated," as Jameson asserts, "of the satiric impulse" [*Postmodernism* 17]), suggest weaknesses in the formulation.

The whole argument rests on a clean and perfectly conventional distinction between parody and pastiche which we might have expected the conditions of postmodernity to have unsettled. In Jameson's discussion, as in Anna's, parody is "the imitation of a peculiar or unique, idiosyncratic style" which communicates the "conviction that alongside [this] abnormal tongue . . . some healthy linguistic normality still exists." Pastiche is "a neutral practice of such mimicry, without any of parody's ulterior motives," a kind of "blank parody" (*Postmodernism* 17). These are highly restrictive definitions, which remove from the range of a mimic's potential comic objects everything but idiosyncracies of style. Jameson cites as an analogue Wayne Booth's distinction between "the 'stable ironies' of the eighteenth century" and "that other interesting and historically original modern thing," the "blank irony" of our times (*Postmodernism* 17). But this parallel merely highlights shortcomings in the analysis. While the mock-heroic parodies of the eighteenth century imitate the language and form of the epic, they do not necessarily indicate the epic as a "stable" object of their ridicule.[52] Are these texts

52. Hutcheon disagrees emphatically with this view and insists that the eighteenth-century mock-epics are examples of parody rather than pastiche. According to her *Theory of Parody*, every text that makes use of "ironic 'trans-contextualization,'" or "repetition with critical difference," is parodic (12, 20). Given Hutcheon's broad definitions of 'ironic' and 'critical,' parody thus covers "a whole range of things. It can be a serious criticism, not necessarily of the parodied text; it can be a playful, genial mockery of codified forms. Its range of intent is from respectful admiration to biting ridicule" (15–16). While this expansive definition enables Hutcheon to include in her study of parody virtually the "whole range" of twentieth-century art, it also leads to the erasure of potentially important distinctions—not only of a distinction between parody and pastiche but of any distinction between modernist and postmodernist forms of imitation. Hutcheon's theory of parody recognizes neither an aesthetic nor a historical shift from the imitations of Beerbohm and Cézanne to those of Barthelme and Rauschenburg.

therefore "blank"? Should they be ruled out of the category of parody? Is a text such as that of Pope, which satirizes social codes other than those with which the linguistic or aesthetic codes of its heroic model are specifically intertwined, a work of pastiche? Is Pope a postmodernist?

One can, of course, choose to adopt these restrictive definitions despite the problems, or provocations, to which they lead. But in that case there is a good deal less at stake in the alleged ascendancy of pastiche over parody than most participants in the postmodernism debate believe. For now pastiche enjoys such considerable latitude that all sorts of comic, satiric, sharply critical forms of imitation are still available to the postmodern. The practice of mimicry can be said to have been neutralized in the postmodern era only as regards idiosyncracies of the language or style being mimicked. To be sure, I would question even this attribution of neutrality to contemporary imitative practice, as well as the supposed stability and intelligibility of earlier parody's "ulterior motives"; where Jameson begins invoking the terminology of Wayne Booth there are bound to be problems.[53] But the point is that neither Jameson nor Lessing is providing grounds for the claim that an aesthetic object or code can be removed from one context to another—transcontextualized—in an ideally neutral way. Such reframings are emphatically not "devoid of laughter," as Jameson wants to believe (*Postmodernism* 17). And when we laugh at them, at the Mona Lisa with a moustache or the *Quixote* rewritten verbatim by Pierre Menard, there is always a tendentious element in our laughter, even if it is directed at our own cultural institutions (at, say, the museum or the university) rather than at Leonardo, Cervantes, or the aesthetic practices of the Renaissance.

Yet even though the "impossibility of parody" turns out to be a much slighter claim than at first appeared, it still raises problems in *The Golden Notebook*. What I have been calling the parodies in that novel still look like parodies and not like pastiche: *Forbidden Love* still presents itself as a critique of a style, an artistic practice, a determinate set of linguistic codes designed to "wring aesthetic pleasure" out of certain materials. And insofar as the text performs this task of critique, there would seem to be a contradiction in Lessing's handling of parody. In advancing thematically the point that parody has become impossible for the contemporary writer, she herself presents recognizable, conventional parodies. We are told that such parody can no longer function, and we see it malfunctioning "in" the novel, but as readers

---

53. For the distinction between "stable" and "blank" (or "unstable") comic practices, see Wayne C. Booth, *A Rhetoric of Irony* (Chicago, 1974).

of the novel we decode it in the usual way—as a technique of ironic ridicule. (This is not the whole story; but the plausability of this sort of argument has done damage to Lessing's critical reputation. Along with other contemporary women writers she has been accused of undertaking only the most superficial, purely thematic departures from the conventional bourgeois novel, naively attempting to present postmodern problems with the worn-out means of premodern fiction.)[54]

Indeed, even the thematics of parody are not unproblematic in the novel. It seems odd that Anna should be so dismayed by the grateful reception of her manuscripts at the film offices and literary quarterlies, since this shows parody functioning just as it is traditionally supposed to. Parody establishes critical distance between itself and what it imitates through irony, and irony always presupposes a divided audience. Every parodic transaction includes (constitutes as its excluded participants) an audience for whom the parody is invisible, an audience so embedded within the imitated discourse that even the exposed defects of that discourse remain hidden to it. Far from being an obstacle to parody, this blindness (the blind spot of ideology) is one of parody's conventional targets. It was, for example, Engels's target in submitting parodic poems to the Biedermeier journal *Stadtbote*. By sneaking these mock poems past the journal's editors, poems that not only imitated the journal's "empty moralising tone" and "glorification of the printed word" but actually consisted of quotations recycled from its own pages, Engels was

---

54. As I argued in the previous section of this chapter, Lessing's use of language is more problematic than her critics have realized. "Realistic" languages are subversively quoted and imitated in *The Golden Notebook*; they are not employed "neutrally" in a naive attempt to resuscitate the bourgeois novel. The text participates in postmodernism as much through its troubled engagement with conventional language as through its disruptions of conventional novelistic form. For an intelligent response to the reading of Lessing as a premodernist, see Dennis Porter, "Realism and Failure in *The Golden Notebook*," *Modern Language Quarterly* 35 (1974): 56–65. Before elaborating his own argument, Porter states the case against Lessing succinctly: "The trouble is that, in spite of the contemporaneity of [Lessing's] themes, there is something distinctly old-fashioned about her determination to evoke twentieth-century reality directly" (56).

Leslie A. Fiedler and John Barth have both generalized that contemporary women writers—at least in America—have failed to move "beyond" the paradigm of bourgeois realism. According to Barth, the "main literary concern" of women writers "remains the eloquent issuance of . . . 'secular news reports.'" See Barth, "The Literature of Replenishment," in Barth, *The Friday Book* (New York, 1984) 195–96; Fiedler, "The Death and Rebirth of the Novel," in *Innovation/ Renovation: New Perspectives on the Humanities*, ed. Ihab Hassan and Sally Hassan (Madison, Wisc., 1983) 228.

using parody as a political weapon—not demonstrating its impossiblity or the impossibility of the "great collective project" of Marxism.[55]

These contradictions between the thematics and the actual functioning of imitation in *The Golden Notebook*, as well as the weakness of an argument that specifies pastiche as the only mode of imitation available to postmodernism, can lead us to a somewhat awkward third term between "parody" and "pastiche" which I have been using intermittently throughout the chapter: (self-)parody. I will now conclude with a brief account of this third term and of its implications for a novel that so sharply highlights the connections between the practice and theory of the postmodern and the concrete failures and frustrations of a postwar political opposition whose subjects are no longer able to say where they belong.

It is true that the presumed political motives of traditional parody such as Engels's would be hampered by the absence of generally recognized linguistic or aesthetic norms; with no stable background against which to display or expose the deviant, no stable ground from which to launch a satiric attack, the parodist is indeed disarmed. The parody itself becomes just another utterance in a discrete language or idiolect. But mimickry need not in these circumstances function according to the supposed logic of "neutral" pastiche. It may rather operate as a kind of radically ungrounded parody, parody without a safety net, parody that is always also self-parody. The ethos of such parody is by no means neutral; the element of mockery, of ridicule, has not lost its bite but merely its supposed stability of orientation. The imitated text or genre is made to look ridiculous, but at the expense also of the mimic, who finds herself always somehow implicated in the ridiculous object of her mimicry.

The parodies in *The Golden Notebook* are all of this sort; they seem at first glance to demand a traditional response, directing our laughter at deviant or substandard productions, but the laughter, once provoked, begins to drift loose from its ostensible target. I have said that *Forbidden Love* (like many other imitations in the novel) mocks the cheap emotional heightening typical of popular films, their translation of painful material realities into the textual *plaisir* of romance and nostalgia. But Anna later recognizes that the irony of the satiric synopsis cuts as deeply into her novel *Frontiers of War* as it does into the proposed film adaptation—that the "unhealthy" emotions that it is the film industry's task to produce and reproduce need not be cynically

---

55. See Margaret A. Rose, *Reading the Young Marx and Engels: Poetry, Parody, and the Censor* (London, 1978) 91–92.

imposed upon "healthy" novels (63). "What made the film company so excited about the possibilities of that novel as a film was precisely what made it successful as a novel":

> The emotion it came out of was . . . the unhealthy, feverish illicit excitement of wartime, a lying nostalgia, a longing for licence, for the jungle. . . . It is so clear to me that I can't read that novel now without feeling ashamed, as if I were standing in a street naked. . . . It is an immoral novel because that terrible lying nostalgia lights every sentence . . . . This emotion is one of the strongest reasons why wars continue, and the people who read *Frontiers of War* will have had fed in them this emotion, even though they were not conscious of it. That is why I am ashamed and why I feel continually as if I had committed a crime.   (63–64)

Anna finds that her parodic imitation of the dishonest and politically irresponsible discourse of popular film can be read equally as a parody of the novel on which it is ironically based (just as Comrade Ted's "serious" version of the Father Stalin myth can be read as a parody of itself and of Anna's own attitudes toward Stalin).

This shameful moment of self-exposure, of authorial nakedness, and not the blind acceptance of the synopsis by a film producer, is the true moment of crisis for Anna as political parodist. For her own work was assumed to represent the aesthetic and political standards against which a lying or immoral film version might be found wanting. If her novel cannot provide these norms then there can be no secure basis for a parody of the deviant adaptation; the film man is in fact justified to call *Forbidden Love* a "perfectly good synopsis." Nor is Anna able to propose other standards that might take the place of those she has subverted through (self-)parody. She admits that "in order to write another [novel], I would have to deliberately whip up in myself that same emotion" (64). Even the Black Notebook, in which Anna attempts to present the "objective," unnovelized version of the *Frontiers* story, is rejected as a sham: "full of nostalgia, every word loaded with it" (153). The very act of writing is an "obscene" practice, an exploitation and falsification of the *material*.

Anna is a postmodern writer in Jean-François Lyotard's sense: for her, "the so-called 'realistic' representations can no longer evoke reality except as nostalgia or mockery, as an occasion for suffering rather than for satisfaction."[56] When her analyst insists that "the artist has a sacred trust" (235), Anna, who "no longer believe[s] in art" (232), can only laugh out loud. Her

56. Jean-François Lyotard, *The Postmodern Condition: A Report on Knowledge*, trans. Geoff Bennington and Brian Massumi (Minneapolis, 1984) 74.

notebooks, with all the imitative "realisms" they contain, are precisely an occasion for suffering and self-mockery; they declare themselves at every turn to be "glossy with untruth, stupid and false" (619). "I'm not," Anna repeatedly acknowledges, "in a position to criticise" (105, 358). Nor does "Doris" place herself in a (pre- or postpostmodern) position from which to criticize "Anna." As I have already pointed out, the inclusion of *Free Women* is precisely calculated as a trap and a disappointment for readers who would rescue "Lessing" from the novel's abyssal structure. Disguised as an authoritative "skeleton, or frame" (vii) external to the problems the novel thematizes, *Free Women* ultimately proves to be another internal, "parasitic" production, perhaps the most compromised and least trustworthy in the whole novel.[57] The "conventional short novel" (vii) can make its appearance only as a critical imitation of itself, framed, recontextualized by the larger text as parody—and as parody of just the kind of Angry realism one might associate with the early Doris Lessing. Though intrinsically realist, honoring all the codes of realist fiction, its frame gives it away as a fake, a self-consciously *retro* production. As Jameson has said of photorealist paintings, which might seem after abstract expressionism to mark a genuine return to realism, they are "false realisms, they are really art about other art, images of other images" ("Consumer Society" 123).

But the fact that *The Golden Notebook*, like so many novels of the last thirty years, puts realisms on display as art about other art should not lead us to understand its postmodernity in narrowly aestheticist terms. Critics of postmodernist fiction have long recognized its (self-)parodic character, its refusal of any stable position from which to criticize. Richard Poirier noted of Borges back in 1968 that "everything in his texts is, in the literal sense of the word, eccentric: he is a writer with no center, playing off, one against the other, all those elements in his work which aspire to centrality."[58] And this "newly developed," uncentered form of parody, said Poirier, is the predominant mode of postmodernist fiction. It is not (to recall Jameson) a literature of "blank" pastiche, "devoid of laughter," but rather (quoting Poirier) a literature that "makes fun of itself," and does so "*as it goes along*": "it proposes not the rewards so much as the limits of its own procedures, it shapes itself around its own dissolvents, it calls into question not any particular

57. Roberta Rubenstein makes this argument in *The Novelistic Vision of Doris Lessing: Breaking the Forms of Consciousness* (Urbana, Ill., 1979): "Just as various sections of *The Golden Notebook* are Anna's self-parody, *Free Women* is Lessing's own self-parody: a pastiche of the flat, somewhat pedestrian style and chronological omniscient narrative form of the earlier volumes of *Children of Violence*" (103).

58. Richard Poirier, "The Politics of Self-Parody," *Partisan Review* 35 (Summer 1968): 352.

literary structure so much as the enterprise, the activity itself of creating any literary form, of empowering an idea with a style" (339).

Similarly, Ihab Hassan, one of the first academics to make postmodernism his field of specialization, has long argued that the postmodern novelist "gives us imitations of the Novel by an author imitating the role of Author" and "parodies [her]self in the act of parody."[59] Such descriptions apply well enough to *The Golden Notebook*. But they understate the extent to which the (self-)parodic text continues to direct criticism beyond itself, and they too strongly suggest that the tensions and contradictions that constitute such a text are those specific to the artist in her heterocosm—that postmodernism is an autonomous phenomenon on the higher plane of art. In fact *The Golden Notebook* is "eccentric," shaped "around its own dissolvents," hopelessly entangled in the logic of (self-)parody, precisely because it will *not* elevate art, will not grant to art a power of synthesis or viable articulation which is lacking on the plane of everyday political practice. The artist and the work of art and the "new laughter" that expresses their (self-)parodic predicament are in and of the world, elements of an actually existing postmodernism, a lived crisis of belonging, of identity and community.

Lessing recognized relatively early that the community invoked within the great modern narrative of emancipation was, like that of the liberals and fascists, "a platonic image, a grail," and that the form of belonging it promised could never accommodate the actual subjects to whom its promise was made. She recognized, too, that merely reconstituting the political subject on an ever more micropolitical level, or merely narrowing the frame within which assessments of effectivity and claims of freedom are made—in short, going local—was a spurious solution by means of which all the same problems would be reproduced in miniature. The effects of these recognitions— on the notions of political commitment, sincerity, and authenticity; on the authority and effectivity of critique; on the social position and role of the writer—are what *The Golden Notebook* traces in the form of a "new laughter" across postwar Britain and across the particulars of its own production and reception. We could say that this new laughter registers both the (fundamental) "impossibility of 'community'" and the (conjunctural, or at least apparent) impossibility of performing progressive cultural work without relying on some telos of community. Though this laughter is no longer new, and indeed might be historicized as the New Left laughter, the laughter that emerged with a dissident and rapidly dis-organizing postwar communism, it is clear that we have not yet heard the last of it.

59. Ihab Hassan, *The Dismemberment of Orpheus*, 2d ed. (Madison, Wisc., 1982) 24.

Six

Community Relations:
Policing Jokes in *The Satanic Verses*

> One of the most grievous sins in Islam is to create discord in the community.
>
> —Mahmoud Ayoub, 1989

> I have fought against communal politics all my adult life. . . . To put it as simply as possible: I am not a Muslim.
>
> —Salman Rushdie, 1990

> We would like to express our solidarity with Salman Rushdie. . . . often it's been assumed that the views of vocal community leaders are our views and their demands our demands. We regret this absolutely. Our lives will not be defined by community leaders.
>
> —Women against Fundamentalism, 1989

> I am Muslim; . . . I am now inside, and a part of, the community whose values have always been closest to my heart.
>
> —Salman Rushdie, 1990

As one reads through the vast entanglement of denunciations, defenses, and apologies which constitutes the *Satanic Verses* affair, it is hard not to be startled by the almost continual appeals to "community." Of the statements collected in the useful volume *The Rushdie File*, for example, nearly all are linked to, or made in the name of, some community or other.[1] On the one hand are the various Islamic communities, ranging from the global—the "whole world community [of Islam]" (*RF* 64), the "international Muslim community" (101), the "Muslim community as a whole" (98)—to the more partial or local: the "Shia community" and the "Sunni community" (93), the

---

1. *The Rushdie File*, ed. Lisa Appignanesi and Sara Maitland (Syracuse, 1990). Hereafter cited parenthetically as *RF*.

"British Muslim community" (105), the "Muslim community in South Africa" (52), the "Muslim community in India" (108), the "Moslem community · in Liverpool" (129). Arrayed against these are a host of liberal and "secular communit[ies]" (239), which likewise assume varying degrees of globalness: the "human community" (102), the "international community" (150), "the non-religious world community" (93), the "international community of writers and intellectuals" (222), the "European Community" (100), "America's literary community" (151), the "community of the UK" (191), and so on. And then there are communities that straddle or disrupt this rigid oppositional scheme: the "religious community" of the Church of England both is and is not in solidarity with the religious community of Islam (190); the "tolerant . . . mixed communities" of an earlier Islamic era are invoked against the ostensibly less enlightened Muslim communities that have succeeded them (214); and the dissident "black communities" of Britain are placed across and between the communities of European liberalism and of Islamic fundamentalism (113).

In some measure this terminological feature of the Affair confirms Paul Gilroy's observation that "the language of community has displaced both the language of class and the langue of 'race' in the political activity of black Britain."[2] But it also should remind us, first of all, that the political activity of Enoch Powell's and Margaret Thatcher's "white" Britain has likewise been pursued through a discourse of community (though one that often mocks or ironizes specifically black versions of this discourse)[3] and, second, that for

---

2. Paul Gilroy, *"There Ain't No Black in the Union Jack"* (1987; Chicago, 1991) 230.

3. The contemporary racist and nationalist discourse of "Britishness" which one associates with Enoch Powell rests heavily on the notion of community. Typical of Powell's rhetoric was his assertion that the British groups that identified themselves as black communities were not in fact part of *the* "national community"; they were "detachments of communities in the West Indies, or India and Pakistan encamped in certain areas of England." Quoted by Errol Lawrence, "In the Abundance of Water the Fool Is Thirsty: Sociology and Black 'Pathology,'" in Center for Contemporary Cultural Studies, eds., *The Empire Strikes Back: Race and Racism in 70s Britain* (London, 1982) 85. In *"Ain't No Black,"* Gilroy notes the use of irony-signaling scare quotes around the phrase "West Indian Community" in a 1976 Metropolitan Police statement to the Home Affairs Select Committee. By means of such "ironic reference," says Gilroy, the official representatives of Britain could distance themselves from the West Indians' self-definition as a community, a self-definition that took place "around the policing question during this period" (92). As I argue below, however, by the early eighties the whole strategics of policing had undergone a shift, whereby the distance between the "two Britains" was maintained not by mocking black communitarianism but by fostering its development along particular lines.

political activists in contemporary Britain the declared turn from a "language of class" to a "language of community" is highly problematic. For, as I have pointed out in earlier chapters, these two languages have long been intertwined in British politics. Not only has "community" served as a god-term for much class-oriented progressive politics in Britain, but a Marxist "language of community" has been repeatedly called upon to displace other languages (of Christianity, of fascism, of liberal nationalism, of modernism, of a discredited orthodox communism) whose own fundamental dependence on "community" is conveniently overlooked. Indeed, the tendency of the new social movements generally, and of black activisms in particular, to distance themselves from the mainstream left by means of this turning replays (with, of course, significant differences) the New Left's own (re)turning to "community" just a generation earlier.

The proliferation of competing communities, community representatives, and community leaders which the *Verses* affair made visible, and to some degree assisted in constructing, tells us also that the general crisis of agency and political identity which Lessing had already indicated in 1962 as *the* postwar problem—the historical cul de sac both for the reiterative artistic productions of postmodernity and for the ever less effectual "movements of various kinds of socialism, or Marxism" (*TGN* xi)—remains a crucial feature of the cultural landscape. The tendency of counterhegemonic activism to stall, as it has done around the Rushdie scandal, in a "mess" of microantagonisms, a disorganized multiplicity of reified "communities," is, as Kobena Mercer puts it in a recent collection devoted to just this problem, the most prominent symptom of "the postmodern predicament of contemporary politics."[4] And this is why it cannot be adequate simply to invoke "community"—even as a goal or telos, an uncompleted and still negotiable entity—as a way of deciphering, much less settling, the problems raised by Rushdie's novel and its reception. We must, rather, number such invocations among the problems themselves.

In this regard I agree with Homi Bhabha, who has argued that one of the most valuable potentialities of the postcolonial perspective—and hence of *The Satanic Verses* itself—is that it can force a rethinking of "the very language of cultural community."[5] But the performance of this rethinking is not

4. A predicament whose emergence Mercer rightly says "should be backdated to the period between 1956 and 1968" (i.e., the period of *The Golden Notebook*). Kobena Mercer, "Welcome to the Jungle: Identity and Diversity in Postmodern Politics," in *Identity: Community, Culture, Difference*, ed. Jonathan Rutherford (London, 1990) 45, 43, 63.

5. Homi Bhabha, "The Third Space," interview with Jonathan Rutherford, in Rutherford, ed., *Identity* 219.

an automatic effect of postcoloniality, always and everywhere. The post-colonial perspective, like the postmodern perspective that is made available in such texts as *The Golden Notebook* (and that, as *The Golden Notebook* indicates, must itself be understood partly in terms of postcoloniality), will always to some degree expose the imaginary and impossible character of the liberal, consensual community, as well as the inadequacy of alternative communitarianisms along classical Marxist, feminist, religious, racialist, or national-liberationist lines. It will always to some degree problematize community, identity, and the prevailing narratives of belonging, on both a theoretical and a strategic level. But, as has become clear in connection with *The Satanic Verses*, the newness toward which this and other postcolonial narratives intermittently gesture, the new thinking of community without organicity, of identity without essence, of solidarity without unity, of a belonging thought *through* rather than *against* the Other—in short, the new oppositional politics of the *organized many* which is not a politics of the *many-as-one*—this is no more the achieved program of postcolonialism than it is that of literary postmodernism. It is rather a question of unfinished business—unfinished business that is at the same time a business of unfinishing: an unworking that is the work-in-progress of postcolonial writing.

That Salman Rushdie should have hoped to advance this project, to perform this work of unworking, through jokes, "pitting levity against gravity," as he expresses it on the first page of *The Satanic Verses*, raises a number of broad questions.[6] I have taken as a starting point for this entire study the idea that comic transactions constitute a field on which the categories and contradictions of community may be most freely set to work and worked upon, a site where the fundamental political operations of inclusion and exclusion, identification and otherization, are performed with special license and often with particular vividness. But I have not on the whole credited the view of laughter as liberation, of joke-work as in itself a form of emancipatory political practice. Though we may agree with Orwell, who remarked that "every joke worth laughing at contains an idea in it—usually a subversive idea,"[7] the work of the joke obviously cannot be reduced to a simple communication of subversive thoughts or dissemination of subversive energies; the joke of the fat anarchist in Conrad's *Secret Agent*, for example, "contains" subversive thinking about anarchy and community in more ways than one. As

6. Salman Rushdie, *The Satanic Verses* (New York, 1989). Hereafter cited parenthetically as *TSV*.

7. George Orwell, "Charles Dickens," in *The Collected Essays, Journalism, and Letters of George Orwell*, ed. Sonia Orwell and Ian Angus (New York, 1968) 1: 425.

I said in the introductory chapter, we have to accept that the sort of work jokes do is multiaccentual rather than programmatic; they resist classification as progressive or conservative events. It is true that, in the interest of what Foucault calls "strategic knowledge," one often proceeds nonetheless to make such a classification, to perform a provisional calculus of political effects. But these instrumental weighings have on the whole suggested to me that joke-work, at least in the literary culture of twentieth-century Britain, answers as well or better to the needs of reaction, domination, and denial than to those of progressive resistance and affirmative action.

Does this generalization apply in the case of Rushdie, a committed writer of the left about whom, notes Timothy Brennan, "the first thing to strike any reader . . . is that, while engaged and pedagogical, his novels are simply funny"?[8] Does the humor in some way limit or compromise the engagement? Brennan has argued (in the best of the many books on Rushdie) that it does, that Rushdie's "insist[ence] on the comic," on a certain "levity" or rising-above as regards human misery, tends, despite its complex insertion into an "essentially religious" structure of imagining (151), to follow a familiar (presumably modernist) logic of "cosmopolitan 'universality'" (165)—affirming the idea "that the 'weightlessness' of the migrant sensibility is universal, . . . that we are all, in a way, migrants because we have all migrated to earth from our home 'out there'" (151). And this cosmopolitan levity, says Brennan, produces a "strangely detached and insensitive" mode of joking as regards not only orthodox Islam but "Britain's black communities as a whole" (165, 164). Rushdie's "cosmopolitan sensibility" can provide us only a "negative and formal parody" of community relations, an overly jocular text that "refuses to take seriously" the communitarian concerns that give the more affirmative (and "very unfunny") work of a June Jordan, a Farrukh Dhondy, or a Roque Dalton its cultural and political potency (166).

Like other critics who have been bothered by Rushdie's commitment to levity, however, Brennan allows that *The Satanic Verses* does perform some politically valuable joke-work on behalf of the "black communities." In particular, it succeeds at least incidentally as a satire of the police state (or at any rate the colonial) conditions that have been fostered by government policies, official and unofficial, in regard to black Britain.[9] From the Commonwealth Immigrants Act in 1968 and the Immigration Act of 1971 (which led to the

8. Timothy Brennan, *Salman Rushdie and the Third World* (London, 1989) 151.

9. Although for Brennan *The Satanic Verses* is more concerned to "capture the immigrants' dream-like disorientation" than to develop a polemical and systematic critique of Thatcherite racism (149), he does acknowledge that "the repressive apparatus of the British state [as regards black Britons] is . . . pictured relentlessly in the novel" (161–62).

establishment of the Illegal Immigration Intelligence Unit at Scotland Yard), to the Nationality Act of 1981 and the ensuing program of computer-aided bureaucratic harassment and expulsions; from the constitution of "black youth" as the central and terrifying object of a new law-and-order discourse during the "mugging" panics of the early 1970s, to the subsequent framing of all inner-city "riots" as expressions of uniquely black behavior which, however, are "not a social phenomenon but crimes";[10] from the abusive exercise of archaic Sus-law prerogatives (which authorized police to harass anyone they deemed a "suspicious person") and the expanded activity of the Special Patrol Groups in the mid- to late-1970s, to the ascendance of the less obviously paramilitary but more deeply interventionist "community policing" paradigm during the Thatcher years—it has been no secret that the black populations that expanded rapidly during England's postwar recruitment of inexpensive African, Asian, and Caribbean labor have been subjected to specially systematic and violent forms of policing by the state. Indeed, as the economisms of the old left have steadily given way in Britain to more complex, neo-Gramscian models of domination, race and policing have come to occupy a particularly prominent place in radical political thought.[11] Even before the full emergence of Thatcherism, Stuart Hall and others at the Center for Contemporary Cultural Studies in Birmingham had seen in the intersection of race and policing the kinds of institutional and discursive practices by means of which a new social and political order was rapidly legitimating itself. With the publication of the center's influential study *Policing the Crisis* in 1978, policing came to be regarded as an exemplary site of neoconservative articulations which brings "race" into strategic relation not only with "law" and "crime" but with such notions as "tradition" and "youth," "family" and "state," "country" and "city," "Britishness" and "for-

10. This was how Douglas Hurd, the Home Secretary, classified the Handsworth riot in 1985. Quoted in John Benyon, "Spiral of Decline: Race and Policing," in *Race, Government and Politics in Britain*, ed. Zig Layton-Henry and Paul B. Rich (London, 1986) 267.

11. Though it just predates the Thatcher years, the Center for Contemporary Cultural Studies' *Policing the Crisis: Mugging, the State, and Law and Order*, coauthored by Stuart Hall, Charles Critcher, Tony Jefferson, John Clarke, and Brian Roberts (London, 1978), remains the most valuable analysis of "race" and policing in postwar Britain. Also indispensable are two pieces by Paul Gilroy: "Police and Thieves," in a later CCCS volume already cited, *The Empire Strikes Back* 143–82, and "Lesser Breeds without the Law," in Gilroy's *"Ain't No Black in the Union Jack"* 72–113. Some useful information can also be found in John Solomos, *Black Youth, Racism and the State* (Cambridge, 1988), and *Black Youth in Crisis*, ed. Ernest Cashmore and Barry Troyna (London, 1982); in the latter collection, see in particular Brian Roberts's discussion of community policing in "The Debate on 'Sus,'" 100–128.

eigness," "community" and "anarchy." To rupture or *dis*organize these articulations, the center compellingly argued, would require a politics of the left more attuned to the hegemonic uses of "race" and to the conditions of life in black Britain, and at the same time a black politics more conscious of the wider social-political framework that has assured the perpetuation and even intensification of British racism.

Rushdie is of course himself a (controversial) figure of the (fragmented) black left, a cultural worker in the new social movements of black Britain. And though his writing throughout the late seventies and eighties seemed to offer few points of contact with the work of the Birmingham center, it is clear that in *The Satanic Verses*, his first book set in England, Rushdie has essentially adapted to novelistic form the center's radical discourse on race and policing. The novel's satiric function is in part to confront that set or system of British institutions which constitutes through acts of ceaseless surveillance and violent containment the very objects of their alarmed attention: "black criminality," "lawless communities," "pathological families" "suspect persons," "illegals." The novel's political agenda is in this respect quite rigid and systematic—despite the fact that Rushdie went on record in 1987, in his scathing review of *Handsworth Songs* (the Black Audio Film Collective's documentary on the 1985 Birmingham uprisings), as being opposed to the kind of black British art that sets out programmatically to "reposition the convergence of 'Race' and 'Criminality,'" accusing such work of arid sociologism, of forsaking the authentic vernacular experiences of black Britons in favor of "the dead language of race industry professionals."[12] (Whether we accept such statements as progressive critiques of an overly remote and academicized form of black cultural production, or rather (following Stuart Hall) as the "lofty, disdainful" pronouncements of the Great Artist, directed at lowly journalistic or documentary cultural forms from a "secure position in the literary firmament,"[13] we confront the basic problematic of the so-called third-world intellectual, whose proximity to street-level struggle is constantly being measured against that of other third-world intellectuals.)[14] Indeed,

12. Rushdie, "*Songs* Doesn't Know the Score," review of *Handsworth Songs*, *The Guardian*, 12 January 1987; rpt. *Black Film British Cinema*, ed. Kobena Mercer (London, 1988) 16.

13. This is how Hall characterized Rushdie's criticisms of *Handsworth Songs*, in a letter to *The Guardian*, 15 January 1987; rpt. *Black Film British Cinema* 17. Ruth H. Lindeborg has analyzed this exchange between Rushdie and Hall over the merits of "documentary," and its relation to Rushdie's own practice in the Brickhall riots section of *The Satanic Verses*, in her fascinating study of Rushdie, still in progress at this time.

14. Running through the whole *Verses* affair is a strong undercurrent of suspicion and

while the *Verses* affair has mostly drawn attention to the policing *of* jokes by the various community representatives who have condemned Rushdie's cosmopolitan levity as blasphemous, obscene, or at the very least "strangely detached and insensitive" toward the "black communities," there has also been a modest countercurrent among black and radical critics consisting of praise for the novel's own policing jokes, which after all provoked the foreign secretary Sir Geoffrey Howe and even Mrs. Thatcher herself to complain of the author's "extremely critical, rude" treatment of their government's policing practices. On the question of race and policing, Howe objected, Rushdie's satire was so intemperately anti-British (read: anti-Thatcherite) as to suggest affinities between Thatcher's Britain and Hitler's Germany.[15] And while the novel does not in fact pursue such an equation (though, as Rushdie said some years ago, the widespread habit of defending Britain's contemporary social order by stressing its points of distinctness from Nazi Germany is in itself a sign that "something must have gone very wrong indeed"),[16] the book's rude mockery of the racist state apparatuses that police Britain's "suspect" populations has weighed in, however slightly, against charges of its offensive levity as regards those populations' common/communal values and concerns.

What I propose to do in the two sections of this chapter is to examine the practice of "policing jokes" in both senses. What kind of work is performed through those of the novel's jokes which take the community-policing of Britain's blacks as an object? What kind is performed through black-

---

hostility toward the postcolonial intellectual, whose status in the Western media as an expert or authority is resented, and whose implicit claims of organic connection are rejected, by black community leaders (whose own status and claims are, however, always subject to challenge along the same lines). From this standpoint no distinction is made between a bitter reactionary like V. S. Naipaul and an outspoken left liberal like Rushdie. Both can be counted among those "'third world' writers and intellectuals who defecate upon the inner ecology of their own people as the agents of secular bigots," to quote Fazlun Khalid, "When Fools Rushed In," in *Sacrilege versus Civility: Muslim Perspectives on the "Satanic Verses" Affair*, ed. M. M. Ahsan and A. R. Kidwai (Leicester, 1991) 244. The special strains on "community" which gather around the figure of the postcolonial intellectual are discussed in Edward Said, "Intellectuals in the Post-Colonial World," *Salmagundi* 70–71 (1986): 44–64; also relevant, despite its focus on the American context, is Cornel West, "The Dilemma of the Black Intellectual" *Cultural Critique* 1 (Fall 1985): 109–24.

15. Sir Geoffrey Howe, BBC Address, quoted by W. J. Weatherby, *Salman Rushdie: Sentenced to Death* (New York, 1990) 173. Mrs. Thatcher's brief statement on the "deeply offensive" nature of Rushdie's novel is quoted in *Rushdie File* 114.

16. Salman Rushdie, "The New Empire within Britain," in Rushdie, *Imaginary Homelands: Essays and Criticism, 1981–1991* (New York, 1991) 129.

community policing of joke-work itself, through critique or proscription of those of the novel's jokes that are judged to be bad for some or all of the black communities? And what does the relationship of these two forms of joke-police-work, the joke presentation of police work and the work of joke-police, both of which announce themselves in this context as oppositional, antiracist political practices, tell us about the hegemony of the right, the problematic of community, and the opportunities for organized resistance and radical social change in end-of-the-century Britain?

Police Work as Joke-Work: The Comic Logic of Crisis Management

> It sometimes seems that the British authorities, no longer capable of exporting governments, have chosen instead to import a new Empire, a new community of subject peoples.
> —Salman Rushdie, "The New Empire within Britain"
>
> *REMEMBER!*
> There is one way that you and your family can be sure of surviving the coming confrontation:
> *Move to a Conservative-controlled borough.*
> —*The Thatcher Papers*

One of the policing questions *The Satanic Verses* is concerned to examine is that of the ideological relation between, as Paul Gilroy expresses it, the thin red line and the thin blue line, the colonial soldiery and the urban police force.[17] To what extent is the law-and-order discourse of contemporary urban Britain a kind of internal and "pre-post-erous"[18] reproduction of the discourse and practice of colonial military occupation, with its imperative to protect white populations, and empire itself, from the always seething and restless natives? Are the black-majority neighborhoods of England's cities

17. "The 'thin red line' of troops in the colonial front line, standing between us and them, between black and white, has been translated into the 'thin blue line' of police, personifying the law. Black transgressions of it become further evidence of their alien character and their distance from the substantive, historical forms of Britishness which are the property of white culture" (*"Ain't No Black"* 110).

18. I take this term from R. Radhakrishnan, "Ethnic Identity and Post-Structuralist Difference," in *The Nature and Context of Minority Discourse,* ed. Abdul R. JanMohamed and David Lloyd (New York, 1990) 50.

the microcolonies of an ever lesser Great Britain—sites where, as on the Falkland (Malvinas) Islands, the colonial drama may still be acted out, perhaps as farce, but nonetheless usefully, securing ideological linkages with an imagined past, affirming the protective and civilizing mission, "the great things which we once did," as Thatcher put it in her triumphant "Falklands Factor" speech at Cheltenham, and the great thing, empire, that "we" still are?[19] The violent urban clashes between black citizens and the police seem inevitably to take on the vivid colors of a grand imperial struggle even while they are officially described as mere outbreaks of "crime"; thus, for example, the Tottenham residents who rose against police in 1985 were widely reported to have "acted on orders" from Moscow,[20] their protest thereby explained in classic colonial fashion in terms of a competing power's move in the Great Game. Are these moments of ideologically and institutionally managed crisis in some sense reassuring to the majority population, enabling the difficult conditions of postcolonial Britain to be processed and familiarized within a stable (colonial) social imaginary?

The Satanic Verses raises these questions by tracing the peculiar (tauto)logics of law and order in contemporary Britain and their role in sustaining an essentially colonial system of categories and borders in the face of a dynamic postcolonial reality. The novel is particularly concerned to draw connections between, on the one hand, the geographical and legal borders of Britain, with the concomitant policing of immigration and citizenship, and, on the other hand, the wider system of imaginary or ideological borders which informs the contemporary (Powellite or Thatcherite) discourse of "Britishness" and structures the everyday policing of the populace. It exposes, that is to say, the essentially colonial framework within which the policing of the urban citizenry and the proscription of "illegitimate" behaviors take place. The book's comic transactions are thus organized around contradictions (the contradictions of imperial democracy) which are reproduced on various registers in the course of policing the "nation," and which among other things mark the gaps between that imagined community and the actual populace and system of social relations it purports to name.

The Satanic Verses begins with the kind of troubled and fantastic crossing-over, the mandatory yet seemingly impossible translation or bearing-across, whose imaginative exploration has become more and more explicitly the

19. Margaret Thatcher, quoted in "'The Fainthearts Were Wrong,'" *Sunday Times*, 4 July 1982, 1.
20. Benyon, "Spiral of Decline" 267.

central project of Rushdie's work since his first novel, *Grimus* (1975).[21] In this case the exemplary postcolonial act of crossing-over is a literal channel-crossing, performed by a pair of literal postcolonial actors, and impeded by all manner of delay and inconvenience. En route to England, the Bombay film star Gibreel Farishta and the Indian-born British TV actor Saladin Chamcha have had to endure 111 days of captivity aboard their hijacked Air India flight, survive a fall from 30,000 feet into the English channel when the hijackers blow up the plane, and then swim or scrape their way ashore. Yet, after facing all these extraordinary difficulties they find that the most formidable obstacles to a successful crossing await them along the border of sane and civilized England. An anonymous phone call reporting a "suspicious person" on the beach has brought three plainclothes Immigration men along with fifty-seven uniformed constables, who have eagerly rushed in with their attack dogs and floodlights from all the surrounding towns in hopes of enjoying a little fun with an illegal. With perfect confidence, these border police descend not upon Farishta, the actual foreigner, but upon the British citizen Chamcha, loading him into a Black Maria, and proceeding with orgiastic hilarity—laughing, hissing, moaning, rolling their eyes—to subject him to various forms of violent indignity.

Of course there is nothing new about satirizing the much-hated customs and immigration services, with their notoriously variable, excessive, and unregulated procedures. Waugh's *Vile Bodies* (1930) begins with very funny channel-crossing and disembarkation scenes, in which British customs officers confiscate the protagonist's "obscene" books (including Dante's *Purgatorio*) and summarily burn the sole manuscript copy of his own just completed magnum opus, all the while submitting his friend Miss Runcible, the daughter of a peer, to an extended strip-search in the next room.[22] But the differences here are more profound than the similarities, and not simply because in 1930 the objects of surveillance and prohibition at the borders are not yet being constituted along fundamentally racial lines. In *Vile Bodies*

21. Salman Rushdie, *Grimus* (London, 1975). Some of Rushdie's most direct statements on the problem of "cultural translation" coincide with his journalistic legitimation as a third-world intellectual in the years immediately following publication of *Midnight's Children* (New York, 1980). See, for example, his remarks in "The Indian Writer in England," in *The Eye of the Beholder: Indian Writing in English*, ed. Maggie Butcher (London, 1983) 75–83. Parts of this paper—a passage on the "translated" status of the postcolonial writer (80) and a popular song celebrating the polyglot-yet-stable nature of Indian subjectivity (83)—reappear in Salman Rushdie, *Shame* (New York, 1984), and *The Satanic Verses*, respectively.

22. Evelyn Waugh, *Vile Bodies* (Boston, 1955).

much of the comic effect lies in the discrepancy between the outrageous actions of the border police and the lack of repercussion on those whom they police. Though the burning of his manuscript deprives Adam Fenwick-Symes of his "whole livelihood" (25) and forces him to cancel his engagement, and though Miss Runcible's "too, too shaming" maltreatment makes a stir in the evening papers (24), life goes on exactly as before for Waugh's Bright Young Things. "Oh, I say, Nina," Adam tells his fiancée afterward on the phone, "there's one thing—I don't think I shall be able to marry you after all." "Oh, *Adam*, you are a bore. Why not?" "They burnt my book." "Beasts. Who did?" "I'll tell you about it tonight." "Yes, *do*. Good-bye, darling." "Good-bye, my sweet" (38).

In *The Satanic Verses* the joke is precisely *not* that of the "Dover ordeal" that leaves everyone and everything within the borders unchanged. The most pronounced incongruity from which these early scenes produce their comic effects is that between Chamcha's longstanding idea of England and his new experience of England. In this respect, the novel presents a postcolonial version of the recognized satiric device of the naive stranger in a strange land. Like Rushdie himself, who says he came to England expecting a gentle green world "composed of Test Matches at Lord's presided over by the voice of John Arlott," Chamcha is both privileged enough and politically naive enough to have accepted the dream-England of Britain's self-mythologizing dominant class—that dream of "the fairest, most just, most decent society ever created upon the face of the earth"—as reality.[23] After living comfortably with this myth during some twenty insular years of residence in England, Chamcha is now for the first time made aware of an utterly incompatible set of circumstances. Bewildered, he can only tell himself that he is not, cannot possibly be, in England. There is no room, he tells himself, in such a decent, common-sensical country for this sinister Black Maria in which agents of the state carry out acts of torture against their fellow citizens. The point of course is that there *isn't* room in the social imaginary of the dominant culture for the realities of much black British experience. Chamcha's crossing has confronted him with what Rushdie calls the unbridgeable "gulf or rift . . . [between] black and white descriptions of society," between black and white "realities."[24]

But this insistence on the significance of the border experience in shaping the (race-specific) "reality" of England itself is taken further in the course of

23. Rushdie, "The Indian Writer in England" 81.
24. Ibid.

Chamcha's grotesque interrogation. For Rushdie's perspective is not simply more critical than Waugh's (in the sense of offering a more total or symptomatological critique of the society's peripheral policing practices); it is critical in a different way. To a considerable extent Rushdie's work reflects the impact on postcolonial writing of Edward Said's Foucaultianism, with its emphasis on the constitutive role of the various institutions that gather, organize, and disseminate knowledge about "race": the universities, the news and entertainment media, the hospitals and social welfare bureaucracies, and the armies and police forces. With the publication, between 1978 and 1981, of Said's three important studies of orientalism, it came to be widely recognized that such institutions do not simply organize or discipline the "whites" and the "blacks," the "Europeans" and the "orientals," and so forth, but supply and manage the discursive system in which subjects take on their "racial" identities and relational positions in the first place.[25]

In the arrival scenes of *The Satanic Verses*, the basic incongruity is between Chamcha's presumed identity as a sophisticated and respectable British citizen, one who in fact has nothing but disdain for penniless and uneducated immigrants from South Asia, and his reconstituted identity as a "suspect person" in the hands of the immigration officials, for whom one Paky is the same as another. The ultracivilized assimilationist finds himself undergoing a grotesque demoniasis, becoming literally an animal, a goatlike creature with actual horns (141), incapable of using language or even of controlling his bowels. When he attempts to address the officers with a properly English demeanor and tone of authority and to impress upon them the enormity of their mistake, he is interrupted by a sudden spilling of his own excrement on the floor around him, and manages only to emit a kind of bleating "Maa-aa-aa" (159).

This is a blacker humor than Waugh's: the young bobbies in the Black Maria are described beating and gouging Chamcha like rampaging hooligans while they carry on a violent quarrel over whether the Tottenham Hotspur double team of the early 1960s was superior to the present-day Liverpool squad (161); their superior officers indulgently look the other way during this bit of "fun," while, among themselves, they consider the football question more solemnly and professionally, stressing the need, in dealing with hooli-

25. Edward Said, *Orientalism* (New York, 1978); *The Question of Palestine* (New York, 1979); *Covering Islam: How the Media and the Experts Determine How We See the Rest of the World* (London, 1981). An interview Rushdie conducted with Said, "On Palestinian Identity: A Conversation with Edward Said," appears in Rushdie, *Imaginary Homelands* 166–84.

ganism, for increaed police vigilance and more thoroughgoing methods of surveillance (162).

And it is a more pedagogical humor as well, making explicit the idea that Chamcha's dehumanization and demonization are the effects of the dominant culture's knowledge of and power over its racial Other. "They describe us," a fellow prisoner explains to Chamcha as he recovers from his injuries in a medical facility at the detention center. "They have the power of description, and we succumb to the pictures they construct" (168). The detention center is filled with the grotesque victims of this discursive power: there is a woman in one of the beds who has been turning into a water buffalo, a group of Nigerian businessmen who have sprouted tails, and some Senegalese vactioners who stopped in London simply to change planes and found themselves transformed into snakes.

These comic transactions make plain, too, the fact that it is by controlling and policing this line of racial difference that the nation sustains the myth of its own (horizontal) community. The police become particularly enraged when Chamcha, whose name they say is no kind of name for an Englishman, calls attention to the heterogeneous names and accents of the immigration officers themselves, which, he points out, don't sound particularly Anglo-Saxon, either. At this impertinence, they turn upon Chamcha with such outraged countenances that he fears they will rip him to pieces. But Officer Novak simply takes hold of him and sternly slaps his face while replying, "I'm from Weybridge, you cunt. Get it straight: *Wey*bridge, where the fucking *Beatles* used to live" (163).

Significantly, when Chamcha challenges the police in this way, threatening the imaginary community of Englishmen whose borders they are charged with maintaining, they suddenly begin to look all alike, "rendered equal and identical by their tension and fear" (163). And when Chamcha is recovering from his ordeal in the detention center, coming to understand the dehumanizing effects of Britain's racialist border policing, he suddenly tells two rebellious detainees who are planning a break-out that they can count on his solidarity with them (170). The whole scene and system of border policing thus unfailingly generates the subjects and objects it requires. An ethnically, geographically, and linguistically heterogeneous group of men (whose fractiousness is unfolded in the football quarrel, which brings them almost to the point of demonstrating on one another what they mean by such hooligan terms as "bollocking," and "bottling," [161]) are transformed into "equal and identical" English subjects, sutured together (and even, apparently, to the subversive expatriot John Lennon) by their fear of alien elements penetrating the borders of their imagined community, a fear that in fact expresses repressed knowledge of unassimilable difference within that "community" itself. And a "British Citizen first class" (164), Oxford educated, politically conservative, even reactionary, an admirer of everything English including the English police (408)—a man who has spent his entire life trying to muster the finer points of Englishness—is transformed into a plotting alien, an "illegal," properly "suspect" and even dangerous, a politicized "ethnic" prepared to transgress English law to secure his human rights (402).

As I suggested at the outset, this whole tauto- and comicological framework through which the policing of borders concretizes both the English nation and the (internal) foreign menace, effecting the rigid communification (nationalization) of an in fact permeable and irremediably differentiated social space, and producing alien objects whose border-crossing transgressions pose the one acknowledgeable decommunifying threat to that space, reproduces itself in *The Satanic Verses* along Britain's *internal* borders, the new intraurban borderlines between black and white, them and us. This internal reiteration is played out most extravagantly in the "Granny-Ripper" subplot that entangles Chamcha as he hides himself away from the authorities in the attic of a "Brickhall" (Brixton/Southall) rooming house. A series of mutilation-murders of elderly women has occurred, and with the energetic assistance of the media this situation quickly produces the kind of urban panic or "crisis" whose management by concerned authorities serves to reinforce the manichean structure of the British social imaginary.

The fact is that these murders have no particular connection to London's black populations; the killer will turn out to be a rather nondescript white man with pale skin, blond hair, and hazel eyes (453). But because the victims have been white, the suspicion of a racial motive immediately passes through the police communication channels (287). (Had the victims been black, a local activist points out, the racial-motive hypothesis would never have arisen [287].) More crucially, the mutilation of the victims, their organs removed and arranged in ritual fashion around the corpses, lungs beside ears and hearts in mouths, suggests a "human fiend" or devil-man: *black* magic, the terrifyingly anticivilized practices of the racial Other. And naturally, as this idea of a satanic black murderer takes hold in the public imagination, the police begin to intensify their detention and interogation of "tints" (288).

But here again, the "fantastic" and comical flavor of the narrative depends on the *constitutive* function of racist policing practices, whose intensification can only intensify the "racial" problem they have constructed, leading to a spiral of intensified resistance to intensified policing. The management or policing of the situation unfailingly produces and reproduces the very subjects of "racial crisis," including, of course, the "black" subjects, whose (communitarian) perspectives and actions also follow the dreamlike or witty logic of the policed panic. White nightmares of a sulphurous black devil, sparked by the murders and intensified by their policing, provide the city's Asian and Caribbean populations, already abuzz with rumors concerning the presence among them of the horned and deformed Saladin Chamcha, with an image they can "occupy . . . inhabit, . . . reclaim" as their own in the form of a "what-else-after-all-but-black-man, maybe a little twisted up by fate class race history, all that, but getting off his behind, bad and mad, to kick a little ass" (287).

In the black-majority neighborhoods this "dream-devil" of colonial revenge begins to catch on (287). Devil tee shirts and buttons proliferate, displayed as badges of black solidarity (352); young people take to wearing rubber devil horns on their heads. But this black appropriation of the white-conjured devil is in turn reappropriated by police community relations officers, who use it adroitly to shift attention from a bizarre racist-secret-society witchcraft scandal in their own ranks to this alarming devil-cult among black and Asian youths (286). Though the latter form of alleged diabolism consists mainly in wearing silly hats, it can easily be made to seem more threatening than the late-night rituals of "working-class Freemasonry" at the local police station (280), since black and Asian youths after all constitute the quintessential criminal class. The police can thus begin issuing statements to the effect that only intensified surveillance and investigation of this new black occultism will lead to the diabolical serial killer, a strategy which justifies violent raids on homes and businesses suspected of involvement in the occultist conspiracy against white society (288). The whole witty process of collective dream-work ultimately produces its inevitable, predictable "suspect"—not the pathetic Chamcha, but Uhuru Simba, a black community leader whose charismatic militancy has already established him in police and media perspectives as both criminal element and diabolical Other. And this key moment in the management of the crisis, which effects not only the criminalization of the contemporary black urban political activist but also his identification with the black-magic "voodoo priest" of the colonial imaginary (289), serves once again to intensify rather than alleviate the conditions of "racial crisis." Gangs of whites begin taking reprisals—beatings, attacks on homes and businesses, and so on (289)—against the people of darkness whose diabolical leader has visited such obscene, primitive-exotic crimes upon the civilized community of white Britain. In response, the various Asian and Caribbean neighborhood groups defiantly close ranks, carefully keeping veiled the widespread dislike of Simba himself (a misogynist bully [415]) and presenting precisely the kind of solidary revolutionary front—the unified and oppositional "black community" committed to remaking British society "from the bottom to the top" (414)—on which the whole imagery and apparatus of the "thin blue line" depends for its continued legitimacy.

Within a few days, during which Simba dies suspiciously in custody (having ostensibly levitated off his prison bunk and crashed to the floor while having a bad dream [449]) and then the actual Granny Ripper is apprehended (not by the Metropolitan Police, but by a Sikh community patrol group), Brickhall is burning and a full-blown "riot" is under way. With this general violence as a screen, the police are able to torch the Brickhall Community Relations Center, thereby killing two more community activists, Chamcha's estranged wife Pamela and her lover Jumpy, who alone are capable of documenting the cult of witchcraft within the Metropolitan Police. The same community liaison officer from the Brickhall constabulary who called Simba's fatal tumble a "million-to-one shot" explains that Pamela and Jumpy, being radical extremists and hence no doubt acting from some obscure far-left political motivation, apparently set a petrol fire in their own Community Relations Center and then were not sensible enough to leave the building before the flames engulfed them (465).

The unfolding of this wildly elaborated racial scenario out of a white man's crimes against white women is typical of Rushdie's bent for comic escalation, by means of which an ever more pronounced incongruity appears between initial and final moments of an event—an incongruity whose preposterous and hyperbolic character can, however, be "resolved," or systematically accounted for, by way of a concrete and recognizable social logic. Much of the humor of "magical" (or "mythical") realism consists of this sort of extravagant but rigorous tracing out of the processes of myth production—that is, of the ways in which a society's interpretive fables or ideologemes are produced and circulated. For no matter how fantastic their products, such processes do conform to specifiable logics and occur along predictable institutional paths.

In this particular instance, the institutional paths along which the racial "crisis" unfolds are those of "community policing" as it has emerged over the last twenty years. Community policing is a term that, like virtually all terms that contain the word "community," is meant to convey a certain warmth. One envisions the unarmed bobby on his home beat, himself an organic member of the community, a known and trusted presence whose genuine connectedness with the neighborhood population—a connection forged through participation in the schools, clinics, and community relations centers—enables him to anticipate and monitor local problems, grievances, antagonisms, and to intervene effectively before these small troubles become larger ones. Though loaded up with nostalgia and traditionalism, this image has something to be said for it over and against the contrasting ideal of the high-tech strike-and-withdraw special force, that team of faceless trouble-shooters storming across the community border to quash or intercept or mop up and then returning to their proper home on the "us" side of the thin blue line. And it is the much greater warmth of the organic-bobby idea, the strong appeal it held not only for black and Asian Britons suffering under the boots of the Special Patrol Groups but for everyone from mainstream liberals to staunch traditionalists and even some key police leaders, that made possible during the early Thatcher years a shift of both rhetoric and policy toward the "community policing" paradigm.

As (among other things) a satire of contemporary policing practices in urban England, *The Satanic Verses* could be expected to represent such a shift in skeptical terms, as one in which the rhetorical dimension is a good deal more pronounced than the practical. It would expose and exploit, that is to say, the gaps between community policing as an ideal and community policing as a set of concrete practices designed to obstruct and defeat truly communitarian efforts on the part of low-income minority populations. But while such gaps are indeed visible in the novel, its policing jokes do not leave unquestioned an *idea* of community policing which needs only to be carried out more faithfully in practice. On the contrary, comic episodes such as that of the Granny Ripper throw this idea itself into doubt and underscore the difficulties involved in appropriating to the advantage of oppressed black populations a discourse of community ("community relations," "community liaisons," etc.) whose historical roots and contemporary functions are essentially colonial.

It is not always recognized that the discourse of community policing originated with the police themselves rather than with any grass-roots or popular "community" initiatives. When the term first began to circulate widely in the aftermath of the early-seventies uprisings (the manifestly collective character of which had put into question the then-dominant articulation of race and policing around the notion of "mugging"), its key promoters were either police officials, such as the chief constable for Devon and Cornwall John Alderson, or social-science ideologues effectively in the service of the police, such as *Shades of Gray* author John Brown. Indeed, years before Brown gained a popular audience with the BBC adaptation of *Shades of Gray* in 1979, his work had become assigned reading for officers-in-training at Bramshill police college (where Alderson had been commandant in 1970).[26] Moreover, as Paul Gilroy and others have noted, in developing what was simultaneously a new set of urban policing practices and a new way for the police to talk about themselves, the promoters of community policing borrowed extensive data and terminology from the Northern Ireland situation and from the literature of counterinsurgency in general.[27] The fundamental aim of community policing (and this is where it diverges from the reactive, strike-and-withdraw strategy, despite many "embarrassing" tactical overlaps) is to occupy the space of the other in such a thorough and integrative way— to so "penetrate the community in all its aspects," as Alderson put it—as to lend the occupation a virtually natural or organic character.[28] The "thin blue line" is not erased but rather woven through the whole fabric of the "community," woven into the very logic of communitarian politics. To achieve their goals, the police must participate proactively in the communitarian process—not mocking the notion of a "black community," as earlier officials had done, but facilitating the construction of a black community in which policing would seem to be horizontally integrated with all other institutional activities (education, social services, and so on) but in fact dominates those activities by overseeing and organizing their increasingly centralized functioning.[29] As a number of social critics have noted, the whole approach rests

26. See Gilroy, "Police and Thieves" 153–82. Before its BBC adaptation, large portions of *Shades of Gray* appeared in *Police Review*, 17 March 1978. But it was John Brown's earlier study, *A Theory of Police/Immigrant Relations* (Cranfield, Bedfordshire, 1974), which had established him as a useful resource for police and found its way onto the syllabi at Bramshill. It was in this study, says Gilroy, that Brown first invokes "community" as an entity "which it has become the burden of the police to reconstruct in the face of crisis and social disintegration" ("Police and Thieves" 157). John Alderson's fullest statement of the community-policing doctrine is *Policing Freedom* (London, 1979).

27. Gilroy, "Police and Thieves" 167, 171–72.

28. Alderson, *Policing Freedom*, quoted by Gilroy, "Police and Thieves" 168.

29. Thus while the phrase "West Indian Community" was (as I mentioned above) still being put in ironic scare quotes in an official 1976 Metropolitan Police statement, Sir David McNee, commissioner of the Metropolitan Police during the first Thatcher term, made broad use of the cooperative, horizontalist language of black communitarianism. In a typical statement of 1982, McNee called for the police to "get alongside the community" and to elicit "the help of the public, particularly the black community," in carrying out "traditional" (i.e., communitarian, preventive, "home-beat") police functions. It is difficult to know what part was played by cynicism and what part by naiveté in the veiling of vertical relations of power behind this language of "alongside"; the same difficulty arises, of

on the direct or indirect "'community leadership' role of the police."[30] For only by setting themselves up "as an alternative source of moral and social authority in the [inner city] areas,"[31] can the police achieve in their occupation of these microcolonies what every program of colonial counterinsurgency ultimately aims at: a "shrinking arena of legitimate politics."[32]

In elaborating this connection between community policing and colonial policing, Rushdie's novel raises questions beyond that of what constitutes proper or acceptable urban police practices. Indeed the book tends ultimately to minimize any supposed distinction between the paramilitary, reactive, "Robo-cop" paradigm and the community or "preventive" paradigm that has come to displace it. The latter continues to leave room for a good deal of reactive violence, after all, and the fact that it takes its conception of police work from the field of military intelligence rather than from that of combat scarcely makes it any less techno-militaristic. What matters, in the Granny Ripper episode and elsewhere in Rushdie's novel, is that the community police work invariably succeeds in a communification that is simultaneously a colonialization of majority-black urban neighborhoods: even and especially at the moments of violently aggravated crisis and determinedly oppositional community action, the "community" is being quite successfully "policed" in this sense. Through the efforts of the novel's Police Community Relations Representatives and the rest of the official apparatus of community construction/occupation, any truly radical black political activity is unfailingly removed from the "arena of legitimate politics" (becoming associated, even among the blacks themselves, not only with insurgency but with diabolism, murder, madness: the "outside" of civilization), and the community activist is unfailingly criminalized, marked out as an extremist and a key offender, not only against white British society but against the "community" on whose behalf he or she is active. (It is the "radical" community activists who, according to the community liaison officer, are responsible for destroying the Community Relations Center.) The apparent softening or blurring of the thin blue line effected by supposed police capitulation to community politics thus in fact reinforces the manichean, and specifically colonial, framework within which that internal border is continually reasserted.

As I remarked earlier, the very success of this police work is a large part of

---

course, in connection with all more or less powerful advocates of community. See "McNee Upholds Traditional Police Methods," London *Times*, 24 June 1982: 3.

30. Roberts, "The Debate on 'Sus'" 116.

31. Stuart Hall, *The Hard Road to Renewal: Thatcherism and the Crisis of the Left* (London, 1988) 79.

32. Gilroy, "Police and Thieves" 146.

what enables such episodes as that of the Granny Ripper to succeed as joke-work: a startling incongruity appears between the seemingly ill-managed and fantastic activities of the various community participants and their actual conformity to a set course of colonial institutional requirements. On the one hand this incongruity underscores the fantastic or mythological element in every production from the colonial imaginary, including the most profession-alized or bureaucratic ones. The more thoroughly rationalized a racist practice becomes, the more grotesque it can be made to appear. But the success of police work as joke-work also points to a serious problem for advocates of community politics, insofar as the community, which is always an entity more or less "in crisis," is always being constructed by a system of crisis manage-ment, whose terms always already occupy the very ground of "community."[33] When "community policing" is seen not as a contradiction (a falsifying label) but as a tautology, policing being a condition of possibility for community, a (dominant) part of the (ostensibly horizontal) framework within which "com-munity" appears, what space remains for a black-community leader, a black-community politics, which is not caught up in a sort of joke-logic of colonial self-perpetuation?

To put this differently (adopting one of Stephen Greenblatt's useful tag phrases): where in the process of postcolonial "self-fashioning" might there by room for radical communitarian agency? If the self of the radically resis-tant black subject, the Brixton or Southall "community activist," is in certain key respects constituted through policing practices and in relation to the community-in-crisis, and if every discursive appropriation effected by this subject disappears into an infinite regress of appropriation/counterappro-priation (such that it is always as true to say that the subject of commu-nitarian resistance is a self or subject fashioned by power, as it is to say that the subject fashioned by power has remade itself as a subject of commu-nitarian resistance), then what forms of identification or solidarity may emerge which are not on some level complicitous and counterproductive? In

---

33. The recognition among those active in black community politics that the "commu-nity" is a negotiable entity "constituted in political institutions and practices" (John Eade, *The Politics of Community: The Bangladeshi Community in East London*, Research in Ethnic Relations Series [Aldershot, 1989] 15) has not prevented a certain blindness in this regard. The problem is that the community is still conceived as the positive side of a struggle for power, the activist's goal and challenge being to build community through participation in local institutions such as neighborhood centers and schools. The intricate relations be-tween the work that goes on in these institutions, the "leadership role" of the police, and the colonial logic of urban communification are thus lost to a politics that will negotiate for community but will not negotiate community itself.

the Foucaultian comedy of *The Satanic Verses*, the "black British" political subject, the *kale angrez*, is always a paradox, an "instant self-contradiction" (which was Christian Metz's phrase for certain forms of joke),[34] never simply a positive term in a diadic contest. And by the same token, the "black communities" have their existence only in the specificities of their impossible and contradictory, their "pre-post-erous" colonial character, never in any secure and prior knowledge of themselves.

This aspect of the novel—its willingness to accept that every available politics of black community resistance is in some sense a kind of joke, a necessary self-contradiction—has perhaps been felt as a provocation and a betrayal, a "cosmopolitan" indulgence, one might say. It no doubt accounts in some measure for the novel's failure, even among non-Islamic community leaders, to generate more than a few murmers of praise for its savage indictment of Thatcherite policies. And as a strategic intervention its effect has so far been largely to bolster narrowly communitarian thinking on both sides of the "line." Nevertheless, the (joke-)work of unworking the well-policed black "community," of unraveling the logic by means of which urban communification, including that which takes place under the auspices of an oppositional community politics, has served the purposes of urban colonialization, is far from frivolous. However much less uplifting this "levity" may be than the gestures of an autonomous or uncontaminated community-in-opposition, it *is* the "serious" postcolonial politics of Rushdie's novel. The text is politically valuable not to the degree that it conveys through satire a black writer's disgust and anger as regards Britain's community police force, but to the degree that it begins to unmake the system of thought which can conceive of the "black community" only as a positive entity that somehow preexists and radically opposes the apparatuses of domestic colonialization.

Systematic Satire and the Politics of Positive Images

> I fear that under the pretext of 'systematic denunciation' a sort of open-ended eclecticism will be installed which will serve as a cover for all sorts of manoeuvres.
>
> —Michel Foucault, "Powers and Strategies"

While I would want to argue that it is ultimately the novel's questioning of the status and function of community in the space of "community policing" and its concomitant problematizing of community politics and community lead-

34. Metz, "Instant Self-Contradiction," in Blonsky, ed., *On Signs*, 259–66.

ers that have made *The Satanic Verses* unpalatable to so many politicized urban sectors of Britain, this is not immediately apparent in the kinds of denunciation and critique that have most often been marshaled against the book and its author. Almost invariably these attacks have focused on the novel's mockery of the underdog and/or on its lack of "positive images." Where is the dignified and uncompromised (not to say sacred) figure of Mohammed? Where are the reverent portrayals of the Prophet's followers and companions? Where are the decent and sensible black activist characters? Where, indeed, is there a single representative of black or Muslim Britain who is not, to some considerable degree, *ridiculous*—either a fool or a freak, a sham or a stereotype?

One needn't support the overzealous joke-police who have called for (and begun to carry out) assassinations of the novel's author, translators, and publishers to recognize a legitimate ground of concern here. What conceivable challenge is after all being met, what desirable aims could possibly be furthered, by humor that confirms the prejudices of the dominant many against the downtrodden few? "Why," Edward Said asked in the *New York Times*, "must a Moslem, who could be defending and sympathetically interpreting us, now represent us so roughly, so expertly and so disrespectfully to an audience already primed to excoriate our traditions, reality, history, religion, language, and origin?" (*RF* 165). This sense of anger and shame at having been mocked before an audience of laughing strangers informs all the many attempts to convey by analogy the impact of the *Verses* on Muslim readers. As one outraged commentator expressed it: "It is as if Rushdie had composed a brilliant poem about the private parts of his parents, and then recited the poem in the market place to the cheers and laughter of strangers! These strangers then paid him money for all the jokes about his parents' genitalia."[35] Just as Said admits that Rushdie's portrait of Islamic culture,

---

35. Ali A. Mazrui, *The Satanic Verses or a Satanic Novel?* (Greenpoint, N.Y., [1989?]) 3. The genre of the *Verses* analogy which sprung up by necessity in 1989 is in itself a fascinating instance of the sort of impeded cultural translation Rushdie's work enacts and thematizes. Mazrui's text, which attempts to supply analogies for every audience and every dimension of the Affair, runs into some typical problems. Just as his secular analogy (the "pornographic betrayal of ancestry" in the marketplace) assumes a certain horror of genitalia, so his Christian analogy ("the last supper described as a homosexual orgy") depends on a certain homophobia. The analogies he uses to legitimate Muslim calls for censorship and execution, which are drawn from actual events (Islamic outcry over the *Verses* is like American outcry over the U.S. flag installation at Chicago's Art Institute; the Ayatollah's *fatwa* is like Reagan's "you can run but you can't hide" speech on terrorism,

while disrespectful, is also expert, this critic charges Rushdie not with mis-representation but rather with the jocular revelation of an embarrassing or suppressed truth (one's parents do, after all, possess genitalia). This is not to say that the writers of such analogies would actually concede the accuracy of Rushdie's representations, only that an overriding emphasis is placed on his indelicate mockery and on the "laughing strangers" who make up his puta-tive audience. Despite the very specific charges of blasphemy, the lists of Rushdie's "lies," and so forth, it may be fair to say that the *Verses* affair has less to do with content than with questions of tone or modality. The humor is the real problem: it is not that Rushdie wrote objectionable things, but that he wrote them with a smirk on his face.

Shabbir Akhtar, a member of Bradford's Council for Mosques and one of the principle organizers of Muslim opposition to the *Verses*, made this argu-ment quite explicitly. Citing the heterodox and heretical traditions in Islamic scholarship, Akhtar observed that even the most "iconoclastic content" could be legitimated by a minimally "reverent tone." But while he allowed that there might be room within such reverence for a certain amount of humor, he made clear that *The Satanic Verses* was scarcely a work that stays within these bounds of legitimacy; Rushdie's humor "moves beyond legitimate sat-ire . . . into forms of parody and caricature wholly motivated by indignation and hatred."[36]

Recent debates, mainly in the United States but spilling over into Britain, concerning "political correctness" and the legal status of "hate speech" have accustomed us to this sort of distinction between "legitimate" comic transac-tions and those whose only effect is to put racist, sexist, or other bigoted sentiments more actively into circulation. We may hesitate to think of Salman Rushdie as the Andrew "Dice" Clay of postcolonial Britain, but in principle the *Verses* affair differs very little from other high-profile disputes over hu-morists whose jokes appear to feed the hostility and resentment felt by established groups toward those on the margins or constitutive outsides of their imagined communities.

I am not concerned here to defend the "rights" of such humorists or to

---

which paved the way for the assassination-by-bombing attempt on Moammar al-Quaddafy in 1986), likewise depend on essentially reactionary—in this case narrowly nationalist and racist—attitudes. For a progressive or even moderately liberal reader these unfortunate "translations" into Western terms can only reinforce the prejudices they mean to amelio-rate.

36. Shabbir Akhtar, *Be Careful with Muhammad! The Salman Rushdie Affair* (London, 1989) 30.

argue for the "higher" value of the "Wog" joke, the "Nigger" joke, as a social safety valve, as a subversion of bourgeois laws governing propriety and politeness, as a manifestation of Western cultural "freedom," or what have you. Humorists who trade in racial or sexual bigotry are neither a precious cultural resource nor, to understate the case, an endangered species. The problem is that the distinction between these humorists and the "correct" or "legitimate" ones is rather more difficult to maintain and to police than most people are willing to admit. Since comic transactions invariably draw upon hostilities and resentments of the most unreasoned character, and circulate these among participants in particularly treacherous, multiaccented ways, no joke is entirely innocent of cultural dirty work. And by the same token no joke is simply or wholly "motivated by . . . hatred" of a particular person or group. As I have been insisting throughout the present book, both the object(s) of the joke and the positioning of the joke's speaking and receiving subjects in relation to the object(s) are to some degree unstable and negotiable. To the extent that the policing of nonlegitimate jokes involves an assertion of (1) the comic object's unitary identity as representative of a particular outgroup or marginalized "community," (2) the subject's unique and fully conscious motive of enunciation, namely hostility, and (3) the transaction's sole or predominant effect on its other participants, namely the dissemination and intensification of that hostility, it precludes any very close examination of the joke-work actually taking place.

Curiously, however, even if we accept as a strategic convenience this very approximate and reductive model of the joke, the politics of humor in *The Satanic Verses* remains more complex than either the novel's critics or its defenders have tended to suggest. To begin with, the text appears to be highly opportunistic, making equal and indifferent use of "correct" and "incorrect" comic objects. Islamic fundamentalists? The character of the Imam (based on Ayatollah Ruhollah Khomeini) attempts to maintain his spiritual purity during a period of exile in the decadent West by drinking water at the rate of two hundred glasses per day—but the water itself is purified in a filtration machine imported from America (209). Christian fundamentalists? There's Eugene Dumsday (also based on an actual religious figure),[37] a "humble foot soldier" in God's army, who hopes to take the American Baptist battle against narcotics, premarital sex, and (above all) Darwinism to India, but manages only to bore a rude and uncomprehending

---

37. According to Rushdie, Dumsday is modeled on an American creationist he encountered in South India, named Duane Gish (*Imaginary Homelands* 368).

audience at the Rotary Club of Cochin, Kerala with his endless slide presentation (75–76). Secular crusaders, revolutionaries of the left? There's Allie Cone, a famous mountain climber, whose radical days in the sixties consisted of going without underwear, holding marginal jobs at "angry" magazines, and sleeping with self-declared revolutionary socialists who made love to her while dreaming about the heroic women they had seen during their radical-chic vacations in Cuba (312). There's Dr. Uhuru Simba, the obese community activist framed up as the Granny Ripper, who is neither a doctor nor from Africa, but just Sylvester Roberts from New Cross (285), evidently unaware that his assumed name, which comes from the "Africa" of Edgar Rice Burroughs, is also that of Tarzan's lion. Or there's Hanif Johnson, an ambitious young black lawyer whose ultrachic radicalism consists of an affected Trinidadian accent and "perfect control of the languages that mattered: sociological, socialistic, black-radical, anti-anti-anti-racist," along with a part-time address in Brickhall where he tends his organic roots when not growing his lucrative downtown practice (287, 281).

All these characters are in a sense political types, and one might sense in the treatment of them, together with that of the police and other officials in the government of "Mrs. Torture" (266), a kind of comic leveling operation of the sort that was effected through "ironic method" in Conrad's *The Secret Agent*: a reaction against all political activity in the name of some "higher," ostensibly apolitical standpoint. Or one could read these jokes as managing a sort of liberal frustration with the lack of decent and sensible political players—deriving, that is, from the politics that rests its whole faith on sound, well-meaning individuals ("if only Labour would put up better *candidates*"). But these readings don't account very well for the comic presentation of other types of characters who are neither leaders nor officials nor activists, but ordinary inhabitants of London's immigrant neighborhoods.

One such character is Hind Sufyan, the talented cook at the Brickhall restaurant/boardinghouse where Hanif Johnson has his chic ghetto address and the deformed Chamcha his temporary hideaway. Though her combination of good business instincts and culinary genius has enabled Hind during fourteen years in London to build the family café into a very successful enterprise, far grander than anything they enjoyed back in Dhaka, her economic success has not meant success in the task of cultural translation. For the tradition-bound Hind, England remains a devil island of strange and poisonous atmosphere, London a demon city whose evil threatens to infect all who inhabit it. She refuses to leave the café even to post a letter or buy groceries. Her husband and daughters do all the shopping and also keep her well supplied with the Bengali and Hindi videos and movie-star magazines that she regards as her link with the "real world."

This comical "traditionalism," which clings to an authentic or undiluted system of values, a true Indian reality, as represented by Bombay fan 'zines, assures Hind's perpetual conflict with her teenage daughters, both of whom identify with "British" values and reality as represented by the productions of London's hybrid, black-inflected musical subculture. The generational feuding reaches its apotheosis when Hind, having learned that her unmarried elder daughter, the punk-haired and braless Mishal, has been having sex with Hanif Johnson, goes after her with a knife—only to be expertly fended off by Mishal, whose "British" cultural life happens to include Bruce Lee movies and martial-arts lessons.

Though played for laughs, the representation of Hind Sufyan could almost be drawn straight from one of the family-pathology features that have been an orientalist staple of the British press since the mid-seventies. In these pop-sociology pieces, the Asian mother is always "locked in the cage" of her home by culturally instilled passivity and fear of change, neglected by her misogynist husband, cut off from the "different world" inhabited by her children, desperately but ineffectually struggling to impede their assimilation.[38] She is said to be particularly resistant to British norms and values where sexuality is concerned, and to stop at nothing to prevent her daughters from surrendering their virginity before marriage. This stereotype of the Asian mother is far from politically neutral; it is a piece of contemporary orientalism which serves the interests of a domestic policing apparatus in much the same way that (as Said argued) the "expert" analyses of the Indian or Arab "national character" served "military-national-security" interests throughout the colonial period.[39] In the seventies and early eighties, for example, this seemingly sympathetic stereotype of the culturally disoriented

38. See for example Karen Thapar, "Asians in Britain," 3-part series, London *Times*, 21–23 June 1982, especially part 2, "Misery of Women, 'Locked in a Cage'" (22 June: 3), and part 3, "Families Growing Up in Different Worlds" (23 June: 3). The sociology of "black family pathology," in both its academic and journalistic forms, is critiqued by Errol Lawrence, "In the Abundance of Water the Fool Is Thirsty: Sociology and Black 'Pathology,'" in Center for Contemporary Cultural Studies, eds., *The Empire Strikes Back* 95–142. For an example of more recent and reliable sociological study of Asian neighborhoods in England, see Eade, *Politics of Community*. On the question of the supposedly extreme "generation gap" in Asian immigrant families, for example, Eade looks beyond the standard litany of divisive tendencies into the neglected "kinship and village ties [that have] linked first and second generation settlers together" (36).

39. Said, *Orientalism* 106.

Asian mother dovetailed very conveniently with the covert but widespread practice of administering intravaginal examinations to determine the marital status of prospective Asian women immigrants. Since, according to the official wisdom, it was "not in their culture for [Asian] women to engage in sexual activity before marriage," this test could "prove" that a husband (and perhaps children) were secretly waiting in the wings and thus serve as a basis for systematically excluding Asian women.[40] The use of such degrading examinations was supposedly curtailed by 1979, but anecdotal evidence says otherwise, and the practice can still be invoked, as it is in *The Satanic Verses*, as one of the grim "truths" about the immigrant experience which no black Briton would dispute (253).

But if Hind is a stereotype of the passive (or perhaps rather passive/aggressive), ultratraditionalist Asian woman, she is also a stereotype of the calculating, entrepreneurial Asian, possessing that shrewd business sense and industriousness which distinguish the "East Indian type" from her West Indian counterpart. Indeed, the Sufyans' major source of income is not the restaurant but the boardinghouse above it, in which Hind provides dangerous and unhygienic lodging to mostly West Indian borough-council families, exploiting the government's temporary accommodation policies to the tune of ten pounds per night per person, or about two thousand pounds a week (264). To Hanif Johnson, this makes her one of the people who denounce Western decadence from the moral high ground while making a tidy capitalist profit off the misery of their own race (290). But for Hind, whose objections to England include its being "a country full of jews and strangers who lumped her in with the negroes" (289), the Caribbean immigrants upstairs are by no means people of "her own" race.

None of this, to be sure, makes for a very "positive image" of the Asian mother. Rushdie's character is an orientalist type or cartoon, recognizable from the popular press, and ridiculous, self-contradictory, complicit with an oppressive system in just the ways we would expect her to be. It is worth noting, though, that Hind Sufyan is herself fully aware of this, and regards as the last and worst of all her difficulties the fact that there is absolutely nothing unique about her situation. She understands that individual identity has receded from her grasp, that she has "sunk into the anonymity, the characterless plurality, of being merely one-of-the-women-like-her" (250).

What needs to be understood about the comic practice of *The Satanic*

Verses (and indeed of all Rushdie's fiction, despite his self-declared liberal concern for the "voices" and "tales" of unique individuals)[41] is that its first principle is to subordinate the individual self to the "characterless plurality" of socially constituted types. Rushdie's characters may strive for an individuality, an authenticity, a unique and sympathetic identity that could be enfolded in an antistereotypic discourse of "positive images." But this quest is always obstructed by their prior (and often self-conscious) insertion into a system of social relations which has only the most unoriginal, compromised, and politically dubious subject positions to offer. It is true that this tension between individual and type (which, again, is the Foucaultian tension of "self-fashioning"—as well as the fundamental tension in Bergson's analysis of "the comic element in character") is constantly producing "freaks" of one kind or another: the "sulphurous" monster growing ever more grotesque in his attic hideaway while he dreams of assimilation; the seven-foot-tall West Indian dub poet of East Indian ancestry whose albino condition and radical raps make him literally a white black man and the star of the black-and-white musical subculture. But even the freakishness in such cases is somehow unexceptional, symptomatic—merely true to type.

This is to say that the effect of what Brennan calls "satiric equal-time" in Rushdie's work derives not from a cosmopolitan and universalist comic practice that regards as equal all the various parties to social struggle, but rather from a practice that is *systematic* in the sense of taking the scene and system of social struggle itself, rather than the more or less worthy individuals who comprise that struggle, as the proper object of comic transaction. Though a kind of leveling of individual roles and performances does occur insofar as no one can finally rise above or emerge from the system whose contradictions drive the text's humor, one does not find here the rigorous reduction to political equivalence which takes place in the work of Conrad and other modernist ironists. Moreover, the political trajectory of this systematic satire is not strictly negative. The contradictions it continually jokes into view—such as those inherent in a "national community" ideologically dependent on internal but alien "communities of resistance" whose policing has become a "community" task—are understood to be the sites from which new, more adequate communitarian strategies and modalities of struggle will have to emerge.

The trouble is that these new strategies remain just beyond the horizon of the novel, and in the meantime those who are carrying on the minority

---

41. Rushdie, "*Songs* Doesn't Know the Score" 16.

struggles for justice and respect are asked to see themselves as constituted by and through a still-colonial or pre-post-erous system of power relations which in effect makes them ridiculous, and the rendering of which would "fail in its object," as Bergson says, "if it bore the stamp of sympathy or kindness" (*Laughter* 187). Those who have had to fight for "positive images" are understandably dismayed by such a text, which is not simply lacking in positive images but is so because its systematic political task is precisely to set *Witz* to work upon the politics of positive images.

It does so openly enough in connection with Uhuru Simba's organized protest against *The Aliens Show*, a hit TV program on which Saladin Chamcha had been co-star. The show is a high-tech semianimated situation comedy featuring a weird and motley crew of extraterrestrials: a belching, vomiting, cactuslike creature from a barren planet on the far edge of the universe who is known as Matilda, the Australien; a gang of hip-hop grafitti artists from Venus who call themselves the Alien Nation, and many others (62). This seemingly pointless riffing on the theme of aliens goes down well with viewers, and the program's computer-aided graphics and machine-processed voice track add greatly to its appeal, making it a prime-time megahit. But as the show grows its market share it also begins to attract political criticism. Right-wing critics denounce it for being too kinky, too deviant, too sexually explicit. Left-wing critics attack it for trafficking in ethnic prejudices and reinforcing the view of aliens as freaks—in short, for "its lack of positive images" (63).

It is the radical critique that sticks. Led by Simba, a group of black-community watchdogs demonstrates against the show, and when its producer, the American ultra-Thatcherite Hal Valance, agrees to make major changes, the protestors believe themselves vindicated. But Valance doesn't see it that way. He is perfectly happy to "depoliticize" the show, firing the immigrant Chamcha and his Jewish co-star Mimi Mamoulian and replacing them with a teutonic Schwarzenegger clone and a curvacious and mindless "shiksa." Valance smugly relates all this to Chamcha, remarking that Dr. Simba and the rest of the protesting black community have been properly screwed once again and that they will have to work a lot harder if they want to wrest power from their cultural and economic overlords (268).[42]

42. Of course, the replacement of a hip-hopping soul brother of the Alien Nation with a Germanic terminator of the Schwarzenegger type is a "depoliticizing" move only in a quite limited sense. There is no organized Germanic British community to protest the recurrence of such types on British TV.

At it turns out, Hal Valance's triumph is short-lived: the new *Aliens* show flops. But the tactical failure of his political adversaries clearly underscores the need for an opposition that works along different lines from those laid down by the politics of positive images. Here is just one of the many places where *The Satanic Verses* anticipates the trajectory of its own reception, both the objections to it raised by black community leaders and the all-too-easy appropriation of those protests by reactionary forces. It was, after all, protests against the lack of positive images in the novel which, to a far greater extent than anything written in the novel itself, were used to reinforce the most negative stereotypes of the (fanatical, terroristic) "Arab" and to foster a whole genre of anti-Asian jokes masked as jokes against censorship (the "I am Salman Rushdie" tee shirts, for example, or the jokes about forthcoming Rushdie novels: *Buddha You Fat Fuck*, etc.). Black-community protest thus served to affirm and stabilize the "white" community, the imagined community of authentic Britons, or of the "civilized West," who were once again presented with the opportunity to brandish their famed "tolerance" as a weapon of racialist exclusion and domination.

What, then, remains available in the way of a community politics, a politics of community, from the standpoint of a postcolonialism that, in all seriousness, finds such practices to be a joke? At this stage, it would seem, very little does remain. What the texts of postcolonialism have done (and in this respect at least the "post" of postcolonialism does seem to me the same as the "post" of postmodernism)[43]—is to trace the logic of "community" in its modern form, to follow its modern trajectory, to the point of crisis or aporia. And of course this is not purely an aporia of theory, but one of praxis: it is the crisis of a paradoxical and a self-defeating politics, a politics of resistance which in practice resists itself. Postcolonial joke-work does not attempt, as modernist joke-work determinedly does, to disguise and manage this crisis in the interest of sustaining a failed and impossible communitarian project. Instead, it attempts to work *through* the crisis point toward a new laughter of community which would not celebrate a common identity, and a new politics of community which would not strive either to realize a common essence or to perform a common work. One cannot simply adduce, from *The Satanic Verses* or any other contemporary writing, successful instances of this process. For the further paradox is that, were this quite new way of thinking and practicing community to be achieved, or successfully presented, in the postcolonial text,

43. See Kwame Anthony Appiah, "Is the Post- in Postmodernism the Post- in Postcolonial?" *Critical Inquiry* 17 (Winter 1991), 336–57.

it would immediately become susceptible of a witty deconstruction; the realization of postcolonialism's thinking of community—in the form of a completed work, a complete vision, a stable and fully articulated bloc—would be its own undoing, would, in fact, be the very site where a new laughter would have to begin once more to erupt.

All of which means that the comic transactions of postcolonialism, of postmodernism—of what perhaps could be called postcommunitarianism—are not demonstrably more useful in pragmatic or strategic terms than those of even the least dissident modernism. They will tend rather to frustrate than to exhilarate those of us who welcome the possibilities of difference while we remain somehow bound to the exigency of community. Or at any rate such exhilaration as they can offer must take the peculiarly negative form of the communitarian experience as described by Bataille: an experience of "the community of those who have no community."[44] This is, I believe, the defining experience of "our" present moment, an awkward moment in political terms but one that could yet prove the starting point for a politics with a real future—a future rigorously unimagined and freed of its obligations to a community of the past.

44. See the closing paragraphs of Blanchot's "The Negative Community," in Blanchot, *Unavowable Community* 25–26.

Bibliography of Works Cited

Abel, Elizabeth. *Virginia Woolf and the Fictions of Psychoanalysis*. Chicago: University of Chicago Press, 1989.

Adelson, Leslie A. "Against the Enlightenment: A Theory with Teeth for the 1980s." *German Quarterly* 57 (Fall 1984): 625–31.

Adorno, Theodor W. "Towards an Understanding of *Endgame*." In *Twentieth-Century Interpretations of "Endgame."* Ed. Gale Chevigny. Englewood Cliffs, N.J.: Prentice-Hall, 1969.

Ahsan, M. M., and A. R. Kidwai, eds. *Sacrilege versus Civility: Muslim Perspectives on the "Satanic Verses" Affair*. Leicester: Islamic Foundation, 1991.

Akhtar, Shabbir. *Be Careful with Muhammad! The Salman Rushdie Affair*. London: Bellew, 1989.

Alderson, John. *Policing Freedom*. London: Macdonald and Evans, 1979.

Amis, Kingsley. "Anglo-Saxon Platitudes." *Spectator*, 5 April 1957.

———. *Girl, 20*. 1971. New York: Ballantine, 1973.

———. *The James Bond Dossier*. London: Jonathan Cape, 1965.

———. *Lucky Jim*. 1954. Harmondsworth: Penguin, 1961.

———. *Lucky Jim's Politics*. Conservative Political Centre Pamphlet 410. London: Conservative Political Center, 1968.

———. *On Drink*. New York: Harcourt Brace Jovanovich, 1973.

———. *One Fat Englishman*. 1963. Harmondsworth: Penguin, 1966.

———. "Pernicious Participation." In Cox and Dyson, eds., *Black Papers*. 170–72.

———. *Socialism and the Intellectuals*. London: Fabian Society, 1957.

———. *Stanley and the Women*. New York: Summit Books, 1984.

———. *Take a Girl like You*. 1960. Harmondsworth: Penguin, 1962.

———. *That Uncertain Feeling*. London: Gollancz, 1955.

———. "Why Lucky Jim Turned Right: Confessions of an Ex-Radical." *Sunday Telegraph*, 2 July 1967.

Amis, Kingsley, and Robert Conquest. "A Short Educational Dictionary." In Cox and Dyson, eds., *Black Papers*. 215–223.

Anderson, Benedict. *Imagined Communities: Reflections on the Origin and Spread of Nationalism*. London: Verso, 1983.

Appiah, Kwame Anthony. "Is the Post- in Postmodernism the Post- in Postcolonial?" *Critical Inquiry* 17 (Winter 1991): 336–57.

Appignanesi, Lisa, and Sara Maitland, eds. *The Rushdie File*. Syracuse: Syracuse University Press and Institute of Contemporary Arts, 1990.

Apte, Mahadev L. *Humor and Laughter: An Anthropological Approach.* Ithaca: Cornell University Press, 1985.

Arac, Jonathan. *Critical Genealogies: Historical Situations for Postmodern Literary Studies.* New York: Columbia University Press, 1987.

———. "Romanticism, the Self, and the City: *The Secret Agent* in Literary History." *Boundary 2* 9 (Fall 1980): 75–89.

Archer, Robin, et al., eds. *Out of Apathy: Voices of the New Left Thirty Years On.* London: Verso, 1989.

Babcock, Barbara, ed. *The Reversible World.* Ithaca: Cornell University Press, 1978.

Baines, Jocelyn. *Joseph Conrad: A Critical Biography.* New York: McGraw-Hill, 1960.

Baker, Houston A., Jr. *The Journey Back: Essays in Black Literature and Criticism.* Chicago: University of Chicago Press, 1980.

Bakhtin, Mikhail. *Rabelais and His World.* 1965. Trans. Hélène Iswolsky. Bloomington: Indiana University Press, 1984.

Barnes, Djuna. *Nightwood.* 1936. New York: New Directions, 1946.

Barreca, Regina, *They Used to Call Me Snow White . . . But I Drifted.* New York: Viking Penguin, 1991.

———, ed. *Last Laughs: Perspectives on Women and Comedy.* New York: Gordon and Breach, 1988.

———, ed. *New Perspectives on Women and Comedy.* New York: Gordon and Breach, 1992.

Barth, John. "The Literature of Replenishment: Postmodernist Fiction." In Barth, *The Friday Book.* New York: Perigree, 1984. 193–206.

Barthes, Roland. "Day by Day with Roland Barthes." In Blonsky, ed. *On Signs.* 98–118.

Bataille, Georges. *The Accursed Share.* Trans. Robert Hurley. Vol. 1. New York: Zone Books, 1988. Vols. 2 and 3. Cambridge: Zone Books, 1992.

———. *Visions of Excess: Selected Writings, 1927–1939.* Ed. Allan Stoekl. Trans. Allan Stoekl, Carl R. Lovitt, and Donald M. Leslie, Jr. Minneapolis: University of Minnesota Press, 1985.

Bateson, Gregory. "The Message, 'This Is Play.'" In *Group Processes, Second Conference.* Ed. Bertran Schaffner. New York: Josiah Macy Jr. Foundation, 1956.

———. "The Position of Humor in Human Communication." In *Cybernetics: Circular Causal and Feedback Mechanisms in Biological and Social Systems.* Transactions of the Ninth Conference on Cybernetics, 1952. Ed. Heinz Von Foerster. New York: Josiah Macy Jr. Foundation, 1953. 1–47.

———. *Steps to an Ecology of Mind.* New York: Ballantine, 1972.

Baudelaire, Charles. "De l'essence du rire." In Baudelaire, *Curiosités esthétiques: L'art romantique et autres oeuvres critiques.* Ed. H. Lemaitre. Paris: Garnier, 1962. English trans.: "On the Essence of Laughter." In Baudelaire, *The Mirror of Art.* Trans. Jonathan Mayne. London: Phaidon, 1955.

Beaton, Alistair, and Andy Hamilton. *The Thatcher Papers: An Exposé of the Secret Face of the Conservative Government.* London: New English Library, 1980.

Beatts, Anne. Interview with Kathleen Beckett. In Collier and Beckett, eds., *Spare Ribs*.

Beatts, Anne, and Deanne Stillman, eds. *Titters: The First Collection of Humor by Women*. New York: Collier Books, 1976.

Beckett, Samuel. *Watt*. New York: Grove, 1959.

Beerbohm, Max. "Laughter." In Beerbohm, *And Even Now*. New York: Dutton, 1921. 303–10.

Bell, Quentin. *Virginia Woolf: A Biography*. 2 vols. London: Hogarth, 1972.

Benjamin, Walter. *Illuminations*. Ed. Hannah Arendt. Trans. Harry Zohn. New York: Schocken, 1969.

Bennett, David. "Parody, Postmodernism, and the Politics of Reading." In *Comic Relations: Studies in the Comic, Satire, and Parody*. Ed. Pavel Petr, David Roberts, Philip Thomson. New York: Verlag Peter Lang, 1985. 193–210.

Benson, Sheila. "Experiences in the London New Left." In Archer et al., eds., *Out of Apathy*. 107–10.

Benveniste, Emile. *Problems in General Linguistics*. Trans. Mary Elizabeth Meek. Coral Gables, Fla.: University of Miami Press, 1971.

Benyon, John. "Spiral of Decline: Race and Policing." In Layton-Henry and Rich, eds., *Race, Government, and Politics*.

Bergson, Henri. *Laughter*. Trans. Wylie Sypher. In *Comedy*. Ed. Wylie Sypher. Garden City, N.Y.: Doubleday Anchor, 1956. 61–190.

Berlyne, Daniel E. "Humor and Its Kin." In Goldstein and McGhee, eds., *Psychology of Humor*. 43–60.

Berman, Jeffrey. *Joseph Conrad: Writing as Rescue*. New York: Astra, 1977.

Berman, Russell A. *Modern Culture and Critical Theory: Art, Politics and the Legacy of the Frankfurt School*. Madison: University of Wisconsin Press, 1989.

Bertelsen, Eve, ed. *Doris Lessing*. Johannesburg: McGraw, 1985.

———. "*The Golden Notebook*: The African Background," In Kaplan and Rose, eds., *Approaches to Teaching Lessing*. 30–36.

Bhabha, Homi, ed. *Nation and Narration*. London: Routledge, 1990.

———. "Of Mimicry and Man." *October* 28 (Spring 1984): 125–33.

———. "The Third Space." Interview with Jonathan Rutherford. In Rutherford, ed., *Identity*. 207–21.

Black, Naomi. *Social Feminism*. Ithaca: Cornell University Press, 1989.

———. "Virginia Woolf and the Woman's Movement." In Marcus, ed., *Virginia Woolf: A Feminist Slant*. 180–97.

Blanchot, Maurice. *The Unavowable Community*. Trans. Pierre Joris. Barrytown, N.Y.: Station Hill Press, 1983.

Blatchford, Robert. *Merrie England*. 1894. London: Journeyman Press, 1976.

Blonsky, Marshall, ed. *On Signs*. Baltimore: Johns Hopkins University Press, 1985.

Booth, Wayne. *A Rhetoric of Irony*. Chicago: University of Chicago Press, 1974.

Bradbury, Malcolm. *Eating People Is Wrong*. 1959. New York: Knopf, 1960.

———. *The History Man: A Novel*. 1975. Boston: Houghton Mifflin, 1976.

_____. "The Novel." In *The Twentieth-Century Mind: History, Ideas, and Literature in Britain.* Vol. 3: *1945–1965.* Ed. C. B. Cox and A. E. Dyson. London: Oxford University Press, 1972.

Brennan, Timothy. "The National Longing for Form." In Bhabha, ed., *Nation and Narration.* 44–70.

_____. *Salman Rushdie and the Third World.* London: Macmillan, 1989.

Bridson, D. G. *The Filibuster: A Study of the Political Ideas of Wyndham Lewis.* London: Cassell, 1972.

Brooker, Peter, and Peter Widdowson. "A Literature for England." In Colls and Dodd, eds., *Englishness.* 116–63.

Brown, Dennis. *Intertextual Dynamics within the Literary Group—Joyce, Lewis, Pound, and Eliot: The Men of 1914.* London: Macmillan, 1990.

Brown, John. *A Theory of Police/Immigrant Relations.* Cranfield, Bedfordshire: Cranfield Institute of Technology, Language and Social Studies, 1974.

Bürger, Peter. *Theory of the Avant-Garde.* Trans. Michael Shaw. Minneapolis: University of Minnesota Press, 1984.

Burke, Kenneth. *Language as Symbolic Action: Essays on Life, Literature, and Method.* Berkeley: University of California Press, 1966.

Butler, Judith. *Gender Trouble: Feminism and the Subversion of Identity.* New York: Routledge, 1990.

Callaghan, John. *Socialism in Britain since 1884.* Oxford: Basil Blackwell, 1990.

Cashmore, Ernest, and Barry Troyna, eds. *Black Youth in Crisis.* London: Allen and Unwin, 1982.

Casillo, Robert. *The Genealogy of Demons: Anti-Semitism, Fascism, and the Myths of Ezra Pound.* Evanston, Ill.: Northwestern University Press, 1988.

Castoriadis, Cornelius. *The Imaginary Institution of Society.* Trans. Kathleen Blamey. Cambridge: MIT Press, 1987.

Center for Contemporary Cultural Studies, eds. *The Empire Strikes Back: Race and Racism in 70s Britain.* London: Hutchinson/CCCS, 1982.

_____, eds. *Policing the Crisis: Mugging, the State, and Law and Order.* London: Macmillan Educational, 1978.

Chapman, Antony J. "Humour and Laughter in Social Situations and Some Implications for Humour Research." In McGhee and Goldstein, eds., *Handbook.* Vol. 1: 135–57.

Chapman, Antony J., and Hugh C. Foot, eds. *Humor and Laughter: Theory, Research, and Applications.* New York: John Wiley, 1976.

_____, eds. *It's a Funny Thing, Humour.* International Conference on Humour and Laughter, Cardiff, Wales, 1976. Oxford: Pergamon, 1977.

Chapman, Graham, et al. "Hell's Grannies" skit, "Full Frontal Nudity" episode. *Monty Python's Flying Circus.* London: BBC, 1969.

Chesterton, G. K. *The Man Who Was Thursday.* 1909. New York: Putnam/Capricorn, 1960.

Cixous, Hélène. "Castration or Decapitation?" Trans. Annette Kuhn. *Signs* 7 (1981): 41–55. Rpt. in *Out There: Marginalization and Contemporary Cultures.* Ed. Russell Ferguson et al. New York and Cambridge: New Museum and MIT Press, 1990. 345–56.

Collier, Denise, and Kathleen Beckett, eds. *Spare Ribs: Women in the Humor Biz* (New York: St. Martin's, 1980).

Colls, Robert, and Philip Dodd, eds. *Englishness: Politics and Culture, 1880–1920.* London: Croom Helm. 1986.

Comstock, Margaret. "The Loudspeaker and the Human Voice: Politics and the Form of *The Years.*" *Bulletin of the New York Public Library* 80 (Winter 1977): 252–75.

Conrad, Joseph. *The Collected Letters of Joseph Conrad.* Ed. Frederick Karl and Laurence Davies. Vol. 3: *1903–1907.* Cambridge: Cambridge University Press, 1988.

——. "A Familiar Preface" to *A Personal Record.* 1912. In Conrad, *"The Mirror of the Sea" and "A Personal Record."* Ed. Morton Dauwen Zabel. Garden City, N.Y.: Doubleday, 1960.

——. *Lord Jim.* 1900. Ed. Thomas Moser. New York: Norton, 1968

——. *Notes on Life and Letters.* 1921. Garden City, N.Y.: Doubleday, 1926.

——. *The Secret Agent: A Simple Tale.* 1907. Garden City, N.Y.: Doubleday Anchor, 1953.

——. *A Set of Six.* 1908. Garden City, N.Y.: Doubleday, 1922.

——. *Typhoon.* 1902. In *"The Shadow Line" and Two Other Tales.* Ed. Morton Dauwen Zabel. Garden City, N.Y.: Doubleday, 1959.

Conroy, Mark. *Modernism and Authority: Strategies of Legitimation in Flaubert and Conrad.* Baltimore: Johns Hopkins University Press, 1985.

Corrigan, Robert W., ed. *Comedy, Meaning and Form.* San Francisco: Chandler, 1965.

Cottom, Daniel. "What Is a Joke?" In Cottom, *Text and Culture.* Minneapolis: University of Minnesota Press, 1989. 3–48.

Cox, C. B., and A. E. Dyson, eds. *The Black Papers on Education.* London: Davis-Poynter, 1971.

Cuddy-Keane, Melba. "The Politics of Comic Modes in Virginia Woolf's *Between the Acts.*" *PMLA* 105 (March 1990): 273–85.

Culler, Jonathan. *Flaubert: The Uses of Uncertainty.* Ithaca: Cornell University Press, 1974.

——. *On Deconstruction: Theory and Criticism after Structuralism.* Ithaca: Cornell University Press, 1982.

Dasenbrock, Reed Way. *The Literary Vorticism of Ezra Pound and Wyndham Lewis: Towards the Condition of Painting.* Baltimore: Johns Hopkins University Press, 1985.

Dayan, Daniel. "The Tutor Code of Classical Cinema." In *Movies and Methods.* Ed. Bill Nichols. Berkeley: University of California Press, 1976. 438–51.

De Lauretis, Teresa. "Desire in Narrative." In de Lauretis, *Alice Doesn't: Feminism, Semiotics, Cinema.* Bloomington: Indiana University Press, 1984. 103–57.

———. *Technologies of Gender.* Bloomington: Indiana University Press, 1987.

Deleuze, Gilles. "Coldness and Cruelty." 1967. In Gilles Deleuze and Leopold von Sacher-Masoch, *Masochism.* Trans. Jean McNeil. 1971. Cambridge: Zone Books, 1989. 81–91.

———. *Foucault.* 1986. Trans. Sean Hand. Minneapolis: University of Minnesota Press, 1988.

Deleuze, Gilles, and Félix Guattari. 1977. *The Anti-Oedipus: Capitalism and Schizophrenia,* 1. Trans. Robert Hurley, Mark Seem, and Helen R. Lane. Minneapolis: University of Minnesota Press, 1983.

———. 1980. *A Thousand Plateaus: Capitalism and Schizophrenia,* 2. Trans. Brian Massumi. Minneapolis: University of Minnesota Press, 1987.

DeLillo, Don. *Mao II.* New York: Viking, 1991.

De Man, Paul. *Allegories of Reading.* New Haven: Yale University Press, 1979.

———. "The Rhetoric of Temporality." In de Man, *Blindness and Insight: Essays in the Rhetoric of Contemporary Criticism.* Minneapolis: University of Minnesota Press, 1983. 187–228.

Derrida, Jacques. "Limited Inc." Trans. Samuel Weber. *Glyph* 2 (1977): 162–254.

Descombes, Vincent. *Modern French Philosophy.* Trans. L. Scott-Fox and J. M. Harding. Cambridge: Cambridge University Press, 1980.

Dodd, Philip. "Englishness and the National Culture." In Colls and Dodd, eds., *Englishness.* 1–28.

Dollimore, Jonathan. "The Challenge of Sexuality." In Sinfield, ed., *Society and Literature 1945–1970.* 64–71.

Drabble, Margaret, ed. *Oxford Companion to English Literature.* 5th ed. Oxford: Oxford University Press, 1985.

D'Souza, Dinesh. *Illiberal Education: The Politics of Race and Sex on Campus.* New York: Free Press, 1991.

Duchowny, Michael S. "Pathological Disorders of Laughter." In McGhee and Goldstein, eds., *Handbook.* Vol. 2.

Eade, John. *The Politics of Community: The Bangladeshi Community in East London.* Research in Ethnic Relations Series. Aldershot: Avebury, 1989.

Eagleton, Terry. *Criticism and Ideology.* London: Verso, 1978.

———. *Exiles and Emigrés: Studies in Modern Literature.* New York: Schocken, 1970.

———. *Walter Benjamin; or Towards a Revolutionary Criticism.* London: Verso NLB, 1981.

Eagleton, Terry, Fredric Jameson, and Edward Said. *Nationalism, Colonialism, and Literature.* Minneapolis: University of Minnesota Press, 1990.

Eco, Umberto. "The Frames of Comic 'Freedom.'" In *Carnival!* Approaches to Semiotics 64. Ed. Thomas Sebeok. New York: Mouton, 1984. 1–10.

———. *The Role of the Reader: Explorations in the Semiotics of Texts.* Trans. William Weaver. Bloomington: Indiana University Press, 1979.

Emerson, J. P. "Negotiating the Serious Import of Humor." *Sociometry* 32 (1969): 169–81.

Empson, William. *Some Versions of Pastoral.* 1935. New York: New Directions, 1974.

English, James F. "The Laughing Reader: A New Direction for Studies of the Comic." *Genre* 19 (Summer 1986): 129–54.

Fiedler, Leslie A. "The Death and Rebirth of the Novel." In *Innovation/Renovation: New Perspectives on the Humanities.* Ed. Ihab Hassan and Sally Hassan. Madison: University of Wisconsin Press, 1983.

Fine, Gary Alan. "Sociological Approaches to the Study of Humor." In McGhee and Goldstein, eds., *Handbook.* Vol. 1: 159–89.

Fish, Stanley. "Literature in the Reader: Affective Stylistics." *New Literary History* 2 (Autumn 1970): 123–62. Rpt. in Stanley Fish, *Is There a Text in This Class? The Authority of Interpretive Communities.* Cambridge: Harvard University Press, 1980. 21–67.

Fishburn, Katherine. "*The Golden Notebook*: A Challenge to the Teaching Establishment." In Kaplan and Rose, eds., *Approaches.*

Fleishman, Avrom. *Conrad's Politics: Community and Anarchy in the Fiction of Joseph Conrad.* Baltimore: Johns Hopkins University Press, 1967.

———. *Virginia Woolf: A Critical Reading.* Baltimore: Johns Hopkins University Press, 1975.

Flemming, Marie. *The Anarchist Way to Socialism: Elisée Reclus and Nineteenth-Century European Anarchism.* London: Croom Helm, 1979.

Flieger, Jerry Aline. *The Purloined Punch Line: Freud's Comic Theory and the Postmodern Text.* Baltimore: Johns Hopkins University Press, 1991.

Forster, E. M. *England's Pleasant Land.* London: Hogarth, 1940.

Foster, Hal. "Armor Fou." *October* 56 (Spring 1991): 64–97.

———, ed. *The Anti-Aesthetic: Essays on Postmodern Culture.* Port Townsend, Wash.: Bay Press, 1983.

Foucault, Michel. *Power/Knowledge: Selected Interviews and Other Writings.* Ed. Colin Gordon. New York: Pantheon, 1980.

———. "The Subject and Power." "Afterword" to *Michel Foucault: Beyond Structuralism and Hermeneutics.* Ed. Hubert L. Dreyfus and Paul Rabinow. University of Chicago Press, 1982.

Freud, Sigmund. *Group Psychology and the Analysis of the Ego.* 1922. Trans. James Strachey. New York: Norton, 1959.

———. "Humour." 1932. In Freud, *Standard Edition.* Vol. 21. 160–66.

———. *Jokes and Their Relation to the Unconscious.* 1905. Trans. James Strachey. New York: Norton, 1960.

———. *The Standard Edition of the Complete Psychological Works of Sigmund Freud.* Trans. James Strachey. 24 vols. London: Hogarth, 1978.

———. "Why War?" 1933. In Freud, *Standard Edition.* Vol. 22: 197–215.

Fry, William F., Jr. *Sweet Madness: A Study of Humor.* Palo Alto, Calif.: Pacific, 1963.

Frye, Northrop. *Anatomy of Criticism.* Princeton: Princeton University Press, 1957.

Gagnier, Regenia. "Between Women: A Cross-Cultural Analysis of Status and Anarchic Humor." In Barreca, ed., *Last Laughs.* 135–48.

Galigan, Edward L. *The Comic Vision in Literature.* Athens: University of Georgia Press, 1984.

Gilbert, Sandra M., and Susan Gubar. *No Man's Land: The Place of the Woman Writer in the Twentieth Century.* 2 vols. New Haven: Yale University Press, 1989.

Gilroy, Paul. "Police and Thieves." In Center for Contemporary Cultural Studies, eds., *Empire Strikes Back.* 143–82.

———. *"There Ain't No Black in the Union Jack."* 1987. Chicago: University of Chicago Press, 1991.

Godkewitsch, Michael. "The Relationship between Arousal Potential and Funniness of Jokes." In Goldstein and McGhee, eds., *Psychology.* 144–50.

Goldstein, Jeffrey H., and Paul E. McGhee, eds. *The Psychology of Humor.* New York: Academic Press, 1972.

Green, Martin. *Children of the Sun: A Narrative of 'Decadence' in England after 1918.* 1976. New York: Wideview, 1980.

Greenblatt, Stephen. *Renaissance Self-Fashioning: From More to Shakespeare.* Chicago: University of Chicago Press, 1980.

Guerard, Albert J. *Conrad the Novelist.* Cambridge: Harvard University Press, 1958.

H. D. [Hilda Doolittle]. "Responsibilities." In Scott, ed., *Gender of Modernism.* 127–29.

Habermas, Jürgen. "Modernity versus Postmodernity." *New German Critique* 22 (Winter 1981). Rpt. in Foster, ed., *Anti-Aesthetic.* 3–15.

———. *The Theory of Communicative Action: Reason and the Rationalization of Society.* Trans. Thomas McCarthy. 1984. Vol. 1 of *The Theory of Communicative Action.* 2 vols. Boston: Beacon Press, 1984–1987.

Hall, Stuart. "The 'First' New Left: Life and Times." In Archer et al., eds., *Out of Apathy.* 11–38.

———. *The Hard Road to Renewal: Thatcherism and the Crisis of the Left.* London: Verso, 1988.

Hall, Stuart, et al. *Culture, Media, Language: Working Papers in Cultural Studies, 1972–1979.* London: Hutchinson, 1980.

Hamilton, Alistair. *The Appeal of Fascism: A Study of Intellectuals and Fascism, 1919–1945.* London: Anthony Blond, 1971.

Harrison, Brian. *Separate Spheres: The Opposition to Women's Suffrage in Britain.* London: Croom Helm, 1978.

Hart, W. C. *Confessions of an Anarchist.* London: E. G. Richards, 1906.

Hartman, Geoffrey. Interview with Imre Salusinszky. In *Criticism in Society.* Ed. Imre Salusinszky. London: Methuen, 1987.

Hassan, Ihab. *The Dismemberment of Orpheus.* Madison: University of Wisconsin Press, 1982.

Hay, Eloise Knapp. *The Political Novels of Joseph Conrad.* Chicago: University of Chicago Press, 1963.

Hazlitt, William. *Lectures on the English Poets and the English Comic Writers*. 1819. London: George Bell, 1884.

Hewison, Robert. *In Anger: British Culture in the Cold War, 1945–60*. New York: Oxford University Press, 1981.

Hite, Molly. "Subverting the Ideology of Coherence: *The Golden Notebook* and *The Four-Gated City*." In Kaplan and Rose, eds., *Doris Lessing: The Alchemy of Survival*.

Hobbes, Thomas. *Human Nature*. 1650. *The English Works of Thomas Hobbes*. 11 vols. Ed. Sir William Molesworth. London: Bohn, 1839–1845. Vol. 4: 1–76.

———. *Leviathan*. 1651. In Hobbes, *The English Works*. Vol. 3. 1840.

Hobsbawm, E. J. *Nations and Nationalisms since 1780: Programme, Myth, Reality*. Cambridge: Cambridge University Press, 1990.

Hobsbawm, E. J., and Terence Ranger, eds. *The Invention of Tradition*. Cambridge: Cambridge University Press, 1983.

Hodge, Bob, and Alan Mansfield. "'Nothing Left to Laugh At . . .': Humour as a Tactic of Resistance." *Language and the Nuclear Arms Debate: Nukespeak Today*. Ed. Paul Chilton. London: Frances Pinter, 1985. 197–211.

Hoggart, Richard. *The Uses of Literacy: Changing Patterns in English Mass Culture*. London: Chatto and Windus, 1957.

Holland, Norman. *The Dynamics of Literary Response*. New York: Oxford University Press, 1968.

———. *5 Readers Reading*. New Haven: Yale University Press, 1975.

———. *Laughing: A Psychology of Humor*. Ithaca: Cornell University Press, 1982.

———. "Style as Character in *The Secret Agent*." *Modern Fiction Studies* 12 (1966): 221–31.

Holloway, John. "English Culture and the Feat of Transformation." "Third Programme." *The Listener* 77 (12 January 1967): 47–49, 85–89, 126–132.

Horkheimer, Max, and Theodor Adorno. *Dialectic of Enlightenment*. 1944. Trans. John Cumming. 1972. New York: Continuum, 1989.

Howe, Florence. "A Conversation with Doris Lessing." In Pratt and Dembo, eds., *Doris Lessing*. 15–22.

Howe, Irving. *Politics and the Novel*. New York: Horizon, 1957.

Howkins, Alun. "The Discovery of Rural England." In Colls and Dodd, eds., *Englishness*. 62–88.

Hutcheon, Linda. *A Theory of Parody: The Teachings of Twentieth-Century Art Forms*. New York: Methuen, 1985.

Huyssen, Andreas. "Mapping the Postmodern." *New German Critique* 33 (Fall 1984): 5–52.

———. "Mass Culture as Woman: Modernism's Other." In Modleski, ed., *Studies in Entertainment*. 188–207.

Hynes, Samuel Lynn. *The Auden Generation: Art and Literature in England in the 1930s*. New York: Viking, 1976.

Irigaray, Luce. *This Sex Which Is Not One.* Trans. Catherine Porter with Carolyn Burke. Ithaca: Cornell University Press, 1984.

Iser, Wolfgang. *The Act of Reading: A Theory of Aesthetic Response.* Baltimore: Johns Hopkins University Press, 1978.

James, Henry. *Portrait of a Lady.* 1881. Harmondsworth: Penguin, 1973.

Jameson, Fredric. *Fables of Aggression: Wyndham Lewis, the Modernist as Fascist.* Berkeley: University of California Press, 1979.

————. *The Political Unconscious: Narrative as a Socially Symbolic Act.* Ithaca: Cornell University Press, 1981.

————. "Postmodernism and Consumer Society." In Foster, ed., *Anti-Aesthetic.* 111–25.

————. *Postmodernism; or, The Cultural Logic of Late Capitalism.* Durham, N.C.: Duke University Press, 1991.

Jauss, Hans Robert. *Aesthetic Experience and Literary Hermeneutics.* Trans. Michael Shaw. Minneapolis: University of Minnesota Press, 1983.

————. *Toward an Aesthetic of Reception.* Trans. Timothy Bahti. Sussex: Harvester, 1982.

Jean-Aubry, G. *Joseph Conrad: Life and Letters.* 2 vols. London: Heinemann, 1927.

Johnson, Samuel. "The Difficulty of Defining Comedy." 1751. *The Rambler.* 4 vols. London: Dodsley Owen, 1794. Vol. 3: 112–14. Rpt. in *The Comic in Theory and Practice.* Ed. John J. Enck, et al. Englewood Cliffs, N.J.: Prentice-Hall, 1960. 10–12.

Johnston, Judith L. "The Remediable Flaw: Revisioning Cultural History in *Between the Acts.*" In Jane Marcus, ed., *Virginia Woolf and Bloomsbury.* 253–77.

Jones, D. A. N. "Kingsley Amis." *Grand Street* 4 (Spring 1985): 206–14.

Joplin, Patricia Klindienst. "The Authority of Illusion: Feminism and Fascism in Virginia Woolf's *Between the Acts.*" *South Central Review* 6 (Summer 1989): 88–104.

Kane, Thomas R., et al. "Humor as a Tool of Social Interaction." In Chapman and Foot, eds., *Funny Thing.* 13–17.

Kant, Immanuel. *Critique of Judgment.* 1790. Trans. J. H. Bernard. New York: Hafner, 1951.

Kaplan, Carey, and Ellen Cronan Rose, eds. *Approaches to Teaching Lessing's "The Golden Notebook."* New York: MLA, 1989.

————, eds. *Doris Lessing: The Alchemy of Survival.* Athens: Ohio University Press, 1988.

Karp, Ivan. "Laughter at Marriage: Subversion in Performance." In *Transformations of African Marriage.* Ed. David Parkin and David Nyamwaya. Manchester: Manchester University Press, 1987. 137–54.

Kayser, Wolfgang. *The Grotesque in Art and Literature.* Trans. Ulrich Weisstein. New York: McGraw-Hill, 1963.

Kedward, Roderick. *The Anarchists: The Men Who Shocked an Era.* Library of the Twentieth Century Series. New York: American Heritage Press, 1971.

Kenner, Hugh. *The Pound Era*. Berkeley: University of California Press, 1971.
____. *Wyndham Lewis*. Norfolk, Conn.: New Directions, 1954.
Khalid, Fazlun. "When Fools Rushed In." In Ahsan and Kidwai, eds., *Sacrilege versus Civility*.
Kierkegaard, Søren. *The Concept of Irony, with Constant Reference to Socrates*. Trans. Lee M. Capel. Bloomington: Indiana University Press, 1968.
____. *Training in Christianity*. Trans. Walter Lowrie. Princeton: Princeton University Press, 1967.
Kimball, Roger. *Tenured Radicals: How Politics Has Corrupted Our Higher Education*. New York: Harper and Row, 1990.
King, Bruce. *The New English Literatures*. London: Macmillan, 1980.
Klossowski, Pierre. "Nietzsche, le polythéisme et la parodie." In Klossowski, *Un si funeste désir*. Paris: Gallimard, 1963.
Knoepflmacher, U. C. *Laughter and Despair*. Berkeley: University of California Press, 1971.
Koestler, Arthur. *The Act of Creation*. New York: Macmillan, 1964.
Kristeva, Julia. "The Speaking Subject." In Blonksy, ed., *On Signs*. 210–220.
Lacan, Jacques. "Function and Field of Speech and Language." In Lacan, *Ecrits*. Trans. Alan Sheridan. New York: Norton, 1977. 30–113.
____. "Sign, Symbol, Imaginary." In Blonsky, ed., *On Signs*. 203–9.
Laclau, Ernesto. "Community and Its Paradoxes: Richard Rorty's 'Liberal Utopia.'" In Miami Theory Collective, eds., *Community at Loose Ends*. 83–98.
____. "The Impossibility of Society." *Canadian Journal of Political and Social Theory* 7.12 (1983): 21–24.
Laclau, Ernesto, and Chantal Mouffe. *Hegemony and Socialist Strategy: Towards a Radical Democratic Politics*. Trans. Winston Moore and Paul Cammack. London: Verso, 1985.
La Fave, Lawrence. "Humor Judgments as a Function of Reference Groups and Identification Classes." In Goldstein and McGhee, eds., *Psychology*. 195–209.
Laing, R. D. *The Divided Self*. 1959. Harmondsworth: Penguin, 1965.
Laing, Stuart. "The Production of Literature." In Sinfield, ed., *Society and Literature*.
Lamb, Charles. Letter to Robert Southey. 1815. In *The Complete Works and Letters of Charles Lamb*. New York: Modern Library, 1963. 799.
Lang, Candace D. *Irony/Humor: Critical Paradigms*. Baltimore: Johns Hopkins University Press, 1988.
Lawrence, Errol. "In the Abundance of Water the Fool Is Thirsty: Sociology and Black 'Pathology.'" In Center for Contemporary Cultural Studies, eds., *The Empire Strikes Back*. 95–142.
Layton-Henry, Zig, and Paul B. Rich, eds. *Race, Government and Politics in Britain*. London: Macmillan, 1986.
Leavis, F. R. *Education and the University*. New York: George W. Stuart, 1948.

————. *The Great Tradition: George Eliot, Henry James, Joseph Conrad.* London: Chatto and Windus, 1948.

Lebzelter, Gisela C. "Henry Hamilton Beamish and the Britons: Champions of Anti-Semitism." In Lunn and Thurlow, eds., *British Fascism.* 41–56.

————. *Political Anti-Semitism in England, 1918–1939.* London: Macmillan, 1978.

Leclerc, Annie. *Woman's Word.* Trans. Gillian C. Gill. Excerpts in Marks and de Courtivron, eds., *New French Feminisms.* 79–83.

Lefort, Claude. *The Political Forms of Modern Society: Bureaucracy, Democracy, Totalitarianism.* Trans. John B. Thompson. Cambridge, Mass: MIT Press, 1986.

Lehman, David. *Signs of the Times: Deconstruction and the Fall of Paul de Man.* New York: Poseidon, 1991.

Lessing, Doris. "A Conversation with Doris Lessing." Interview with Florence Howe. In Pratt and Dembo, eds., *Doris Lessing.* 15–22.

————. "Doris Lessing at Stony Brook." Interview with Jonah Raskin. *New American Review* 8 (1970): 166–79. Rpt. in Lessing, *A Small Personal Voice.* 61–76.

————. *The Golden Notebook.* 1962. New York: Bantam, 1973.

————. *In Pursuit of the English.* New York: Simon and Schuster, 1961.

————. "One off the Short List." In Lessing, *A Man and Two Women.* New York: Simon and Schuster, 1963.

————. *Retreat to Innocence.* London: Michael Joseph, 1956.

————. *A Ripple from the Storm.* Vol. 3 of *Children of Violence.* 1958. New York: New American Library/Plume, 1970.

————. *A Small Personal Voice.* Ed. Paul Schleuter. New York: Knopf, 1974.

Levenson, Michael H. *A Genealogy of Modernism.* Cambridge: Cambridge University Press, 1984.

Lewis, Jane. *Women in England, 1870–1950: Sexual Divisions and Social Change.* Bloomington: Indiana University Press, 1984.

Lewis, Wyndham. *The Apes of God.* 1930. Santa Barbara, Calif.: Black Sparrow Press, 1981.

————. *The Art of Being Ruled.* 1926. Ed. Reed Way Dasenbrock. Santa Rosa, Calif.: Black Sparrow Press, 1989.

————. *The Childermass.* London: Chatto and Windus, 1928.

————. *The Complete Wild Body.* 1927. Ed. Bernard Lafourcade. Santa Barbara, Calif.: Black Sparrow Press, 1982.

————. *Hitler.* London: Chatto and Windus, 1931.

————. *The Hitler Cult.* London: Dent, 1939.

————. *Men without Art.* 1934. Ed. Seamus Cooney. Santa Barbara, Calif.: Black Sparrow Press, 1987.

————. *Paleface: The Philosophy of the "Melting Pot."* London: Chatto and Windus, 1929.

————. *The Roaring Queen.* Ed. Walter Allen. New York: Liveright, 1973.

————. *Rotting Hill.* 1951. Ed. Paul Edwards. Santa Barbara, Calif.: Black Sparrow Press, 1986.

_____. *Rude Assignment: An Intellectual Autobiography.* 1950. Ed. Toby Foshay. Santa Barbara, Calif.: Black Sparrow Press, 1984.

_____. *Time and Western Man.* 1927. Boston: Beacon Press, 1957.

_____. *The Writer and the Absolute.* London: Methuen, 1952.

_____. *Wyndham Lewis on Art: Collected Writings, 1913–1956.* Ed. C. J. Fox and Walter Michael. New York: Funk and Wagnalls, 1969.

_____, ed. *Blast* 1 (1914). Santa Rosa, Calif.: Black Sparrow Press, 1989.

Little, Judy. *Comedy and the Woman Writer.* Lincoln: University of Nebraska Press, 1983.

Lodge, David. *Changing Places.* 1975. Harmondsworth: Penguin, 1978.

_____. *Nice Work.* Harmondsworth: Penguin, 1988.

_____. *Small World.* Harmondsworth: Penguin, 1984.

_____. *Working with Structuralism: Essays and Reviews on Nineteenth- and Twentieth-Century Literature.* Boston: Routledge and Kegan Paul, 1981.

Lombroso, Cesare. *Crime: Its Causes and Remedies.* Trans. Henry P. Horton. Boston: Little Brown, 1911.

Lovell, Terry, ed. *British Feminist Thought: A Reader.* London: Basil Blackwell, 1990.

Lowe, Roy. *Education in the Post-War Years: A Social History.* London: Routledge, 1988.

Lukács, Georg. *The Theory of the Novel.* Trans. Anna Bostock. Cambridge: MIT Press, 1971.

Lunn, Kenneth. "Political Anti-Semitism before 1914: Fascism's Heritage?" In Lunn and Thurlow, eds., *British Fascism.* 20–40

Lunn, Kenneth, and Richard Thurlow, eds. *British Fascism: Essays on the Radical Right in Inter-War Britain.* London: Croom Helm, 1980.

Lyotard, Jean-François. *The Postmodern Condition: A Report on Knowledge.* Trans. Geoff Bennington and Brian Massumi. Minneapolis: University of Minnesota Press, 1984.

McCarthy, Mary. "A Bolt from the Blue." Review of *Pale Fire* by Vladimir Nabokov. *New Republic,* June 1962: 21–27. Rpt. in *Nabokov: The Critical Heritage.* Ed. Norman Page. Critical Heritage Series. Boston: Routledge and Kegan Paul, 1982. 124–36.

Macciocchi, Maria-Antonietta. "Female Sexuality in Fascist Ideology." *Feminist Review* 1 (1979): 67–82.

McDermott, John. *Kingsley Amis: An English Moralist.* New York: St. Martin's, 1989.

MacEwen, Malcolm. *The Greening of a Red.* Concord, Mass.: Pluto, 1991.

McGhee, Paul E. "The Role of Arousal and Hemispheric Lateralization in Humor." In McGhee and Goldstein, eds., *Handbook.* Vol. 1: 13–38.

McGhee, Paul E., and Jeffrey H. Goldstein, eds. *Handbook of Humor Research.* 2 vols. New York: Springer-Verlag, 1983.

Malcolm, Janet. "Graven Images." *New Yorker,* 8 June 1987: 102–8.

Mann, Thomas. "Joseph Conrad's *The Secret Agent*." In Watt, *Casebook*. 105–8.

Marcus, Jane. *Art and Anger*. Columbus: Ohio University Press and Miami University, 1988.

———. "'No More Horses': Virginia Woolf on Art and Propaganda." *Women's Studies* 4 (1977): 265–90.

———, ed. *Virginia Woolf: A Feminist Slant*. Lincoln: University of Nebraska Press, 1983.

———, ed. *Virginia Woolf and Bloomsbury: A Centenary Celebration*. London: Macmillan, 1987.

Marcus, Leah S. *The Politics of Mirth*. Chicago: University of Chicago Press, 1986.

Marcuse, Herbert. *The Aesthetic Dimension*. Boston: Beacon Press, 1977.

Marks, Elaine, and Isabelle de Courtivron, eds. *New French Feminisms*. Amherst: University of Massachusetts Press, 1980.

Martineau, William H. "A Model of the Social Functions of Humor." In Goldstein and McGhee, eds., *Psychology*. 117–25.

Marwick, Arthur. *British Society since 1945*. Harmondsworth: Penguin, 1982.

Maugham, Somerset. "Books of the Year." *Sunday Times* (London), 25 December 1955: 4.

Mazrui, Ali A. *The Satanic Verses or a Satanic Novel?* Greenpoint, N.Y.: Committee of Muslim Scholars and Leaders of North America, n.d.

Mellencamp, Patricia. "Situation Comedy, Feminism, and Freud: Discourses of Gracie and Lucy." In Modleski, ed., *Studies in Entertainment*. 80–98.

Mercer, Kobena. "Welcome to the Jungle: Identity and Diversity in Postmodern Politics." In Rutherford, ed., *Identity*. 43–71.

Meredith, George. "An Essay on Comedy." In *Comedy*. Ed. Wylie Sypher. Garden City, N.Y.: Doubleday Anchor, 1956. 3–60.

Meredith, Isabel [Helen Rossetti and Olive Rossetti]. *A Girl among the Anarchists*. London: Duckworth, 1903.

Metz, Christian. "Instant Self-Contradiction." In Blonsky, ed., *On Signs*. 259–66.

Meyers, Jeffrey. *The Enemy: A Biography of Wyndham Lewis*. London: Routledge and Kegan Paul, 1980.

Miami Theory Collective, eds. *Community at Loose Ends*. Minneapolis: University of Minnesota Press, 1991.

Miller, F. C. "Humor in a Chippewa Tribal Council." *Ethnology* 6 (1967): 263–71.

Miller, J. Hillis. *Poets of Reality: Six Twentieth-Century Writers*. Cambridge: Harvard University Press, 1965.

Milner, G. B. "Homo Ridens: Towards a Semiotic Theory of Humour and Laughter." *Semiotica* 5 (1972): 1–30.

Mitford, Nancy. "The English Aristocracy." 1955. *A Talent to Annoy*. Ed. Charlotte Mosley. London: Hamish Hamilton, 1986. 92–105.

Modleski, Tania. "Rape vs. Mans/Laughter: Hitchcock's *Blackmail* and Feminist Interpretation." *PMLA* 102 (May 1987): 304–15.

_____, ed. *Studies in Entertainment: Critical Approaches to Mass Culture.* Bloomington: Indiana University Press, 1986.

Monkhouse, A. N. Review of *The Secret Agent* by Joseph Conrad. *Manchester Guardian*, 12 September 1907. Rpt. Sherry, ed., *Conrad; The Critical Heritage.* 181–84.

Monro, D. H. *Argument of Laughter.* Melbourne: Melbourne University Press, 1951.

Morreall, John, ed. *The Philosophy of Laughter and Humor.* Albany: State University of New York Press, 1987.

Morrell, John. "Arnold Leese and the Imperial Fascist League: The Impact of Racial Fascism." In Lunn and Thurlow, eds., *British Fascism.* 57–75.

Morrison, Blake. *The Movement: English Poetry and Fiction of the 1950s.* London: Methuen, 1986.

Moser, Thomas C. *Joseph Conrad: Achievement and Decline.* 1957. Hamden, Conn.: Archon, 1966.

Mosley, Oswald. *My Life.* London: Nelson, 1968.

Mouffe, Chantal. "Democratic Citizenship and the Political Community." In Miami Theory Collective, eds., *Community at Loose Ends.* 70–82.

Mudrick, Marvin, ed. *Conrad: A Collection of Critical Essays.* Twentieth Century Views Series. Englewood Cliffs, N.J.: Prentice-Hall, 1966.

Nairn, Tom. *The Break-up of Britain: Crisis and Neo-Nationalism.* London: New Left Books, 1977.

Nancy, Jean-Luc. *The Inoperative Community.* 1989. Trans. Peter Connor et al. Minneapolis: University of Minnesota Press, 1991.

_____. "Of Being-in-Common." In Miami Theory Collective, ed., *Community at Loose Ends.* 1–12.

Nicholson, Linda J., ed. *Feminism/Postmodernism.* London: Routledge, 1990.

Nietzsche, Friedrich. *Beyond Good and Evil: Prelude to a Philosophy of the Future.* Trans. Walter Kaufmann. Harmondsworth: Penguin, 1979.

_____. *The Birth of Tragedy and the Genealogy of Morals.* Trans. Francis Golffing. Garden City, N.Y.: Doubleday, 1956.

O'Brien, Flann. *At Swim-Two-Birds.* New York: Viking Compass, 1967.

Oliver, Hermia. *The International Anarchist Movement in Late Victorian London.* New York: St. Martin's, 1983.

Orwell, George. "Charles Dickens." In *The Collected Essays, Journalism, and Letters of George Orwell.* 4 vols. Ed. Sonia Orwell and Ian Angus. New York: Harcourt Brace Jovanovich, 1968. Vol. 1: 413–60.

Owens, Craig. "The Discourse of Others: Feminists and Postmodernism." In Foster, ed., *Anti-Aesthetic.* 57–77.

Pankhurst, E. Sylvia. *The Suffragette Movement: An Intimate Account of Persons and Ideals.* London: Longman's, 1931.

Parkin, Frank. *Class Inequality and Political Order.* London: Paladin, 1972.

Parmar, Pratibha. "Gender, Race and Class: Asian Women in Resistance." In Center for Contemporary Cultural Studies, eds., *The Empire Strikes Back.* 236–75.

Paulos, John Allen. *Mathematics and Humor.* Chicago: University of Chicago Press, 1980.

Pirandello, Luigi. *On Humor.* Trans. Antonio Illiano and Daniel P. Testa. Chapel Hill: University of North Carolina Press, 1960.

Poirier, Richard. *The Comic Sense of Henry James.* London: Chatto and Windus, 1960.

———. "The Politics of Self-Parody." *Partisan Review* 35 (Summer 1968): 342–55.

Polhemus, Robert M. *Comic Faith: The Great Tradition from Austen to Joyce.* Chicago: University of Chicago Press, 1980.

Porter, Dennis. "Realism and Failure in *The Golden Notebook.*" *Modern Language Quarterly* 35 (1974): 56–65.

Pratt, Annis, and L. S. Dembo, eds. *Doris Lessing: Critical Studies.* Madison: University of Wisconsin Press, 1973.

Price, Richard Geoffrey George. *A History of Punch.* London: Collins, 1957.

Price, Richard N. "Society, Status, and Jingoism: The Social Roots of Lower Middle Class Patriotism, 1870–1900." In *The Lower Middle Class in Britain, 1870–1914.* Ed. Geoffrey Crossick. New York: St. Martin's, 1977. 89–112.

Pritchard, William. *Seeing through Everything: English Writers, 1918–1940.* New York: Oxford University Press, 1977.

Quail, John. *The Slow Burning Fuse: The Lost History of the British Anarchists.* London: Paladin, 1978.

Radcliffe-Brown, A. R. "A Further Note on Joking Relationships." In Radcliffe-Brown, *Structure and Function in Primitive Society.* New York: Free Press, 1965. 105–16.

———. "On Joking Relationships." In *Structure and Function.* 90–104.

Radhakrishnan, R. "Ethnic Identity and Post-Structuralist Difference." In *The Nature and Context of Minority Discourse.* Ed. Abdul R. JanMohamed and David Lloyd. New York: Oxford University Press, 1990. 50–71.

Raskin, Victor. *Semantic Mechanisms of Humor.* Boston: Reidel, 1985.

Ray, Martin. "Conrad, Nordau, and Other Degenerates: The Psychology of *The Secret Agent.*" *Conradiana* 16 (1984): 125–40.

Redwine, Bruce. "Deception and Intention in *The Secret Agent.*" *Conradiana* 11 (1979): 253–66.

Richards, I. A. *Principles of Literary Criticism.* New York: Harcourt, Brace, 1948.

Richardson, Dorothy. "The Reality of Feminism." 1917. In Scott, ed., *Gender of Modernism.* 401–7.

Riffaterre, Michael. *Text Production.* Trans. Terese Lyons. New York: Columbia University Press, 1983.

Roberts, Brian. "The Debate on 'Sus.'" In Cashmore and Troyna, eds., *Black Youth in Crisis.* 100–128.

Rose, Margaret A. *Reading the Young Marx and Engels: Poetry, Parody, and the Censor.* London: Croom Helm, 1978.

Rose, Phyllis. *Woman of Letters: A Life of Virginia Woolf.* New York: Oxford University Press, 1978.

Roth, Philip. "Introducing Milan Kundera." "Introduction" to *Laughable Loves* by Milan Kundera. New York: Knopf, 1974.

Rowe, Marsha, ed. *Spare Rib Reader.* Harmondsworth: Penguin, 1982.

Rubenstein, David. *A Different World for Women: The Life of Millicent Garrett Fawcett.* New York: Harvester Wheatsheaf, 1991.

Rubenstein, Roberta. *The Novelistic Vision of Doris Lessing: Breaking the Forms of Consciousness.* Urbana: University of Illinois Press, 1979.

Rushdie, Salman. *Grimus.* London: Knopf, 1975.

_____. *Imaginary Homelands: Essays and Criticism, 1981–1991.* New York: Viking Granta, 1991.

_____. "The Indian Writer in England." In *The Eye of the Beholder: Indian Writing in English.* Ed. Maggie Butcher. London: Commonwealth Institute, 1983. 75–83.

_____. *Midnight's Children.* New York: Knopf, 1980.

_____. *The Satanic Verses.* New York: Viking, 1989.

_____. *Shame.* New York: Vintage, 1984.

_____. "*Songs* Doesn't Know the Score." Review of *Handsworth Songs.* *The Guardian,* 12 January 1987. Rpt. in *Black Film British Cinema.* ICA Document 7. Ed. Kobena Mercer. London: Institute of Contemporary Arts, 1988. 16–17.

Rutherford, Jonathan, ed. *Identity: Community, Culture, Difference.* London: Lawrence and Wishart, 1990.

Sacks, Harvey. "Some Technical Considerations of a Dirty Joke." In *Studies in the Organization of Conversational Interaction.* Ed. Jim Schenkein. New York: Academic Press, 1978. 249–69.

Said, Edward. *Covering Islam: How the Media and the Experts Determine How We See the Rest of the World.* London: Routledge and Kegan Paul, 1981.

_____. "Intellectuals in the Post-Colonial World." *Salmagundi* 70–71 (1986): 44–64.

_____. *Orientalism.* New York: Pantheon, 1978.

_____. *The Question of Palestine.* New York: Times Books, 1979.

Said, Edward, and Salman Rushdie. "On Palestinian Identity: A Conversation with Edward Said." In Rushdie, *Imaginary Homelands.* 166–84.

Salwak, Dale. "An Interview with Kingsley Amis." *Contemporary Literature* 16 (Winter 1975): 1–18.

_____. *Kingsley Amis: A Reference Guide.* Boston: G. K. Hall, 1978.

Samuel, Raphael. "Born-Again Socialism." In Archer et al., eds., *Out of Apathy.* 39–58.

Schlack, Beverly Ann. "Fathers in General: The Patriarchy in Virginia Woolf's Fiction." In Marcus, ed., *Virginia Woolf: A Feminist Slant.* 52–77.

Schopenhauer, Arthur. *The World as Will and Idea.* 1859. Trans. R. B. Haldane and John Kemp. 2 vols. London: Routledge and Kegan Paul, 1957.

Scott, Bonnie Kime, ed. *The Gender of Modernism: A Critical Anthology*. Bloomington: Indiana University Press, 1990.

Sears, Sallie. "Theater of War: Virginia Woolf's *Between the Acts*." In Marcus, ed., *Virginia Woolf: A Feminist Slant*.

Sherry, Norman, ed. *Conrad: The Critical Heritage*. Critical Heritage Series. London: Routledge and Kegan Paul, 1973.

———. *Conrad's Western World*. Cambridge: Cambridge University Press, 1971.

Shipley, Peter. *Revolutionaries in Modern Britain*. London: Bodley Head, 1976.

Showalter, Elaine. "Towards a Feminist Poetics." In *Women Writing and Writing about Women*. Ed. Mary Jacobus. London: Croom Helm, 1979. 22–41.

Silver, Brenda R. "Virginia Woolf and the Concept of Community: The Elizabethan Playhouse." *Women's Studies* 4 (1977): 291–98.

Silverman, Kaja. *The Subject of Semiotics*. New York: Oxford University Press, 1983.

Simon, Brian. *Education and the Social Order, 1940–1990*. London: Lawrence and Wishart, 1991.

Simon, Richard Keller. *The Labyrinth of the Comic: Theory and Practice from Fielding to Freud*. Tallahassee: Florida State University Press, 1985.

Sinfield, Alan. *Literature, Politics, and Culture in Postwar Britain*. Berkeley: University of California Press, 1989.

———, ed. *Society and Literature, 1945–1970*. London: Methuen, 1983.

Slatoff, Walter J. *With Respect to Readers*. Ithaca: Cornell University Press, 1970.

Sloterdijk, Peter. *Critique of Cynical Reason*. Trans. Michael Eldred. Minneapolis: University of Minnesota Press, 1987.

———. "The Twilight of False Consciousness." Trans. Michael Eldred and Leslie A. Adelson. *New German Critique* 33 (Fall 1984): 190–206.

Solloway, Richard. "Counting the Degenerates: The Statistics of Race Deterioration in Edwardian England." *Journal of Contemporary History* 17 (January 1982): 137–64.

Solomos, John. *Black Youth, Racism and the State*. Cambridge: Cambridge University Press, 1988.

Sorrentino, Gilbert. *Mulligan's Stew*. New York: Grove, 1979.

Spencer, Herbert. "The Physiology of Laughter." 1860. *Essays: Scientific, Political, and Speculative*. 3 vols. London: Williams & Norgate, 1868. Vol. 1: 204–7.

Spielman, H. H. *History of Punch*. London: Cassell, 1895.

Sprague, Claire, and Virginia Tiger, eds. *Critical Essays on Doris Lessing*. Boston: G. K. Hall, 1986.

Stallybrass, Peter, and Allon White. *The Politics and Poetics of Transgression*. Ithaca: Cornell University Press, 1986.

Stedman Jones, Gareth. *Outcast London: A Study in the Relationship between Classes in Victorian Society*. Oxford: Clarendon, 1971.

Steedman, Carolyn Kay. *Landscape for a Good Woman: A Story of Two Lives*. New Brunswick, N.J.: Rutgers University Press, 1987.

Steele, Murray. "Doris Lessing's Rhodesia." In Bertelsen, ed., *Doris Lessing*. 44–54.

Stephen, Adrian. *The Dreadnought Hoax.* 1936. London: Chatto and Windus/ Hogarth, 1983.

Sukenick, Lynn. "Feeling and Reason." In Pratt and Dembo, eds., *Doris Lessing.* 98– 118.

Suls, Jerry. "A Two-Stage Model for the Appreciation of Jokes and Cartoons: An Information Processing Analysis." In Goldstein and McGhee, eds., *Psychology.* 80–92.

Sutherland, John. "The Politics of English Studies in the British University, 1960– 1984." *Historical Studies and Literary Criticism.* Ed. Jerome J. McGann. Madison: University of Wisconsin Press, 1985. 126–40.

Tanner, Tony. *Adultery in the Novel.* Baltimore: Johns Hopkins University Press, 1979.

Taylor, A. J. P. *English History, 1914–1945.* New York: Oxford University Press, 1965.

Taylor, Jenny Bourne. "Raymond Williams: Gender and Generation." In Lovell, ed., *British Feminist Thought.* 296–308.

Thapar, Karen. "Asians in Britain." Three-Part Series. London *Times,* 21–23 June 1982.

Theweleit, Klaus. *Male Fantasies,* 1. *Women, Floods, Bodies, History.* Trans. Stephen Conway. Minneapolis: University of Minnesota Press, 1987.

———. *Male Fantasies,* 2. *Male Bodies: Psychoanalyzing the White Terror.* Trans. Erica Carter and Chris Turner. Minneapolis: University of Minnesota Press, 1989.

Thompson, E. P. *The Poverty of Theory and Other Essays.* New York: Monthly Review Press, 1978.

———. "Preface." In MacEwen, *Greening of a Red.*

Thompson, John B. *Studies in the Theory of Ideology.* Berkeley: University of California Press, 1984.

Thomson, Philip. *The Grotesque.* Critical Idiom Series 24. London: Methuen, 1972.

Tiger, Virginia. "Candid Shot: Lessing in New York City, April 1 and April 2, 1984." In Sprague and Tiger, eds., *Critical Essays.* 221–23.

Tillyard, E. M. W. "*The Secret Agent* Reconsidered." *Essays in Criticism* 11 (July 1961): 309–18. Rpt. in Mudrick, ed., *Conrad.* 103–10.

Todorov, Tzvetan. *The Fantastic.* Trans. Richard Howard. Ithaca: Cornell University Press, 1973.

Van Den Abbeele, Georges. "Introduction." In Miami Theory Collective, eds., *Community at Loose Ends.* ix–xxvi.

Vlastos, Marion. "Doris Lessing and R. D. Laing: Psycho-Politics and Prophecy." *PMLA* 91 (March 1976): 245–58.

Volosinov, V. N. *Marxism and the Philosophy of Language.* 1929. Trans. Ladislav Matejka and I. R. Titunik. Cambridge: Harvard University Press, 1986.

Walker, Nancy. *A Very Serious Thing: Women's Humor and American Culture.* Minneapolis: University of Minnesota Press, 1988.

Watt, Ian. *Conrad in the Nineteenth Century.* Berkeley: University of California Press, 1979.

———, ed. *The Secret Agent: A Casebook.* Casebook Series. London: Macmillan, 1973.

Waugh, Evelyn. "An Open Letter to the Honble Mrs Peter Rodd (Nancy Mitford) on a Very Serious Subject." 1955. In *The Essays, Articles and Reviews of Evelyn Waugh.* Ed. Donat Gallagher. Boston: Little, Brown, 1983. 494–502.

———. *Vile Bodies.* 1930. Boston: Little, Brown, 1955.

Weatherby, W. J. *Salman Rushdie: Sentenced to Death.* New York: Carroll and Graf, 1990.

Webber, G. C. *The Ideology of the British Right, 1918–1939.* New York: St. Martin's, 1986.

Weber, Samuel. "The Divaricator: Remarks on Freud's *Witz.*" *Glyph* 1 (1977): 1–27.

———. *The Legend of Freud.* Minneapolis: University of Minnesota Press, 1982.

Weiler, Peter. *British Labour and the Cold War.* Stanford, Calif.: Stanford University Press, 1988.

West, Cornel. "The Dilemma of the Black Intellectual." *Cultural Critique* 1 (Fall 1985): 109–24.

Widmer, Kingsley. "Conrad's Pyrrhonistic Conservatism: Ideological Melodrama around 'Simple Ideas.'" *Novel* 7 (1974): 133–42.

Wiener, Martin J. *English Culture and the Decline of the Industrial Spirit, 1850–1980.* Cambridge: Cambridge University Press, 1981.

Wilde, Alan. *Horizons of Assent: Modernism, Postmodernism, and the Ironic Imagination.* Baltimore: Johns Hopkins University Press, 1981.

Wilden, Anthony. *System and Structure: Essays in Communication and Exchange.* London: Tavistock, 1972.

Williams, Raymond. *The Country and the City.* London: Chatto and Windus, 1973.

———. *Culture and Society, 1780–1950.* London: Chatto and Windus, 1958.

———. *The English Novel from Dickens to Lawrence.* London: Chatto and Windus, 1971.

———. *Keywords: A Vocabulary of Culture and Society.* Rev. ed. New York: Oxford University Press, 1985.

———. *The Long Revolution.* 1961. Westport, Conn.: Greenwood, 1975.

———. *The Politics of Modernism: Against the New Conformists.* Ed. Tony Pinkney. London: Verso, 1989.

Wilson, Christopher. *Jokes: Form, Content, Use and Function.* London: Academic Press, 1979.

Wilson, Elizabeth. *Only Halfway to Paradise: Women in Postwar Britain, 1945–1968.* London: Tavistock, 1980.

Woodcock, George. *Anarchism: A History of Libertarian Movements and Ideas.* New York: New American Library, 1962.

Woolf, Virginia. *Between the Acts.* 1941. New York: Harcourt Brace Jovanovich, 1969.

———. *Collected Essays.* Ed. Leonard Woolf. 4 vols. New York: Harcourt Brace, 1967.

_____. *"Death of the Moth" and Other Essays*. 1942. Ed. Leonard Woolf. New York: Harcourt Brace Jovanovich, 1970.

_____. *Diary of Virginia Woolf*. Ed. Anne Oliver Bell with Andrew McNellie. 5 vols. New York: Harcourt Brace Jovanovich, 1984.

_____. *"The Moment" and Other Essays*. Ed. Leonard Woolf. New York: Harcourt Brace Jovanovich, 1948.

_____. *Orlando*. 1928. New York: Harcourt Brace Jovanovich, 1956.

_____. *Three Guineas*. 1938. New York: Harcourt Brace Jovanovich, 1966.

Young, Iris Marion. "The Ideal of Community and the Politics of Difference." In Nicholson, ed., *Feminism/Postmodernism*.

Zillman, Dolf. "Disparagement Humor." In McGhee and Goldstein, eds., *Handbook*. Vol. 1: 85–108.

Zillman, Dolf, and J. R. Cantor. "A Disposition Theory of Humor and Mirth." In Chapman and Foot, eds., *Humor and Laughter*.

Žižek, Slavoj. *The Sublime Object of Ideology*. London: Verso, 1989.

Zwerdling, Alex. *Virginia Woolf and the Real World*. Berkeley: University of California Press, 1986.

Index